THE COMPLETE MANUAL OF
WOOD VENEERING

By the same author:

THE ART & PRACTICE OF MARQUETRY

THE COMPLETE MANUAL

OF

WOOD VENEERING

W. A. LINCOLN

Fully Illustrated

STOBART & SON LTD
LONDON

TO KATHY

Published 1984

ISBN 0 85442 022 3

Stobart & Son Ltd 67-73 Worship Street London EC2A 2EL

Printed in Great Britain by A. Wheaton & Co. Ltd., Exeter, Devon

From a plaque

on the wall on the Paseo Carlos Faust

in the botanical gardens at Blanes, Spain.

PASAJERO: Tu que pasas y levantas contra

mi tu brazo antes de que me hagas

                     daños oyeme bien ...

Translation:

     PASSER BY:
     Ye who pass by and would raise your hand
     against me, harken ere you harm me.
     I am the heat of your hearth on the cold
     winter nights.
     I am the friendly shade which you find when
     you walk in the August sun.
     My fruit quenches your thirst on the road.
     I am the beam that holds your house,
     the board of your table,
     the bed on which you repose
     and the wood of your boat.
     I am the handle of your spade
     the door of your dwelling
     the wood of your cradle
     the shell of your coffin.
     I am the bread of kindness and
     the flower of beauty.
     Ye who pass by,
     Listen to my prayer
     Harm me not!
                       'Jardines del Beso' (Jativa)

CONTENTS

PREFACE

The word 'veneer' has acquired some unfortunate connotations. In Roman times it was derided by Pliny as 'bestowing upon the more common woods a bark of a higher price'.

Since then it has been misused to suggest a thin covering to conceal something inferior, cheap or shoddy, or to hide poor workmanship.

Charles Dickens delivered the *coup de grâce* when he wrote in 'Our Mutual Friend' (Chapter 2) when describing the family of Mr & Mrs Veneering:

'Mr & Mrs Veneering were bran-new people in a bran-new house . . . all things were in a state of high varnish and polish. And what was observable in the furniture, was observable in the Veneerings; the surface smelt a little too much of the workshop and was a trifle sticky.'

Even the dictionary is no comfort: 'to put a superficial polish, or to disguise, to gloss over'.

We can thank the industrial revolution for the misconception. It is true that in Victorian times, much of the first factory-made furniture, often from small cottage industries, used crudely produced plywood of unbalanced construction, decorated with amateurishly matched veneers which were finished with the little understood technique of french polishing. This mass of poorly produced veneered furniture rapidly brought the craft of veneering into disrepute.

Even in this enlightened age, the belief still persists, that hand-made furniture, built by craftsmen from solid timber is superior to, and is to be preferred to, furniture made from veneered construction.

It is believed that solid timber is more durable, and, probably because it is much heavier, far more substantial. Because it is undoubtedly more expensive, and the modern attitude suggests 'you only get what you pay for', it follows that if it is more costly, it is superior.

The truth is, that the majority of the greatest masterpieces of cabinet craftsmanship of the golden ages, treasured by the world's leading art museums, are of veneered construction.

For nearly two hundred years, master craftsmen have realised the severe limitations of working with solid timber. It is subject to shrinkage, warping, casting, splitting, twisting, and insect and fungal attack.

It is especially vulnerable in centrally heated homes, where the superdry atmosphere can adversely affect the furniture. Also in locations of varying humidity, or in extremes of climatic conditions, both circumstances affect the natural moisture content of the timber.

There are many other technical reasons why veneered construction is far superior to solid timber.

For example the most highly prized, beautifully figured woods are the burrs of hardwoods. These are often wild grained, very brittle, full of knots and unmanageable in small sizes. In attempting to use this material in the solid, especially if the required curvature is great, the piece would be short or end grained and lack strength; the surface would comprise a multitude of joins and be structurally weak. But the same timber sliced into veneers would be easily worked. Matching consecutive leaves would enable the craftsman to create beautiful patterns which would be impossible if the material had been used in the solid.

If a cabinet were to be made from solid ebony, it would be exceedingly expensive to make, almost too heavy to move, subject to all the inherent weaknesses of construction described, and be aesthetically tasteless in appearance.

Conservationists would argue that by converting precious species into veneers, they are preserving dwindling stocks of rare woods.

There is no doubt at all that modern techniques and processes enable us to produce furniture today which is far more durable and as attractive, than the solid wood furniture it has largely superseded.

A correctly balanced plywood panel is far stronger than solid timber of the same thickness; it will not warp, twist or split, and will not suffer from stresses and strains. This means, that a piece of furniture may be made from thinner material, with a saving in material, weight and cost.

Humidity changes are compensated for, as the natural tendency to expand and contract is cancelled out by opposing layers equalising the strain in the opposite direction.

The modern veneer craftsman has the opportunity to use an ever increasing number of natural, rare and exotic woods.

A magnificent array of colourful woods is being converted into veneers, aided by computerised plant backed by scientific research and development into every specialised aspect of wood technology.

Today, even after a lifetime in the business, whenever I hold a piece of veneer in my hands, to feel its lustrous texture, admire its beautiful figure, peculiar markings or attractive contortions of grain, or to smell its aroma, I never cease to be filled with admiration and reverence for the wonder of wood.

Although this is a technical book, I hope my own enthusiasm is infectious and that you too, will share my pleasure in working with these wonderful woods of the world.

W. A. Lincoln, London 1984

ACKNOWLEDGMENTS

At Dalston, in the East End of London in 1946, I set up a small veneer business. I felled logs in the woods with a telesaw, hacked off the bark, and peeled them into veneer to make ice cream spoons, lollipop sticks and pipe smoker's wood spills.

This led, first to installing a plywood plant to make furniture, and then into supplying decorative veneers for marquetry, a hardwood mill, and a chemical dyeing plant for veneers.

Eventually to a mail order business supplying wood craftsmen all over the world: The Art Veneers Co Ltd of Mildenhall, Suffolk, and World of Wood Ltd — supplying the needs of antique restorers.

Thirty years later, I sold the business to Mr L. Reed, C.Eng., B.Sc., M.I.Mech.E.

The production of this book, would not have been possible without the invaluable assistance given to me by my successor, and his tireless enthusiasm and co-operation.

He made available to me the extensive use of AVCO copyright material which I wrote during my thirty year stint, including *The Veneer Craftman's Manual, Wood Technology,* and material from *Forest Products Review* and *Techniques of Intarsia.* Also for use of the archive materials from the International Woodcraftsman Competition for the Lincoln Awards. He also personally selected all the veneers, created the veneer matches and undertook much of the photography for this book.

I would also like to express my thanks to Ernie Ives, editor of *The Marquetarian* and Mr Richard Shellard of the distribution office, for supplying back numbers of the magazine and putting me in touch with members of the Marquetry Society.

Very special thanks are also due to companies and friends in the trade, for their generous help and advice in providing up-dated information on equipment, materials and techniques. The Adjustable Clamp Co Inc of Chicago for 'Jorgensen' clamps and 'Pony' press screws; Beresford & Hicks Ltd of Kings Lynn for Regency furniture; Karl Danzer Furnierwerke GmbH of Reutlingen, West Germany, for information on veneers from around the world.

Gibbs Constructor (1961) Ltd of Edmonton and Pye Thermal

Bonders Ltd of Cambridge for information on low voltage heating of presses; Messrs Interwood Ltd of Chelmsford for information on veneering tools, equipment and presses; McIntosh of Kirkcaldy, Scotland, for modern and reproduction furniture; Georg Ott of Ulm, West Germany, for veneering tools; Messrs F. R. Shadbolt & Sons Ltd of Chingford—'The Master Veneerers'—for technical advice.

Greatful thanks are also due to the following editors, and librarians for splendid research facilities made available to me.

British Museum (Natural History) Department.

Building Research Establishment, Department of the Environment, Princes Risborough, Bucks.

Commonwealth Forestry Institute, Furniture Industry Research Association, Stevenage.

Hackney Public Library, Pitfield Street, Shoreditch.

Timber Trades Journal and Wood Processing, London.

Timber Research and Development Association, High Wycombe, for their library, bibliographies, 'red booklets' and 'teaching aids'.

World Wood magazine of Brussels.

Plywood and Panel World, Timber & Processing Industry, Timber Harvesting of Montgomery, Alabama, USA.

Mrs Giuditta Dolci-Favi of the Photo Library, Food and Agricultural Organisation, of the United Nations, Rome, Italy.

Consiglio Nazionale delle Richerche, Florence, Italy.

Deutche Gesellschaft für Holzforschung, Stuttgart, Germany.

Centre Technique du Bois, Paris, France.

Lastly, a special word of thanks to Jon Harrison of Sutton who produced all the line drawings for the book, and to Brian Davies of Stobart & Son Ltd, for his patience in bringing the manuscript into print.

Fig. 1 Craftsmen at work — Tomb of Rekh-mi-Re,
Thebes, c 1950 BC

1

A Look at the Past

VENEERING is a craft as old as civilised man. Hieroglyphic evidence discovered in the form of low relief limestone wall murals, in the Valley of the Kings, depict Egyptian craftsmen squatting at their tasks of cutting veneers from logs, applying glue to groundwork, with heavy flat stone weights at hand to serve as cauls and other stones to act as abrasive grinders to smooth and finish the work.

They used the axe for felling and the adze for shaping and slicing their veneers.

The Egyptians imported veneer logs from Phoenicia, Syria and the Lebanon, including cedar, cypress, sandalwood and ebony from Punt in East Africa. Other woods used were ash, beech, boxwood, elm, fir, lime liquidambar, maple, oak, pine, plum and yew.

The illustration is from the tomb of Rekh-mi-Re at Thebes, c 1950 BC, but even earlier examples were discovered at the cemetery at Ur, where fragments of inlaid decoration on a harp were found dating to 3500 BC, and from the tomb of Hemaka at Saqqarah, 1st dynasty, 3200 BC, veneer inlays resembling basket weave on a casket.

In the later classical Graeco-Roman period, between 500 BC-500 AD, the Greeks and Etruscans brought the craft of veneering to a high state of development. Veneers were called *sectiles laminae*, and the acme of Grecian elegance of style was reached in the 5th century BC. A rapid deterioration took place in the 4th and 3rd centuries when the Romans adopted the technique, and made over-lavish use of exotic woods imported from their far reaching empire.

The Romans prized the wood *tetraclinis articulata* which grew on the slopes of the Atlas mountains in Morocco, especially the burrs which attacked the roots below ground.

Pliny tells us that Cicero paid a fortune for one table veneered in the wood, which has a wild grain and beautiful figure. It was used to produce 'tiger tables' with striped figure; 'panther tables' with spiral figure; the burr was described as 'swarm of bees' or 'leopard spots', or resembling 'the eyes of a peacock's tail', and the curls as 'filaments of a feather'. The Romans invented the bow-saw which enabled them to cut much thinner veneers as the saw was angled to enable the frame to avoid passing through the saw kerf as in the case of the rigid frame saw.

After the collapse of the Roman Empire, Europe was plunged into the 'Dark Ages'—six centuries of turmoil which saw the ravaging of Teutonic tribes, Goths, Huns, Danes, Vikings and Vandals. The lamp of knowledge was kept flickering in isolated monastic orders such as the Carthusian, Cistercian and Benedictine.

Fig. 2 Box with vaulted cover, veneered in ebony, inlaid with ivory—c 1950 BC *(Ashmolean Musuem, Oxford)*

The Age of Oak

Although the Norman invasion of Britain in 1066 ended the Dark Ages, they did not practise the art of veneering, and all furniture was of simple but sturdy construction comprising tables, chests and stools built by carpenters, and blacksmiths.

The framework of medieval furniture made in the period 1200 to 1450 was assembled with mortise and tenon joints and panels were grooved into framework; square pegs driven into round holes in the joints. The monks had re-discovered the techniques of the Egyptians, who were using dovetails in 2960 BC and really advanced joinery (as in the sarcophagus of Queen Meryet-Amen in 1440 BC).

It was the Italians who kept the veneering craft alive and Florence and Venice became thriving art centres. Venetian noblemen built their splendid palaces along the canals in Gothic style.

The banking town of Siena became the home of the 'cloistered intarsiatori'—and they were sent out from Siena to decorate other cathedrals throughout northern Italy with intricate pictures featuring biblical scenes, figures of saints, buildings, courtyards, and cupboards revealing their contents. In the cathedral of Orvieto, twenty-eight craftsmen created the first known intarsia panel of this type completing in 1431 the work begun in 1331. The thickness of decorative veneers during this period was between ⅛ inch and ³⁄₁₆ inch (3mm-4.5mm) thick, and were fashioned into intarsia patterns with a shoulder knife. The long wooden handle was placed on the shoulder which acted as a fulcrum so that the whole weight of the body could be thrust behind the knife cut.

The Renaissance (1450-1650)

Late in the 14th century the Florentines re-discovered the heritage of their classical past and culture and enjoyment of life here and now became the theme, mixed with pride in the past.

The first national style of furniture evolved, made in solid walnut, with flat surfaces decorated with inlaid bandings and motifs featuring landscapes, interiors, human figures, arabesques, grotesques, fantasies and garden scenes.

Certosina mosaic intarsia and parquetry became popular and furniture manufacturing centres were established at Urbino, Bologna, Verona and Naples, each developing their own styles.

By the period of High Renaissance, carved decoration in ebony and walnut enriched with ivory, mother of pearl and tortoise shell and high relief carving brought about the demise of veneering.

Spanish Renaissance (1500-1700)

The Mohammedan Moors, during their long occupation of the Spanish peninsular from the 8th century until their expulsion by Philip II in 1607, firmly imprinted their style of geometric *mosaico de madera*. The fusion of Christian and Moorish art is known as the *Mudejar* and to this day Hispano-Mauresque styles are still a feature of Spanish veneered cabinetwork.

The sixteenth century was Spain's Golden Age. Charles V (1519-56) introduced the Plateresque style of minute ornamentation resembling the art of the silversmith, and Philip II (1556-98) brought the Italian styles of Palladio and Vignola to Spain and, when interpreted by

Juan de Herrera, became walnut veneered furniture with geometric inlays peculiar to Spain. The *sillón de caderas* (chair) the *vargueño* (writing desk); *taquillón* (chest); *papelera* (desk) and the *arqueta* (casket) are typical items of furniture of the period.

Germany (1525-1620)

Around 1562 the fretsaw was invented in Germany. Fine saws were cut from clock spring steel and used in wooden box frames. This permitted the interchange of two contrasting veneers cut simultaneously and brought veneering, decorated with marquetry into popularity.

For centuries, logs had been sawn into veneers by the pitsaw. Then, around 1420 in Breslau, an enterprising pitsaw operator harnessed the power of the water mill to drive the saw. In 1560, Georg Renner founded, in Augsburg, the first veneer mill driven by water power, to produce veneers in $\frac{1}{8}$ inch (3mm) thickness which stimulated the importation of exotic hardwoods from all over the world. His brother-in-law opened the second veneer mill in Nuremburg and the two towns became Germany's leading centres of cabinetmaking. They founded an industry of ebony cabinets, lavishly decorated with arabesque marquetry.

The popularity of ebony has its origin in pieces imported by the Portuguese and the Dutch from their East Indian colonies.

Flemish Styles (1520-1636)

With the severance of the Netherlands from Burgundy in 1477 the Dutch continued to produce carved oak furniture but in Flanders, Flemish craftsmen introduced Italian walnut furniture; also, ebony cabinets were produced in Antwerp in Augsburg and Nuremburg styles, but decorated with beautiful Flemish floral marquetry.

France

Successive French invasions of Italy brought the Italian Renaissance styles to France. During the reign of Henri II and his Florentine wife Catherine de Medici, impetus was given to Italian walnut furniture.

The Bourbon dynasty of French monarchs, of whom the first was Henri IV (1589-1610), planned to establish France as the world's leading centre for culture and the arts. The French cabinetmaker became known as a *menuisier en ébène* or *ébéniste*, and started to produce lavish ebony veneered cabinets.

Louis XIV (1643-1715)

Louis XIV established the first royal furniture factory at the Gobelins in Paris, and from it, all furniture for the palaces was produced. In addition to free workshops in the Louvre, additional accommodation was provided at the Arsenal and at the Temple in Paris, for *artisans-privilégies*, who were freed from supervision by the trade guilds. He also established a refugee haven at the Abbey de Saint Antoine des Champs, which gave right of refuge to foreign craftsmen as *artisans-libres* or free craftsmen. Special techniques were perfected in great secrecy and passed from father to son.

Andre Charles Boulle (1642-1732) became the greatest *ébéniste* of his age, specialising in tortoise shell and brass counterchange marquetry to decorate his ebony cabinets with gilt bronze mounts in baroque style.

The brass motif in the dark shell background was known as the *première partie* and the reverse effect as the *contre-partie*.

English Renaissance

The end of the Wars of the Roses and the victory of Henry VII at the battle of Bosworth Field in 1485 saw the end of feudalism in England. After his long exile the King brought with him walnut furniture from Italy and Burgundy, and the middle class homes were furnished from Antwerp and Bruges with walnut furniture decorated with floral inlays of fine veneers.

The introduction of renaissance ideas to Britain was attributed to Henry VIII who brought Italian craftsmen to work on his father's tomb, and when he later suppressed the monasteries in 1538, much of the oak furniture disappeared and wealthy merchants were given land by the Tudors from the confiscated properties of the monasteries and Tudor mansions were built and filled with walnut furniture.

By the time of the accession of Elizabeth I (1558-1603) all Italian influences had gone and Flemish styles were the vogue. Flemish craftsmen were joined by the Huguenots who fled from the St. Bartholomew Massacre in France in 1572, and who were given refuge by Elizabeth I. They made an immediate impact on contemporary cabinetmaking. Elizabeth ordered the plantation of walnut forests in England, and an exuberant, vigorous style developed, reflecting an age of unparalleled expansion. It was in this period that Sir Walter Raleigh, in 1597, tore up the rich red planks of the deck of his ship, which had been admired by Elizabeth, and presented her with a desk made from the first imported mahogany.

As a variation from Gothic tapestries, Inigo Jones introduced linenfold oak panelling for walls, which harmonised with beamed ceilings, and balustraded staircases. The panelling was ornamented with renaissance details such as the Tudor rose, medallions and armorial bearings. It was a period of solid oak furniture, with carved decoration during which the 'Age of Oak' reached its pinnacle.

James I of England and VI of Scotland (1603-25) and his successors, saw years of surging prosperity.

Furniture was lavishly decorated with veneers of walnut and ebony, ornamented with marquetry of fine veneers. But with the beheading of Charles I in 1649, all Flemish styles were banished and were replaced with bleak, severe, Puritan oak furniture, which was devoid of any veneered decoration until the restoration of the monarchy in 1660.

Fig. 3 English 17th century oak box with lignum vitae, walnut and boxwood decoration *(V & A Museum, London)*

The Age of Walnut (1660-1714)

The era of 'King's walnut' veneered furniture and the age of the designer had arrived. Instead of joiners making the furniture the work was sub-divided and cabinetmakers produced the furniture. The cabinetmaker did not design the furniture but employed specialist designers to create new styles. The term cabinetmaker came to mean 'employer of many specialists'.

Now the craft of decorative veneering came into its own. Veneer matching from consecutive leaves became the vogue, inset with panels of brilliant floral marquetry, and a unique form of veneering peculiar to England, oyster parquetry.

Saplings of walnut, laburnum, mulberry, yew, kingwood, olive, maple and lignum vitae were cut tangentially to produce small oval 'oyster' shaped veneers which were cut into polygons and fitted together to form a symmetrical parquetry. They were used to form border surrounds, backgrounds into which boxwood lines were inlaid, or eventually to completely cover the surface.

This Carolean style was Baroque at its most flamboyant, with dark walnut or ebony in shaped panels, surrounded by oystering, with lighter crossbandings to form a background for colourful floral marquetry.

When William of Orange became king in 1689, Dutch influence was paramount, further established when Daniel Marot, the Huguenot craftsman, became chief architect to the King. The Baroque styles proved to be too ostentatious for English taste, and was refined into foliated acanthus marquetry known as 'seaweed marquetry', a remarkably intricate arabesque style, which consisted of minute scrolls of boxwood or holly inlaid into a walnut background and still considered to be the acme of craftsmanship bringing the Baroque style to its greatest heights in England.

The rectilinear lines of the William and Mary period, gave way to the graceful curving lines of the Queen Anne style which introduced the cyma curve. Furniture of charming simplicity was veneered in matched leaves of walnut, although the marquetry decoration was relegated to the splat backs of chairs.

Louis XV (1723-74)

The lavish Baroque style of the Sun King now matured into *le style Rocaille* (from the artificial grottoes using pebbles and shells) which we know as the rococo style. The court was highly sophisticated, but its corruption, decadence and extravagance sowed the seeds of the French revolution. The era of the boudoir ushered in a period of soft curves and flowing lines. Baroque ebony styles, were swept away, and replaced with a vogue for lighter woods such as kingwood (*bois de violette*), tulipwood (*bois de rose*), purpleheart (*amaranthe*) and rosewood (*palissandre*). These purplish woods were ornamented with geometric parquetry decoration and bronzed gilt mounts.

The intimate cosiness of purpose-built rooms demanded new types of furniture. Music rooms, games rooms, sitting rooms, reading rooms, boudoirs, dressing rooms, tea rooms etc., became the vogue with especially built furniture.

In 1743 the Guild of *Menuisiers-Ébénistes* had over 1,000 *maîtres* in the guild and were using 23 native woods and 48 imported woods.

Famous ébénistes of the period were J. F. Oeben (1720-63) who was appointed *ébéniste du Roi*, and his protégé Jean Henri Riesener

(1734-1806), whose joint masterpiece is the famous *Bureaux du Roi* on view at the Wallace Collection in London.

The vintage years of the Louis XV style were around 1755-60 when the discoveries of Pompeii and Herculaneum aroused universal interest in the classical past.

The multi-curvilinear *bombé* shapes became old fashioned, and were modified to accomodate neo-classical motifs.

It is this period of refinement that is now rated as the best of all French cabinet styles, as the furniture became light and graceful with rectangular symmetry softened by elegant marquetry ornament. This superb style was known as *l'antique*.

David Roentgen (1743-1807) was acknowledged by his contemporaries as the leading cabinetmaker of his time, and in 1779 was given the title of *ébéniste-mécanicien du Roi*. The French revolution brought an end to the period in 1789.

Fig. 4 Louis XV 18th century lady's small veneered writing desk *(National Gallery of Art, Washington)*

The Age of Mahogany

Most of the walnut forests on the continent were destroyed by the severe winter of 1709. The English imported 'Virginia walnut' (*juglans nigra*) from America, but this proved to be disappointing. The cabinet-makers turned to the 'new' imported red mahogany. Sir Robert Walpole repealed the duty on mahogany in 1733 and this led to a huge demand for Spanish, Cuban and Honduras mahoganies. Matched figured mahogany was laid over pine groundwork; striped mahogany crossbanded surrounds were used with herringbone veneer bandings and boxwood lines.

During the reign of George I, two new developments took place: the emergence of a new style of architect, who planned the house, garden and furniture; also the arrival of the 'upholder', who employed craftsmen from every field of specialisation to carry out the architects' plans, right down to the candlesticks and table cruets. Chippendale, Vile and Cobb were upholders and George Seddon 1727-1801, employ-ed over four hundred journeymen. Thomas Chippendale (1718-79) was the son of a cabinetmaker and woodcarver from Worcester. He came to London in 1737 and opened his own shop in 1749, moving in 1753 to No 60, St Martin's Lane, where he remained for the rest of his life.

In 1754 he published the first edition of *The Gentleman and Cabinet-Maker's Director*—a furniture catalogue—upon which his great reputat-ion was founded. A second edition followed in 1755 and a third enlarged edition in 1762. He was a craftsman of great versatility who sought his inspiration from many sources. He employed the Queen Anne-style ball and claw foot and cabriole leg; Gothic quatrefoil and trefoil and geometric forms; and from the French rococo style he inter-preted and modified furniture to suit English taste. When Sir William Chambers published a book on Chinese architectural designs, he introduced pagoda cabinet tops and square fretted legs and table aprons.

Chippendale's speciality was the riband back chair, the carved splat of which shows a knotted ribbon with four loops. He was the first to introduce mahogany plywood when he found that solid mahogany had severe limitations when used on cabinets with delicately pierced or fretted galleries, slender curving traceries and glazing bars. Mahog-any's cross grained weaknesses prevented delicate styling, however, in attempts to overcome this he laminated three layers of mahogany to form a strong plywood which could be worked without breakage and also to form shaped plywood panels. This technique was used in succeeding styles.

(The earliest known use of plywood was found in an Egyptian sarcophagus of Dynasty 111 (2700 BC) in which six layers of thin veneers were laminated in alternate grain directions. The woods used were cypress, pine, juniper, and sidder, held together with pegs and glue).

The Director deliberately set out to capture the imagination of its contemporaries with the playful ingenuity of its designs. They were intended to arouse interest and they succeeded, although he was obliged to modify the design considerably when executing an order for a client. Because most cabinetmakers used *The Director* as a blueprint, it became difficult to distinguish between a genuine Chippendale piece and other contemporary work—but a new style had emerged which was completely indigenous to England.

It has since been widely accepted that Henry Copland designed most of the carver's pieces in the book, and Matthias Lock designed most of the individual pieces for special clients that were illustrated, but because the book was widely read, Chippendale gave his name to practically all the furniture made in the mid-eighteenth century based upon designs in *The Director*.

It is ironic that Chippendale's true greatness and genius was to be revealed in a style opposite to that by which his name is popularly identified—the style of Robert Adam. It was in this second phase of his career, that his greatest works were created, and veneering replaced carving as the form of decoration.

The Age of Satinwood (1760-1830)

There were many other outstanding cabinetmakers in the mid-eighteenth century worthy of special mention. William Vile and his partner John Cobb produced fine veneered furniture in the style of Louis XVI. William Hallet, Giles Grendey, Benjamin Goodison, John Bradbury, William Gates, William Bradshaw, John Linell and George Seddon were considered to be among the finest of the period and as the public grew tired of the curved sinuous lines of the rococo style, they began to experiment with the use of satinwood veneer.

Robert Adam (1728-92)—one of four brothers who all became architects—had made an intensive study of antiquity and was attracted by the archaeological discoveries at Pompeii and Herculaneum dating back to 79AD. He returned to England in 1758, and in 1762 he was appointed the sole architect to George III—an office he vacated in favour of his brother James who was his close collaborator and partner throughout the Adam period.

They jointly published a series of engravings in 1773 featuring many of their celebrated designs in *Works of Architecture* which greatly popularised the Adam style.

They designed everything including the house, its furniture, curtains, carpets, lamps, tea services and candlesticks. They were the first interior decorators.

So great was their impact upon fashion, that their contemporaries, who had themselves been dictators of fashion, abandoned their own ideas and worked to designs supplied by Robert Adam, in the neo-classic style.

The Adam style developed independently from the French *l'antique* style. The classic contours, the lightness and elegance and tasteful delicacy of ornament were the inspiration and dominating influence on the remaining years of the eighteenth century.

Adam brought the craft of veneering back into popularity. Satinwood was used in conjunction with contrasting veneers of tulipwood, king-wood or rosewood for bandings. He also specified silver harewood as an alternative to satinwood. Particular attention was paid to the beeswing mottle of satinwood and the fiddleback figure of harewood to obtain rich and beautiful effects in matched panels. He made extensive use of inlay lines and bandings.

Because the Adam style was rectilinear in outline, in contrast to the rococo curvilinear forms, he was able to arrange his decorative ornaments in small oval panels and friezes.

He revived marquetry as the major form of ornamentation and the semi-circular fan, the oval and circular paterae and the oval shell inlays typify Adam style motifs. The parts were sand shaded and the leaves were engraved.

Adam also employed bouquets of flowers tied with ribbons, lightly woven garlands, ribboned paterae, festoons of husks, urns and medal-lions and classical figure studies. In 1770 he introduced painted furniture—to match his tinted stucco walls and painted ceilings which brought veneering into decline.

After 1775 Adam changed his style yet again, and in its final stages corresponded closely with the French *l'antique* style bringing veneering back into popularity.

Chippendale's workshops produced large quantities of Adam style furniture, which had to be considerably modified to suit everyday needs and although he did not conform exactly to Adam's specification the chairs and furniture made by Chippendale were superior in construction due to his talent and technical knowledge. Robert Adam was buried in Westminster Abbey—perhaps the highest honour a subject can receive from his monarch and fellow countrymen.

The style of George Hepplewhite became popular around 1780-1795 and was also based upon a book of designs, which was published in 1788. Not a single piece of furniture has ever been identified as having been made by him. The true value of Hepplewhite's book '*The Cabinet Maker and Upholsterer's Guide*' which contaned 300 designs, was that it translated 'court style' Adam designs of his *l'antique* style period, for the everyday cabinetmaker.

They formed a perfect link between the best ideas of the French Louis XVI style and mature Adam style in a form any cabinetmaker could use, favouring neither the curved style of Chippendale nor the straight classical lines of Sheraton.

Hepplewhite adhered to rectilinear lines, although he did use oval and circular panels occasionally. Pier tables and Pembroke tables were his speciality, with *fleur de lis* motifs on chairbacks which also included heart, hoop, shield, oval and lyre shapes.

Thomas Sheraton (1751-1806) was a trained cabinetmaker but he lived as an eccentric in penury and died in poverty. He published the *'Cabinetmaker's and Upholsterer's Drawing Book'* between 1791 and 1794 in four parts and more than 600 cabinetmakers subscribed to the book on publication.

Fig. 5 Sheraton Pembroke table of veneered mahogany with marquetry in a satinwood crossbanding *(V & A Museum, London)*

The work was not original. He drew freely upon the ideas of Adam, Chippendale and Hepplewhite, and the Louis XVI style although he had a special genius for imparting a gracefulness which was remarkable for its elegant proportions, and delicacy of ornament. He had a greater sense of proportion than Hepplewhite, and his best drawings have never been surpassed in English furniture design. His inventive ability led him to design furniture with secret compartments and mechanical devices.

Sheraton used mahogany, satinwood and harewood extensively and relied on skilful application of veneer matching combined with inlay bandings and lines, and exquisite marquetry set in oval panels.

In 1806, Marc Isambard Brunel patented the first veneer peeling machine, making possible the production of constructional veneers, for plywood manufacture, and in 1818 Henry Faveryear patented the first veneer slicer to produce decorative veneers.

Until these times, all veneers had been sawcut and at last the craft of veneering was freed from the limitations imposed by sawing, and all the techniques of cutting through logs in various ways to extract the best figure could be employed.

The English Regency period was the final phase of the 'Age of Mahogany' ending in 1830. It was dominated by Roman, Egyptian, Greek and Chinese influences sponsored from many different sources.

By 1820, mahogany and rosewood veneers had become so popular that much of the furniture produced was veneered from those woods and decorated with brass inlays which suited the dark backgrounds.

Foliated ornaments and endive scrollwork in brass on ebonised wood veneers became so widespread that it quickly led to the production of stamped and extruded brass rosettes and bosses, a development which brought the style into decay.

Directoire and French Empire

Immediately following the French revolution of 1789, every royal household was looted and sacked, and all court furniture was piled high on bonfires. After the fall of Robespierre, France was governed by a Directorate of five directors (1795-99) of which Napoleon was First Consul. He later overthrew the Directorate and became Emperor.

The Louis XVI *l'antique* style, which was so hated by the revolution-aries persisted, but with changed motifs. During the Directoire, the revolutionary motifs of Fraternity, Equality and Liberty were quickly changed to Greek motifs, but Napoleon changed them to Roman, glorifying the Corsican Caesar's egotism, with winged victory emblems such as laurel wreaths incorporating the Napoleonic 'N'.

When his Egyptian campaigns were in full swing, the French Empire style emerged, featuring the Egyptian motifs of the sphinx, lotus and the lilly.

The veneers used were mahogany, with brass inlays featuring the swan's neck, Athenian bees, the acanthus, the honeysuckle, torches, fasces, the eagle and the lion.

The furniture observed the principles of symmetry and became angular in form.

At the same time, the new American republic severed its colonial links with Britain and adopted the French Empire style, substituting the American eagle and stars for its brass motifs.

The Victorian Period & Arts and Crafts Movement (1837-1901)

Following the Regency period a short lived German style called Biedermeier became the vogue. It was a combination of French Empire and English Regency, but devoid of brass inlays, and using lighter veneers with highly figured matching.

The height of the Victorian period saw the first spate of mass produced ornament which flooded the market. As the wheels of this new machine age began to hum, fads, whims novelties and vogues overlapped each other in confusion.

The best furniture made for the wealthy was of rosewood; for the masses, an avalanche of cheap, shoddy mahogany furniture spewed out from mushrooming backstreet factories.

The affluent middle classes spurned mahogany furniture and preferred American black walnut. Matched leaves of walnut were used to cover inferior wood and indifferent workmanship and was french polished. This relatively new technique of finishing was not properly understood by many, and resulted in a treacly high gloss sticky finish which brought 'factory made' or 'veneered' furniture into disrepute.

The firm of William Morris (1834-96) during this period, introduced a style of cottage furniture, hand made from oak, in the 'arts and crafts' style, and also a new style of Gothic oak furniture.

This led to the Arts and Crafts Furniture Movement of the 1890's and later to the Cotswold school. Many new designers emerged toward the end of the Victorian era; the firm of Morris, Bruce Talbert, C. L. Eastlake, Philip Webb, T. E. Collcutt, W. R. Letheby, Ernest Gimson, C. F. A. Voysey, C. R. Mackintosh, Ambrose Heal are among many eminent furniture makers using veneers in their work, particularly for inlays and design motifs in oak, walnut, mahogany and satinwood furniture.

A splendid example of an *escritoire*, decorated with sycamore marquetry, designed by George Jack for Morris & Co. in 1893, is displayed in the Victoria and Albert Museum, London.

At the turn of the century, the *Art Nouveau* style started in France, later followed by the Art Deco style in England; both failed to enjoy more than a passing vogue, despite the fact that many brilliant new designers emerged producing innovative work in a wide variety of materials. The fact that pieces from these short lived but important periods are widely sought after is a testimony to their greatness.

Between the two world wars from 1920 to 1940, veneering and plywood manufacture developed in countries all over the world.

Architects specified veneered wall panels for shopfitting, restaurants, offices, banks, insurance companies and public buildings.

There was also a huge demand for veneered panels for the railways, and most carriages were decorated with veneers. Marine architects specified almost exclusively, veneered panelling for shipbuilding, and most of the cabins, public function rooms, and staterooms on luxury liners were decorated with veneers. The Queen Mary and Queen Elizabeth were both lavishly decorated with exotic veneers and marquetry murals.

Logs of architectural panel length were imported from all over the world to meet the demand, and many rare and exotic woods were used.

Luxury cars were provided with walnut burr fascias and cappings.

The use of plywood from constructional veneers to produce thin shaped panels for aircraft also led to the production of 'hydulignum' multi-layered plywood from which propellers were turned. In the second world war, the famous Mosquito aircraft were fabricated from plywood panels.

In the first half of the present century, almost all domestic furniture, including the early 'wireless' and 'gramophone' cabinets, were of veneered construction, chiefly in oak, walnut and mahogany, with some bedroom furniture in bird's eye maple; and during the Second World War, 'Utility' furniture was introduced which was veneered mainly in oak.

The post-war years has seen many changes with the widespread use of plastics and metals in furniture design—so much so, that in some quarters a mini-revolt against 'the plastics age' has taken place.

Something better than plastic was demanded. A technique was evolved of printing exotic wood grains such as rosewood, upon plain veneers such as makoré. The panel would have the appearance of rosewood and the feel of real wood. Even so, the plastics industry decided to concentrate upon white melamine board production, which would suit bedroom suites for built-in fitments, and also the DIY 'knock-down' furniture for the home handyman.

More bedrooms and kitchens in Britain today have white melamine-surfaced chipboard built-in fitments and cupboards than any other type. And similarly, living rooms and dining rooms have more modern furniture in completely matching suites in teak veneers than in any other style or type of finish.

Now, there is a rising and persistent vogue for reproduction traditional Regency period furniture featuring mahogany curl veneers and yewtree veneers for dining room and lounge furniture, incorporating boxwood inlay lines.

In the commercial field almost all office blocks and public buildings utilise veneered wall panelling and flush door panels. Office furniture reflects the trend, and combines metal framework usually ebonised, with veneered chipboard panels.

Many company boardrooms today, are proud of a magnificently veneered Brazilian rosewood boardroom table with matching chairs, with the walls panelled to match or in luxurious contrasts, such as satinwood, maple, aspen, cherry or avodire.

This has, in turn, led to a demand for wall panelling for the home and a huge range of random V-grooved veneer wall panels are available.

The general public awareness of the virtues of real wood veneers has made the craft of veneering more popular than ever, and more appreciative of the skills involved in the production of matched veneered furniture, and its future is virtually assured.

Fig. 6 Modern use of mahogany curl veneers, crossbanded in sapele and with boxwood inlay
(McIntosh & Co, Kirkcaldy)

2

From the Tree to You

PAUSE for a moment, while admiring a beautifully figured veneer, and think of the real-life adventure story — the romance of logging — that perhaps brought that piece of timber from far-away lands to you.

Many of the woods we use as veneers for decorative purposes, grow in the heart of dense tropical rain forests; in remote jungle locations, or on high, bleak mountainsides.

Men have penetrated the most forbidding forest sites on earth in search of rare woods. They do not grow in cultivated forests on plantations such as pine, fir, spruce and other more common softwoods. Many valuable hardwoods may be widely scattered in forests of other species which are much less valuable, and grow in solitary isolation and obscurity, and such trees are extracted from their natural environment with great difficulty.

The men who work as loggers endure physical hardships in the most primitive conditions. In addition to climatic hazards, they are often exposed to real danger from wild animals, poisonous reptiles, and the ever-present threat of tropical diseases.

Felling a tree is a highly skilled job. The tree fellers often have to erect pole scaffolding high above the ground to get to a height above the sloping buttress of the tree, which may have a diameter up to twenty feet and over, and which has stood undisturbed for a century or more. (The Californian redwood tree has reached diameters over 36ft (11 metres).

Some massive teak logs are far too heavy to be moved. They are girdled and left to die where they stand, so that their weight decreases before being felled. Then the log, which could weigh four tons or more,

Fig. 7 A buttressed tree. Felling with chain saw at Botambi near Nabgui, Central African Republic

Fig. 8 Felled logs being dragged out of the rain forest near Ratnapura, Colombo, Sri Lanka

Fig. 10 Elephants employed as force workers in Thailand

Fig. 9 Rosewood log being manhandled over rock-strewn rapids in Brazil

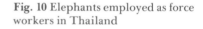

Fig. 12 Bulldozer loading giant makoré
log in Africa

Fig. 11 Logging with cable-crane in
jungle, Sri Lanka

Fig. 13 Log convoys on the road in
Gabon, West Africa

Fig. 14 Mahogany logs floated downriver
to Abidjan harbour

may be dragged by elephant, through jungle tracks to a clearing, possibly over rocky mountainsides.

In tropical South America as many as ten yoke of oxen are used to haul a single log over crude trails to the bed of a stream to await the time when the water is in full spate to carry the log downstream to deeper water.

Men with crowbars have to wrestle logs around boulder strewn rapids. In alpine countries, logs are sent rattling down mountainsides in huge log chutes where they are eventually brought to the caterpillar trucks that load them on to great timber trucks for transportation to river beach-heads. The floatable species are then lashed together into enormous rafts. The non-floaters, such as afrormosia and wenge, are loaded on to pontoons or barges. The rafts are towed by tugboats to the timber wharves where the logs are kept in log harbours or ponds to protect them from attack by insects, fungi, or from rotting or splitting.

In Finland, steam heat has to be injected into the log ponds to prevent them from freezing over.

After grading into veneer or timber logs they are assembled into 'parcels'. A parcel of logs is a carefully balanced assortment to prevent the logyard accumulating unsaleable logs and often log parcels are sold by auction. Veneer logs have to be of a far higher quality than logs for conversion into timber. They must have a clean, cylindrical stem or bole, free from all outward visible defects, and with parallel sides from a point just above the root buttress to below the first limb. The log should have about nine feet of perfect length to enable the mill to extract architectural panelling veneers of a minimum 8 feet 3 inches (2515mm) length.

The log buyer has to stake his judgement and experience on the outward appearance of the log in the round, as the log will keep most of its secrets until it has been sold and the opening cut made on the bandmill saw.

When logs are exported from the country of origin in the round it is one of the most difficult jobs in the veneer business and often a commercial gamble for the buyer, since he may be obliged to purchase a mixed parcel of logs containing good, fair and indifferent examples, some of which he may have to convert into lumber, profile boards or other stock.

He has to assess what type of figure the logs will produce and whether the figure extends throughout the log or only in part; if it is too strong it may not be cut into veneer; and similarly if there are stains visible on the end of the log, whether they penetrate throughout. He has to know if the log will produce a saleable striped figure, and whether it is likely to be a broad or narrow, mottled or roe figure. He will be concerned about how much sapwood the log may possibly contain in relation to heartwood, and he will have to examine the log externally for tell-tale signs of thunder shakes caused by tropical storms; ring checks or cross breaks caused by compression or tension during the life of the tree; whether there are likely to be gum pockets, calciferous deposits or flint-hard knots.

In some cases the buyer may be allowed to make one bore hole to a depth of a few inches with a special auger bit which contains a glass phial in which the withdrawn wood can be examined to see how much sap the log contains before the heartwood is reached. But this is a risky business and can be very misleading and very few buyers of my acquaintance trouble to use the auger. What is certain is that the buyer needs a sound knowledge of wood science to back his judgements.

To increase your pleasure in working with veneers and to ensure success in creating your own veneered projects, it will be rewarding for you to acquire a basic understanding of wood technology.

DEFINITION

A veneer is a thin slice of wood; its thickness is determined by the end use. There are two classifications: (a) constructional (b) decorative.

Constructional veneers are produced for three different purposes: (1) plywood (2) corestock (3) utility articles.

Plywood is an odd number of laminations of veneer bonded at right angles to each other to equalise shrinkage. It has three components:

(i) A central core veneer known as the balancing point.

(ii) An equal number of laminations of veneer on each side of the central core veneer, laid at right angles to each other.

(iii) Two outer casing veneers, known as the face and backing, also laid at right angles to the underlaying veneer, but parallel to the core veneer.

The central core veneer may be the same thickness as the other laminations, but is usually thicker. The outer casing veneers are graded according to their end use. The complete panel is graded according to the type of species used in its manufacture, the type of bond and its durability. A plywood panel is produced as a complete product ready for use.

It may be used as a groundwork for a decorative panel, provided that the outer casing veneers are suitable; it may be further worked upon and treated as corestock and provided with outer casing veneers suitable to receive decorative veneers. Plywood may be manufactured complete with decorative face and backing veneers.

Corestock is a laminated component of a decorative panel requiring further work. It would not be produced and sold as plywood. It is laminated from constructional veneers and may be in flat, shaped or compound curvilinear form. It has three elements:

1.   A central core veneer which may be thicker than the remaining veneers.

2.   An equal number of laminations of veneer, laid at right angles to the core veneer and to each other.

3.   Two other casing veneers known as crossbandings, also laid at right angles to the other veneers.

But unlike plywood, the grain direction of the crossbanding veneers must be *opposite* to (and not parallel with) the grain direction of the core veneer. This is to allow the decorative face and backing veneers to be laid at right angles to the crossbanding veneers, and parallel with the core veneer for panel strength.

Groundwork may be produced with a central core other than constructional veneer, for example: (a) solid wood (b) hardboard (c) flaxboard (d) particle board (e) plywood (in which case it would fulfill both items 1 and 2 above).

Groundwork would require the application of crossbandings prior to receiving face and backing veneers.

Substrates comprise all layers of material below the face and backing veneers including crossbandings, groundwork and corestock.

Utility articles are constructional veneers used in two ways;

(a)   For lamination as components of other articles such as snooker cues, tennis rackets, table tennis bats, emery board nail-files, decorative wood turnery, wooden jewellery and the like.

(b)   The manufacture of chip baskets, battery separators, pipe smoker's spills, ice cream spoons, lollipop sticks, firework rocket sticks, medical spatulas, glassblower's spills and similar items.

DESCRIPTION AND DIMENSIONS

The descriptions 'constructional' and 'decorative' veneers, are simply convenient categories of their end uses. A single species may be either or both, entirely depending upon the *thickness* into which it has been cut; the type of cut through the log; the surface appeal of figure displayed after cutting.

(a)   Walnut (*Juglans regia*) for example, may be cut in one thickness, in nine different ways to produce entirely different visual surface figures.

(b)   Birch, Canadian (*Betula alleghaniensis*) is cut into 'scale' thickness of 0.1mm; for utility purposes in all thicknesses up to 3mm; for decorative purposes from 0.5mm to 0.9mm; for corestock and plywood purposes from 0.9mm to 1.625mm; for outer casings from 0.9mm up to 2.032mm; for centre core purposes up to 6mm thick.

Veneers are produced in lengths up to about 5.5 metres.

Decorative veneers are produced to display aesthetic surface appeal. This depends on several characteristics, the proportion of sapwood to heartwood in the veneers and the visual differences in the heartwood zone caused by growth considerations. The *way* the veneer was cut from the log; the type or cut, (i.e.: the angle of the knife to the longitudinal axis of the log) will produce a different surface appearance. The colouration of the veneer is important—not the 'fresh cut' hue, but the mature fading or darkening that occurs according to species.

The combined effect of colour, texture, grain, figure, markings, lustre and working potential for matching, laying and finishing due to the absence or presence of resin, latex, calcium or other matters; the durability of the species after exposure to light, and ability to maintain these features into maturity, all affect the value of decorative veneers.

Some species are not suitable for constructional purposes, and others are not suitable for decorative purposes. If a constructional veneer log unexpectedly produced a wonderful figure the mill would change gauge and convert it into a decorative veneer, and, conversely, a usually decorative veneer may offer such an uninteresting figure, that the cutting would be stopped, the cutting gauge altered, and the log converted for constructional purposes.

VENEER DIMENSIONS

Thickness   *Europe* All decorative veneers produced in Europe are cut into 0.6mm to 0.9mm thickness for face quality, average thickness 1/40th inch (0.7mm).

Backing grade veneers, vary from 0.5mm to 0.7mm average 0.6mm.

U.S.A. and Australia Most veneers produced are cut 0.9mm (1/28 inch).

Africa and Asia Veneers are produced in the thickness of the country to which the domestically produced veneers will be exported, Europe 0.7mm and USA 0.9mm.

Micro-thin veneers are cut from 0.1mm to 0.25mm.

Length   Architectural panel grade face veneers are 8 feet 3 inches long (2515mm minimum).

Veneers over 6 feet 9 inches (2055mm) and under 8 feet 3 inches (2515mm) are suitable for flush doors.

Veneers under 6 feet 6 inches (1980mm) are suitable for cabinetmaking and the price of the veneers of equal figure and grade will increase according to length.

Widths   *Rotary cut* veneers are widest but are produced mainly for constructional purposes with a few notable exceptions: bird's eye maple, kevazingo and masur birch for example. Rotary peeled veneers are clipped to any convenient width from 8 inches to 24 inches (200mm-600mm). Average 12 inches to 15 inches (300mm-380mm).

Crown Cut (flat sliced). These are the widest decorative veneers, the full width of the log or flitch and vary from 8 inches to 24 inches (200mm-600mm) according to species. The best half of the log would contain bundles of a fair average width of 12 inches to 15 inches (300mm-380mm) but the other half would contain many half-width bundles from 5 inches to 10 inches wide (125mm-250mm). Fair average 8 inches (200mm).

Half Rounded (Stay log) Average widths from 10 inches to 24 inches (250mm-600mm). Fair average: 12 inches (300mm).

Quartered (radial, tangential etc). These striped veneers vary from 5 inches to 12 inches (125mm-300mm) according to species, with a fair average width of 8 inches (200mm).

Shorts　　Fancy butts or stumpwood, are usually about 36 inches to 54 inches (915mm-1375mm) by 10 inches to 18 inches (250mm-450mm) wide. Fair average about 36 inches × 12 inches (915mm × 300mm).

Curl Veneers (Crotches)

Curls vary from 12 inches up to 54 inches in length (300mm-1375mm) with a fair average leaf measuring 30 inches × 12 inches (765mm × 300mm).

Burr Veneers (Burls)

These precious veneers are in small, irregular shaped leaves which vary from about 6 inches × 4 inches (150mm × 100mm) up to 36 inches × 18 inches (900mm × 450mm) according to type. Fair average dimensions are only 18 inches × 9 inches (450mm × 225mm).

Narrows　　Narrow billets are sometimes cut from woods such as Macassar ebony, satinwood, tulipwood, kingwood, boxwood, lignum vitae for decorative crossbandings. These are from 4 feet to 6 feet long (1220mm-1830mm) and from 3 inches to 6 inches (75mm-150mm) wide.

Sawcut　　Very few species are cut by saw today, but those which are available are about 1mm thick and similar dimensions to 'narrows', from billets too small for slicing.

HOW A TREE GROWS

A background knowledge of how a tree grows will prove invaluable to the veneer craftsman. The way in which the tree grows, affects its structure and thus its appearance when cut for veneers.

A seed contains an embryo seedling, which feeds upon food stored in the seed and begins to grow, splitting the seed case; the shoot elongates towards the sky and the rootlet thrusts into the soil to begin performing its function of anchorage, and food storage. The seedling's leaves may remain within the seed case as in oak, or may rise with the shoot as in maple. At the tip of the shoot is the terminal bud or growing point known as the *apical meristem.*

The root develops in one of two ways; either in the form of fibrous spreading roots which grow near to the surface, or by a deep vertical tap root which, in some species grows down as deep as 18 feet (5.5 metres) or more. Firs, maples and beeches have fibrous roots, and pines, hickory and oaks have tap roots for example. A giant sequoia tree in California had a fibrous root system which covered three acres.

During the first year of its life, the sapling develops another growth tissue as an internal sheath of generative cells which is called the vascular cambium. It produces layers of wood on the inside and layers of bark on the outside causing the tree to increase in diameter.

The roots have minute hairs that take up minerals in water solution, which passes up through the sapwood cell structure, and along the branches to the leaves. The sap rises in the spring and ends a month or so before autumn in temperate climates, and it is during this interrupted growth cycle that a distinguishable wood layer is formed called a growth ring.

The view that the age of a tree can be told by counting the number of 'annual' rings is not always true. Cold winters, periodic droughts, and severe climates can interrupt the growth cycle and in certain climates, the cycle can be interrupted several times a year and the number of rings formed may not correspond with the age of the tree. In the tropics, growth may be continuous and the wood may appear to the naked eye to be homogeneous from pith to bark without growth rings. (The pith is formed in the tree's early sappy years, when a small hole forms in the centre of the trunk.)

Apart from these exceptional cases, in temperate climates the age of a tree can be estimated fairly accurately from the number of growth rings provided that they are counted at the base of the trunk. False rings due to frost or caterpillars and other causes are often recognised as such. In moist tropical climates, growth rings may be unrecognisable and are an unreliable indication of age, and only some trees—teak for example—have recognisable rings.

The tree produces its food in its leaves by a process called photosynthesis, from the heat and light of the sun; the carbon dioxide of the air, and the water drawn up through the tree from the soil, which contains minerals. The leaves give off moisture by transpiration. The food produced by the leaves is then carried back through the branches, down the trunk to the roots through the inner bark called the phloem.

Suitably nourished, the cells grow to full size and then divide to form new wood by the vascular cambium which begins at the bases of the buds and extends downwards throughout the tree.

The solid matter of the tree is a chemical compound mainly of cellulose and lignin, and minerals, which contribute to the hardness of the wood. A new layer of wood is formed by the cambium and the inner and outer bark increases in diameter; a new growth ring is formed.

In each growth ring there are two distinct zones. The earlywood cells have thin walls and big cavities, while the latewood cells have small cavities with thick walls. It is the contrast between these two layers, which makes it possible to disinguish them with the naked eye, when viewing the end section of timber, that forms the growth ring.

When seen on the longitudinal surface, especially in softwoods, there is also a distinct colour difference between earlywood and latewood.

As the tree grows larger in diameter, after a few years, the centre of the tree becomes inactive and ceases to conduct sap. Most of the cells in the sapwood die, and only the parenchyma lives until the affected wood forms a darker colour and becomes heartwood. The function of the heartwood is to give the tree its strength and support. It is far more durable than the soft sapwood and of better appearance; it is the heartwood which is valuable commercially and the lighter coloured water-carrying sapwood of little value in comparison.

The wood anatomist studies the number of growth rings to the inch and the proportion of earlywood to latewood within each ring to form an indication of the structural strength and durability of the timber. The widths of the growth rings vary according to the available amount of moisture, and will show changes not only in trees from area to area where more or less rainfall occurs, but within the same tree according to year-to-year variations in the climate. In the case of tonal woods, the heartwood and number of rings to the inch are an indication of their resonant properties.

To provide an example, the number of growth rings to the inch may vary from six to twenty-four in the case of ash, depending on the rate of growth. The strongest ash would be selected from timber with from eight to ten growth rings to the inch and with an average of 70 per cent of latewood across the growth ring.

The specialised study of the systematic measurement of growth, age and biography of trees, for example, in order to determine the timing of past events such as the age of a building, or the date of a climatic change or fire, is embodied in the science of dendrochronology.

The cell structure

The accepted means of wood identification is by a study of the cell structure; the arrangement of these cells into tissues, and the visual

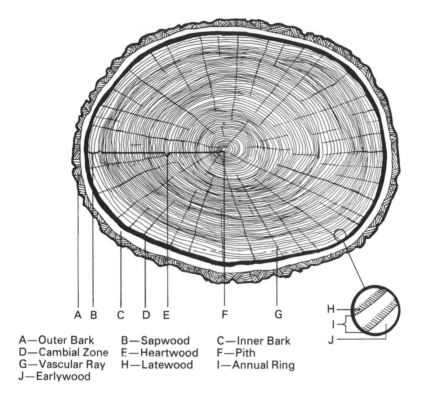

A—Outer Bark   B—Sapwood   C—Inner Bark
D—Cambial Zone   E—Heartwood   F—Pith
G—Vascular Ray   H—Latewood   I—Annual Ring
J—Earlywood

Fig. 15 Cross section of a tree trunk

appearance of these tissues. Wood is created with tube-like cells, which differ in appearance depending upon their functions.

There are three main functions: (a) Vessel cells, which are conductive and carry the sap through the tree, (b) Supportive cells, which provide mechanical support and strength, and (c) Food storage cells, which are in the form of soft tissues that radiate around the centre of the tree like spokes of a wheel and are known as axial parenchyma, and originate at the cambium. They form rays and comprise up to twenty per cent of the total volume of the tree. These three types of cells form certain character patterns in every species and are used as identification aids by the wood anatomist. However, identification often stops at the genus, or part of a genus including a number of species.

Some types of cell perform both the functions of vessel cells and supportive cells. These thin, blunt tipped cells with pitted walls are known as tracheids and are found in softwoods, which do not contain separate vessel cells.

Softwoods and Hardwoods are terms universally applied and are accepted as conventional for the two main classes of commercial timber. But the descriptions can be very misleading. For example, balsa wood is one of the lightest and softest woods known—but it is a hardwood; pitch pine is much harder than many 'hardwoods' but is a softwood. So how do we distinguish one from the other?

The division between the two rests on a botanical distinction. There are two main types, both of which are seed bearing spermatophytes. The first type are *gymnospermae*—naked seeded trees (not having seeds in a closed pod). These are the cone bearing types with evergreen needles or scale-like leaves which we know as conifers, such as pine, spruce, fir, larch, hemlock, cedar and yew. They form extensive forests in cool temperate regions and mountain districts and supply the bulk of the world's commercial timber. They are soft, easy to work, light and strong for most practical purposes.

But the group from which the majority of commercial hardwoods for veneering are found is the *angiospermae*; types which hide their seeds in fruit seed cases and produce broad leaved trees with fruits and flowers which are deciduous, by which we mean that they shed their leaves every year in the autumn, in the temperate zones. The type from which the majority of veneers is produced encase their seeds in two lobes and are called *dicotyledoneae*, which sub-divide into two groups. The polypetalous group, which possess both a calyx and a multi-petalled corolla, produce the most beautiful flowers and fruit such as the apple, pear, peach, plum, cherry and almond, and excellent hardwood veneers such as horse chestnut, maple, lime, cedar, avodire, mahogany, sapele and African walnut.

The other is the apetalous group, whose inconspicuous flowers lack the corolla and often the calyx, but which produce the strongest and most durable of hardwoods such as oak, elm, beech, walnut, willow, and hickory.

The structural features of softwoods, under microscopic examination, appear as a honeycomb structure made up of cells called tracheids, with thin, pitted sidewalls and large open cavities with rounded ends. The earlywood cells have tracheids which overlap, and the pits of adjoining tracheids connect to each other forming a means whereby sap can pass from one to the other. The latewood tracheids develop much thicker walls with smaller pits in their sides, and smaller cavities, and these tracheids are to provide strength rather than for conducting the sap.

Therefore in all softwoods, water conduction and mechanical support are carried out by earlywood and latewood tracheids. There is a gradual transition between the two with no sharp demarcation line. Tracheids are about ⅛ inch (3mm) long.

With hardwoods there are two distinctly different types of cell for

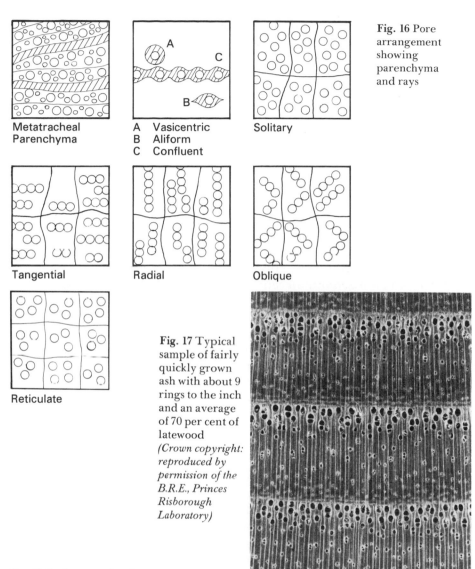

Metatracheal Parenchyma

A Vasicentric
B Aliform
C Confluent

Solitary

Fig. 16 Pore arrangement showing parenchyma and rays

Tangential

Radial

Oblique

Reticulate

Fig. 17 Typical sample of fairly quickly grown ash with about 9 rings to the inch and an average of 70 per cent of latewood *(Crown copyright: reproduced by permission of the B.R.E., Princes Risborough Laboratory)*

Fig. 18 Caricature of end grains

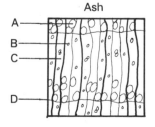

Ash

A
B
C

D

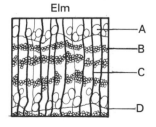

Elm

A
B
C

D

A) Earlywood
B) Latewood
C) Ray
D) Parenchyma

water conduction and for mechanical support. The sap is conducted through vessel cells, which are thin walled, open ended cells arranged one above the other like short lengths of drain pipe, and appear on longitudinal surfaces of planed wood or veneers as fine grooves or grain. The cross section of a vessel cell is called a pore, and on cross grained end surfaces, these pores are visible to the naked eye as tiny holes. In fine textured wood such as sycamore, the pores cannot be seen without a magnifying glass. In hardwoods where the earlywood pores are distinctly larger than the latewood pores, and form a well defined growth ring, they are called ring-porous, e.g., ash, elm, chestnut, teak. In other types where the pores are scattered across the growth ring without much difference between earlywood and latewood pores, they are described as diffuse-porous,—beech, sycamore, birch, lime, poplar, cherry, horse chestnut, willow are examples.

Pore arrangements in hardwoods are described as 'solitary' if isolated from each other; 'clusters' of a given number, or 'chains'—in which case, the general direction of the pore-chain is an identification feature.

The mechanical support of hardwoods is provided by the fibres; long, narrow, minutely pitted thick walled cells, sharply tapered at each end, which make up the bulk of the woody tissue. They are similar in structure to the latewood tracheids of softwoods, but are only about 1mm long. Therefore the vessel cells of the hardwoods are equivalent to the earlywood tracheids of softwoods; the hardwood fibres to the softwood latewood tracheids.

A major diagnostic difference between softwoods and hardwoods is the absence of pores in the growth ring in the former and their presence in the latter.

The function of food storage in both softwoods and hardwoods is carried out by the parenchyma; thin, brick-shaped cells of soft tissue which form into vascular rays, which run horizontally across the grain in a radial direction at right angles to the growth rings. According to species these rays vary from extremely fine in appearance to wide and broad. They may appear all of the same width as in chestnut, or of two distinctly different widths as in oak, or they may combine to form an aggregate ray formation as in alder, for example. There are two main groups of parenchyma. The first group contains (a) vasicentric parenchyma which forms a complete sheath around a pore, (b) aliform parenchyma also forms a sheath but develops elongated winged ends, and (c) confluent parenchyma which is a series of aliform tissues joined to form a continuous band surrounding pores. This group is called paratracheal parenchyma.

The second group is apotracheal parenchyma which forms independently without enclosing pores, and comprises (d) terminal parenchyma where the tissues form a line parallel to the grain fibres and appear as the boundary of the growth ring on the end grain cross section, (e) metatracheal parenchyma forms in lines or bands, (f) reticulate gridwork, or mesh-like arrangement with the rays at right angles to the metatracheal parenchyma.

There are other types of axial parenchyma beyond the scope of this book to examine, such as (g) diffuse parenchyma which takes the form of minute dots scattered over the end grain. The absence or presence of parenchyma, its type, form and distribution are valuable diagnostic features for identification.

Some softwoods such as spruce, larch, Douglas fir and all true pines, possess resin ducts, which are channels surrounded by secretory parenchyma cells which exude resin into channels.

These resin ducts are also found in hardwoods such as meranti, seraya and many of the mahoganies.

Another feature which occurs in many trees is a thin walled secondary growth called tylosis. This anomaly in the normal cell function produces a bubble-like in-growth that fills the vessels during the change from sapwood to heartwood and is sometimes visible on the surface of sawn woods and veneers, showing as a high lustre, thus adding to the decorative effect of the timber. Also, because the vessels fill with this foam-like substance, it is inclined to make the wood less permeable and more difficult to penetrate with preservatives, chemicals or wood dyes.

3

The Grain and Figure
of Veneers

THE GRAIN of timber is an expression often misunderstood and wrongly applied.

The terms 'cross grained' or 'coarse grained' and 'fine grained' actually refer to the *texture* of the wood surface.

A hardwood with large open pores in the earlywood part of the growth ring, or a softwood with a marked difference between the earlywood and latewood zones, will both have a coarse textural feel.

Also, on occasions, 'grain' is used incorrectly to describe the figure, for example when referring to 'silver grain' on quartered oak, which shows a prominent ray figure.

The various cuts through a log will expose a different surface and these three surfaces are often wrongly described as 'end grain', 'side grain' or 'flat grain', when referring to the transverse cross cut surface; the tangential surface cut parallel with the growth rings; or the radial surface cut at right angles to the growth rings.

THE GRAIN

This is the natural arrangement of the wood fibres in relation to the main axis of the tree and there are eight types:

1. *Straight grain*
   The fibres run parallel to the vertical axis of the tree.
2. *Irregular grain*
   The fibres contort around knots, swollen butts, curls etc.
3. *Cross grain*
   The fibres are *not* parallel to the main axis of the tree.
4. *Wavy grain*
   The fibres form short, undulating waves in regular sequence.

5. *Curly grain*
   The fibres form short undulating waves in *irregular* sequence.
6. *Spiral grain*
   The fibres form a spiral around the circumference of the tree giving the trunk a twisted appearance. A flitch cut from a log would have diagonal grain.
7. *Diagonal grain*
   Either the result of a true flat cut board of spiral grain, or a milling defect in otherwise straight grained timber.
8. *Interlocked grain*
   Where the angle of the fibres change from a right-handed spiral to a left-handed spiral and back again at intervals of a few years.

TYPES OF FIGURE

The pattern seen on the surface of a veneer is known as the figure. It results from two main factors: (a) the interaction of several natural features; or (b) the way the log is cut to achieve the desired figure.

Natural features can be any of the following: the scarcity or frequency of growth rings; the colourtone variations between early-wood and latewood; the peculiarities of the combinations of grain types; pigments and markings in the structure; contortions around knots, swollen butts and the stunted growth of burrs; and the tree's reaction to the effects of tension or compression during its life.

The variation in density between earlywood and latewood produces a fine striped figure when the log is radially cut; the greater the variance, the more pronounced the striped figure.

In wavy grain timber or curly grain, we obtain the 'fiddleback' figure as in sycamore, or the 'beeswing' figure in satinwood, further enhanced by the effects of light refraction at different viewing angles.

Where wavy grain is also combined with spiral growth, the log yields a block mottled figure as in eucalyptus; a roe figure is produced by a combination of interlocked grain and wavy grain, as in afrormosia.

When the reverse spiral growth, which produces the interlocked grain, is radially cut, it produces alternate light and dark striped veneers, which will change places when inverted, or when viewed from a different position, with the lighter stripes now appearing darker than the others, a feature which is invaluable for veneer matching.

A variation in the natural pigmentation of veneer can cause a very attractive figure when cut radially, as in the case of zebrano. Irregular grain yields 'blistered' or 'quilted' figure; other combinations provide such attractive effects as pommelle, moiree, 'plum pudding', snail, etc.

Radially cut veneers, cut parallel with the rays produce a strong ray figure on the surface such as 'raindrop' or 'splash' figured oak, 'lacewood' figure in planetree, 'lace' sycamore, and Australian silky oak.

The many descriptive names given to types of veneer figure by the trade cannot always be relied upon since no two trees are ever identical.

Butts   The butt or stump of the tree is the section above ground nearest to the roots. Normally a veneer log is felled from a point above the buttress, but where butt figure is desired, the cut may include part of the buttress. At this juncture of the trunk with the roots, the fibres of the wood are distorted by the changes in direction, and also by the effects of compression, due to the weight of the living tree. These butt ends are difficult to machine, and are not normally cut into veneer. There are certain rare exceptions, such as figured walnut stumpwood, and highly figured burry-butts in ash, for example. Butts are usually cut by half rounding on rotary lathes.

Burrs (Burls)

These are wart-like growths which appear on trees and when cut into veneer have the appearance of tightly clustered dormant buds, each with a darker pith, which, through stunted growth—possibly caused by an injury to the tree in an early stage of growth—failed to develop into twigs or branches.

Figured burr veneers appear as groups of tiny knot formations, like masses of small eyes, surrounded by swirling, contorted lines and pigmented veins and are the most treasured of all precious fancy figured veneers, and are the most expensive.

Because of the surface of burr veneers presenting a mass of brittle knots and short end fibres, they require special treatment in cutting and handling. They are usually dried with a slightly higher moisture content than ordinary veneers, which renders them less liable to crack or break in handling. However, this can result in a 'dross' or fungal growth to the surface—especially in the case of amboyna burr and maidu burr. It is not serious, and is easily removed at a later stage.

Burry-butts

As burrs form mostly near the buttress of a tree, some of the most attractive figure is obtained from burry-butts, which contain the advantages of beautiful swirling figure and burrs which are less figured but are also less brittle and easier to handle.

Curls (Crotches)

Veneer logs are cut from the tree from a point just above the root buttress, to a point just below the intersection of the first limb or fork of the tree.

Above that point, the wood fibres in the trunk of the tree begin to suffer from reaction of either compression or tension caused by the weight of the limb. When this section is cut into veneer, it produces a

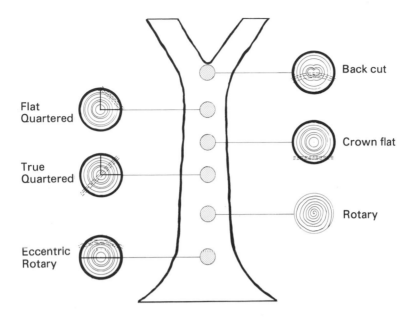

Back cut

Flat
Quartered

Crown flat

True
Quartered

Rotary

Eccentric
Rotary

Fig. 19 Different cuts through the tree shown by
the dotted lines *(see also page 59)*

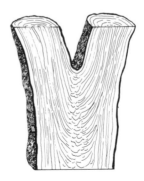

Fig. 20 A burr growing on a trunk

Fig. 21 How a curl is formed

very distinctive 'curl' or 'feather' figure elliptical in outline but with a strong central plume.

In cabinetwork, the curl is usually inverted so that it appears upside down from the position it occupied in the growing tree.

Curl Front and Backs

During the cutting process, the true curl figure is not immediately apparent from the first few slices into the wood from the outside. The first leaves may be devoid of curl figure, which gradually becomes stronger and more pronounced as cutting continues.

These perfectly sound veneers are the curl fronts, possessing a swirling figure, and are usually very sound and flat. Then the beautiful curl figure appears. As cutting continues through the curl, the figure becomes less distinct and gradually disappears and produces curl-backs, with swirl figure again.

When a complete stock of curls is purchased, it will usually contain a few fronts and backs, but often these may be sold separately.

Ideally, veneers should be cut from the sappy outside, towards the heart. In the case of curls, a special technique of cutting is adopted which cuts from the 'double-heart' (caused by the joint of the limb and the trunk) out towards the sappy outside. This 'stay-log' half round back-cutting takes a cut at a greater sweep through the log in a direction across the growth rings to produce the desired figure. However, it can result in one half of the leaf of curl being smoothly cut, and the other half having a rough texture which may tear out.

By its nature, curl veneer tends to buckle in the centre after drying as it tries to return to its natural shape.

Texture

This refers to the variation in the size of the spring and summer cells. For example, diffuse-porous woods with narrow vessels and fine rays are described as 'even textured'; ring-porous woods with wide vessels and broad rays are 'coarse textured'.

Oak is coarse textured; mahogany, medium textured; and sycamore is fine textured.

Lustre

This is the ability of the wood cells to reflect light and is closely related to the texture. Close, smooth textured woods are likely to be more lustrous than coarse textured woods such as oak. However, the ability of the wood to take a high degree of polish does not equate to its degree of lustre.

Odour

Many woods have a strong natural odour when freshly cut into veneer. Whilst the majority of veneers lose their odour in the pre-conditioning, cutting and drying phases of production, others retain their characteristic odour and may sometimes be put to good use.

Camphor and cedar may be used to line the interiors of clothes closets; cigar box cedar is used in making cigar boxes and humidifiers to retain the aroma of cigars.

The resinous pines and spicey aromas are pleasant, but others are fetid and can be unpleasant.

Mineral stains

Timbers coming into contact with iron compounds in the soil may suffer from mineral stains. The chemical reaction between iron and tannins or related compounds such as polyphenols, which are present in wood, are likely to cause severe staining. Veneers such as obeche, oak and afrormosia are examples of wood that can be affected.

Insect and fungal attack

All sorts of insects attack the living tree. Leaf mining, gall mining, twig boring and seed eating types do not affect the veneers, but cambium eating, wood eating and sap sucking types certainly do. The *lyctus* beetle usually attacks the sapwood of hardwoods for example. The sapwood of the tree provides starch and food for insects and fungi; the higher moisture content, especially in softwoods, renders the tree more likely to fungal attack.

Certain veneers are affected by a mould type of fungus which attacks the surface of the veneer, and serious discolouration can be caused by wood destroying fungus which also brings about decay.

In most cases they are very destructive, however, in a few cases, such as in maple, oak, chestnut, birch etc., they increase the decorative value of the timber.

False heart

Many species with a light coloured heartwood show a 'false heart' caused by natural mineral stains from the soil. Examples are black heart in ash, and brown heart in beech, but these render the heartwood equally as strong as the more usually coloured heart and is not a defect.

REACTION WOOD

A tree normally grows erect, against the force of gravity. If it is forcibly displaced or bent, its natural response is to develop a reaction, to counteract the forces tending to deform it, and to restore itself to the normal position.

During the tree's struggle to assert itself over the force that tries to bend it, the tree develops what is known as reaction wood.

In hardwoods, the reaction wood forms on the upper side of leaning or crooked stems, and is known as tension wood. Softwoods, by contrast, develop a reaction on the lower side and is known as compression wood.

Both tension wood and compression wood differ from normal wood in many respects, and both impair the quality of the timber. They are

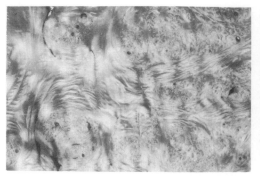

Fig. 22 Maple burry butt

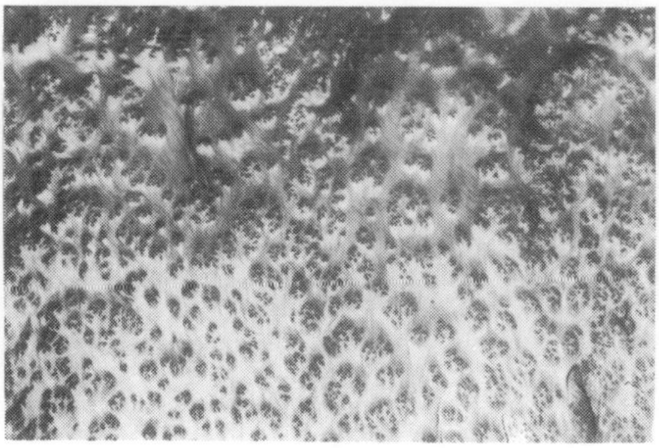

Fig. 23 Thuya burr

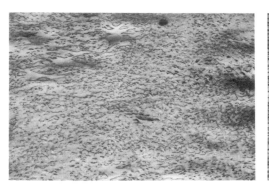

Fig. 24 Rotary cut, freak
figured, Masur birch

Fig. 25 Zebrano

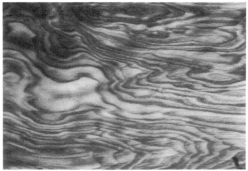

Fig. 26 Ash curl

Fig. 27 Olive ash butt

Fig. 28 Flat sliced crown cut
fruit cherry

Fig. 29 True quartered, radially cut
Australian silky oak with ray figure

Fig. 30 Flat quartered, tangentially
cut Macassar ebony

Fig. 31 True quartered oak, with
"splash" raindrop ray figure

Fig. 32 Faux quartered diagonally cut wenge

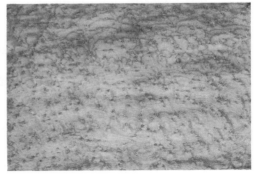

Fig. 33 Rotary cut bird's eye maple

characterised by exceptionally high longitudinal shrinkage in drying and a subsequent large expansion when moisture is re-absorbed, which brings about severe distortion within the tree.

Tension wood

Any hardwood which grows on a hillside, or on exposure to strong prevailing winds may become a leaning tree and subject to tension. When it is bent or tilted bodily by a hurricane for example, a very strong development of tension wood is initiated to try to restore the tree to the vertical.

Obviously, the veneer log is a well rounded cylindrical butt, with a straight stem, but tension wood growth is quite often discovered, when the log is opened, reflecting a tortuous struggle to attain the vertical in its early growth.

Top logs—higher in the tree above the first limb—suffer much more commonly from tension wood problems, but as utilisation dictates the conversion of lower grade veneers, the problem becomes more widespread for the veneer merchants.

Any indication of irregular growth is a danger signal, and is quite common in mis-shapen home grown logs of elm, oak, beech, poplar etc.

Tension wood can be recognised if the end of a crosscut log is examined; it appears on the side with the larger radius as concentric, crescent shaped zones, following around the growth rings but differing in colour and texture.

In beech and poplar, the zones of tension wood have a lustrous silvery appearance. In other woods it may appear as a darker crescent shaped growth, harder than the rest of the material. The fibres tend to tear instead of cutting on the saw, and appear like woodwool. It is especially noticeable in veneers, which have a rough woolly surface which is most pronounced in woods of irregular grain.

Under the microscope, the wood fibres contain a thick gelatinous inner layer which gives a cellulose reaction and stains instead of the normal lignin reaction; where the gelatinous layer is missing the fibre walls give a cellulose staining reaction indicating a lack of lignification.

Tension wood causes veneers to buckle and split due to collapse in drying.

Compression Wood

This is found in softwoods in trees growing out of the vertical, exposed to strong prevailing winds, or tilted by hurricane, or even the sheer weight of snow and ice on hillsides; even in an erect stem it can be found under a large branch. This abnormal wood tends to be more pronounced in rapidly growing trees.

In appearance on the crosscut end of a log compression wood forms in bands of concentric growth on the longer radius in the same way as tension wood in hardwoods. It is denser and darker in colour than normal wood and is more distinct in spruce than in the darker heartwood of pine, or larch and it is difficult to detect in veneers which are naturally darker and have streaks such as Parana pine.

Abnormally high shrinkage along the grain causes transverse fractures and rough woolly patches, and are to be considered bad defects in veneers.

4

How Veneers are Cut

I N order to extract the greatest commercial value from the log, it is the veneer cutter's task to decide *how* the log is to be cut.

The structural features and natural characteristics of each log are studied; from the end grain, he can see mirrored in the cell structure, all the events and hazards that the tree was subjected to in its lifetime. Whether it enjoyed years of plenty or drought; hunger or maltreatment; attacked by insects, plagued by disease or burned by fire. Whether extremes of climate and the tree's fight for life have induced tension or compression wood; or evidence of fungal attack.

No two logs are ever identical; there are differences of grain, figure, texture and markings which will vary in the same species and even in the same log. But even more fascinating, is that every cut through a log at a different angle, will produce a veneer with a visual surface pattern difference.

This is vitally important, because the commercial and aesthetic value of a decorative veneer depends both on the peculiarities of its structure, and, even more, on *how* the veneer was cut from the log.

DECORATIVE VENEERS
There are three basic methods of cutting decorative veneers, they are: sawing; slicing; and rotary peeling.
Sawing
This has largely been superseded by knife cutting methods. It is still used today for cutting exceptionally hard species such as lignum vitae, greenheart and Gabon ebony. Also for cutting timbers of a diameter too small for economic knife cutting and for the production of 'oyster' veneers from small limbs.

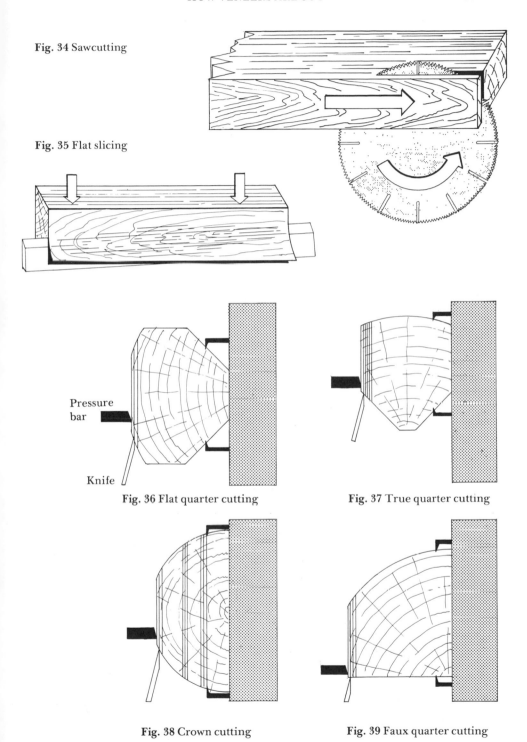

Fig. 34 Sawcutting

Fig. 35 Flat slicing

Pressure bar

Knife

Fig. 36 Flat quarter cutting

Fig. 37 True quarter cutting

Fig. 38 Crown cutting

Fig. 39 Faux quarter cutting

Home craftsmen also use small circular saws for cutting up domestic limbs for small quantities of narrow decorative veneers.

Normally, huge segmental circular saws are used, in a very wasteful process, where almost as much wood is lost in sawdust as is converted into veneer.

Slicing

There are four methods of slicing decorative veneers.

Flat sliced crown; True quartered, radial; Flat quartered; Faux quartered.

Flat sliced crown

The log is sawn in half, and slicing begins at the sappy crown to produce a pattern of sappy edges and a very attractive heartwood display of loops in the centre of the leaf.

The familiar wide figured leaves of walnut, rosewood, teak, elm and ash are produced in this way and are so useful for traditional cabinet making, flush doors and architectural wall panelling.

Ideally, as in flat sawn timber, the growth rings should meet the face of the veneer, at an angle of less than 45 degrees.

True quartered, radial

The log is sawn into quarters, or sections known as 'flitches' which are roughly a quarter of a log—but may be much less according to the diameter of the log concerned, in order to produce a flitch where the rays are generally in the same direction.

The flitch is cut across at 90 degrees to the growth rings, and generally parallel to the medullary rays.

Obviously, if an actual quarter of a log were used, the rays would be parallel with one cut, but would gradually be angled like the spokes of a wheel, around to 90 degrees from the first cut. Therefore, flitches are cut from the log to maximise the number of rays approximately at 90 degrees to the growth rings.

This produces the beautifully striped veneers such as sapele, and the attractive silver grained, 'splash', and 'raindrop' figured oak, silky oak, and the lacewood figure in plane tree.

Flat quartered, tangential

The flitch is cut in a direction parallel to the growth rings and at 90 degrees to the rays. The cut produces a veiny, heart type figure in the leaf centre, with stripey edges. The tangential cut produces veneers which are narrower than those flat sliced crown cut, being only half the width.

Although sometimes superior in figure to full width crown cut veneers, the quartered log or flitches will not provide the equivalent quantity of continuous sequential figure for matching purposes.

Faux Quartered, diagonal

The quarter log or smaller flitches of a large log are sliced in a

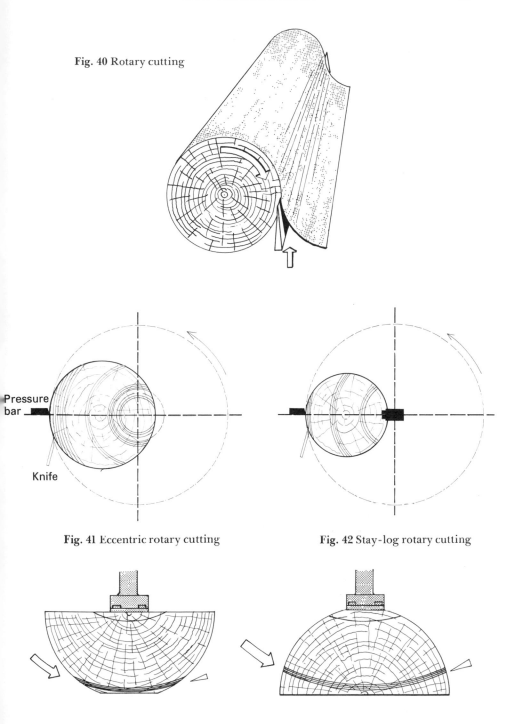

Fig. 40 Rotary cutting

Pressure bar

Knife

Fig. 41 Eccentric rotary cutting

Fig. 42 Stay-log rotary cutting

Fig. 43 True half rounding (stay-log)

Fig. 44 Back cut half rounding (stay-log)

compromise between radial and tangential cutting. The line of cut runs at 45 degrees to both the growth rings and the rays.

This provides a little heart type figure at one side of the leaf and a rather curved striped figure across the leaf. These leaves make up well in veneer matches.

Rotary Peeling   There are five methods:

The complete log-in-the-round, is mounted in a giant lathe and is peeled off against the knife in a sheet, the length of the log and in a continuous width.

The log is forced against a pressure bar, and the knife advances by one veneer thickness for every revolution of the log.

The veneer peels off in a long sheet rather like unwrapping a roll of paper.

Rotary cutting is the method used universally for the production of constructional veneers for plywood manufacture and corestock, and also for a very wide range of utility purposes, such as chipbaskets, battery separators, tennis racquets etc.

It is also used to produce many freak figured decorative veneers, where the figure cannot be extracted by any of the other cutting methods, such as bird's eye maple; figured betula, masur birch, kevasingo, for example.

The surface pattern on the veneer shows a swirly grained figure as the line of cut follows around the path of the growth rings.

Rotary eccentric cutting: By locating the round log off-centre in the lathe chucks, the eccentrically mounted log meets the knife for only about a quarter of its revolution, gradually increasing as the log diameter reduces.

By this method, extra wide veneers can be produced with the general appearance of sliced crown cut, with sappy edges, and a flowery looped heart figure in the centre. The line of cut does not follow around the growth rings, but takes a progressively wider sweep across them as the cutting proceeds.

Stay-log cutting: A slab-cut is taken off one side of the round log, to enable the log to be mounted on a stay-log in the chucks of a rotary lathe.

The resulting cut takes a more shallow sweep across the growth rings than eccentric cutting, but wider veneers than would have been possible with flat cut crown slicing.

Stay-log true half rounding: Up to about half a log may be mounted in the stay-log on a rotary lathe, so that cutting commences at the *sapwood* side of the log.

This method produces wider veneers than quarter sliced by the flatcut method, as the line of cut takes a longer sweep across the growth rings in a curved direction, in woods with prominent rings.

Stay-log half rounding back-cutting: A flitch, a third, or about half a log, is mounted in the stay-log of a rotary lathe, at the sappy outer edge, so that cutting commences at the *heart* side.

The line of cut follows a path at an even greater angle than true cutting and is used for cutting fancy butts and stumps.

Logs which have a double-heart feature, such as curls (crotches) are usually back-cut on the stay-log.

THE CUTTING PROCESS

The logs are de-barked, and then pass through electronic metal detecting machinery to discover the presence of metal fragments it may have picked up, or may even have grown around. This is one reason why hedgerow or back garden timber is seldom used for veneer production. Such logs are often found to contain rusty nails from old clothes lines; parts of horse shoes or the tip of a penknife broken off while carving initials into the tree.

The log is clamped to a moving carriage and travels on rails to meet the giant bandsaw. The blade may be 14 inches (355mm) wide and fifty feet (15.25 metres) long, and travelling at eight thousand feet (2438 metres) a minute.

A slab-cut is removed—a small tangential cut from one side of the log to provide a flat base. (This only applies to logs which are not intended for rotary peeling, which are dealt with in the round). The log is then turned over on to its flat base. Sometimes this slab cut is quite large, in order to reduce the height of the log to clear the upper limits of the saw carriage.

The next cut is the opening cut. The heart of a log is seldom dead centre, especially in trees grown in temperate zones where there is more wood on the side of the tree that grew facing the sun. The 'opening cut' takes this into account and is aimed at cutting out the pithy wood at the heart, if any. Now the exposed surface is examined for figure, grain, texture, defects, and evidence of insect or fungal attack, mineral stains etc. It is at this point that the veneer cutter decides how best to cut the log to extract the greatest yield, by one of the methods described. The log is then marked accordingly and offered to the bandsaw again for cutting into the required section.

The halved, quartered, or flitched log sections are taken from the bandsaw to pre-conditioning log softening vats where they are steamed or given hot water baths for periods varying from a day up to two weeks, depending upon the species, size, hardness or thickness to be cut.

This treatment softens the tissues and reduces the possibility of the fibres being torn during the cutting process. It also protects the valuable knife edge from dulling too quickly.

Certain species such as sycamore and horse chestnut, which produce white veneers, would immediately suffer from discolouration if steam or hot water treated, and have to be cut 'cold'.

Veneer mills do not like cutting veneers without pre-treatment, because even small knots, which would slice easily if boiled, could be as hard as flint, and would have to be hacked out with an axe. The resulting hole reduces the yield of sound veneer from the log. Even worse would be the loss of production which would result from a chipped knife, which would have to be changed.

The flitches of logs are brought by overhead crane into the veneer mill for cutting. (In modern mills, the whole process is now fully automated and computer controlled). The flitch is either fastened to the flitch table with clamps, or held against a flitch bed with vacuum pressure, for slicing. It is held at an angle to the horizontal and is moved up and down bringing the flitch against the veneer knife in a shearing motion which cuts the veneer into the pre-set thickness. With every stroke of the machine, the flitch moves forward by the same thickness as the veneer being cut, at from 80 to 100 veneer strokes per minute.

The rotary cutting logs or sections are mounted in the lathe.

After cutting by rotary lathe, in continuous peeling, the veneers would pass through automatic electronically controlled clippers, to be cut into pre-set widths as required to suit production. All decorative veneers are kept in the precise sequence as cut from the log or log section to provide matching consecutive leaves. The 'set' from the cutter then passes through a mechanical drier where they are jet-air dried to an exact moisture content.

The water in the veneer cells is known as 'free water' and in the cell walls as 'absorbed water'.

When you consider that the weight of a newly felled 'green' log can amount to more than double its dry weight, plus the fact that the flitch or section has been steamed or boiled, the veneers are in a saturated condition when entering the drier. The drier operates at between 80 to 160 degrees C and removes the moisture down to a point known as 'fibre saturation point', where the veneer loses the free water in its cell cavities, but leaves the cell walls intact. Beyond this point, the cell walls would begin to shed their water and shrinkage would result.

By a scientifically regulated process, the veneers are dried to about 12½ per cent moisture content for all normal domestic purposes, and to 14 per cent or 18 per cent external use. The aim is to bring them into equilibrium with local atmospheric conditions, and this will vary with local humidity and climatic conditions in different locations. Fortunately, as wood is hygroscopic, it will absorb moisture from the atmosphere or shed its water in super dry conditions. The immediate purpose in a veneer factory is to store the veneers without risk, and without waiting for a period of natural acclimatisation.

The veneers are now transported to the clipping and grading department where irregular shaped or waney edged leaves, as cut directly from the flitch, are clipped to widths in bundles of 16, 24, 28, or 32 leaves—always in units of four for matching purposes. These giant clippers are up to 17 feet (5180mm) in length. Wide veneers with a sappy edge and a wandering stripe, may be 'trued-up' by being cut at an angle to produce a narrower leaf with a stripe parallel to the newly clipped edge. It is at this stage that veneer grading takes place, and where the commerical value of the veneers is determined.

Veneer Grading

The first requirement is that the veneers should be structurally sound and free from natural defects such as knots, holes, in-growing bark, thunder shakes, compression or tension wood, shell, worm holes, mineral stains etc. Next an examination for milling defects such as knife scour marks across the leaf caused by a chipped knife, evenness of cutting gauge at each side of the leaf and at each end.

Sometimes the log hardness can result in some leaves of veneer being thicker and others thinner, as the machine compensates for the unequal pressure. The drier may have left roller marks imprinted on the face of the veneer and in the case of veneers with a high tannin content, may penetrate through the leaf leaving a blue stain. This occurs on obeche, oak and afrormosia.

Assuming that the veneers have no natural or milling defects, the physical appearance of the veneer becomes important in grading, in particular the colouration and figure, markings and texture and particularly the length.

The importance of veneer length is widely misunderstood. Veneers sold for architectural panelling must be a minimum of 8 feet 3 inches (2515mm) in length to allow for trimming down for panels 8 feet × 4 feet, (2438 × 1219mm). As only a small percentage of all logs cut, produce perfectly graded 'A' quality face veneers in 8 feet 3 inches (2515mm) lengths, completely sound and free from all defects, they are, naturally, the most expensive.

Next in order of requirement, from a veneer cutter's viewpoint, is a veneer which will suit the 'flush door' market, which must be about 6 feet 9 inches × 7 feet (2057 × 2133mm). Cabinet making veneers may be shorter. But this does not mean that they are of a lower *quality*, only of a shorter length. In fact, the most precious and highly prized veneers ever produced are small in length, such as burrs, butts, curls etc. It is also true that from a 'face quality', top grade viewpoint, many veneers of 6 feet (1828mm) in length are far superior to architectural veneers of 8 feet 3 inches (2515mm) length and comparatively are worth much

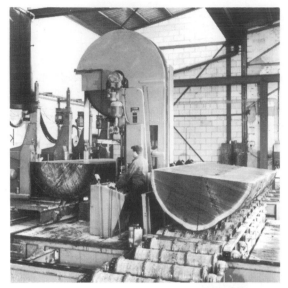

Fig. 45 A log is sawn on the giant bandmill into flitches

Fig. 46 Stored flitches awaiting overhead crane for transport to conditioning vats

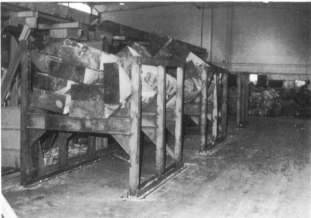

Fig. 47 Veneers are fed through a mechanical drier

Fig. 48 Flitches being sliced in veneer factory

Fig. 49 Logs of veneer in humidity controlled warehouse

more.

Another problem with architectural length veneers is that an architect may take a small sample from a log and specify the log in his plans, and it may take two years or more before the contractor calls to purchase the specified log. During that long period the log has to be stored and protected, all of which reflects in the price of the log.

Many logs from temperate zones, which have an off-centre pith, produce a good half and a bad half, when cut into veneers. The opening cut provides a large sound half; and after the core wood has been cut out, the back of the log appears as narrow width bundles, while the best half may possess a large number of wide, face quality veneers. For this reason, veneer mills and merchants will not 'break' logs, and allow individual flitches or bundles to be sold from the log.

In cases where this is permitted, bundles have to be bought 'as rising from the pile' i.e., without selection, or the result would be that the best bundles would be taken, and the residue would become unsaleable.

Veneer craftsmen may be able to persuade a veneer merchant to 'sweeten' the appearance of a log which contains a poor 'back half' by selling off the short and narrow bundles. The 'shorts' may be wide and well figured; the 'narrows' may be long but possess defects which can be trimmed out.

The grading department decides, whether the quality is of 'face' or 'backing' grade, and in the case of striped veneers the mill has a list of grades depending on the straightness and closeness of the stripe, and the type of 'ribbon' or 'pencil striped' effect etc.

The details of the length, width, number of leaves in the bundle, the bundle number, number of bundles in the flitch, flitch number, number of flitches in the log, log number etc., are all recorded on the computer, which provides a complete print-out of the total log specification in square metres. Sometimes the price is printed in code, with a summary of defects and negotiable selling prices; whether the log could be 'broken' etc.

The log is then fork lifted and stored in a humidity controlled warehouse for palletising or crating, shielded from natural daylight and with every leaf of veneer in exactly the same position that it occupied in the log.

CONSTRUCTIONAL VENEERS

The business of converting logs for constructional veneer purposes for corestock or plywood manufacture is also a highly specialised one and in the forefront of scientific and technological innovation.

Whereas decorative logs are fairly huge in diameter and are handled individually as previously explained, the lower grade logs intended for constructional purposes can be handled in a far more mechanical way.

Huge plants are established in locations where the maximum conversion of the timberland 'mix' within that catchment area can become a viable commercial proposition.

Research into the ratio between softwoods and hardwoods in the region is the key factor. As total utilisation of every twig and branch and every bit of bark comes into the calculations it is essential that the softwood/hardwood ratio is marketable.

There would be no point in having to import into the region extra hardwoods if the ratio was wrong, or have an excess of softwood if the market demanded hardwood faces for example.

As a typical instance of how maximum utilisation of a quarter of a million acres of forest was tackled by the Boise Cascade Corporation Inc. of America in North Carolina, they began with a forestry survey which revealed that the timberland mix was 35 per cent hardwood and 65 per cent softwood. Market research proved that softer hardwoods could be used as corestock; hardwood faces could be supplied with softwood plywood, and that hardwood plywood had a market.

In addition to a veneer plant, there would be a backup of other units such as an attendant sawmill, a plywood factory, and a chipboard factory. In other cases a pulp mill and a paper mill would be possible, which would ensure the total consumption of all timber, offcuts, trimmings, chipping, shavings and bark.

Fineline veneers

This type of man-made veneer became commercially available in the 1950's, intended for the furniture and architectural panel trade.

Veneers of constructional thickness up to ⅛ inch (3mm) were cut from various logs and bonded together to form a man-made flitch. This was returned to the slicer and cut at right angles to the layers of veneer into a wide leaf of ribbon straight striped veneer.

The commercial possibilities of this type of veneer were great. A furniture manufacturer could register for his own exclusive use, a precise pattern of stripes; the veneers could be jointed at the factory without waste. The tonal appearance was guaranteed from month to month, to assist quality control and the finishing department.

Perhaps the biggest advantage was to produce man-made close substitutes for scarce or expensive veneers. African walnut, agba, and afrormosia were used to imitate teak; utile, gaboon, meranti, cipo and others were used to imitate sapele.

Sadly, the novelty caused firms to abuse the idea and all sorts of wild and weird combinations were tried, and although the vogue enjoyed a limited popularity it rapidly disappeared.

No doubt, after a period of experiment and research, a more natural

Fig. 50 Stay-log cutting
half-round

Fig. 51(a) Logs peeled down to
4″ (101mm) cores

Fig. 51(b) Four tray deck system
taking continuous veneer
sheets

product may emerge and might find favour with the public.

Injected veneer

Also during the 1950's an idea originated in Germany which was to inject the living tree with aniline dyes. The sap carried the dye through the tree to its branches and leaves. After a few years, with successive growth layers, there would be a diffusion of colour through the heartwood. When the log was cut into veneers, a more remarkable effect was obtained naturally, than by the chemical dyeing of veneers of a monotone colour.

Some experiments involved injecting a tree with a different dye each year to produce rainbow effects in the cut veneer. This proved to be too garish and had limited aesthetic value. Further experiments involved injecting different shades or strengths of the same hue to produce subtle shades of pinks, reds, maroons, or various shades of blues or greens.

The original characteristics of the tree, such as grain, texture, figure, rays, markings etc., were unaffected. However, the experiments were not always successful, for example, it was found that the ray figure in beech did not take the dye. Its best application was for architectural wall panelling to create an ambience otherwise unobtainable. Injected fineline veneers also enjoyed a brief vogue.

HAREWOOD

Centuries ago, when logs for veneers were cut with the pit-saw, into boards ¼ inch (6mm) thick, the log was conditioned by soaking in artesian well pools—some of which contained salts of iron. The effect of these salts on various species was different. Sycamore became silver grey; maple turned grey-green; oak became purple and walnut almost black.

This accidental discovery enabled craftsmen in those days to widen the spectrum of colour tones used. What they had found was the chemical reaction between the natural tannin in wood and metallic sulphates of various kinds.

When tannic acid (which is used as an astringent) is mixed with metallic sulphate, the reaction forms a salt which rapidly oxidizes upon exposure to the air and turns black. Of the various sulphates of iron, copper and zinc, the one used to produce harewood commercially is ferrous sulphate (copperas) which will react with tannin in veneers at room temperature in tap water. The other sulphates require the addition of sulphuric acid or an ammonia mordant, and higher temperatures; copper sulphate is an irritant and is poisonous.

Tannin concentration varies throughout the tree during its annual growth cycle and the tree has to be felled when the sap is at its height, rather than in the spring or winter. Tropical trees do not enjoy the seasonal rise and fall that trees in the temperate zones experience; but the sap rises and falls according to the phases of the moon and are felled according to lunar cycles. Therefore the amount of tannin in the tree depends on several factors, not least of which is the type of soil (sand, clay, chalk etc.) and the felling cycle.

Another problem is the pre-conditioning of logs by boiling or steaming prior to cutting into veneers, which draws the water soluble tannin out of the sap. Which is why logs for harewood production— almost exclusively sycamore—are selected from nurseries in specific locations where soil conditions are known. They are felled when the sap has risen, never pre-conditioned and always cut cold. This has a very detrimental effect on the veneer knives and few firms specialise in sycamore production for harewood.

To produce harewood, the first essential is a non-metallic container (a glass jar with a screwtop would suffice for very small leaves). A domestic fibreglass water storage tank is ideal for 3 feet (914mm) lengths; a plastic dustbin is also suitable as the veneers may be coiled around to fit inside, in 8 feet (2438mm) lengths.

Never use warm or hot water as this will deepen the tone. Fill the bath from the tap with cold water, but measure the quantity in gallons or litres.

Make a solution of ferrous sulphate in water, using 1.3 ozs (36 grammes) to the gallon (4.5 litres), in a separate container and stir until completely dissolved before introducing the solution to the dyebath. Submerge the veneers, coiled round if necessary to fit the bath, and weigh them below the water level with heavy wooden weights—do not use iron weights. After a few hours, remove the bundle from the bath and use a sponge to wash the surface of every leaf on both sides. This is to remove a sludge that will form on the top leaves, and to ensure complete penetration through the entire bundle. Always keep the veneers in bundle sequence.

The real secret of producing a pearly light silver-grey harewood, is to use only a little of the chemical over a long period, with regular washings. The entire process should be completed overnight. Smaller quantities of a few leaves only take an hour for complete penetration.

After removing the first bundle from the dyebath, (and the solution will work for weeks) successive immersions of new stock can be made, but the tone will get progressively darker.

To produce slate harewood, or dark charcoal harewood, heat the solution or throw a handful of washing soda into the bath to achieve instant penetration; the more soda and the hotter the water the darker the shade.

Always keep a scrap piece of veneer from each bundle as a test piece. Take it out periodically and run it under the tap, dry it carefully, and cut off a sliver with a sharp knife. If the test piece is not dried properly the knife will carry the solution with it and misguide you. Then break the veneer in half and tear it across the grain—the fibres should be completely penetrated and none of the original colour showing through.

The amount of natural tannin in the sycamore decides the colour—not the time left soaking in the dyebath. Once penetration is achieved there is no point in leaving the veneer in the bath.

Why not soak sycamore veneers in a tannin solution to make silver harewood? A tannin solution made from steeped tea, or tannin powder, or from tannic acid, will turn the veneer light brown and when immersed in copperas will produce a slate or dark harewood.

Harewood is light sensitive, and should be air dried and wrapped against light under heavy weights. It should not be allowed to come into contact with acidic substances, or the silver-grey will immediately bleach back to white.

For this reason, all acid catalytic adhesives and finishing materials must be tested for compatibility when using harewood on a project.

Anything with a pH factor below 7 will have this effect. In practice, the veneer craftsman who intends to tackle making his own harewood or dyed woods, should equip himself with a pH meter, in order to control the three variables (a) the veneer, (b) the water supply and (c) the dyebath solution.

The water locally may be hard or soft and should be de-mineralised to neutral. A scrap of the veneer to be used (the fresh whitest veneer possible) is then tested in a glass of de-mineralised water, and the reading obtained, and this is matched with the copperas solution for perfect results.

Otherwise the process is just a 'hit or miss' guesswork project with widely varying results.

DYED VENEERS

With harewood, we were dealing with a chemical reaction. Although other chemicals may also be used in water to produce different colours, the range is limited and the colours are very basic.

For example, brown shades may be attained by using a solution of potassium permanganate; potassium bichromate gives a warmer shade of brown.

Many dyestuffs require spirit solvents, such as white spirit, methylated spirits or naptha solvents, but most of these pose two problems, one of penetration and the other of permanency to light.

The Society of Dyers and Colourists have prepared a 'Fast to Light' set of eight standards, each one being twice as fast as the preceeding one. Most basic colours have a low rating. But *acid dyes* (used for wool) and *direct dyes* (used for cotton) achieve ratings of 6 or 7 and are therefore the best for veneering.

This is how dyed veneers are produced commercially.

(a)   Selected veneers are placed in an autoclave under vacuum pressure to remove the air, and free cell water from the veneers, and also much of the resins, tyloses, tannin, etc., which would hinder complete penetration.

(b)   The pH readings are taken and the three components are scientifically adjusted for neutralised and de-mineralised water; the veneer and the dyebath acidity/alkalinity adjustments made.

(c)   When the vacuum process is complete, valves are opened to permit the dyestuffs to fill the autoclave, and obtain partial penetration.

(d)   A re-circulating process begins in which the dye is fed from the (sometimes heated) reservoir tank, through the autoclave to assist penetration.

(e)   The pressure pump now applies up to 120 psi, (351.19 Kg/cm^2) for maximum penetration, and this is maintained for a calculated length of time.

(f)   The autoclave is emptied and the veneers rinsed thoroughly.

(g)   They are then given a Fixanol PN (ICI) treatment for one hour at 50 degrees C to fix the surface colour. The colour tends to migrate to the surface and be a darker shade than the centre of the veneer. However, when laid, sanded and polished the shade of colour is restored and this is taken into account.

From the above description, the home veneer craftsman can see that attempts to satisfactorily dye veneers in a tin bath are not likely to obtain the desired results!

A good tip is to slightly heat the veneers first to reduce their moisture content, and this makes penetration easier. Add up to 2 per cent urea to increase the solubility of acid dyes, and add 'wetting agents' such as Lissapol N, or Perminal BX and penetrating agents such as Calsolene Oil HS or Turkey Red Oil PO — all of which are from ICI.

The veneers should be brought to the boil and then simmered for up to eight hours and then left in the cooling liquid overnight. Rinse in cold water and thoroughly air dry to 10 per cent moisture content before replacing in the correct numbered sequence.

The veneers best for dyeing are, in order of priority: sycamore, horse chestnut, maple, bird's eye maple, poplar, ash, birch, aspen, abura and peartree. The three most difficult colour groups to obtain are dyed black, snow white, and pastel shades, and they are best left to professionals.

To obtain snow white the veneers are bleached in a reducing agent, then an oxidizing agent such as hydrogen peroxide 120 vols., neutralised to end the chemical action and thoroughly rinsed.

For pastel shades, unless the fresh, cold-cut sycamore is used, other veneers will have to be bleached first, and then dyed.

Dyed black is the most difficult colour to obtain and is achieved with the autoclave impregnation plant previously described, dyeing the veneer (sycamore, peartree or agba) in a solution of logwood extract. At the end of the first stage, the resulting colour is brown.

The second stage is another pressurised impregnation of 'iron liqueur', a solution of sulphate of iron with additives, which causes a strong chemical reaction to take place and a jet black colour permeates through every fibre of the veneer. In fact this process is used to dye planks of wood up to 4 inches (101mm) thick in the autoclave as the penetration is partly achieved by chemical reaction. The product has to be rinsed in a strong mordant such as isinglass to seal in the colour and prevent it discolouring everything it comes into contact with.

All black lines, stringings, and purflings etc. are made from this material.

The home craftsman cannot produce dyed black to this depth of tone. However, he can obtain a black acid dye and produce a very dark brown, using the following method:

After carefully sealing other adjacent veneers, the surface can be treated with carbon black VS paste (ICI), which will only produce surface penetration to sufficient depth to permit a very light sanding, and then a fixative coat to seal in the colour.

Generally, the production of harewood and dyed veneers is, as earlier mentioned, a highly specialised professional job and is best left to experts in their own field, especially as these are freely available in a wide range of fast to light colours to suit most purposes.

5

Measuring and Storing Veneers

THE MAJORITY of decorative and constructional veneers are clipped and trimmed into square edged bundles at the veneer mill, but in certain cases, it is trade practice to leave bundles which contain defects such as 'waney-edged' and irregular shaped edges exactly as cut from the flitch or log.

There are two reasons for this. In the case of expensive burrs, which are mostly used in small pieces, every inch that can be yielded from the cutting must be sold. It is not trimmed to a convenient squared edge but left as it came from the irregular shaped burr. Other species such as yew, contain so many holes, ingrowing bark, knots etc., that bundles are sold waney edged. These waney bundles often contain sap on both sides of the heartwood. There are other cases, where a log may have exposed a large knot, which the mill operative hacked out with an axe, leaving a large man-made hole, which will appear in several bundles of veneer until the defect clears as cutting proceeds.

These bundles contain excellent veneer, even though the hole may prevent its use as architectural panelling grade.

If the clipper operator had attempted to clip or trim these bundles, far too much veneer would have been wasted, and in many cases, very short bundles would result. Instead, the mill 'measurer' marks on the top leaf of such bundles, in chalk, the limits of his measurement to enable the buyer to check the measurement of contents.

It is safer to 'measure out' defects, than to cut them out.

For example, if a bundle of walnut veneer was 15 inches (380mm) wide at the butt end, tapering down to only 8 inches (203mm) at the outer end, with wide irregular sappy edges, the measurer's chalk marks may have been drawn at 'half-sap' at each end, and if the bundle

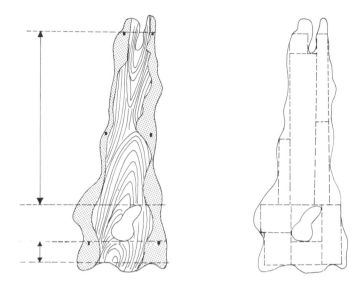

Fig. 52 Measuring a 'waney-edged' log

had a narrow waist, in the middle, three sets of chalked 'widths' would then occur, say at 12½ inches (317mm) 8 inches (203mm) and 6½ inches (165mm). The mill would probably charge this as a 9 inches (228mm) bundle. Where a large defect has been cut out of the centre of the bundle, there may be measurer's chalk marks in the length as well.

Quite often you will find width and length marks. Therefore when buying waney-edged bundles from your supplier be careful to check the measurements and the contents.

Example: 24 leaves 8 feet × 9 inches (2438 × 228mm) contains:

  8 × 9 ÷ 12 = 6 × 24 = 144 square feet (13.37 sq. metres)

Sometimes a veneer bundle is an awkward shape, without a convenient taper from one to the other, or with an hour glass waist in the middle. Check the measurer's chalk marks carefully to see how he has assessed the contents. If you disagree, let the physical shape of the bundle guide you in making your own assessment, if necessary measuring in four places, and averaging the width.

In my own experience, a log of teak measured by a salesman can contain hundreds of square feet difference between the measure of the buyer! A 'tight' measure often results from a low price; a fairly generous measure from a moderately high price. The integrity of your supplier is all important.

Specialist mail order veneer stockists, with published list prices for veneers simply cannot afford to have disputes with valued customers over the measurement, and *always* err on the customer's side.

The measurement problem is mentioned here, in case you happen to have access locally to a source of supply where veneers are sold subject to your own choice and selection.

There is always the temptation for a veneer merchant who has reasonable veneer logs for sale, to 'sweeten' the overall appearance of the logs by disposing of separately, to small users, short, narrow or otherwise defective bundles which 'spoil' the log. Buyer beware. In veneer buying 'penny wise is pound foolish'. It always pays to buy the best you can afford.

VENEER DEFECTS
The first rule for the veneer buyer is to examine the veneers in a good light with his bare hands. Even in mid-winter, he must take his gloves off!

Pick up the bundle at each end in turn and look to see that the leaves all appear to be the same thickness; then, compare the sides of the bundle. The veneers should be the same gauge at each side and each end of the leaf.

'Wandering gauge' is a milling defect. Many logs contain hard and soft parts, which react differently under the pressure bar of the machinery, and this results in a thicker or thinner cut than programmed, with a compensating cut on the next stroke, alternately thick and thin. Reaction wood can cause this when present in timber.

Naturally, this type of defect is usually sorted out in the veneer mill, but many such bundles get past quality control, especially if a very expensive log is involved.

Now run your fingers over the leaf to ensure that the face side is smooth, with no torn grain, or plucked rays, due to milling defects.

Be especially careful with radially cut quartered oak for example, which has a pronounced ray figure. It is quite common for this to become raised and to pluck out. They would appear as coarse raised bumps to carefully questioning fingertips.

Rub the ball of your thumb across the end of a leaf, and you will feel a sharp, smooth edge on the face side and a loose ragged edge on the underside or the back.

Feel for tiny surface scratches across the leaf caused by a dull knife which may be difficult to paper out. Also, be especially guarded against finding a raised score or blip mark diagonally across the face of the veneer, caused by a chipped veneer knife. Turn the leaf over, and you will see a matching indentation or scratch into the back. Discard the leaves so marked.

The more slanted the grain to the veneer surface, the greater the danger of dry checks, especially on burr veneers. Tiny hairline checks cannot be avoided on rotary cut veneers, as the veneer has been 'torn' from around the circumference of the log and than flattened out, thereby opening out the underside of the leaf. For this reason, most rotary cut veneers are laid with the face side uppermost, and not 'turned over' for matching purposes, with the exception of bird's eye maple, which should be laid face side down, to ensure that the masses of 'eyes' do not fall out, as they are funnel shaped.

Check to ensure that the bundle has not been 'dressed.' What happens in a veneer mill is that the top leaf of a bundle—especially one in stock for a long time—becomes soiled with chalk marks recording samples taken from the log; measurement marks, spillages, spots from water dripping through condensation, etc. It is not unknown for the veneer warehouseman to untie the bundle and slip the dirty leaf inside the bundle to 'dress' the appearance. Worse than this, you may find the mill have cut 'samples' from leaves inside the bundle, or even that the pattern continuity has been shuffled, with a pattern jump between top and bottom leaves. Untie the bundle and fan it open to ensure there is no evidence of dressing, and that the pattern sequence is undisturbed.

Look through the leaves to ensure that no signs of 'thunder shakes' are visible—small cracks running across the leaf as though someone had tried to bend the leaf and it has cracked. These are caused by tropical storms, and are quite prevalent in some tropical timbers such as agba, obeche, etc.

Compression or tension wood will show either at the edges which will have a fine woodwool stranded appearance, or in a ripple of buckling on one half of the leaf caused by irregular drying; in others it appears as a series of bumps or blisters.

Many woods are resinous or contain gum pockets and as you separate the leaves they tend to stick together. Agba and zebrano are examples. Other woods have calcium deposits and appear as white chalky deposits in the grain.

Curl or crotch veneers require careful handling and inspection. One half of the leaf is smooth and the other may be rough to the touch. Ideally, the veneer knife should travel from the outer sappy edge of the log towards the heart. As explained, curl veneers are usually back cut by stay-log cutting, and the knife travels right across the log from side to side. The fibres tend to tear out. If you examine a complete stock of curls from front to back, you will discover that the smooth flat plainish veneers of the front gradually adopt the smooth-rough feel as the pattern becomes more pronounced, and the veneers become more buckled as a result, and when the curl gradually disappears and the back bundles are reached, the swirl figure is flat again. For this reason curls require to be carefully handled, and flattened before use.

Burrs, are usually very brittle, may be full of holes and may have patches of in-growing bark. If held up to the light, they may have thousands of tiny pinholes and you can see through the very short end grain. Such burrs must be thoroughly glue sized and flattened before use.

Mineral stains

Some mineral stains are welcome in decorative veneers if required for architectural work or marquetry. Blue stained obeche, mineral stained sycamore, olive ash, and maple are examples. But the majority of mineral stains are defects caused by the tannin of the wood reacting to iron or chemical compounds in the soil. Heavy, blue or black stains may result in woods with a high tannin content such as oak, sweet chestnut, afrormosia, idigbo, makore and walnut. Ferrous metals produce a blue-black stain in some woods and a grain stain in others. Softwoods contain little or no tannin, but tannin-like substances do occur in Douglas fir and Californian redwood and dark staining may result.

The effect of iron on Western red cedar is to cause a red stain, while Canadian yellow cedar turns brown, and iron reacts most strongly against oak which, if left in the ground where iron deposits are in the soil will turn the log into black bog oak.

Veneers with a high tannin content may show blue or black lines of stain across the face of the veneer caused by traces of iron picked up from the veneer knife, while the veneer was wet.

Many other veneers pick up stains from the rollers in the mechanical driers, which are usually noticeable along the length of the veneer in a regular series of patterns like a tyre mark.

There is always a risk of veneers becoming mineral stained in a veneer mill immediately following a holiday shut down, when the plant has been allowed to become cold, and condensation forms on the machinery.

Insect attack

A patch of tiny holes in a veneer leaf caused by pin worm, can be ignored, as they can be easily filled during the later stages. However if worm holes of a fair size are present, insist on running through the bundle, flitch or log to make sure that the defect does not gradually get worse. These are usually trimmed out at the mill.

Be eternally vigilant for any sign of white worm casts which indicate live worm, as this pest could not only destroy your bundle of veneers, but could infect your total stock.

Paradoxically, one of the most treasured veneers for decorative purposes is masur birch from Finland. It is regularly attacked by sap eating insects every year, but when rotary cut into veneer reveals an entire surface covered with tiny brown clusters and markings against the cream white background and is most attractive.

Fungal attack

A filmy covering of fungus known as 'dross' forms on many species, such as canella, padauk, narra, maidu burr etc. This is not a defect and wipes off easily and does not affect the final polishing stages. But veneers stored in humid or damp conditions may suffer from 'doat' a form of wet rot caused by either poor drying or bad storage and should be firmly rejected.

Moisture Content

The 'decay safety line' is a moisture content of 20 per cent, as fungal decay or doat cannot develop below this moisture level.

When veneers are stored in a particular environment the moisture content will attain a steady state. As air conditions and humidity vary through the year, the veneers will make compensating adjustments. If stored in a humid atmosphere, dry veneers will absorb moisture and swell; if overdry they will buckle or split.

As a guide, the moisture content of veneered furniture in a living room varies between 10 per cent to 14 per cent throughout the year. In centrally heated homes the range narrows between 9 per cent to 12 per cent.

Therefore veneers are dried to suit the average of the conditions of service and seasonal variations are not troublesome.

It is trade practice to produce burrs and curls to a slightly higher moisture content than ordinary veneers, to make them easier to handle and less brittle.

Provided that the veneers are reasonably flat and feel dry to the touch, they will adjust naturally to their correct environmental moisture content if stored correctly.

Weathering

Veneers should be kept covered and not exposed to either natural or artificial light. Many colourful veneers fade quickly and lose their original brilliance when exposed to light; some darken, while others change colour. Many veneers such as sycamore, maple, and birch, are light sensitive and will 'weather' from a cream to a tan colour.

If you find that the colour of the log when viewed at the edges, is different from the leaf colour when opened up, this will give a guide to the way the veneer colour will weather in later life.

Toxic Woods

Some species contain dust which may be toxic—Indian laurel and dark mansonia being two examples. Barrier creams may have to be worn when handling them.

Splinters from these species have been known to produce allergies in veneer craftsmen.

STORAGE AND FLATTING

Not everyone is fortunate enough to be able to make a personal visit to a veneer mill or merchant to buy their veneers. The majority of veneer craftsmen have to rely upon the integrity and experience of their suppliers to fill their required specification with the best veneers available at the time of the order.

It is essential therefore to enquire well in advance of your need for suitable stocks of veneer, as availability will fluctuate according to many factors, and it is always good advice to buy more than you need in case of accidents, as identical veneers may be impossible to obtain.

When your veneers are received they will either be in flat crated condition or rolled, if obtained from mail order suppliers. Do not leave your veneers rolled up. Open the parcels immediately upon receipt and inspect them to ensure that they are suitable for your requirements, and free from defects.

It is essential to reduce the amount of handling to an absolute minimum. Every time you handle a leaf of veneer there is a risk of splitting it, and remember that a bundle of veneers, rolled at a suppliers despatch department, may have the effect of a coil spring and if carelessly undone, may split from each end. This is why your supplier will have carefully protected both ends of the bundle with veneering tape. However, distrust the precautions, and ensure that you are prepared for the veneer to unwrap suddenly.

Locate one end of the bundle on the outside of the roll, and press this down on the floor or bench, then gradually allow the roll to unwind keeping downwards pressure on the veneer until it has lost its spring and you can lay it flat.

Action must now be taken to protect the veneers. Most complete bundles from your supplier will be tied securely at each end of the bundle. It is good practice to fasten a length of veneer tape across the end of the top and bottom leaves of veneer on every bundle, immediately upon receipt. If you have bought a flitch or small log, this would not take too long to accomplish.

Normally, every bundle will bear a chalked or crayoned number in continuity sequence, also with the log and flitch number and side or half number, e.g.: 719/2, 17/B, 32/256, would indicate Log No. 719, second half, (usually the worst half!) Bundle No 17 from the B half of the log; 32 leaves in the bundle containing 256 sq. feet (23.78 sq. metres). Store the veneers in *bundle number* sequence. This will enable you to check the delivery against the computer print-out specification.

If you have bought a few odd bundles from a supplier, so that the sequential numbering is irrelevant, it is good practice to chalk your own sequential numbers on the bundles in case you are obliged to store them out of sequence.

As we have previously learned, veneers are hygroscopic and will shed or absorb the moisture of the atmosphere. Veneers are kept in humidity controlled warehouses which keep them in equilibrium to suit atmospheric conditions. It is therefore essential that you should store your veneers in a well ventilated area, with a good circulation of cool, *dry* air around and below the veneers. They must be kept away from every heat source, and as previously mentioned, be kept covered with a dust sheet to protect them from light. They should be kept well away from contact with walls or from any form of condensation, as water dripping from an iron roof would cause mineral stains in veneers containing tannin.

Keep veneers lightly weighted down. Build a platform, or pallet by placing a plank on bricks to keep them off the ground. Make sure the plank is wide enough to take the widest bundle in flat condition. Stack the veneers with the widest at the bottom, tapering upwards into a pyramid, but with the front built square, with varying lengths to the rear.

In many cases, the mill will have completely discarded the pith or hearty centre of the log, which would create a log with a few very wide bundles at the bottom, a pile of narrow bundles at one side, and an equal number of wider bundles at the other side, and a few more wide bundles at the top. This is because the heart is seldom in the centre of the log.

If you attempt to stack the log in the correct sequence it will topple over. Therefore stack one half of the log in sequence, and the other half beside it, both with the widest bundles at the bottom.

When you have two stocks of veneer side by side, place wooden struts—short pieces of scrap timber—between them, propped between the veneer bundles to act as 'ties'. These will anchor the two stocks and prevent them from toppling over.

This becomes important should you decide to break the log continuity for economic reasons, and select a bundle out of sequence. This would involve turning over bundles of one or both piles, to find a bundle of the required width.

Never stand short bundles, or butts or curls against a wall; always lay them flat.

If you have built 'dexion' type metal racking or shelving to hold your veneers, never put more than one bundle per shelf, as this can lead to torn or damaged veneers. If a few leaves are removed from a bundle, always re-tie the bundle at each end, otherwise loose leaves will snag and tear each other and the stock will degrade.

In a veneer mill, you will always see two people handling veneers. Never try to drag or manoeuvre a bundle of veneer from the bottom of a pile unaided. One person handling veneers can wreak havoc in a veneer store. It is always advisable to obtain a helping hand when handling your veneer stocks.

Upon inspection, you may find that the veneers have become slightly dried out in transit and appear wavy or even buckled. Burr veneers may have become brittle, with small pieces breaking off at the ends and edges despite ultra care in handling. In fact the more wildgrained and interesting the burr figure, the more short grained it is likely to be. Always tape burrs all around every edge of the leaf. Curl veneers possess a natural weakness in the leaf centre and need taping.

The flatting process

For the majority of normal run-of-the-mill commercial veneers, the flatting process is very simple. If they appear wavy or buckled, sprinkle them with water—do not wet them thoroughly—only shake a few drops of water across the leaf and wipe them off with a cloth, and cramp the veneer between boards overnight or until dry and flat. Do not soak the veneers or they might turn spotty.

The process is aided by the addition of a small quantity of animal glue (one part glue to ten parts water). Sprinkle on this 'size' and wipe off quickly with a rag, and cover the surface with a sheet of polythene before cramping under pressure.

If you have a source of heat to warm up the two boards before clamping, this will speed up the flatting process and also draw out any oiliness in teak or rosewood.

If the veneers are very resinous, or contain gummy patches, wipe the leaf with carbon tetrachloride to remove the resin.

With a veneer press, use heated metal cauls, and get them hot enough to handle without gloves.

Obviously, the more difficult the veneer or the more brittle it feels, the more drastic the flatting process needs to be.

The addition of adhesive to the water will give additional strength to weak veneers; glycerine will provide greater flexibility and alcohol will accelerate the drying time.

Here is a time honoured recipe which will flatten the most stubborn veneers:

Cascamite One Shot adhesive	2 measures or 1 part by weight.
Wheat flour (not self-raising)	1 measure or ½ part by weight.
Water	3 measures or 2½ part by weight.
Glycerine	1½ measures or 1¼ part by weight.
Methylated spirits	1 measure or ½ to ⅔ part by weight.

Thoroughly mix the ingredients. The mixture should be used cold.

Immerse the offending veneers in a shallow tray containing this mixture and then hang them up to dry to the touch. Cover the leaves with polythene to prevent sticking and aid their later separation, and place between two heated sheets of aluminium and clamp in a press, or place between boards under a heavy weight overnight. If burrs or curls are very buckled, (even bundles of oak or zebrano or walnut may be very buckled,) do not attempt to flatten them in one operation.

When tightening the press, only exert moderate pressure, so that the veneers only partially compress but not enough to split or crack them. Allow time for the mixture to penetrate and soften them before slightly increasing the pressure. Repeat the heat treatment after 24 hours and the next time you will find that you will be able to tighten down the press completely.

Allow the veneers to remain under pressure after removing them from the press, by heavy weighting down, until they have become acclimatised to their new environment.

The writer has successfully used commercial decorator's wallpaper paste for many years, instead of the above mixture, and this has rendered even the toughest buckled burrs malleable and flat.

The flatting process also makes veneers easier to cut, without a trace of brittleness which would otherwise cause small fragments to splinter off.

The process should be carried out immediately before veneer matching or laying. If the veneers are to be returned to storage for any length of time, keep them interleaved with polythene sheets to prevent sticking, and ensure that they are kept weighted down.

Another safe way to protect veneers is to cover the face side with clean white paper or even thin kraft wrapping paper.

The glue size will cause the paper to adhere, and enable you to handle the burrs or curls with ease without risk of splitting or buckling.

Never use newspaper, as the newsprint offsets on delicate veneers and spoils others by imprinting to the point that some penetration of the ink takes place which is almost impossible to remove.

6

Tools & Clamps

NIVES: Ask ten veneer craftsmen to name the ideal knife and you will get ten different answers. There is no such thing. Knives are personal tools, like pens, and give a different result when used by different people.

A knife has a 'feel' peculiar to the individual, and will produce a slightly different type of cut. You might have a tight grip on the handle, or perhaps a loose grip but very firm finger pressure on the knife point. Others like to have a long handle for balance, especially when making a heavy cut through several thicknesses.

The first lesson with a knife is the craftsman never cuts himself with a sharp knife—only with a blunt one. Most accidents occur when the edge has dulled; when pressure is exerted in the expectation that a cut will result—it doesn't. The knife does not bite into the wood but slips off into the nearest finger!

Commercially available knives are handy aids to have in the workshop for specific purposes, and it is a good idea to stock a few different types and use them according to the job in hand. For example, when trimming veneers along the grain for jointing, the knife point wants to wander in the grain. A long blade, sharpened only on one side will cut through several thicknesses with a shearing motion, holding the flat edge against the straightedge. For crosscutting, you would prefer to use a knife with a 45 degree bevel, or wane, on each side; for intricate cutting a 30 degree bevel. For marquetry work a long pointed surgical scalpel blade is ideal.

A high speed hacksaw blade, as used by engineers, can be broken in half and filed down to make an excellent knife. File off the teeth and grind a 45 degree wane on one side, which can then be sharpened and honed on an oilstone. Fit the blade into a hardwood handle into which a suitable sawcut has been made to receive it. This sawcut should only be ⅞ths of the way through the handle. Bind the handle with adhesive tape, or drill through and pin with two rivets.

Another veneer craftman's tip is to shape the end of the wooden handle into a rounded knob. It makes an ideal rubber for pressing down veneer tape, small fragments of veneer which may lift or tear at the joints, or for coaxing small inlays into place.

Try to design a knife handle where the back of the handle protects the blade, with only a fraction of the blade protruding.

The Swann Morton No 11 surgical scalpel blade which is very finely pointed, is best used in the craft tool handle, rather than the correct No 3 scalpel blade handle, as too much of the blade protrudes and the blade's tip will snap off under pressure.

When making up home-made knives, remember that it is the *width* of the hacksaw blade that provides the knife with strength, so file away only the end of the blade to a fine point, at an oblique angle, to enable you to bring the maximum amount of pressure on the blade safely.

The double knife

This is an inlayer's home-made favourite. Make a hardwood handle which will accommodate two blades, with an adjustable spacer between them when tightened. The spacer is used as a width gauge.

The knife cuts twin grooves into a panel to receive inlay lines; and also cuts the inlay lines for a perfect fit. This type of knife comes into its own when cutting freehand designs.

Scratch stock

Another home-made tool made from two pieces of hardwood 6 inches × 3 inches × ¾ inch (152 × 76 × 19mm) screwed together with a notch cut out in both pieces to form a fence or shoulder. The two pieces enclose a steel cutter filed from a hacksaw blade the exact width of the inlay line or banding. Chapter 17 describes its use.

Veneer inlay cutter

The Ulmia 728 Veneer inlay cutter is designed for the accurate cutting and removal of straight, shaped and circular veins of any required depth from 2mm to 8mm in width, and has two cutting blades and a third cutter which acts as a clearing cutter to remove the wood.

For cutting grooves, the blades are mounted with bevels inside, and for cutting inlays, with the bevels outside. The clearing cutter is mounted in an adjustable tool holder and can be set at the optimum clearing angle. The blades are easily adjusted to any width with shims. The tool has a detachable guide head extension for cutting long grooves, and curved edges, with radii from 1 inch to 6 inches

(25-152mm) (No 728/1) and 6 inches to 22 inches (152-558mm) (No 728/2).

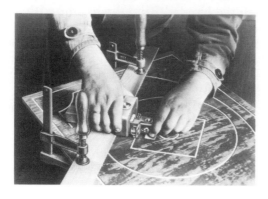

Fig. 53 Inlay line cutter

Veneering clamps

The clamps are used in pairs for flattening buckled veneers and comprise two pieces of hardwood about 20 inches (508mm) long, cut from 2 inch × 1½ inch (50 × 38mm) and drilled at each end to take bolts and wing nuts.

Three or four sets of these pairs of clamps are made up. The inner surfaces of the battens are slightly rounded so that pressure is brought to bear first in the centre, as the wing nuts are tightened at the ends.

The veneers are treated with glue size, or special flattening formulation and placed between two wooden cauls. The clamps are then set at each end and in the centre of the cauls to provide the pressure.

The centre clamp is tightened first, and then progressively outwards towards the end pairs.

Fig. 54 Veneer edge trimmer

Edge trimmer

This handy tool cuts in either direction without the danger of tearing cross grained veneers and is made for trimming off surplus veneer around the panel after laying.

Combined joint and strip cutter

This is another useful tool for veneer work in which the left hand side cuts perfect joints both with and across the grain when used against a straightedge. The right hand side is used to cut inlay strips from 2mm to 8mm wide by means of spacers. The blades can be set to the required depth of cut.

Fig. 55 Combined joint and strip cutter

Veneer trimming chisel

Another tool for trimming off surplus veneer from panel ends and edges without risk of breaking cross grain or for following pronounced strong grain of edge veneers. It is fitted with a nylon triangular guide block.

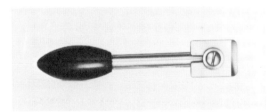

Fig. 56 Veneer trimming chisel

Veneer saws

There are two types. The first has a wooden sawhandle grip, with a curved steel sawblade. The teeth face inwards at each end, towards the centre, and in the middle there is a single central tooth.

When veneers are compressed under a batten on the shooting board the saw is rocked backwards and forwards and a straight clean cut will result even on thick sawcut veneers.

The other popular type has a wooden tool handle and a double-edged reversible sawblade, with teeth of different size to suit various woods. It will cut perfectly square edged joints for veneer matching, when used against a straightedge.

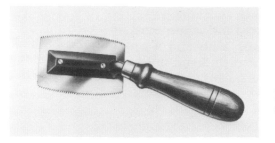

Fig. 57 Veneer saw with reversible saw blade

Planes

It is assumed that you will already possess a cabinetmaker's basic toolkit containing a standard block plane, smoothing plane, and a small trimming plane for planing the edges of veneers for jointing.

Toothing plane

This is a wooden plane, usually with a hornbeam sole. The plane blade stands almost vertical, and has a series of fine grooves like a saw edge. It planes tiny corrugated teeth marks into the surface. When being sharpened, only the bevel is worked on the stone. The plane is worked from corner to corner of a corestock panel, removing any highspots, and passing over depressions by leaving them unscored. The surrounding surfaces have to be further worked to reduce them to a perfect level. The surface forms a perfect mechanical lock for adhesion.

Fig. 58 Smoothing plane with hornbeam sole

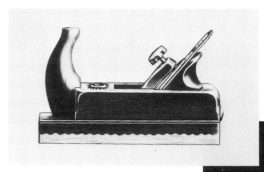

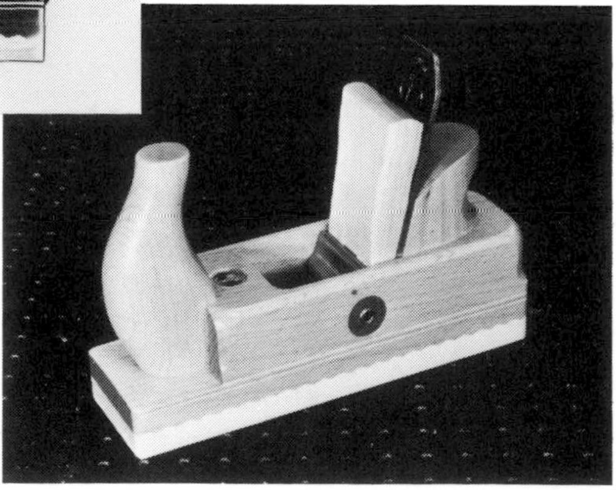

Fig. 59 Toothing plane with hornbeam sole

Veneer hammer

This is a handmade tool, and is not used like a hammer but as a squeegee. It is simply a wooden holder about 6-7 inches (152-177mm) wide by 3½-4 inches (89-101mm) deep, and about ⅝ inches or ¾ inches (16 or 19mm) thick, into which a brass or aluminium strip is let into a saw kerf, about 1 inch × ⅛ inch (25 × 3mm) wide. The edges and ends are rounded to avoid digging in. The tool is fitted with a dowel handle. It is used in zig-zag fashion to squeeze out the air and surplus glue from hand veneered panels.

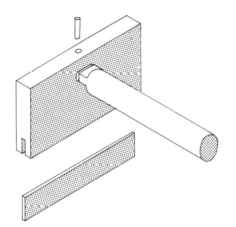

Fig. 60 A home-made veneer hammer

Electric veneer hammer

This is a double-sided professional tool powered by electricity, with one large flat surface for heating the glueline under the veneer, and a rounded veneer hammer edge for pressing down. It is ideal for repairing blisters or relaying joints.

Non-slip safety ruler

For small jobs, this has an M shaped section, so that downward pressure anchors the ruler and prevents it from slipping. The ruler may be obtained in black with white graduations.

Steel straightedges

Made from heavy duty steel with a perfectly machined straightedge, this is the ideal tool for veneer jointing when making matches. Straightedges are available in many lengths, from 18 inch, 24 inch and 36 inch upwards in imperial measure, and 500mm and 1 metre and upwards in metric measure. The thickness of the straightedge varies with the length, (the longer, the thicker) and consequently the more expensive. The 36 inch or 1 metre length covers most workshop requirements.

Fig. 61 Straightedges and measuring instruments

Measuring instruments

Carpenter's steel try-square for testing the accuracy of corners, T-squares, and a combination try and mitre square for checking mitred corners.

An extending spring steel ruler for measuring incoming veneers. For usual workshop jobs a 24 inch boxwood folding ruler is ideal, and/or a 36 inch/1 metre (dual measurement) boxwood straight ruler.

A range of set squares for 30, 60, 45 and 90 degree angles and a 180 degree transparent protractor are essential items for marquetry or parquetry cutting, and for laying out certain veneer matches.

Dividers

A pair of dividers, with one leg sharpened into a cutting edge is a useful tool for cutting out corners for inlay motifs etc.

Cordix measuring gauge

Circular gauge with black dial calibrated to 1/10 of mm for accurate testing of thickness of veneered panels up to 1 inch (25mm) thick.

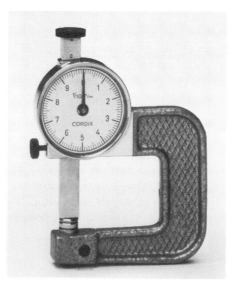

Fig. 62 Cordix veneer and groundwork thickness gauge

Marking gauge

The head is fitted with a fine needle point which marks a line parallel to the edge of a panel for crossband border surrounds.

The best types have brass strips let into the face to prevent wear.

Cutting gauge

The head is fitted with a sharp knife blade, which will cut into the veneer for easy removal. The width from the edge of the work may be up to 6 inches (152mm). The face of the head should have brass strips.

Mortise gauge

This has two knives to make a double cut of the required width to receive inlay stringings, lines or bandings.

Firmer chisel

Useful for cleaning out the corners of solid groundwork before being worked with a scratchstock, to prevent the crossgrain from splintering out. Also handy as a scraper for removing glue squeeze-out in places where a cabinet scraper may be too cumbersome.

Cabinet scraper

A rectangular flat steel blade about 4½ inches × 2½ inches (114 × 63mm). The edge is burred over to form a cutting edge. The steel is then flexed between both hands with thumb pressure and held at an angle. It is used for scraping off gummed veneer tape, glue spots, stopping from joints, and levelling the surface prior to sanding.

Scraper blade sharpener

The triangular shaped finely ground tool is used to form the required edge to the steel cabinet scraper.

Fig. 63 Scraper blade sharpener

Scraper burnisher

This special tool comprises a wooden handle with a pivoting steel disc, having an angle section of steel with a recessed corner to protect the formed cutting edge of the steel scraper.

Veneer punches

Hollow steel cutters in the form of a punch with spring loaded ejector. Used to remove an irregular shape around a veneer defect, and an identical shape may then be punched from a sound leaf to effect an invisible repair. The punches come in a range of sizes and shapes from ⅝ inch to 2 inches (15mm to 50mm).

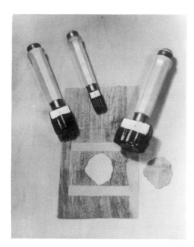

Fig. 64 Ulmia veneer punches

Fig. 65 Veneer pins with large heads

Small router plane
Known as the 'Old Woman's Tooth', this is used for removing parts of solid groundwork to receive inlay motifs.
Small bullnosed rabbet plane
When an inlay line of square section is required on an edge, and the cutting gauge has been used in both width and depth, the waste is removed with the bullnosed rabbet plane.
Veneer pins
There are two types: thin wire pins similar to panel pins, which are nipped off, and driven into the work below the surface before laying; and those that have large plastic heads and are used to hold matched leaves together. By leaning the pins towards the join, the joint is held tightly together until the veneer tapes are affixed, when the pins are removed for further use.
Shooting board
This is a simple home made tool for trimming veneers. The veneers are placed on a board and compressed under a batten which is held by a backstop. The protruding veneer edges are then planed. For several thicknesses of veneer, they are compressed between battens and clamped to the shooting board. The finely set plane will remove a fine shaving from both the battens and the veneers when 'kissing' the veneer edges.
Workboard
To protect the surface of the workbench from score marks of veneer knife, saws etc., select a piece of particle board the length of the workbench and about 9 inches wide by ½ inch thick (228 × 12mm). Use this for veneer preparation, jointing etc. When one surface is com-

pletely scored with knifemarks, turn it over. When both sides are worn, it may be coarse sanded, crossbanded, toothed and used as corestock.

Sanding block-scraper

This beech handled tool enables finishing garnet papers etc. to be wrapped around a cork pad for sanding. It may be turned on its side and used as a scraper for cleaning up.

Ulmia precision mitre boxes

Invaluable for cutting mitred frames etc. Available in 2 inch (50mm) cutting width by 2⅜ inch (60mm) depth; or 4 inch width by 4 inch depth (101 × 101mm).

Portable trimmer

This Scheer HM7 trimmer is used for trimming any overhang and will also smoothly trim plastic laminates.

Fig. 66 Sanding block and scraper

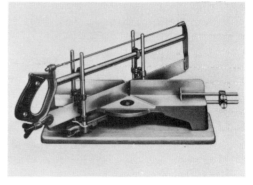

Fig. 67 Ulmia precision mitre box

Fig. 68 Portable power trimmer

Fig. 69 Fretsaw frame with double tooth fretsaw blades

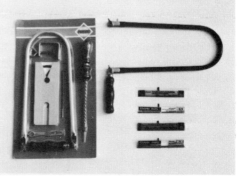

Soft brush

A soft decorator's brush is ideal for keeping veneer surfaces free from sanding dust and the worktop free from grit and veneer splinters or fragments.

Fretsaw frame and fretsaws

A tubular fretsaw frame with 12 inch (305mm) deep throat, suitable for bevel cutting fretsaw marquetry work. Fretsaw blades are available in four basic types:

Single tooth blades for general veneer cutting, with rounded backs for easy manipulating around curves, in size from 8/0 down to 2/0 and up to No 2 (thick).

Double teeth blades for marquetry 8/0, 4/0, 2/0, No 1 and No 3.

Helical spiral piercing blades 2/0, 0 and 1 — chiefly for tough work on metals and plastic sheets for Boulle-work etc.

Metal piercing blades 8/0, 6/0, 4/0 and 2/0 No 1, for use on copper, brass, aluminium and other alloys in combination with veneers.

Pliers and nippers

For tightening wing-nuts, and cutting-off heads of veneer pins.

Tweezers

For holding delicate parts of veneer assemblies; inserting components of motifs; holding veneers for sand scorching and — for removing splinters!

Scales & volume measures

For accurate weighing of pre-mixed powder adhesives, etc; and for use when resins and catalysts have to be mixed by volume. (Use a glass or stainless steel mixing bowl for mixing adhesives).

Seam roller

6 inch (152mm) wide rubber coated roller with wooden handle, is ideal back up tool for hammer veneering. A boxwood decorator's seam roller is useful for rolling down joints and edges.

Glue brush

Available in sizes from 6 up to 24.

Sanding block

Prevents edges of panels from being dubbed over and is made of cork to hold half a sheet of garnet or finishing paper.

Veneer tapes

Gummed veneering tape 1 inch × 800 feet (25mm × 243 metres) reels. Also in other widths and lengths. (See Chapter 12 for other temporary-holding and protecting tapes).

Chalk

For numbering veneers in sequence (use a sponge for wiping clean).

Sharpening stone

Small carborundum stone for keeping knives and edge tools sharp.

Fig. 70 Tapes, brushes, firmer chisel, cabinet scraper and emery board nail file

CLAMPS AND CLAMPING

The correct clamping (also termed cramp and cramping) of veneer assemblies and in assembling curved work can be a source of trouble for the veneer craftsman.

It is far too late to discover that you have the wrong type of clamp, once the work is glued up and ready for clamping, so always make a dry-run before gluing up and go through the motions with the clamps, to make sure you have everyting right before applying the adhesive. Make sure that the clamps you have will fit the work and will hold on an irregular surface or will accommodate the shape you want to hold.

It is good practice when cutting out curved work, to save the offcut, and number both pieces. Use the waste offcut as a clamping caul for edge veneering, as it is difficult to cut out a shaped caul to fit a required shape. The offcut will also provide a flat side to clamp against and avoid slipping. The trick is to make sure the saw kerf is wide enough to accommodate the glueline and the edge veneer.

The golden rule for all clamping is that clamping pressure must always be *at right angles to the glueline*.

Sometimes, steps may have to be cut in the outer face of the clamping cauls, to make sure the step is parallel to the glueline. Where this is not possible, small wedge shaped pieces are used in the jaws of the clamp tacked into place. This prevents them from slipping out when pressure is applied. Otherwise, glue shaped pieces temporarily to the surface of the work, with a piece of paper between the work and the wedge—the same process used for gluing up mitred corners in cabinet making.

If the clamps are the slightest angle out of right angles, the veneer may slip out of line when the pressure is applied and this may be unseen if the work is concealed by the cauls. Securing the work with tapes is not the answer as the pressure from clamps will burst the tapes open.

There are a wide variety of clamps to suit every purpose, and the following is a guide to their usefulness for veneering.

Clamp heads

Comprising a tail-stop and stationary head, with screw and sliding head, these are fitted to any hardwood bar 1 inch (25mm) thick to make bar clamps. Some types have multiple disc clutch for fast adjustment and quick release.

Band clamps

The actual band may be of pre-stretched canvas, thin steel, or nylon; the principle is the same. The band encircles the work and is pulled tight through a screwhead, with self locking cams holding the band securely from slipping. Ideal for clamping irregular or round shapes, such as drum tables, mitred corners etc.

Spring clamps

Spring operated jaws open with hand pressure and spring pressure grips the work. For quick temporary holding where fast application and removal are important. Opening capacities 1 inch up to 4 inches (25mm to 101mm).

Edge clamps

For applying pressure to work edges, or the centre of wide surfaces. They attach to any steel bar and apply pressure at right angles to it. Single screw type has a ⅝ inch (15mm) diameter screw; double screw types which apply pressure on each side of the bar have 1 inch (25mm) screws with 4 inch (101mm) between centres.

Record edging clamp

Opening capacity 2⅜ inches (60mm) and throat depth of 1¼ inches (31mm) with twin screws for edging.

Corner clamp

For clamping mitred corners, with clamping capacity of 2 inches (50mm)—leaving joints fully exposed for nailing, gluing, dowelling etc.

Three-way edging clamp

Enables right angle pressure to be applied to edges, or the side of the work. The right angle screw can be made to grip off-centre on varying thicknesses of work.

Piling clamps

These are purpose-made for the small veneer workshop where a number of veneered panels need to be stacked, or for a stack of edge glued corestock strips etc.

The 'pile' may comprise stock of different lengths, widths and thicknesses. The clamp is actually a steel frame with two in-dependently operated screws; one clamps the work below the frame, and the other, the work above. This holds the pile secure from buckling and may be built to any convenient height. The clamps are

Fig. 71 Assorted clamps

Fig. 72 Flexiformer band clamps

Fig. 73 Edging clamps also used as holdfast clamps in panel centre

applied from one side only of the pile and there is only 1 inch (25mm) between each panel.

Jaw openings from 6 inches to 24 inches (152-609mm) are the smallest in the range, up to 54 inches up to 72 inches (1370-1828mm) maximum for the largest type.

Steel bar clamps, (fixed head type)

These are the familiar 'sash clamps' with I-section steel bars. Recommended for edge veneering, where great pressure is not required. Opening capacity 18 inches up to 42 inches (457 to 1066mm).

Steel bar clamps, (sliding head type)

All adjustment is in the sliding head for close up work, widely used in place of traditional 'C' clamps because of instant adjustment to work and quick easy release. Opening capacity from 6 inches up to 36 inches (152-914mm).

Steel bar clamps (hinged type)

A swivel plate at the foot end enables the clamp to be mounted anywhere and will swing in an arc up to or away from work and can be fitted under the workbench. Opening capacity 6 inches up to 30 inches (152-762mm).

C-clamps

There are various types of C-clamps, according to the load limit required. Use the correct size C-clamp. A large clamp on small work throws an abnormal strain on the clamp screw and frame. Use C-clamps having as small a depth of throat, or reach, as the work will permit. The greater the depth of throat, the greater the leverage on the clamp frame by the same force at the screw. Available in opening capacities from ⅝ inch up to 12 inches (15-304mm) in light or heavy duty types. (Also known as G-Clamps or Cramps).

Hold-fast clamps

These can be mounted anywhere that a holding bolt ⅜ inch × 3½ inches (9× 89mm) can be fitted to the workbench. The clamp slides on to the pre-spotted holding bolt and slides off when not in use. Instant pressure can be applied anywhere, and it swivels through 360 degrees; when removed the workbench top is clear and uncluttered. (Also known as 'bench hold-down').

Spindle Handscrews

These are wooden clamps and will not mar highly finished surfaces, and will grip irregular shapes without twisting or crawling. Two wooden screwthreads adjust the opening and closing, and final pressure is applied from the 'outside' screw, with the centre screw acting as a fulcrum. Make sure the pressure is applied all along the jaws not just at the end or the edge of the work. Available with jaw openings from 2 inches up to 14 inches (50-355mm), length of jaws from 4 inches up to 24 inches (101-609mm).

7

Workshop Equipment and Veneer Presses

HAND operated veneer guillotine

The knife blade is 4 feet 6 inches (1370mm) long and will cut through a bundle of veneers up to 2 inches (50mm) thick. A handwheel operates a heavy pressure bar for clamping the veneers, and the knife is activated by a long manually operated handle in a shearing movement. A safety fence swivels to all angles to permit accurate cutting of veneers for geometric parquetry cutting, and veneer matching etc. The cut is perfect for jointing.

Belt sander

The universal working sander for the veneer shop: the table height is adjustable and has a vertical working stroke of 470mm. The table size is from 950mm up to 2800mm. It is driven by a 5.5hp motor at 1,500 rpm. The machine has a dust extractor fan with 1,200 cubic metres per hour air extraction capacity.

Hand veneer taping tool

A reel of gummed veneering tape is held in a special holder, and is moistened as it feeds through to a pair of inward tracking rollers which pull the veneers together to ensure a tight fitting joint.

Moisture meter

A Hydrometer, with direct reading scale, calibrated from 6 per cent up to 24 per cent moisture content, suitable for testing timber and surface testing of veneers and veneered panels, groundwork, etc.

Edge rotary gluer

It has a sponge rubber spreading roller fitted with a built-in device for edge veneer gluing. The panel is fed against the roller for rapid gluing.

Fig. 74 Interwood belt sander

Fig. 75 Portable sander

Fig. 76 Edge gluer

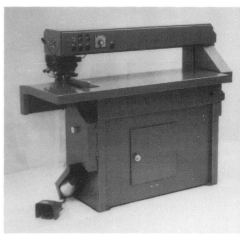

Fig. 77 Veneer stitching machine

Fig. 78 Single or double-sided glue spreading machine

Fig. 79 Contact adhesive applicator

Trimming and jointing machine

The machine has a precision guideway, with pneumatic pressure clamping bar, and a 3hp motor driven saw which runs along the guideway the length of the machine. The saw will cut bundles of veneers, chipboard, plywood, laminated board, solid timber or plastic sheets, even metal sheets, down to strips only 22mm wide with perfect accuracy. The veneers are suitable for jointing straight from the jointing machine. An automatic version of the machine is available with crank fed chain drive, with a pole changeable saw motor for two speeds. This permits cutting veneers up to 35mm stacked height, crossbandings and boards up to 60mm thickness.

Veneer jointing machine

Two leaves of veneer are fed through twin, inward tracking rollers, to make a tight joint, within a thickness range from 0.3mm to 3mm. A glue thread is used as a gluing medium, fed from underneath, leaving the veneer face visible at all times. The thread stitches the two leaves together with a zig-zag line, alternating on each side of the joint, at the rate of 45 metres per minute. It can also 'sew' across the grain to protect the ends of leaves. The glued-sewn joint remains inside the bonded veneers when laid, and melts with the heat of the press.

Spot jointing machine

A Japanese machine 'spot welds' a glue coated fibre, either as a glue-spot, or glue-stitch at about 6 inch (152mm) intervals across two veneers to form a permanent joint suitable for corestock or face veneer purposes. The spots hold the veneers together until bonded in the press and the heat melts the fibre glue spots or stitches.

Glue mixer

These are for short pot-life resin adhesives with catalyst hardeners. The shaft is of heavy industrial chrome plate; the interior and six paddles are given a nylon protective coating designed for rapid, easy cleaning.

Glue spreader

Spreaders are available from 24 inches wide up to 63 inches (609 to 1600mm) wide and comprise twin rollers; the top roller is spring loaded to accommodate various thicknesses of veneers or panels. The machines will give a single or double-sided glue coating. A glue-mixer with a capacity of up to 3.5 gallons (15 litres) can be incorporated in some models.

Hand glue spreader

This is a hopper-head tank, fitted with a dispensing roller in the feed tank connecting with a rubber roller which spreads the glue to the panel. Available in 3 inch and 6 inch (76mm and 152mm) widths.

Contact or cold glue spreader

Comprising a cannister with removable head on a pistol grip. An adjustable spreading lip and comb ensures a correct spread. There are two sizes: one with a working width of spread of 150mm/6 inches with adjustable reduction pieces down to 40mm/1½ inches and another size for edge applications down to 5mm/¼inch wide.

Fig. 80 Hand glue spreaders

VENEER PRESSES

There are veneer presses on the market to suit every type of veneering operation. They range between the small hand-clamp rig to screw presses through to multi-daylight hydraulic platens, heated by electricity, steam, hot water or oil.

For the smaller workshop where professional or amateur craftsman need only moderate equipment the following should encompass average needs.

It is all a question of size: for a small panel about 12 inches × 9 inches (300 × 225mm), a simple press can be made from two pieces of ¾ inch (19mm) blockboard 15 inches × 12 inches (381 × 304mm), with three 2 inch (50mm) crossbearers at the bottom, and three more for the top. The top bearers should be slightly rounded on the bottom surface so that the pressure begins at the centre and the glue forced outwards towards the edges. Drill ½ inch (12mm) holes through the six bearers, and fit coachbolts, washers and wingnuts for tightening. For panels a little larger, say up to 18 inch × 12 inches (457 × 304mm), you will need something more substantial. An old bookpress of the type found in solicitor's offices is ideal, and can usually be extended with pieces of angle iron and C-clamps.

Convenient ready-made press frames are also available complete with cold-drawn steel press screws. Inside width of press frame 18 inches (457mm), inside height 6 inches (152mm), screw diameter 11/16 inches (17mm), number of screws per frame 2, weight of steel frame with screws 36lbs (16 kilos).

Two such frames have a capacity of 18 inches × 18 inches (457 × 457mm) panel size.

Four frames have a capacity for 18 inches × 36 inches (457 × 914mm).

The next larger size press frames have an inside width capacity of 36 inches (914mm), inside height 6 inches (152mm), number of screws per frame 4, weight per frame 56lbs (25 kilos).

Two such frames have a capacity for 36 inch × 18 inch (914 × 457mm) panels.

Three such frames have a capacity for 36 inch × 27 inch (914 × 685mm) panels.

Four such frames have a capacity for 36 inch × 36 inch (914 × 914mm) panels.

For narrower panels, the distance between frames may be increased proportionately to allow for 80 sq. inches (516cm²) of work *per screw*. Pony Press frames come complete with steel frames.

Press screws

If you would prefer to make up your own press, but to purchase only the cold drawn press screws 11/16 inch (17mm) diameter, they are available in 9 inch, 12 inch and 18 inch (228, 304 and 457mm) lengths.

The size of the work will determine the dimensions of your frame members, and the quantity, diameter and length of the Jorgensen Press Screws.

For every 9 inches (228mm) of work *width*, you will require one press screw in each frame. And for every 9 inches (228mm) of *length*, you will need one complete frame. The height of the side members is governed by the distance the screw will travel through the top cross member, plus the thickness of the work, beds and cauls.

If you are going to construct an all purpose press, for most panel requirements, sketch out the length and width you propose to construct, calculate the number of *frames*, screws, and length of screws required and follow the next sequence:

1.   For each frame, select two correct-length side members, and top and bottom members at least 4 inches × 4 inches (101 × 101mm)in dark oak, or similar hardwood. Smaller stuff is not recommended.

2.   Prepare mortise and tenon joints and drill holes for carriage bolts. (For the convenient insertion of long work into the press from the side, one side member of each frame can be rounded so that the frame will open up when the top bolt is removed).

3.   For press screw installation, spot holes along the top member at 9½ inches (241mm) centres. Bore ¾ inch (19mm) diameter holes for the 11/16 inch (17mm) diameter press screws. Countersink the underside of top member 1 inch (25mm) diameter for the nut of the 11/16 inch (17mm) diameter screws.

4.   Assemble frame and secure corner bolts.

5.   Remove swivel and nut from each press screw. Secure each nut into countersunk holes on the underside of the top members. Insert press screws from the top, through the nut, and replace swivels.

Fig. 81 Two 'Pony' veneer press frames

Fig. 82 Jorgensen press screws used in self-made wooden frame press

Fig. 83 Jorgensen press screws used to create a large flat press

6.   The lower and upper cauls, should be ¾ inch (19mm) blockboard or laminated board, and may also be fitted with removable metal plates which may be heated as required.
7.   One such press frame is used for every 9 inches (228mm) of length. But as they are not permanently fixed to the workbench, may be moved closer or further apart to suit the project.

Single and multi-screw presses
A wide range of quick acting screw veneer presses is available. The smallest (Type FS1) has a total pressing area of 39 inches × 43 inches (990 × 1092mm). This press has only one spindle and pressing table; the bottom table may be withdrawn.

The next size has two tables, two spindles (Type FS2) and can cope with panels 39 inches × 84 inches (990 × 2133mm) long.

The FSO 3 type press, has three spindles and three pressing tables, one side with an open end for veneered panels exceeding the length of the press.

Presses with two or more spindles are fitted with an auxiliary screw to keep the end top pressing table level, when the total press area is only partially taken up.

The range of presses available cater for sizes from 43 inches up to 87 inches (1092 to 2209mm) and from 50 inches up to 146 inches (1270 to 3708mm).

Excellent work can be carried out in these screw presses. Where several press screws need to be tightened down, even when two people are assisting for speed, it is best for one person to go around and make the final tightening, to ensure that all screws are given the same degree of uniform pressure which is essential. Pressure tends to slacken off after the first half hour, and the slack has to be taken up by re-tightening the screws.

Pressures
For edge veneering, pressures as low as 30 lbs psi (88 kg/cm²) are permissible, but for most cold press work in screw presses 60 lbs psi (176 kg/cm²) is required. For laminating, compound or curved work from 150 lbs psi (439kg/cm²) up to 300 lbs psi (878 kg/cm²) are required—or the maximum up to the crushing strength of the veneers, or elements in the case of heated presses.

These pressures perform three functions. Firstly, they ensure a perfectly closed gap between veneer and groundwork; secondly, they force a thin glueline, and the thinner the glueline the stronger the bond; thirdly, the glueline moisture tends to foam at high temperatures and cause delamination problems—the high pressure prevents this from happening.

Hydraulic press

The upstroke, single opening hydraulic press, ideal for all cold pressing (or can be converted into a hot press with low voltage heat) has three large diameter rams for raising and lowering the three bottom pressing tables. Each table can press independently, or all three can lock together as one large press.

HOT PRESSES

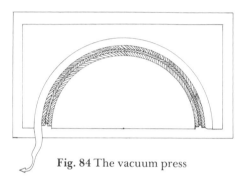

Fig. 84 The vacuum press

The twin vacuum press (see fig. 86)

This is the 'Jack-of-all-Trades' for the smaller veneer shop. It may be used for all flat, curved, shaped or compound work and laminating multi-glueline assemblies. The press is capable of full continuous production and maximum pressure is instantly obtained, with controlled top and bottom heating. The sequence of use is as follows:

1. A panel with waterfall edges and a suitable tailored veneer is carefully placed on the jigs; the frame containing the thick rubber sheet is brought down and clamped over the work; the vacuum turned on. The heated top dome is rolled forward on slides, over the work.

2. The timing clock is set to the required curing cycle, and the balanced frame with the rubber sheet on the second table automatically opens ready for loading.

3. Immediately the time clock alarm signifies that the glueline on the first assembly has cured, the dome is rolled back over the second table, and vacuum and heat applied and the timing clock re-set.

4. The frame rises on the first table and the work is removed from the press and the jigs are re-loaded ready for the load on the second table to complete its cycle.

The capacity of the twin press is 40 inches × 82 inches (1016 × 2082mm), with a working height of 12 inches (304mm). Total electric

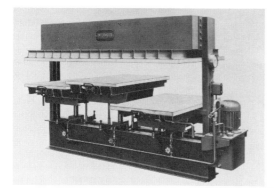

Fig. 85 Hydraulic upstroke press with three bottom tables

Fig. 86 Twin vacuum dome press, electrically heated

Fig. 87 Universal single daylight hydraulic press

Fig. 88 Multi-platen hydraulic press

load is 15 kw but thermostatic control ensures low electricity consumption. Pressure about 15 lbs psi (44 kg/cm²). This type of press is the workhorse of the industry for bow fronted doors, headboards, fascia boards, serpentine drawer fronts and the like.

Hydraulic single daylight press

Model IMP Universal Hydraulic press is suitable for the small to medium veneering workshop. It has four sides open for easy loading from any postion. Six rams give an even distribution over the entire surface, yet two rams can be isolated for smaller workloads.

Two 9 kw electric platens each with independent temperature indicator and controller, and a contact pressure manometer, ensure that the desired pre-set pressure is maintained. Very fast cycle times can be secured.

The platen size is 54 inches $\times$ 100 inches (1346 $\times$ 2540mm) and the press develops a total thrust of 88 tons (89 tonnes). The maximum pressure over the full platen area is 2.6 kg/cm², or over two thirds of the platen area, 3.9 kg/cm².

HEP Multi-Platen Hydraulic Press

This is a side loading electrically heated press, with each platen individually thermostatically controlled and each platen can be isolated to reduce power consumption, when fewer daylights are being used. The platen temperature and pressure is automatically controlled. Platen sizes 39 inches $\times$ 78 inches (990 $\times$ 1981mm) with a 4 kw heating per platen is available up to 62 inches $\times$ 122 inches (1574 $\times$ 3098mm) size, which requires 8 kw per platen.

PRODUCTION PRESSES

For general interest, here is a short list of other types of veneering presses available.

Flow line Press: This is a flat press for use with fast setting adhesives, in which work is loaded on one side and removed from the other for continuous working.

Shuttle Press: As one tray is being unloaded with a completed panel and re-loaded with the next panel to be pressed, the second tray is inside the press completing its time cycle, when the trays are reversed.

Multi-Daylight Hydraulic Presses:

Up to about 6 'daylights' can be loaded by hand, but presses up to 16 or more platens have to be loaded with automatic stacking and insertion machinery.

Nip Roller Press: The panel is fed between adjustable rollers which apply single line pressure as the panel traverses the table. It is used with heated rollers for hot melt adhesive applications.

Dome Press: Pneumatic pressure is applied to a flexible non-porous rubber sheet, which flows to the shape of the workload. Another type has a rubber bag into which the workload is inserted and the air pumped out.

The dome is lowered on two pistons, clamped and inflated to 35 lbs psi (102 kg/cm²) for about eight minutes for flat panels, and up to 100 lbs psi (292 kg/cm²) for shaped work, in ten to twenty minutes cycle curing times.

The dome also contains heating elements which can raise the temperature to 93 degrees C (200F) for very rapid curing in under two minutes.

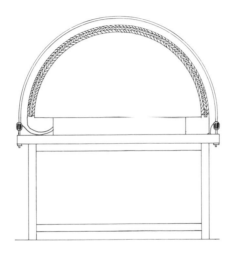

Fig. 89 A pneumatic press

LV and RF Presses

Low Voltage heated presses, and Radio Frequency heated presses operate hydraulically for heavy laminated work and are available in single or two-bay types. Presses can be offered which work on steam, oil, pneumatic or electricity in a wide variety of specially built types to suit every veneering function.

8

Low Voltage Heating

TO UNDERSTAND the value of low voltage heating we have to consider the setting action of modern adhesives: hot glues attain their strength on cooling, and the application of heat will soften the glue and weaken its bonding strength; cold adhesives, which set by evaporation of their solvents or by chemical reaction can be rapidly cured by the application of heat. The value to the veneer craftsman therefore, is that by the use of LV heating a great deal of time in terms of curing times of adhesives can be saved, along with the advantage that modern synthetic adhesives, with short pot-lives may be used, and increased output can be achieved at lower cost.

Among the adhesives recommended for low voltage heating are Polyvinyl acetate; modified animal and fish glues; and the synthetic adhesives UF (Urea formaldehyde) PF (Phenol formaldehyde) RF (Resorcinal-formaldehyde) and MF (Melamine formaldehyde)—also combinations of any of the synthetics.

Curing times of just over a minute are attained with interior gluing and with exterior bonding under two minutes, using RF adhesive and it is extensively used for edge veneering.

The heated element comes in contact with the edge veneer or lipping and has to raise the temperature of the material and conduct the heat through it to the glue line; the thicker the material the longer it will take.

The curing time is calculated at one minute per millimetre of veneer thickness, plus the curing time of the adhesive at the heat setting. UF takes half a minute to cure at 200 degree Fahrenheit (93 degrees Centigrade) and therefore with 0.7mm (1/40th inch) thick veneers the assembly can be removed from the jig in 1¼ minutes, and with 1mm thick veneers in 1½ minutes.

The Theory

When a voltage is applied across the ends of a strip of metal, a current will flow in it. The *value* of the current for a particular voltage depends upon the material's cross section and length. When current flows in metal, heat is generated in it and the amount of heat is proportional to the square of the current multiplied by the resistance of the strip. This means, by doubling the current, the heat becomes *four times* as great. By using a thinner strip of metal with a smaller cross section, the resistance is greater and the heat increased. The resistance of the metal also depends on the type of metal used—copper being the lowest and mild steel or stainless steel much higher. By using high resistance material for the element strip, a lower current can be used to produce the required heat without excessive loss in the connecting leads.

The current per inch width of the element strip governs the amount of heat and the wider the strip the more current is needed. A 3 inch (76mm) wide strip requires three times the current of a 1 inch (25mm) strip. The voltage required to cause the current-flow in a strip of known thickness and type, will depend upon its length.

Elements

There are materials with a very high specific resistance, but they are expensive. For our purposes, an inexpensive and easily obtainable element material is mild steel. As we must not let this come in contact with veneers with a high tannin content such as oak or afrormosia, the mild steel must be tinned, which will also prevent it from rusting. Use this for elements up to 6 inches (152mm) wide.

For greater widths use a grade of stainless steel which is flexible and of high resistance, e.g. Firth Vicker's F.1.17. Stainless steel is used for elements over 6 inches (152mm) wide.

As the resistance increases, the thickness reduces, therefore we want to use the thinnest strip possible which will withstand the pressures it will be subjected to. The most practical thickness to use is 26 swg (0.018 inch, (0.4572mm) which will withstand continuous use.

Power requirements

(a) When the length is greater than the width say 72 inches × 1 inch (1828 × 25mm) and a mean final temperature of 212 degrees Fahrenheit (100 degrees Centigrade) is required the power rating should be 350 watts per square foot (32.5m²).

(b) In a flat or shaped press where large areas of say 12 square feet (1.1m²) are to be pressed, also at 212 degrees Fahrenheit (100 degrees Centigrade), the rating would be 250 watts per square foot (23.2m²).

(c) When the length is greater than the width as in (a) but lower

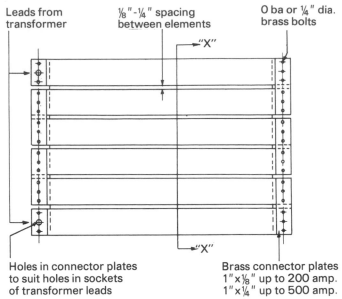

Leads from transformer

⅛"-¼" spacing between elements

0 ba or ¼" dia. brass bolts

→"X"

←"X"

Holes in connector plates to suit holes in sockets of transformer leads

Brass connector plates 1"x⅛" up to 200 amp. 1"x¼" up to 500 amp.

Note:- brass fixing bolts to be as near to the edge of the element as possible at all joints.

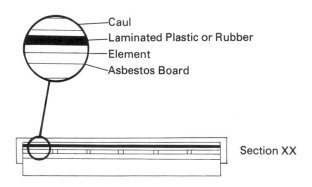

Caul
Laminated Plastic or Rubber
Element
Asbestos Board

Section XX

Fig. 90 Typical assembly of low voltage heating jig
The procedure for connecting strips in series and the general arrangement of building a heated platen, either curved or flat

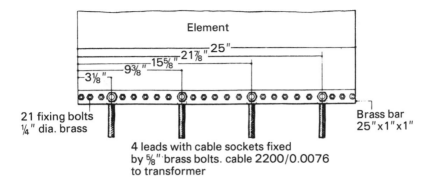

Fig. 9l(a) How four leads are connected to a brass bar when feeding a wide element. Note the 21 fixing bolts to ensure good connection between the brass and the element

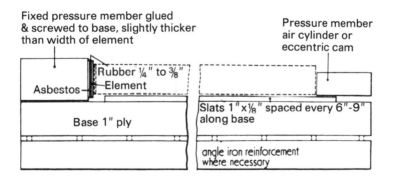

Fig. 9l(b) A general view òf a simple jig showing the relative positions of the asbestos, rubber and element

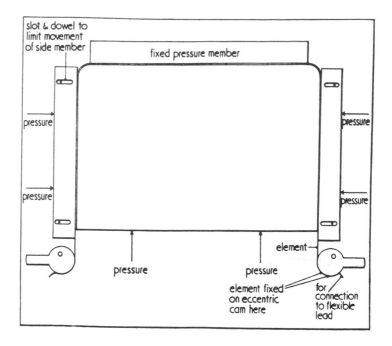

Fig. 92 The basic arrangement for a jig to edge-band the three sides of a panel, with radiused corners, at the same time

temperatures of 160 degrees Fahrenheit (71 degrees Centigrade) are required for edge banding with plastic laminates the power rating is 250 watts per square foot (23.2m²).

(d) Where the area is square or near square as in (b) but lower temperatures are required for veneering with plastic laminates (for kitchen surfaces) the power rating becomes 175 watts per square foot (16 watts per m²).

(e) When the length is four to six times the width, and higher temperatures are required of 392 degrees Fahrenheit (200 degrees Centigrade) as for scarf jointing, the power rating would be 500 watts per square foot (46 watts per m²).

In practice it is easier to deal with voltages and lengths of strip than with currents.

TABLE FOR USE WITH 26 GAUGE ELEMENT MATERIALS

		MILD STEEL TINNED				STAINLESS STEEL F.I.17			
Power (Watts) per Sq. foot	Power (Watts) per Sq. metre	Volts per Foot run	Volts per metre run	Amps per inch width	Amps per mm width	Volts per Foot run	Volts per metre run	Amps per inch width	Amps per mm width
175	16.26	.28	.919	53	2.08	.49	1.607	30	1.18
250	23.23	.33	1.085	63	2.48	.58	1.902	36	1.42
350	32.52	.39	1.279	75	2.95	.69	2.263	42	1.65
500	46.45	.54	1.771	83	3.27	.82	2.697	51	2.00

Example: What voltage is required to heat 6 feet × 3 inch (1828mm × 76mm) wide mild steel tinned, at 250 watts per sq. ft. (23.23m²)? The volts per foot run are shown as 0.33 (1.08 per metre) so the voltage across the ends of the element is 6 × 0.33 = 1.98 volts. (1828mm × 1.085 volts per metre = 1.98 volts approx.) The current per inch of width is given as 63 amps (2.48) so that 3 inches (76.2) wide element will need 63 × 3 = 189 amps (2.48 × 76.2 = 189).

To this required voltage of 1.98 in the example, we have to add the voltage drop suffered by the cable lead from the element to the transformer. This table determines the cable voltage losses:

VOLTAGE DROP IN 10 feet (3048mm) OF FLEXIBLE CABLE LEADS

Cable Current	490/0076 125 amp	770/0076 190 amp	1330/0076 275 amp	1680/0076 300 amp	2200/0076 375 amp	1248/018 700 amp
.75	0.36	0.22	0.15	0.12	0.11	0.08
1.00	0.49	0.30	0.20	0.17	0.15	0.11
1.50		0.49	0.32	0.26	0.23	0.16
2.00		0.69	0.44	0.37	0.31	0.21
3.00				0.59	0.48	0.31
4.00					0.70	0.41
5.00						0.51
6.00						0.62
7.00						0.73

In the above example where we need 1.98 volts at 189 amp, we find that we will require 770/0076 cable, which at our required current of 1.98 volts would have a voltage drop of 0.69 divided by 2.00 and multiplied by 1.98 = .68 volts. Therefore we add 0.68 volts to the 1.98 volts which is 2.66 volts required from the transformer.

Connections

Socketed leads are clamped to the element by brass bolts and nuts with brass washers under the bolt heads and nuts.

When the element is 2 inches (50mm) wide or less, the sockets are clamped direct to the element. When the element is 6 inches (152mm) or wider, two brass connecting strips are used, one on either side of the element, with brass nuts and bolts at 1 inch (25mm) intervals; the outer bolts as near to the edge as possible. Very wide elements require several connecting leads (depending on the calculated current in the strip) and these are attached to brass connecting strips at each side of the element.

On a wide platen press, heating elements are laid parallel, and connected in series, and brass connecting strips used for the leads.

Transformers

Alternating voltage transformer of the 'step-down' type is used, where the output is less than the input. There are two types: one has only one fixed output voltage and is used for heating wide strips or platens. (For edge veneering only 2 kw is required).

The other type has the output tapped so that six different lengths of element may be used, but not all at the same time.

Energy regulators

These are of various types and permit the heat in the element to be controlled and to protect the transformer. The 'Simmerstat' switches the transformer on and off to a predetermined timescale. The 'Regavolt' regulator permits any length of element to be used (up to the maximum of the transformer).

Jigs for edge banding

The object of the jig is to hold the element in its correct position as well as the components to be assembled, and to apply the necessary pressures. The pressure members of the jigs may be straight or shaped, and are made of laminated plywood, to withstand constant heat.

On the working surface side of the pressure member, a strip of asbestos millboard is fixed to protect the pressure member. Next to the asbestos millboard, a strip of 4mm to 6mm rubber which allows for variations in the panel acting as a pressure pad and laid directly on the rubber comes the heating element; then the edging strip of veneer. The asbestos strip, rubber and element are usually extended beyond the length of the pressure member and pinned or clamped outside the working area, to avoid marking the veneers.

When edging a rectangular panel, two edges are veneered simultaneously, which means two pressure members, asbestos and rubber strips and two elements. One member is permanently fixed, and the other is movable to allow for variously sized panels.

The movable pressure member may be in three sections, and by the

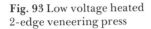

Fig. 93 Low voltage heated
2-edge veneering press

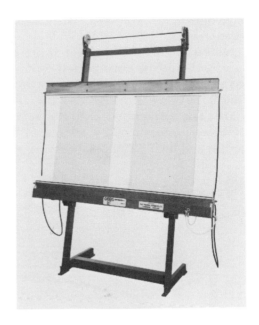

time the craftsman has loaded all three the first section is finished and ready for unloading.

For larger bench jigs, the pressure can be applied by eccentric cams, air cylinders etc. For small panels, the pressure may be applied with sash clamps on a bench jig.

It is important to insert small strips of wood or veneer packing pieces to keep the other side of the panel about ⅛ inch (3mm) from the surface of the jig, to allow the veneer to overhang the panel edge for subsequent trimming off.

When using sashclamps for the pressure, secure them to the bench, and check that they all have the same spacing of the back stop holes. They should not be more than 20 inches (508mm) apart on panels over 36 inches (914mm) long.

Curved pressure members are simply cauls made to the shape of the edge to be veneered, with the thickness of the asbestos and rubber sheet and the element taken into account.

If a *portable* LV press is wanted to tackle many edging projects, it can be attached to a piece of stout section timber, and G-clamped to any suitable edge.

For veneering panels with radius corners, the elements are extended beyond the fixed member and attached to eccentric cams, which are rotated, thereby bringing the element tightly around the curved corners of the panel, and then side pressures are introduced to veneer the long edges.

Large flat presses

To create a single daylight heated press for veneering, the two main press cauls should be constructed from 1½ inch (38mm) thick resin bonded exterior grade plywood to form the upper and lower platens. The lower surface is covered with a sheet or strips of asbestos millboard. The element strips are attached to the plywood with small gaps between each strip, by means of short pins with large heads knocked in at 9 inch (228mm) intervals, making sure the elements are

Fig. 94 Hydraulic veneering press with LV heated top platen

pulled tight. The ends of the elements are connected. Next an electrical insulating material is placed over the elements and nail heads—ideal for this purpose is a reject sheet of very thin plastic laminate such as 'Wareite'. Finally, a smooth sheet of 16 gauge (1.5mm) or 18 gauge (1.2mm) aluminium half-hard completely covers the platen and is turned down over the edges of the plywood about ½ inch (12mm) deep all round. By including a regulator in the mains circuit, the surface temperature can easily be controlled.

When making a press to take compound or shaped panels, the elements may be made in the form of strips as described, and inserted in both male and female formers and to take up any irregularities in the mating of the two formers, a sheet of 6mm rubber is inserted in the lower former instead of the sheet of 'Wareite' plastic. Both formers are covered with aluminium to act as cauls.

As an alternative to using a series of narrow mild steel tinned strips, one wide stainless steel element, the full width of the assembly can be used. This eliminates the need for insulating material and the aluminium cauls altogether.

For example, on a 25 inch (635mm) width assembly, using mild steel strip elements, a current of 1,575 amps would be required, whereas in F.I.17 stainless steel, the current reduces to only 900 amps—although slightly higher cable losses result.

In the famous 'Schreiber System' for making 'wrap-around' shells for TV cabinets and drawer units in one operation, a one piece stainless steel element was used to pull the veneers around a central block.

Fig. 95 100 ton, two bay hydraulic press with mould for radio frequency (R/F) heating producing chair arms from laminated veneers

RADIO FREQUENCY HEATING

Transverse radio frequency heating employs two flat electrodes to heat the press. There are two basic methods of RF heating. The first is known as 'stray field' and uses a diagonal grid system to heat the formers. This is extensively used for laminating chairbacks and seats, but it means heating the whole assembly, i.e. corestock, veneers and gluelines. On large flat panels this would result in wasted energy and on thick material it would not be very quick. The other method uses electrodes to heat the glueline only up to about 6 inches (152mm) wide. The equipment for this is expensive and outside the scope of all but the large manufacturer.

V.H.F. heating

Dielectric heating by VHF, operating at 10 Mc per second, is also used in some factories but requires high capital outlay, and, like the above, is outside the scope of all but large manufacturers.

9

Substrates

ALL LAYERS of material below the face and backing decorative veneers, including crossbandings, corestock and groundwork are collectively known as substrates.

(a) **Corestock** is the central core of a veneered panel, which will require further work *before* face and backing veneers are bonded to it, ie, the addition of crossbanding laminations.

(b) **Groundwork**, is the completed corestock base of the panel, including crossbandings, and ready to receive the face decorative veneer and compensating back veneer.

There are ten forms of substrate in general flat panel use:

1. Solid boards (hardwood or softwood).
2. Solid strips (hardwood or softwood).
3. Plywood.
4. Laminboard.
5. Blockboard.
6. Battenboard.
7. Particle board (flat pressed).
8. Particle board (extruded).
9. Hardboard.
10. Frame core construction

Whichever form of corestock is used, the final success of the veneered panel depends upon the correct preparation of the groundwork.

The hygroscopic nature of wood makes it subject to variations in moisture content with changes of atmospheric humidity. These humidity changes can have a wide range even in one geographic location and relative humidity can vary from 20 per cent to 65 per cent between winter and summer, with a corresponding variance in the moisture content of wood from 8 per cent up to 18 per cent or more. This could result in shrinkage in a 6 inch (152mm) wide board, of about ³⁄₃₂ inch (2mm).

The moisture content of timber in the United Kingdom is controlled down to 8-13 per cent for normal interior use. The lower range of 8 per cent is intended for use in centrally heated homes, and for shelving near radiators; for most other purposes 10-13 per cent is normal.

It is important to use only well seasoned timber which has been allowed to acclimatize naturally in the locality of its ultimate use, or at least in conditions where it can shed its moisture to maintain its equilibrium before being worked for corestock purposes.

Solid boards

A log tends to shrink along the direction of its growth rings, and when cut into boards this produces shrinkage in a direction away from the heartside of the log. By examining the end grain of a board, you will see the pattern of growth rings, and can easily determine which is the heart side, by imagining their curvature projecting on either side of the board.

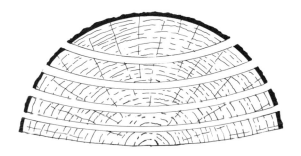

Fig. 96 A log shrinks away from the heart side

Fig. 97 Project the grain to determine the heart side

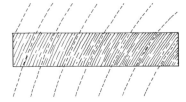

A radially cut board, with growth rings at right angles to the surface and parallel to the rays will shrink in its *thickness*, and is therefore the best for corestock purposes. A tangentially cut board, cut across the rays and in the general direction of the growth rings will shrink across its *width* and this is the worst possible type to use in its full width. A board cut part radially and part tangentially with growth rings at 45 degrees to both, would cause the board to warp and wind.

If repairing an antique and you have no choice but to use the wide board, veneer the surface on the *heart* side, so that the pull of the veneer when drying, will be opposite to the natural tendency to shrink away from the heart. Solid wood used on the ends of cabinets should have the heart side outwards to receive the veneers.

The ideal way is to veneer *both* sides, of radially sawn boards. Honduras mahogany or yellow pine are ideal for corestock. If they contain small knots or other defects, these should be chopped out and plugged. Cut a diamond or rectangular shaped plug or pellet, and glue it to stand up proud of the surface and in the same grain direction as the board, to be planed level when the glue has dried. Never use dowels where the grain would run at right angles to the surface, and would stand proud, even when planed, if the panel shrank in thickness.

Be careful of softwoods, as they absorb more adhesive and the surface must be well sized with glue which is compatible with the adhesive to be used to bond the panel. This will seal the pores of the wood before veneering takes place and prevent undue suction.

Radially cut boards are best to avoid the shrinkage problem but they can create their own problems. Radially cut oak for example may have a pronounced ray figure. The rays are harder than the surrounding wood and could telegraph through the face veneer to the surface.

American whitewood, Honduras mahogany, obeche, poplar and many softwoods are suitable, but try to avoid woods with a very strong figure.

Fig. 98 Solid wood strips with alternate grain

Solid strips

The best form of solid wood corestock is produced by cutting solid timber into strips, and alternate them head-to-tail with heart side up and down to equalise shrinkage tendencies. This may be done either from one board, or even from a variety of boards of the same thickness; mixed indiscriminately.

The way to ensure that the growth rings are assembled alternately up and down in adjacent strips, is to mark the top surface of the boards before cutting with a clear chalk mark on one side and a double chalk mark on the other. When assembled, look for the double mark on alternate strips. The reason that we do not chalk mark only one side, with the other side blank, is that strips tend to fall on their sides when being assembled, and a blank top may look like a blank side. By having a double chalk line on every other strip, and a single chalk line (a few inches further down the strip) on adjacent strips, the danger of a strip turning over is removed. (Waste timber containing mineral stains, bad colour, and other minor defects can be used up in this process).

Another advantage is gained when placing sawn strips in the vice for planing true. By keeping the chalk (or pencil) lines on the outside, you will ensure that mating edges are planed true and square. There must be no hollows or humps along the mating edges. For practically all corestock purposes, a rubbed butt joint is usually sufficient. Special panels which might be subjected to stress would be considerably reinforced if the corestock strips were to be tongued and grooved. This is very rarely done and for most domestic internal purposes simply glue and rub the strips together.

In bonding the core strips, do not use a thermo-plastic adhesive if the panel will be exposed to heat in subsequent veneering processes. Use cold thermosetting adhesive which is available in two main types: either a pre-mix powder containing resin, catalyst hardener, and extenders, which may be applied in a single operation to both mating edges; or a double application, where liquid resin is applied to one edge, and the liquid catalyst to the other. This greatly extends the pot life of the adhesive for quantity production.

The core strips are then clamped together with bar sash clamps. Usually one clamp is fitted at each end of the assembly on one side, and a third clamp on the opposite side to prevent any possibility of warping during the drying out period. The curing time is affected by the type of adhesive used, the size and the thickness of the panel and the number of joints. Local radiant heat can speed the curing time and is widely used for this purpose. But the introduction of water with the adhesive and localised drying by radiant heat, both disturb the moisture content of the strips and tend to make it unstable.

When removing the panel from the clamps clean off any adhesive seepage at the joints and edges and store the panel vertically in racks to allow a free circulation of dry air around the panels and time for them to restore their equilibrium.

After the panel has dried out, test it for flatness and plane it true in each diagonal direction. It should be toothed with a toothing plane ready for the laying of outer casing veneers. These are constructional veneers known as crossbandings and will complete the corestock operation, resulting in groundwork ready for decorative veneering.

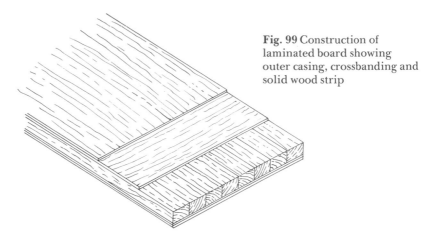

Fig. 99 Construction of laminated board showing outer casing, crossbanding and solid wood strip

Plywood

Because veneers have a natural tendency to shrink across their width, they are always laid in opposing grain directions at right angles in alternate layers. This is known as balanced construction.

Plywood is therefore made from an odd number of laminations; 3-ply, 5-ply, 7-ply, 9-ply etc. and the balancing point is the central core veneer with an even number of laminations on each side. If the central core veneer was thinner than the other layers, the tremendous pull they would exert when drying would cause the panel to warp or twist. This is especially true of factory produced plywood where constructional veneers used to form the layers are 'composed' or butt jointed together to avoid waste, and may possess a different shrinkage potential within parts of a single lamination. These joints are sometimes effected with a 'zig-zag' stitching machine which actually sews the two sheets together along the joint with a special nylon twine; or the latest Japanese layup composer which 'spot-welds' the veneer sheets together with up to sixteen spots of adhesive coated fibre along the joint. By having a thicker central core veneer and thinner outer casing veneers, the panel is kept in balance. Plywood has a very high strength to weight ratio, and is ideal where this ratio is important.

There are many advantages in making up your own corestock in plywood. Firstly, you would ensure that the laminations were of sound construction, free from defects and well jointed; you would also ensure that the crossbanding outer casings were treated before the application of the face and backing veneers. It is also possible to plan the fabrication so that the outer faces and centre core were in the same direction to suit the project. The number of laminations could be increased within the same overall thickness if the face veneer is likely to be short grained or difficult, such as a burr or curl. Furthermore, you can use up narrow or otherwise waste veneers in the core construction.

The important point to remember is, although the terms 'face', 'backing', 'crossbanding', or 'corestock' are used, they are constructional veneers, all cut from a log, and there is nothing to prevent you from using any veneer for corestock purposes, except the cost.

Commercial Plywood

There are several types of plywood, each graded according to its intended end-use.

INT (Interior Grade)

This is the cheapest type of plywood, usually bonded with casein, animal or blood albumen adhesive, and may delaminate in damp conditions due to micro-organic attack.

Even higher quality interior grades bonded with water resistant or fully waterproof adhesives may use sub standard veneers for the inner laminations, which could result in localised glueline weaknesses when panels are subjected to humid conditions.

Grade C veneers are used, which permit knotholes from 25mm across the grain up to 38mm; synthetic or wood repair patches; discolouration and sanding defects that do not impair strength and even limited splits are allowed.

Grade D panels allow knotholes up to 63mm wide across the grain and up to 75mm within specified limits; areas of white pocket rot sterilised during manufacture and therefore inert. These panels are intended for only a very short life chiefly for packing cases, and are not suitable for veneering corestock.

M.R (Moisture Resistant)

These panels are bonded with urea-formaldehyde, which has a high resistance to acids and alkalis; is immune to micro-organic attack and is excellent for veneering corestock purposes.

M.F. (Melamine Formaldehyde)

This plywood is resistant to boiling water; immune from micro-organic attack, and is also heat resistant. It is ideal for veneering corestock, and for laminating plastic sheets.

P.F. (Phenol Formaldehyde)

This bond produces plywood classified as weather and boil proof (WBP) grade. WBP adhesives are defined in BS 1455 as being adhesives which by systematic tests and by their records in service have been proved to make joints which are highly resistant to weather, micro-organisms, cold and boiling water, steam and dry heat.

Exterior Grades

Marine plywoods have to conform to BS 188 or BS 4079 (1966) and there are three types:

1.   Exterior High Hazard: driven rain or full sunlight with fluctuating relative humidity, fungal decay risk, heavy frosts, insect attack, chemical pollution etc.
2.   Exterior Low Hazard: the end use requires protection from direct soaking by rain, and no direct sunlight.
3.   Interior High Hazard: conditions of high humidity, exposure to condensation, leaking roofs, extremes of temperature in the daily cycle in industrial buildings etc.

These exterior grades use special formulations of phenolic adhesives in combination with resorcinol (PF/RF) mixes, and epoxy resins. They are all suitable for corestock purposes but naturally rather expensive. They will withstand extremes of most external and all internal hazards.

It is important to remember that the designations INT/M.R/ M.F/P.F etc. refer only to the bonding adhesive and not to the veneers which are obviously subject to normal timber behaviour.

F.R (Fire retardant)

Many substrates are required to be 'flame retardant' or 'fire retardant' for building construction and architectural panelling purposes. There are stringent tests for such material and also the surface treatment of veneered panels which have flame retardant finishes applied. This does not affect the original bonding adhesive, except that experiments are in hand to produce fire retardant adhesives and therefore plywood offered with the F.R grading is likely to be suitable for such purposes.

GRAIN DIRECTION

In planning a project in which you intend to use commercial plywood, remember when specifying the plywood that the first stated dimension is always 'with' the grain. A panel 24 inches × 36 inches (609 × 914mm) would be 24 inches (609mm) long by 36 inches (914mm) wide across the grain.

This is very important when you plan to apply crossbandings to the plywood and then face and backing veneers. In this case the 24 inches (609mm) direction of the core panel, would then receive a 36 inch (914mm) long by 24 inch (609mm) wide crossbanding lay-up, followed by the 24 inch long × 36 inch (609mm × 914mm) wide face and backing veneers. But if you decided to apply the face and backing veneers direct to the plywood panel, without underlaying crossbandings, you would need to order a 36 inch (914mm) long by 24 inch (609mm) wide plywood core.

More important is the *number* of laminations.

If the plywood panel was 36 inches (914mm) long by 24 inches (609mm) wide but only in 3-ply, the centre core veneer would also be only 24 inches (609mm) long (to enable the outer laminations to run in the 36 inches (914mm) length direction). This would be ideal for veneering in the 24 inches (609mm) grain direction with the outer decorative veneers. The finished 5-ply panel would therefore have 3 laminations in the 24 inches (609mm) direction and two in the 36 inches (914mm) direction.

But if you bought a 5-ply panel, 36 inches (914mm) long by 24 inches (609mm) wide, the outer laminations would be in the 36 inch (914mm) as would the central core veneer.

By laying the face and backing veneers in the 24 inches (609mm) direction to suit your project, three laminations would result in the 36 inchs (914mm) direction and four in the 24 inches (609mm) direction.

The following chart (over page) will illustrate the position:

In the first example we wish to complete a panel in which the face veneer and backing veneer will both have a 24 inches (609mm) grain direction; we need to order plywood in the correct size.

(A)   These columns show face and backing veneers without cross-bandings. Left-hand columns indicate 3-ply, right hand columns indicate 5-ply.

(B)   Shows grain direction where crossbandings will be used in addition to face and backing veneers. Left-hand columns indicate 3-ply, right-hand columns indicate 5-ply.

You can substitute your own dimensions when referring to the chart.

*   *   *

There are three important considerations before deciding on the specification for commercial plywood:

<u>Balanced construction</u> for your project means that the veneers on either side of the core must be in pairs of equal thickness; of the same species; the same distance from the core and at the same moisture content prior to manufacture. This means, that even if the central core veneer in the case of 3-ply is twice as thick as the outer casings, it is best for the complete panel to be constructed from veneers of the same species (except for face and backing decorative veneers), and made at the same time. For this reason, many craftsmen prefer to make their own groundwork. (Continued after chart, p. 129)

Grain Direction of Face and Backing Veneers to be in the 24 inches (609mm) Direction

A

- 24"/609mm face
- ─ ─ ─ ─ ─
- 36"/914mm outer case
- 24"/609mm core
- 36"/914mm outer case
- ─ ─ ─ ─ ─
- 24"/609mm backing

Order Plywood
36" × 24"
914mm × 609mm

B

- 24"/609mm face
- 36"/914mm cross band
- 24"/609mm outer case
- 36"/914mm core
- 24"/609mm outer case
- 36"/914mm cross band
- 24"/609mm backing

Order Plywood
24" × 36"
609mm × 914mm

A

- 24"/609mm face
- ─ ─ ─ ─ ─
- 36"/914mm outer case
- 24"/609mm inner case
- 36"/914mm core
- 24"/609mm inner case
- 36"/914mm outer case
- ─ ─ ─ ─ ─
- 24"/609mm backing

Order Plywood
36" × 24"
914mm × 609mm

B

- 24"/609mm face
- 36"/914mm cross band
- 24"/609mm outer case
- 36"/914mm inner layer
- 24"/609mm core
- 36"/914mm inner layer
- 24"/709mm outer case
- 36"/914mm cross band
- 24"/609mm backing

Order Plywood
24" × 36"
609mm × 914mm

Grain Direction of Face and Backing Veneers to be in the 36 inch (914mm) Direction

A

- 36"/914mm face
- ─ ─ ─ ─ ─
- 24"/609mm outer case
- 36"/914mm core
- 24"/609mm outer layer
- ─ ─ ─ ─ ─
- 36"/914mm backing

Order Plywood
24" × 36"
609mm × 914mm

B

- 36"/914mm face
- 24"/609mm cross band
- 36"/914mm outer case
- 24"/609mm core
- 36"/914mm outer case
- 24"/609mm cross band
- 36"/914mm backing

Order Plywood
36" × 24"
914mm × 609mm

A

- 36"/914mm face
- ─ ─ ─ ─ ─
- 24"/609mm outer case
- 36"/914mm inner layer
- 24"/609mm core
- 36"/914mm inner layer
- 24"/609mm outer case
- ─ ─ ─ ─ ─
- 36"/914mm backing

Order Plywood
24" × 36"
609mm × 914mm

B

- 36"/914mm face
- 36"/914mm outer case
- 24"/609mm inner layer
- 36"/914mm core
- 24"/609mm inner layer
- 36"/914mm outer case
- 24"/609mm cross band
- 36"/914mm backing

Order Plywood
36" × 24"
914mm × 609mm

Thickness: If you are making a project where all the panels are to be produced with a finished thickness of 19mm, it is necessary to work inwards from the face and backing veneers, and crossbandings, to find the thickness of commercial plywood to order. This is especially important if utilising offcuts from another job and crossbandings have to be used to throw the face veneer in the correct grain direction.

Example: Face and backing veneers each .7mm   1.4mm
            Crossbandings each .9mm   1.8mm
                                                         ───────
                                                          3.2mm
            Plywood thickness maximum   15.8mm
                                                         ───────
            Total overall thickness is 19mm   19.0mm
                                                         ───────

The availability of plywood panels is as follows:
1.5mm; 3mm; 4mm; 5mm; 6mm; 9mm; 12mm; 15mm; 18mm; 22mm; 25mm.

Economy: In some cases, the glueline is almost as valuable as the veneer content; the more laminations and gluelines, the more costly the plywood. Therefore, when the cost of multi-plywood is being considered, it will pay to compare the price with other groundwork substrates which may be more economical.

Laminated boards are universally used for decorative veneering. There are three basic types, all of similar construction, using strips of solid timber, cut into strips and assembled head to tail, and with thick outer casings of constructional veneer laid at right angles to both faces.

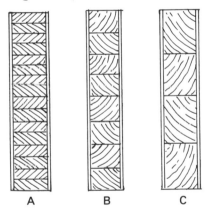

Fig. 100 A: Laminboard,
        B: Blockboard,
        C: Battenboard

A   B   C

Laminboard

The solid wood strips are only 3mm to 7mm maximum width, with heart sides up and down alternately. This means that you would lay the decorative face veneer opposite to the outer casing grain direction and in line with the corestrips for maximum strength.

Laminboard is the most expensive groundwork of the three laminated boards, but undoubtedly the best.

Available in thicknesses:
    12mm; 15mm; 18mm; 22mm; 25mm; 32mm and 38mm.

Blockboard

This is of similar manufacture except that the solid core strips are from 22mm-25mm maximum width.

Available in thicknesses:
    12mm; 15mm; 18mm; 22mm; 25mm; 32mm and 38mm.

Solid core door blanks are also available in thicknesses:
    38mm; 45mm; 50mm and 54mm.

Battenboard

The solid core strips are 25mm to 75mm wide. The danger is that unequal shrinkage in the wider strips might result, and this could telegraph through to the face veneers. When battenboard is used, it is safest to apply crossbandings. However, this poses a problem because the crossbandings would be laid opposite to the outer casing veneers, (i.e. in the same direction as the strips) and the decorative face and backing veneers would then have to be laid across in the shorter direction.

For this reason, battenboard is chiefly used for partitioning and wall panelling. It is available in the same range of thicknesses as blockboard and laminboard.

Battenboard is available in panel sizes 48 inches × 84 inches (1200 × 2135mm); 48 inches × 96 inches (1200 × 2440mm); 60 inches × 120 inches (1525 × 3050mm) and 60 inches × 178 inches (1525 × 4500mm) up to other specially jointed panel sizes. The first stated dimension is the grain length of the outer casing veneer, and should be specified in that way similarly to plywood.

Particle board

This is a manufactured board familiarly known as chipboard or flaxboard, made from wood chips, shavings and sawdust.

There are two basic types. The first is *flat pressed*. The mixture is compressed between platens, causing the wood fibre particles to lie parallel with the surface of the board. By factory processes of progressive refinement of the particles some superfine surfaces are achieved, suitable for veneering.

Extruded particle board is forced out under pressure and the chips lie at right angles to the surface of the board. This type is far less dense; has lower strength, coarser texture, and is subject to moisture content variations. There are three varieties of particle board.

(a)   Single layer boards, which have a uniform density throughout due to chips being graded to the same size.

(b)   Graded density boards, which utilise varying chip sizes, with the largest in the centre and the smaller on the surface.

(c)   Sandwich construction boards which have three layers with the centre layer of large loosely packed chips, with smooth smaller chips on both surfaces.

These boards have only a medium density, but lend themselves to bending.

Particle boards range from 600 to 800 kilograms per cubic metre, in density, and offer a wide range of uses. They are subject to moisture absorption, which could affect thickness, especially the flame retardant types, due to salts used in manufacture. This becomes extremely important when edge lippings or facings are to be applied, which is usually the case with all particle boards. Always buy the strongest density and superfine grades. Panels are available in 6mm; 9mm; 12mm; 15mm; 18mm; 22mm and 25mm;

Flame resistant particle board

Approximate density expressed in kg/M^3. Class 0 is in accordance with BS476 parts 5, 6 and 7, and Class 1 refers to the surface spread of flame.

Class 0	10mm	12mm	16mm	19mm	22mm	25mm
	795	790	775	—	—	—
Class 1	745	740	730	700	680	665

Hardboard

Superfine wood fibres are bonded together under very high pressure and temperature to produce a board of uniform strength in every direction and no grain direction.

Three types of hardboard are produced suitable for veneering: *Medium grade*—only suitable for interior partitions and thin panels. *Standard grade* for most normal veneering corestock purposes in 6mm thickness. *Tempered grade*, exceptionally strong, can be used for door facings and for panels in regular use, rather than interior partitioning.

Available in many thicknesses from 1.5mm; 3mm; 4mm; 6mm; and in flame retardant surface finishes, Class 1, in 3mm and 6mm.

Flaxboard with Hardboard faces

This special combination board is made for partitioning and wall panelling in 46mm, 49mm and 54mm thickness.

Wastage

Groundwork substrates of whichever type you choose, are an expensive item, and one of the first considerations is the elimination of waste. Therefore consider the advantages of jointing the corestock.

Plywood can be half-lapped or scarf jointed; laminated boards half-lapped, tongued and grooved, fitted with loose tongues, or butt jointed. Butt jointing should only be used on panels which are not load bearing and *not* on everyday working surfaces subject to stress.

Frame core construction

This is a form of hollow corestock which is very much lighter in weight than solid corestock. This form of construction is valuable when large doors, shelving, partitions, or table tops are to be made, which would otherwise be extremely heavy. The frame assembly can be put together with mortice and tenon joints; tongued and grooved; dowelled joints; or butt jointed, or held with industrial staples or corrugated strip joints.

The hollow core frames are then covered with thin hardboard or plywood 'skins' to complete the panel ready for veneering. The interior may be filled with slotted hardboard or plywood strips in egg-box fashion; or a honeycomb in cardboard or hardboard; corrugated cardboard strips; wood shavings or chips; or extended polyurethane or polystyrene. Constructional veneers in ⅛ inch (3mm)

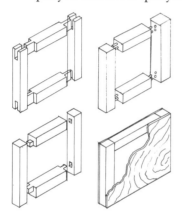

strips slotted together make excellent inner fillings, but care must be taken to ensure that the packing does not telegraph through to the surface of the veneer.

When it is intended to fit cabinet fittings such as hinges, locks, rim furniture, escutcheons, door knobs, letterboxes etc., include suitably sized pieces of hardwood within the hollow frame construction to accept subsequent drilling and screwing of the fitting.

The same construction method is used to create deep thickness coffee tables, desks, dining room furniture, which would have an appearance of being solid and heavy, but in fact would be very strong and light to handle.

Fig. 101 Hollow frame construction showing various joints

Telegraphing

This problem is even more actute with the hollow frame construction and it is always best to overlay a skin of hardboard or thin plywood to prevent it. If you employ constructional veneer crossbandings instead, avoid those with a coarse figure such as fir or pine, or crossbandings with several joints, or dovetailed corestock, as these details could telegraph through to the surface of the face veneer. It is therefore essential that the crossbanding veneer immediately below the face veneer should cover all joints or strong surfaces likely to telegraph through. Take especial care of dovetail joints which tend to show through, and instead employ lapped dovetails which will not.

One of the most common causes of telegraphed damage to face veneers, is the careless application of edge lippings or facings.

10

Shaped Groundwork & Wood Bending

S HAPED and curved groundwork enables the cabinetmaker to tackle projects which would not otherwise be practical, or structurally sound in solid wood. He would encounter short grain and cross-grained parts in the solid as well as an increased number of joints. On the other hand, by creating compound or contoured groundwork the project can be given increased strength, lightness, and at the same time, enjoy the full advantages of veneer matching by exploiting the beauty of the woods.

SHAPED GROUNDWORK

There are seven ways of making shaped groundwork and which you choose will depend partly on the nature of the project and partly upon the tools and other equipment available to you.

1. Cut from solid
2. Cut from laminated boards
3. Brick construction
4. Coopered units
5. Wood bending
6. Laminated veneer bending
7. Hollow frame construction

Solid Wood

The shape might be bandsawn from the solid if the curvature was shallow, but there are three good reasons why this method is rarely used: (a) the wastage encountered is usually uneconomic; (b) the crossgrained part of the shape is weak; and (c) there may be areas of end grain on the surface which will create finishing problems.

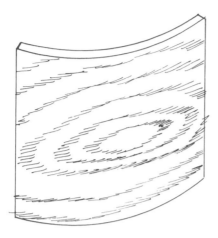

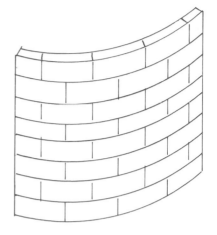

Fig. 102 Solid wood is weak caused by crossgrain and endgrain problems

Fig. 103 Use brick construction as an alternative to solid wood

Laminated board

Two or more boards of laminated construction are glued together and the required shape bandsawn. This would overcome difficulties (a) and (b) above, although it is still quite wasteful.

In both the above methods, save the male and female offcuts to be used as cauls in the later veneering process.

Brick construction

This eliminates short and end grain problems on the curvature, and is constructed from a series of small 'bricks' of solid timber laid in courses; the vertical joints of which are staggered, as in common brickwork, to provide shape and strength.

This method is widely used by the smaller craftsman who lacks the more expensive equipment required for series production. By this simple brick method, curved drawer fronts, kidney shaped rims for tables and dressing tables, and circular rims for tables are created easily.

The required shape is first drawn on to a piece of plywood, and pencil lines marked in to show where the vertical lines in the courses of brickwork are to come. Two templets are required, as the courses are built 'out of course' or staggered. If required by the project, the top and bottom layers may be bandsawn from solid hardwood, otherwise the assembly and gluing takes place on the plywood setting-out board.

There are two ways of proceeding depending on whether you have a bandsaw available or not. If you have a bandsaw, make the bricks wider than required, and after you have laid a complete course, bandsaw the work to shape. Otherwise, make the bricks only a trifle oversize and after assembly, clean them up with a spokeshave or circular plane. Allow each course to dry, and then plane the work true before the next course is added to it.

Coopered units

Unlike brickwork, (where the ends are rub jointed together) the *edges* of solid timber are planed to suitable bevels and glued together. This is done by making a cradle carefully cut out to a drawing of the

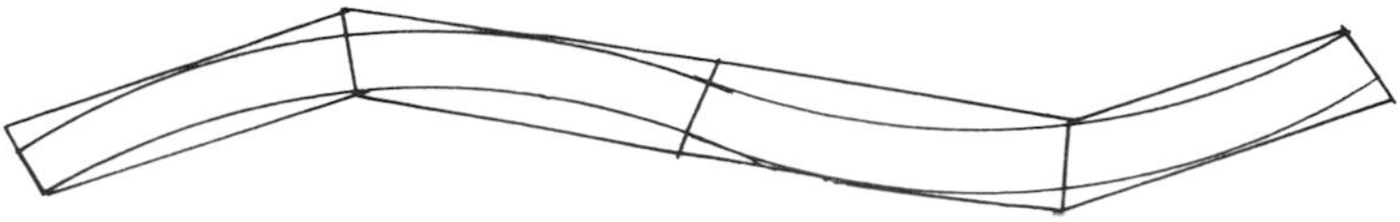

Fig. 104 Serpentine shape from coopered groundwork

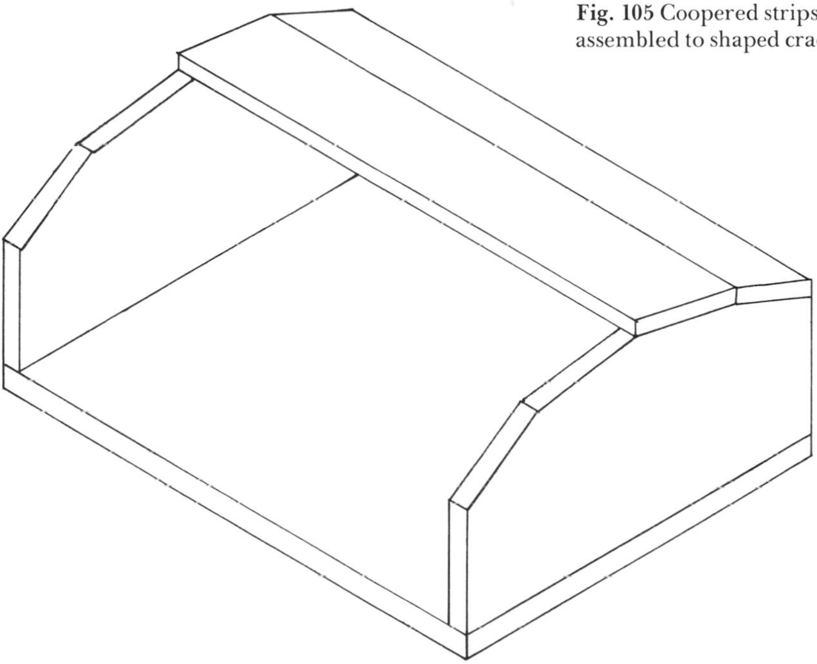

Fig. 105 Coopered strips assembled to shaped cradle

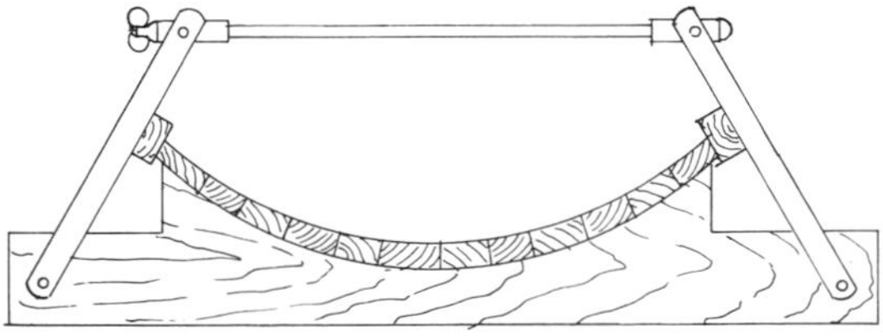

Fig. 106 Pivoted jaws clamp coopered strips on saddle

curvature, and assembling the strips on the cradle; or, laying the strips after gluing, on shaped saddles, with pressure applied by tightening pivoted jaws which bring pressure to bear on the strips which are protected at each end with a waste piece of hardwood. The outer face can be cleaned up with planes or rasps, and the inner curves with a compass plane. Serpentine shaped fronts and doors are made in this way using extra thick stuff to allow for shaping.

Dry coopering is another technique for very shallow curving doors. Make a simple cradle to the inner curve of the door, and bend (or steam and bend) a thin sheet of plywood over the shape and clamp it in position until dry.

A series of battens about 3 inch (19mm) wide are laid and glued to the plywood with a second sheet of plywood clamped on top and glued to the top of the battens.

If the curvature is great, the surface of the battens would have to be planed to remove the peaked joints, otherwise they might telegraph through—but for most shallow curves this is not a problem.

Remember to be careful about the possibility of actually breaking the fibres of the plywood surface when bending, and also avoid overheating or excessive moisture when steaming or delamination may take place. Also check that the inner core of the plywood does not crack.

Sometimes hardboard may be used instead of plywood.

When making bearers for bending shaped groundwork of a slight curvature, ensure that they are more curved than the finished shape to allow for the groundwork to spring back a little.

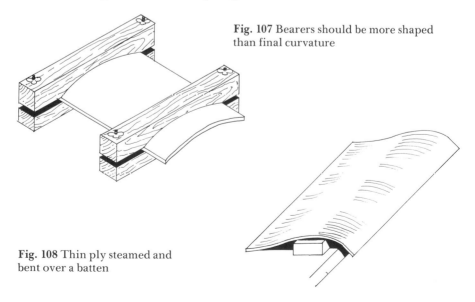

Fig. 107 Bearers should be more shaped than final curvature

Fig. 108 Thin ply steamed and bent over a batten

If steaming plywood, make the preliminary bend over a batten on the workbench to part-form the shape before clamping. For more acute curves, the process might be repeated by making up two sets of bearers, one more sharp than the other, and after steaming and bending on the first bearer, repeat the process on the second bearer until the correct curvature is reached.

WOOD BENDING

There are four methods of wood bending for groundwork purposes:
(a) force fit, (b) slitting, (c) cold bending and (d) steam bending.

(a)   *Force fit:* When the radius is gentle in relation to the thickness of the panel, and the panel can be fixed and held permanently in position by adjacent parts of the structure, the panel, after veneering, may be forced manually into shape and held by glue and joints by the structure itself.

(b)   *Slitting:* Use a thick sawblade in the circular sawbench, and cut a series of slits in the groundwork about ¾ inch (19mm) apart, and right through about ¾ of the panel thickness. For example, cut through 5 laminations of a 7ply panel, or 3 laminations of 5ply.

The more acute the curve, the closer together the sawcuts need to be. Manually bend the panel around bearers, bandsawn to the required shape. Then temporarily fix a batten across as a tie to secure the shape. The sawn surface should then be glued and veneered with constructional veneer crossbandings laid across the sawcuts.

(c)   *Cold bending:* Green timber with a high moisture content can be bent without steaming. Normally, bending stretches and lengthens the timber, however, if this is prevented by end stops, supported on the convex face with a metal strap and held until dry, it will retain its shape. Steaming increases the pliability, enabling much smaller radii; also, brittle woods which will not bend 'cold' will respond to steam. Cold bending is only suitable for shallow curves.

(d)   *Steam bending:* Prepare the workpiece by machining on all surfaces before steaming or boiling. Ideally the blank piece of timber for bending should be straight grained, free from knots, grain changes, surface or end checks, in-growing bark or fungal growth.

The wood may be green or air dried. In fact, air dried stuff takes more pressure to bend and green timber is preferred. Fibre saturation point is about 25 per cent for air dried timber up to the green state.

Green timber has the advantage that no pre-drying period is required, requires less effort for manual bending, very little risk of surface or end checking and no distortion in the heating process.

Its disadvantage is the longer drying and setting time after bending; supporting straps and tie pieces are needed for longer periods; there is a tendency for the piece to distort or split in drying out and for moisture filled cells to rupture when bending to small radii.

Partially seasoned timber has the advantage that there is no danger of hydraulic rupture; rapid drying and setting time; requires support pieces, tie pieces, length restriction blocks, etc., for a shorter time, and there is a marked reduction in the tendency to distort or split. However, the disadvantage is that it takes more effort to bend; there is a danger of compression failure due to unobserved surface checks in drying, and the risk of distortion during heat treatment or immediately afterwards.

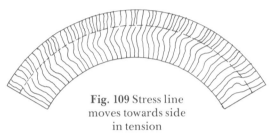

Fig. 109 Stress line
moves towards side
in tension

Cutting the blank

Remember the shrinkage factor when drying out and possible distortion in cross section which might deviate from the required shape, also the additional length for fixing tie pieces to hold the bend when preparing a smoothly finished rectangular blank suitable for shaping after bending.

Steaming

The temperature of the workpiece has to be raised to the boiling point of water (212 degrees F or 100 degrees C) without affecting the moisture content of the wood.

In factory conditions this is achieved by exposing the wood to saturated steam at atmospheric pressure for ¾ hour for every inch (25mm) of thickness. Prolonged steaming has no advantage.

This heat treatment actually *reduces* the moisture content of green timber, but not of the 25 per cent partially air dried timber.

Home craftsmen will not be able to use steam heat (which requires a special cabinet with a safety valve in the roof and a tap for running off the condensation at the bottom). However, hot wet sand and boiling water is the ideal method for the home craftsman.

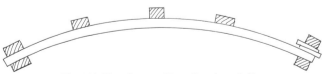

Fig. 110 Simple wood bending bench jig
showing blocks and wedges to righthand side

Manual bending

There are two types of manual bending: either without supporting straps, or with supporting straps.

Without straps:

(a)   Where the radius of curvature is large compared with the thickness of the wood, a set of pegs may be fixed to a suitable backplate and the piece forced around these by hand.

(b)   Shaped blocks can be mounted on a bench to supply a skeleton former, and the piece forced to shape between the blocks by means of wedges or clamps.

(c)   Male and female cauls can be bandsawn, and the workpiece clamped between them.

(d)   The workpiece may be forced over wooden or metal forms, and clamped in position. It is even better when the metal form is heated. This is the preferred method as it does not present the setting problems posed by methods (a) and (b), both of which will leave tell-tale marks caused by the pegs or blocks where the workpiece was pressed against them, and (c) method takes much longer to set because both faces are covered by the cauls.

The main reasons for using the heated bending method are that it makes the timber more pliable because the fibres soften; the stress line through the timber moves nearer to the convex face decreasing the number of fibres in tension; the limiting radius may be much smaller as breaking point on the compression face is increased and as the timber cools, the fibres set into the newly formed pattern. Provided that the new shape is fixed, it will remain as set, whereas a bent shape that is not fixed will tend to move back towards its original shape.

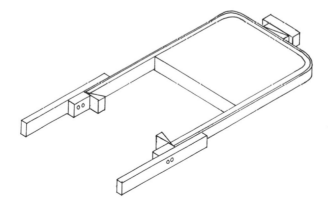

Fig. 111 A simple wood bending jig with wood end-stops and wedges

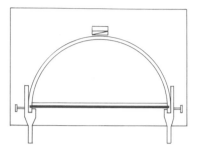

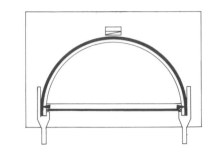

Fig. 112 (Above) Unsupported bending jig with metal tie-rod

Fig. 113 (Right) Supported bending jig with tie rod

With Supporting Straps:

The metal straps should be made of either mild steel in 18 swg, or spring steel in 14 swg. The 18 swg is suitable for timber thicknesses up to 25mm and the 14 swg for thicker material. The strap should be wider than the width of the workpiece, and it is fitted along the convex side to be stretched. The inner part of the bend, naturally, will be placed, unsupported, against a wooden or metal former around which the shape is to be bent. Sometimes handles may be fitted at each end of the workpiece with turnscrews, and these provide excellent leverage in bending and also support the wooden blank during bending.

After the simultaneous bending of both halves of the workpiece around the former a tie rod is fitted across to secure the bend. The handles are removed leaving the wooden blank and its metal strap still attached, to be removed from the former and allowed to set.

Prior to making the bend the workpiece is held tightly against the former with wedges. Sometimes the pressures induced are likely to cause the metal strap to slip. To prevent this, metal or wooden end stops are attached to the strap and pressure applied by inserting tapered wedges between the stops and the ends of the block to tighten the strap.

For some bends these end stops are made adjustable to control pressures along the length of the timber during the bending operation by means of an adjustment screw. This is necessary when the cross section of a piece is small compared with its length and could result in snaking or back bending. It is controlled by regulating the end stop to allow very slight stretching of about 2 per cent of the total length.

End stops are made not only adjustable but also detachable, and this is particularly useful for series production, or even when bending in two planes or when S-bends are formed.

If the shape to be bent is assymetrical use two tie pieces, one at the top and the other at the bottom to hold the shape.

Setting and drying

This is a two stage process. The workpiece, with the tie pieces and straps not removed, are placed in a 'setting' room. This is a heated, well ventilated room, with a flow of hot, dry air, with temperatures up to 100 degrees F (38 degrees C) and a means of removing the moisture laden air.

Green beech up to one inch (25mm) thick will set in 24 hours and air dried beech of the same thickness would take only nine hours. Test the tie bars, and when you can feel that the work has slackened off, the tie pieces and straps can be removed, and the blank taken to a room with temperature about 75 degrees F (24 degrees C) and allowed to dry out for three weeks.

This has to be a slow process, otherwise longitudinal changes may occur with changing atmospheric conditions.

Bending Properties for Various Timbers

The most important factor is the minimum radius of curvature for a given thickness of wood without breaking.

The following table provides the safe radius—with only 5 per cent failure rate of fracture. The material is air dried, 25mm thick and steamed at atmospheric pressure for 45 minutes.

TIMBERS FOR WOODBENDING

Standard Name of Species	Approximate radius (mm)	
EXCELLENT	Supported by strap and end stop	Unsupported
Ash European (home grown)	64	300
Ash European French	51	340
Beech European (Danish)	43	370
Beech European (home grown)	38	330
Elm, Dutch (home grown)	13	240
Elm, English	38	340
Elm, American white	43	340
Oak, American	13	330
Oak, European (home grown)	51	330
Oak, Japanese	38	320
Planetree	51	430
Sycamore (home grown)	38	370
Walnut, European	25	280

GOOD

Ash, American	110	330
Celtis, African	270	860
Chestnut, horse	150	460
Chestnut, sweet	150	380
Guarea	190	510
Mansonia	250	390
Myrtle, Tasmanian	180	430
Olive, East African	290	760
Yewtree	220	420

AVERAGE

African Walnut	460	810
Afrormosia	360	740
Agba	510	410
Alder	360	460
Douglas Fir	460	840
Greenheart	460	910
Hemlock, Western	480	910
Iroko	380	460
Larch, European	330	460
Larch, Japanese	420	790
Lime, European	360	410
Makore	300	460
Obeche	460	430
Purpleheart	460	760
Rauli	420	420
Teak	460	890

POOR

Abura	790	890
Avodire	910	970
Idigbo	810	1120
Mahogany, African	970	890
Pine, Corsican	860	740
Poplar, French	810	660
Ramin	910	940
Sapele	760	940
Seraya, White	840	890
Utile	910	120

LAMINATED VENEER BENDING

There are a tremendous number of advantages in making corestock from laminated veneers. Constructional veneers of any thickness up to about 3mm (⅛ inch) may be used successfully. They are bonded with cold setting urea formaldehyde adhesives in a press, between male and female cauls. The veneers are flexible and can therefore be bent into smaller radii than solid timber.

There is no restriction on length, and each veneer slides over the adjacent piece, lubricated by the adhesive, free to take up its own location without over stretching the wood fibres on the convex face, and without excessive compression on the concave face. There is no deformation of the cell structure; any species may be used providing it is free from decay, knots, checks, wild grain, in-growing bark etc. For the inner core, relatively cheap inferior veneers, or jointing waste veneers may be used. The laminations do not all have to be of the same thickness, for example, the central core may be twice as thick as the adjacent veneers; the crossbanding veneers may be a different thickness. The only vital factor is that veneers are in 'pairs' on each side of the core.

True face

Each of the laminations has a loose and a tight 'true' face. This is caused by the action of the rotary knife in shearing the veneer from the log and causes fine hairchecks to occur in the veneer which run from the underside, through to the face. Crossbanding veneers should be laid with the 'true' face outwards ready to receive the decorative veneers, otherwise the heat in the press, and subsequent drying can cause these hairchecks to telegraph through to the face veneers.

Corestock laminations

For corestock laminations—not the crossbandings—keep the loose face of the veneer towards the concave shape of the bend which comes under compression. The thicker the corestock, the greater the pressure to be exerted by the press, as much greater pressure is needed to laminate a curved panel than a flat one for two reasons: (a) the larger number of gluelines to be squeezed out in one operation; and (b) the larger area of veneer to be compressed in bonding.

It is therefore necessary to add the exact thickness of the veneers used for the corestock, plus the crossbandings on each side, plus the face and backing veneers—and then add to that, the thickness of the number of gluelines.

The pressure is not precisely distributed in a home-made press especially when using home-made cauls and the glueline tends to be thicker.

Let us take an example: to construct a 19mm panel.

Five core veneers of 3mm thickness	15.0mm
Two crossbanding veneers of 0.8mm	1.6mm
Two decorative veneers of 0.7mm	1.4mm
Eight gluelines of 0.125mm	1.0mm
	19.0mm

Choose obeche or mahogany for this type of corestock work, which is available in a range of thicknesses. Too great a variation in the thickness of laminations can cause bond failure. This does not mean that they should all be of the *same* thickness, but of *uniform* gauge throughout the layer, and arranged in pairs in balanced construction on each side of the central core.

Do not rely on gap filling adhesives to compensate for veneer thickness inequalities, they will result in doubtful bonds. Also, the pressure exerted must never exceed the crushing strength of the veneer. This is unlikely in home made presses unless the panel area is small.

Jointing the laminations

The constructional veneers used in laminations must be jointed. Although corestock veneers are usually obtainable from the mills in great widths (in fact the rotary lathe produces unlimited widths and the reels have to be clipped to convenient sizes for ease of shipment by road and rail), these veneers are delivered to you in short widths and will have to be jointed to make up panel sizes. Consider the problem of a panel to be made, say 60 inches × 15 inches (1524 × 381mm).

1	Face veneer	60 inches × 15 inches (1524 × 381mm)
2	Crossbanding	15 inches × 60 inches (381 × 1524mm)
3	Outer casing	60 inches × 15 inches (1524 × 381mm)
4	Inner substrate	15 inches × 60 inches (381 × 1524mm)
5	Core veneer	60 inches × 15 inches (1524 × 381mm)
6	Inner substrate	15 inches × 60 inches (381 × 1524mm)
7	Outer casing	60 inches × 15 inches (1524 × 381mm)
8	Crossbanding	15 inches × 60 inches (381 × 1524mm)
9	Backing veneer	60 inches × 15 inches (1524 × 381mm)

Veneer No 5 may be jointed from two leaves 61 inches × 8 inches (1549 × 203mm). This joint would have to be *tapeless*, or made with perforated tape (see (a) below). Veneers 4 and 6 may be prepared from veneers 16 inches (406mm) long by five leaves each 12¼ inches (311mm) wide, requiring four joints in each layer.

After bonding these three layers in the press, the 3-ply would have to be removed from the press and the tapes removed.

Layers 3 and 7 would then be bonded and removed from the press for their tapes to be removed; similarly layers 2 and 8 would have to be pressed and removed for tape clean off before the decorative veneering phase (layers 1 and 9).

All very time consuming and unnecessary. For corestock purposes we have to dispense with veneering tapes. There are three ways:

(a)   Perforated veneer tape, used in 4 inch (100mm) straps is left inside the glueline in layers 4, 5 and 6. Stagger the location of the tapes in each layer to avoid them telegraphing to the surface.

(b)   Corestock veneers are compressed between battens in a clamp, and the edges shot with a finely set plane, coated with a contact adhesive, and allowed to dry. The veneers are then butt jointed together without tapes.

(c)   Joint the veneers together by stapling the ends of the oversize leaves, to be trimmed off later. One staple in the centre of the leaf, tapped flat with a mallet, will not telegraph through to the surface.

Hollow frame core construction

Curved doors can easily be made with a frame core of hollow construction, similar to that previously described for flat construction.

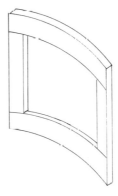

Fig. 114 Hollow frame with curved members

The top and bottom door members are bandsawn to shape, and the frame put together with mortise and tenon joints, or tongued and grooved, or dowelled, etc. It is usual to cover the hollow framework with hardboard or thin plywood, rather than with constructional veneer crossbandings. The gentle curve of the door is therefore veneered on plywood or hardboard in any of the methods previously described by hammer, cauls or tambours.

CAULS AND TAMBOURS

There are various ways of making wooden cauls for shaped work. The simplest is to cut the crossbearers to the required contours, and use

Fig. 115 Press ready to receive crossbanding veneers

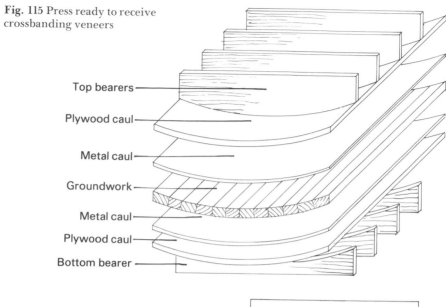

Top bearers

Plywood caul

Metal caul

Groundwork

Metal caul

Plywood caul

Bottom bearer

Fig. 116 Contoured crossbearers with thin plywood cauls

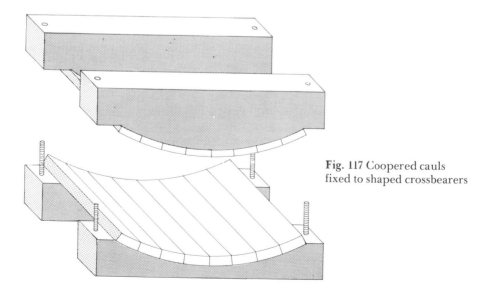

Fig. 117 Coopered cauls fixed to shaped crossbearers

thin plywood sheets as cauls. The panels should have a pressure blanket, such as a rubber sheet to take up any unevenness. Heated metal cauls of ⅛ inch (3mm) thick zinc are used for hot pressing, or low voltage heating elements (see Chapter 19).

The crossbearers should be fitted with handscrews or clamps and tightened in sequence uniformly.

Another method, when coopered strips have been made for the groundwork in saddles, clamped together with pivoting jaws, is to use the same rig-up to clamp more strips to form the cauls. The lower caul is allowed to rest on 2 inch × 2 inch (50mm × 50mm) crossbearers fitted with long bolts at each end; the upper caul is drilled to accommodate the bolts.

In either case, the crossbearers are cut from 2 inch (50mm) stuff, after carefully outlining the required contours on drawing paper. The contour has to allow for the thickness of the cauls used, including the ⅛ inch (3mm) thick zinc heated cauls if used; the thickness of the groundwork, say ¾ inch (19mm), the thickness of the decorative veneers and also the thickness of the pressure blanket used to equalise the pressure and distribute the load. This should permit sufficient room for laminating the corestock in one operation without the decorative veneers, and for laying the decorative veneers according to their required sequence in a second operation. Packing is used in the press to make up the thickness of the face and backing veneers in the first operation.

Bandsaw sufficient crossbearers to space them about 9 inches (228mm) apart and about 4 inches (101mm) longer than the panel length to be pressed. Drill and bolt the crossbearers together with tie rods, using four rods per bearer, and ensure that you have at least two inches (50mm) of timber below the lowest point of the curve to take the pressure.

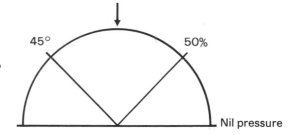

Fig. 118 Never veneer more than a quadrant of a circle: the loss is 50% of the top pressure at 45°; this reduces to virtually no pressure at the base line

45°   50%

Nil pressure

Quadrant curves

Never attempt to press corestock of a radius up to or exceeding a quadrant of a circle. The pressure at 45 degrees is reduced to 50 per cent of the pressure exerted on flat panels, and at 90 degrees, the quadrant angle, the pressure is non existent.

Adapt the design of the project to a multiple of the overall shape, or change the shape to an ellipse. One carefully designed caul, used four times can make an oval or elliptical shape.

If this is impossible and you *do* require a quadrant or greater radius shape, the female former has to be abandoned and other forms of pressure employed, such as hydraulic, pneumatic or vacuum.

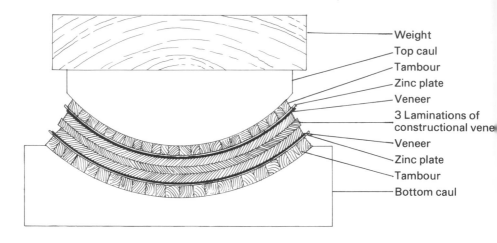

Fig. 119 A tambour press for shaped veneering

Tambours

Tambours work in the same way as cauls, but are multi-purpose and form to any shape; they are only suitable for pressing fairly thin panels.

The required contour of the crossbearers is again drawn on paper, with the required top and bottom radius, this time allowing for ½ inch (12mm) square sticks or tambours, (instead of caul strips, which are usually about 1 inch (25mm) thick).

Bandsaw the upper and lower cradles, this time from 1 inch (25mm) stuff, and space them 9 inches (228mm) apart as before, dowelled together to form a set about 4 inches (101mm) longer than the panel to be pressed. The cradles should be cut from 2 inches (50mm) stuff; ensure that 2 inches (50mm) of material is below the lowest part of the curvature to take the pressure.

The tambour sticks are cut in the same way as corestrips, by alternating them for reasons of strength. Draw one pencil line on one side of the board and two on the other before cutting the tambour strips, to enable you to assemble them correctly without turning a stick over on its side accidentally. This is especially important if the sticks are not perfectly square. Drill holes in three or four places in the length of the tambour sticks and thread a nylon cord through and tighten securely, or glue the tambour sticks to canvass, and they can be rolled up and used again on a future project.

Whether using tambours or the heavier cauls, place a 2 inch (50mm) pressure plank on top and begin tightening with handscrews or clamps in the middle of the panel, to start the outflow of air and glue, and then tighten down at the edges in sequence.

The zinc or aluminium sheet, in addition to supplying heat to speed the pressing time, also protects the surface of the veneers during bending.

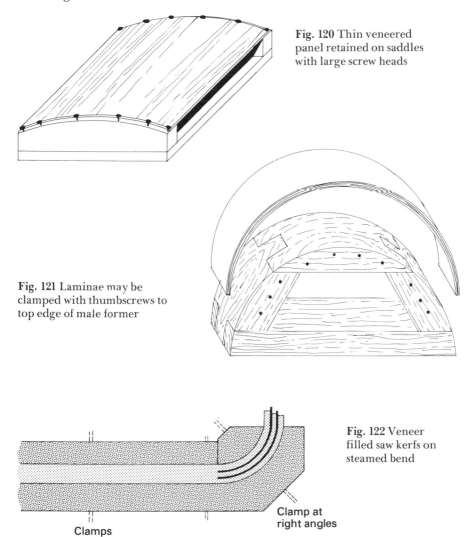

Fig. 120 Thin veneered panel retained on saddles with large screw heads

Fig. 121 Laminae may be clamped with thumbscrews to top edge of male former

Fig. 122 Veneer filled saw kerfs on steamed bend

Clamp at right angles

Clamps

Formers or jigs

Most curves that do not require making up cauls or tambours can be made over a former or jig of the male shape. The laminae are bent around and clamped to the former.

Another type of former for narrow edge veneers, has holes drilled below the top edge of the former, to allow thumbscrews to be fitted, which are tightened from the centre outwards to force out the air and glue.

If you have a plinth or frieze which is straight but with curved ends, make sawcuts in the ends through the width, and steam bend the ends. After clamping, fill the saw kerfs with veneer, re-heat and re-clamp after gluing, and the shape will be retained when the glue cures.

Problems to avoid

(a)   *Thickness:* More pressure is required to bond a curved panel than a flat panel of the same thickness and number of laminations. The press expends part of its energy in overcoming the compression and tension stress factors in addition to the pressure required for adhesion.

A curved panel will be fractionally thicker than a flat panel with all other factors being equal. When both flat and curved panels are required for use in the same project this could lead to a problem.

To overcome this, use thinner crossbandings when laminating curved panels. The larger the number of gluelines and the thicker the panel, the more important this factor becomes. This is another reason why the decorative veneer phase is always carried out as a separate operation, to enable you to rectify any discrepancy before it is too late.

(b)   *Inherent Movement:* There is a natural tendency for laminae to return to their original shape, particularly at the ends of a bend. Overcome this by increasing the number of laminations and thinner veneers. This means more gluelines, so check the final thickness of the groundwork before laying the decorative veneers.

(c)   *Shrinkage:* Moisture content can cause problems, especially if laminae are of higher moisture content than the working humidity. Overcome this by leaving the veneers in the workroom environment to acclimatize before use.

(d)   *Adhesive Mix and Spread:* If the adhesive mix is wrong and too much water is introduced into the gluelines, it will penetrate into the wood fibres and will not dry out until after the groundwork has been released from pressure. This will cause distortion. Check the mix and the adhesive spread.

(e)   *Distortion:* A differential in shrinkage between laminations leading to distortion can result from a variation in grain direction and veneer thickness. Ideally, the best laminations are all of the same thickness (apart from the centre core veneer) and of the same species, and from the same log.

Alternating the grain at right angles in adjacent layers is not the problem. But when odd waste veneers, from different stocks which might be nominally of the same thickness, but possess slight variations, have been butt jointed together to make up corestock laminae, these variations can cause distortion of the bonded panel.

This is overcome by being very selective in your choice of corestock veneers; check thickness and grain direction when jointing and wherever possible use 'pairs' of the same thickness on either side of the core, of the same species, from the same flitch or log.

Preparation of groundwork

When the groundwork panel has been allowed a period of curing time for stabilisation, it is ready to be cleaned up and trued ready for surface veneering.

Work over the surface with a panel plane, to ensure that it is true in length and width, and from diagonal corner to the opposite corner. Place two planed strips of wood across the panel and 'sight' under them against a good light to test for winding. Use the toothing plane diagonally across the panel in each direction. This will remove the panel plane marks and prepare the surface to receive the decorative veneers. It will also reveal any hollows or depressions, and remove any high spots. Where parts are free from toothing marks, the surrounding area needs further work to reduce it. Care should be taken near the edges not to dub them over, and it is good practice to leave corestock panels a fraction oversize to avoid edges being slightly damaged during this keying process.

11

Adhesives

ADHESION is caused in one of two ways:

    (a)   Specific adhesion

    (b)   Mechanical adhesion

Specific Adhesion

This is caused by the natural attraction of similar molecules held in close contact, depending upon their compatability, making it difficult to separate them.

For example, two sheets of polished optical glass or plastic will cling tightly together and cannot be pulled apart—they would have to be slid apart. But if their surfaces were exposed to the air for a period of time to allow foreign bodies of dust or grease to settle on the surface, the molecular attraction would become impaired and the bond would fail—the two sheets would pull apart easily.

Wood has a rough, uneven porous surface when viewed under a microscope, and when brought together, the surfaces only touch at random places and can easily be pulled apart. Therefore, for an effective bond by specific adhesion, an extremely close contact of very smooth similar surfaces is vital, and both surfaces must be clean, free from dust, grease, chalk marks etc.

The action of an adhesive is two-fold. Firstly, it has to wet both surfaces; secondly, it has to solidify in order to hold them together. For example, if both wooden surfaces were wet with water, they would pull apart, but if immediately frozen, the water would have become ice and an adhesive as it completed the second requirement.

Mechanical Adhesion

A physical or mechanical 'lock' is caused, when the adhesive is forced under pressure into the pores of the wood. When magnified, the glueline would appear as thousands of vertical prongs in both directions penetrating into the wood structure.

The purpose of 'keying' a surface with the toothing plane is widely misunderstood. It is not to provide for mechanical adhesion. It serves a useful purpose by increasing the surface *area*, and helps remove grit and grease etc., by cleaning the surface, thereby preventing interfacial failure. It should be borne in mind that coarse sanding can create dust and loose fibres and can actually encourage bond failure if not brushed away.

Bond failure

The test of a strong adhesive bond is *how* it breaks up when forced apart. If the glueline fractures it is an indication that the wrong adhesive was used; the remedy is to change the adhesive. If the break is at the surface it is caused by one of the following: inadequate coating of the two surfaces; incorrect timing; temperature or pressure; stress; or incompatability of the adhesive with the surface. If the work surface itself fractures it proves that the adhesive bond is actually stronger than the wood, and is the ideal strived for.

From the above it is obvious that the surface fracture is the most difficult to cure and requires special study. If the surfaces flex in service; shrink or swell due to humidity changes, or suffer bond creep under sustained loading, it is important to use a thermo*plastic* adhesive, which will yield to any changes.

Fig. 123 Adhesives

Thermo*setting* adhesives will crack, craze or become brittle if subjected to stresses and loadings they are not designed to cope with.

The Glueline

As a generalisation, remember that the thinner the glueline the stronger the bond. Pressure from press or clamps greatly assists in achieving a thin glueline, but the number of gluelines being pressed simultaneously will increase their thickness and cause problems. Therefore, for thin, close contact gluelines a perfectly flat, smooth surface is essential; but for multi-gluelines on porous, pervious surfaces, a gap-filling adhesive should be used. Gap-filling adhesives do not shrink when setting due to the addition of chemical additives in the mix.

A close contact glueline, when set, does not exceed 0.13mm; whereas a gap-filling glueline can be successful up to a maximum of 1.3mm.

The Time Factor

Some bonds are designed to be as permanent as possible; others are required to be temporary, and to permit immediate further work on the surface such as re-heating and re-laying.

The time cycle of the adhesive operation has challenged industrial chemists to develop a wide range of adhesives to suit every type of requirement.

Shelf life

Some adhesives deteriorate in storage. Others are stable indefinitely —until their container is opened, and then rapid oxidisation takes place giving a limited shelf life. Careful storage in dry conditions is very important.

Pot life

Once mixed, an adhesive has a limited 'pot life' until it begins to coagulate and set; when the end of the life has been reached it has to be discarded. When used in glue mixing machines and glue spreaders, this can be a major problem.

Assembly time

This depends on the type of solvent and workroom temperature. Adhesives with a very fast setting time due to the rapid evaporation of volatile solvents will only provide a few minutes assembly time for the groundwork and veneer to be loaded into the press.

It is therefore important for the veneer craftsman to choose an adhesive which will provide him with sufficient time to mix and apply the adhesive to groundwork and/or veneers, and to carefully load the press and put it under uniform pressure within the assembly time.

Setting time

Certain types of adhesive achieve very fast setting times, and if applied without the correct equipment would actually set faster than the adhesive could be spread by hand methods and the work assembled and loaded into the press. For hand spreading, a slow setting adhesive is required.

Pressure time

There are various phases of 'tack'; some adhesives do not have a period before they tack, while others require that a period of time elapses for the solvent to evaporate from the adhesive to tack before pressure is applied.

For example in multi-daylight platen presses, one of the press cycle timing problems is that the adhesive may begin to cure before all the platens are loaded. The gluelines may then have to remain under accurately controlled pressure for a period of time until the second phase of setting is completed before the panel is removed from the press.

Curing time

A further period of time must be allowed for the glueline to cure and harden; for the panel to dry out and stabilise before being ready for further work or use.

Therefore, working with adhesives is a question of being time conscious, and acquiring a working knowledge of the various timescales to suit your own equipment, project and working environment.

Temperature

Unless you have press facilities in which the operational temperature can be controlled, always select an adhesive which will cure at a room temperature of about 70 degrees Fahrenheit (21 degrees Centigrade).

Pressure

Similarly, your choice of adhesive will depend on the pressing equipment available. If you have to rely on screw press or clamp pressure, select an adhesive which will cure under low pressure over a longer timescale — in hours rather than minutes.

Strength

The adhesive must be strong enough for the project. Not only to resist the pulling power of the veneers, but also to hold resinous, oily or gummy veneers without the risk of delamination.

Discolouration

Many adhesives leave a dark or coloured glueline. This does not matter if an edge lipping is to be applied to conceal it, but could spoil the appearance of the project if exposed in a conspicuous area. This is even more serious if glue penetration occurs through the veneer pores to the surface and spoils the delicate face veneers.

Another problem is caused by the 'squeeze-out' at the edges during the pressing cycle and you should determine whether or not the adhesive can be cleaned off without disturbing the press-load before possible discolouration ruins the edges.

Viscosity

Most resin adhesives contain additives or extenders made from cereals, aimed at preventing adhesive penetration; if used in close contact adhesives rather than in gap filling types, the additives can weaken the strength of the bond.

Thermoplastic adhesives, can be re-heated after bonding for further work, and can then be submitted to further pressure for a repeat bond.

Thermosetting adhesives, set very hard and become impervious to boiling water, cold water, steam or dry heat, micro-organic attack or fungal attack and are used extensively for Weather and Boil Proof (WPB) bonds and for all exterior grade and marine plywood manufacture.

TYPES OF ADHESIVE

Animal Glue This is the oldest type of glue known to man and was used by the Egyptians 5,000 years ago. It is collagen based, or protein extracted from animal bones, tissues or hides of animals. The resulting bond can be stronger than the wood. Commonly known as 'scotch glue' it is available in cakes, granules, jelly or powder. It is soaked in water, heated to 140 degrees Fahrenheit (60 degrees Centigrade). When correctly mixed the glue should run freely off the brush without forming into drops. Only sufficient for the job in hand should be prepared as re-heating causes rapid deterioration. It is neither heat nor water proof but possesses many advantages for the veneering of panels for interior furniture use. Any defects in the laying operation can easily be rectified. The thermoplastic bond allows the glueline to breathe and flex with changes of humidity. It is used for 'hammer veneering' techniques, where leaves of veneer are re-heated, peeled off and re-layed. It also permits repairs and restorations to be made.

The glue is applied hot, and time allowed for it to tack for the evaporation of the water solvent. As the water diffuses into the wood the full strength of the glue develops. The bond is resistant to organic solvents but is not moisture resistant and is also subject to bacterial or fungal decay in humid conditions unless treated with chemical additives.

Scotch glue must not be used where the joint will be subjected to heat at a later stage of production. For example, if scotch glue was used to laminate corestock and crossbandings the face veneer would have to be bonded in a cold press, or the groundwork might delaminate.

Fish glue

This has most of the properties of scotch glue except that it is sold in liquid or gel form for use direct from the tin in cold condition. It must be used in a cold press and remain under pressure until set, up to 24 hours, with a further period for curing. It has unlimited shelf life, long pot life, and extended assembly time. Re-heating for further work deteriorates the bond.

The addition of flake white powder to both fish glue or scotch glue will whiten the glue and prevent surface discolouration due to penetration.

Casein glue

This is made from the curds of skimmed sour milk, after the removal of acids, and with alkaline chemical additives. It is strongly alkaline in nature and possesses a one year shelf life, and, when mixed with water, a pot life of only a few hours. It is mixed with hydrated lime and caustic soda, which increases the properties of water resistance, and shortens the pot life. The water diffuses into the wood as chemical reaction takes place and the bond will set at room temperature in a few hours. Heat introduced to the press will shorten the press time.

Gluelines can be from 0.13mm up to 0.75mm thick. The strongly alkaline nature of the adhesive reacts with those veneers possessing a high acid content, such as oak, mahogany, obeche and afrormosia causing dark staining and discolouration.

Casein glue is available in premixed dehydrated form and the mix will vary depending on the application required. For instance, with a higher proportion of lime its water resistance can be increased, or with a higher proportion of caustic soda, the opposite effect is achieved, less water resistance but extended pot life.

It is used in the cold press and the resulting bond is permanent and cannot be re-heated or further worked. Assembly time is about twenty minutes, allowing for the surfaces to tack; the pressure required is about 100 to 150 lbs psi (292 to 439kg/cm^2) and the press time from four to twelve hours depending on workshop temperature, and curing time outside press a further three to four days.

Staining can be removed by brushing with a solution of one part oxalic acid to nine parts water, then neutralised with borax, but it is best to avoid these problems of staining whenever possible.

Vegetable protein glue

Made from ground nuts and soya beans, with chemical additives it produces an adhesive with a high degree of water resistance and can be used to bond veneers with a high moisture content. However, they possess an even greater risk of veneer staining and discolouration.

Vegetable starch glue

This is made from extracts of the cassava root, and the glue is water soluble. It has little resistance to mould or fungal attack and has been superceded by synthetic resin adhesives.

SYNTHETIC RESIN ADHESIVES

These are the most widely used of all veneering adhesives for the lamination of corestock, crossbandings and decorative veneering. However, the moisture content of the materials, correct mixing of the adhesive, the thickness and timing of the spread, assembly times, temperature and pressure timing for setting, are all critical for success. More than 80 per cent of all cabinet and furniture trade adhesives are from the Urea Formaldehyde (UF) type.

Urea Formaldehyde

UF comes in the form of a syrup and is relatively inert with a long shelf life. It is activated by the addition of a hardener or catalyst; an alternative form is a premixed powder of resin and catalyst, which is activated by the addition of water.

The resin is prepared by heating the urea and formaldehyde under weak acid conditions, but halting this reaction at an intermediate stage before complete polymerisation has occurred. By subsequently adding a weak acid (or acid producing salt) catalyst, the partial polymerisation can be re-started.

By the addition of other chemicals, the rate of this further reaction can be slowed to increase the pot life of the adhesive, with a corresponding increase in both the assembly time and setting time. But by applying heat in the press, the rate of polymerisation increases to shorten the setting time.

In all cases, the manufacturers mixing ratios must be strictly followed, but extension of pot life, or more rapid setting times are adjusted by using different grade catalysts.

Extenders

Most synthetic resins claim to possess 'gap-filling' properties as they contain additives. This does not mean that poorly made joints or bonds in the laminations will be taken up by the thickness of the glueline, but minute differences in the gauge of veneers, when laid in a perfectly flat caul will not cause a weakened bond, as the resin will flow and take up minor undulations up to about 0.75mm.

The high cost of resins can be reduced by the addition of cereals in the form of rye, tapioca, or wheat flour, by from ten to twenty per cent of the dry weight of the resin. This greatly improves the viscosity and should eliminate any tendency for the adhesive to penetrate through to the veneer surface. However, the reverse effect is possible, as a fully extended glue can only be spread as a thick film due to its higher viscosity, and this can result in higher penetration as the glueline is thicker; whereas the thinner original resin mix, unextended with additives, will spread more easily, thinly, and therefore be less likely to bleed through.

The spreading life of the adhesive or assembly time, is from half down to one third of the pot life. Therefore the ideal is to extend the pot and assembly time and reduce the setting press time. It is striking the right balance between these variables that presents the veneer craftsman with his most critical task. In practice he aims for an acceptable pot life, and shortens the press time cycle by adjusting the press temperature. Since the most vital moment in the whole sequence is when resin and catalyst are mixed together, by delaying that moment it is possible to control the pot life and assembly time by avoiding the single operation sequence of mixing the resin and catalyst together, as one mixture, and applying as an ordinary adhesive to both surfaces. (Only sufficient adhesive would be mixed for the work in hand and the residue discarded).

Alternatively, you could use a double application method by coating one surface with the resin and the other surface with the catalyst; the pot life is greatly prolonged, since chemical reaction cannot take place until both surfaces are joined. Also, a faster acting catalyst can be used for rapid setting made even faster by higher press temperatures.

Cold pressing types

The small veneer workshop, without veneer presses equipped with high temperature and pressure controls, has to rely on cold pressing with a screw press, and on adhesives which may be used without heating.

UF adhesives are specially formulated to cure at, or slightly above, normal room temperature. The resulting bond is suitable for all types of furniture and wall panelling but not for interior high-hazard locations or exterior panels. They are usually supplied with the resin and catalyst pre-mixed in powder form, requiring only the addition of water. There are of course other variations available such as resin in syrup form and catalyst in liquid form etc.

Workshop temperature should be at about 70 degrees Fahrenheit (21 degrees Centigrade) which will give a pot life of up to four hours and an assembly time of up to half an hour. This assembly time will shorten as the workshop temperature increases.

At 90 degrees Fahrenheit (32 degrees Centigrade) the pot life comes down to an hour, assembly time down to ten minutes, and the pressing time of twelve hours can be reduced to five hours.

Cold pressing UF is not intended for a hot press. The heat provided by heated metal cauls cannot be compared with a hot press and serves only to shorten the press time slightly.

Once bonded, the panel cannot be re-heated. It has to be right first time.

Although the panel may be worked on to remove glue squeeze-out and be superficially cleaned up when removed from the press, the curing time takes several days. Panels should be stored on their end, with a free circulation of warm dry air around them to allow their moisture content to equalise with the environment.

When weighing UF powder on scales, remember to adjust the tare screw to zero. First check the weight of the powder and then add water in proportion. Only add sufficient water to stir into a thick creamy paste before adding the rest of the water. Leave it to stand for a few minutes and then give it a thorough stirring to remove all lumps; it must be smooth and creamy in consistency.

Polyvinyl acetate (PVA)

The adhesive is an emulsion of particles of polymerised vinyl acetate in water, with the addition of plasticisers and other chemicals.

The water disperses into the wood leaving the PVA adhesive bond. This is a thermoplastic adhesive and the joint must be allowed to remain under pressure until set. Extenders are added to the mix increasing viscosity, thus preventing penetration; at the same time the spreading ability is increased.

PVA adhesives can form a bond at room temperature without the use of a catalyst, and the pot life is counted in days. It should not be used where the bond is to be subjected to high temperatures, or where the bond may have to be re-heated. For example, if used for corestock purposes, the face veneering must also be cold pressed. Care must be taken to ensure that finishing materials do not contain solvents which will affect the PVA glueline.

PVA Catalysed adhesives

Special formulations of PVA are also obtainable which employ a catalyst hardener to achieve 'cross-linking', to enable their setting time to be greatly increased with heat. This is to combine the advantage of several days pot life, and long assembly times, to rapid pressing cycles.

Generally, PVA adhesives are not suitable for conditions of high temperature or moisture hazards, or where the bond may be subject to stress loadings. There is no visible glueline and the adhesive will not stain delicate veneers. Brushes and equipment may be cleaned with warm water.

Aliphatic emulsion

This adhesive is popularly known as 'yellow' glue to differentiate from PVA which is commonly known as 'white glue'.

Aliphatic emulsion is sold ready-mixed in cans, and has a fast tack—hence a short assembly time. It has a higher solid content than PVA and is more difficult to spread, giving less time for assembly. The room temperature required is between 70 and 80 degrees Fahrenheit (21 and 26 degrees Centigrade) and uniform pressure is required for about two hours, after which the panel should be cleaned up and the squeeze-out wiped off because of the tendency to stain white veneers; the panel is then returned to the press for twelve hours or overnight.

For bonding non-porous, dense woods, or hardboard, it is superior to PVA and is also ideal for corestock purposes. It is also a thermoplastic adhesive and may be subject to bond creepage in extreme changes of humidity or sustained loading. Brushes may be cleaned in warm water.

Contact adhesives

These are based on synthetic or natural rubber formulations in a volatile solvent and have a long shelf life if undisturbed.

The solvent evaporates into the atmosphere, giving off a heavy inflammable vapour and must never be used near a naked flame, radiant fire, spark or pilot light. Good ventilation in the workroom is essential with temperatures between 70 and 90 degrees Fahrenheit (21 and 32 degrees Centigrade).

Some types include fillers or additives, others in the form of a gel, or thixotropic to enable the adhesive to spread easily. It is usually applied with a comb, brush or spray, and both surfaces have to be allowed to become touch dry. The surfaces should be covered to prevent dust settling, and, after an hour, a second coat should be applied to both surfaces. After about half an hour both surfaces are brought together with a 'slip-sheet' separator between, which is gradually withdrawn and the two surfaces bonded together evenly.

In factories, the two treated surfaces are fed through a 'Nip' roller press, where two rollers, set one above the other, bring the required pressure to ensure an even but firm pressure. An exceptionally strong bond results.

Clamping is unnecessary, but it does help if weights or clamps are used since the bond rapidly increases in strength for up to three hours and the resulting glueline is invisible. Blisters can be cured by re-applying adhesive to both surfaces.

Contact adhesives are ideal for veneering shaped, curved or compound work; veneering around corners or small radii etc. They are universally used for the application of edge veneers and for bonding panels without presses, clamps or weights, and on panel sizes too large for existing equipment.

Some finishing materials have solvents which penetrate through the veneer and will adversely affect contact adhesives. It is therefore necessary to test the finishing material on a scrap piece of veneer bonded with your chosen adhesive.

Brushes have to be cleaned in lacquer thinners.

Balsa cement

Synthetic adhesives sold as 'Balsa Cement' or 'Marquetry Cement' in small tubes, are extremely fast setting. They have a restricted use for butt jointing small veneer components for motifs, or for mixing veneer dust to form a wood stopping for filling open joints.

Epoxy resins

These very expensive resins are not normally associated with veneering because of cost, but they are excellent adhesives which, when mixed with the appropriate catalyst set without the evaporation of the solvent, and entirely by chemical reaction. For this reason they are ideal for bonding non-porous materials.

They can be supplied with gap-filling extenders. The pot life is very short—perhaps half an hour. The assembly time can be regulated from a few minutes to a few hours depending on the formulation, but both are reduced by increasing the temperature. There is little if any tack, and joints must be kept under pressure until set.

Epoxy resins will produce panels up to BS1455 WBP specification.

Hot pressing types

These synthetic resins are also supplied with various resin and catalyst combinations, either in syrup, powder, or pre-mixed forms. The pot life will vary from twelve to twenty-four hours or more. The single application process is adopted, and the spread of the resin is about 2.5 to 4lbs per 100 sq. ft. (0.12 to 0.19kg/m²). Temperatures of 194 up to 230 degrees Fahrenheit (90 to 110 degrees Centigrade) are common, with pressures from 150 to 300 lbs psi (439 to 878kg/cm²).

Most hot pressing types are in the phenolic resin group.

The Phenol resins are in three forms: (a) liquid, (b) powder, and (c) film.

Phenolic film is absorbant tissue paper impregnated with resin at a ratio of 2 resin to 1 of tissue paper. Under heat and pressure the resin hardens into a permanent bond. The two surfaces must be perfectly flat and true as for specific adhesion as the film has no gap-filling qualities at all. The heated press must compress the laminae by up to ten per cent of their thickness. To do this with hardwoods such as oak, beech and ash would require pressures of up to 300 lbs psi (878kg/cm²) and on low density woods such as obeche or horse chestnut the pressure would be 150 lbs psi (439kg/cm²). With pneumatic pressure, about 100 lbs psi (292kg/cm²) is sufficient. Temperatures vary according to the time cycle of the press from 280 degrees Fahrenheit (138 degrees Centigrade) to 310 degrees Fahrenheit (154 degrees Centigrade).

A problem with hot pressing is the moisture content of the veneers which must be down to between 7 per cent and 10 per cent as a higher moisture content would result in blistering.

The range of phenolic resins is being widened to include low temperature phenolic resins which will bond at 212 degrees Fahrenheit (100 degrees Centigrade). Powders are available which may be mixed with water, alcohol, or acetone, to make a liquid resin.

The recommended spread is 2.5 lbs to 3.5 lbs per 100 sq. ft. (0.12 to 0.17kg/m²) with half of this quantity applied to each surface of bonding area. Extenders of walnut flour are used to avoid penetration, and dried blood to speed curing times.

PF/RF resins are used to produce panels to BS1455 which are WPB Standard, (weather and boil proof), which, by systematic tests and their record in service have been proved to make joints which are highly resistant to weather, micro-organisms, cold and boiling water, steam and dry heat. They are bonded at temperatures from 239 to 293 degrees Fahrenheit (115 to 145 degrees Centigrade).

These panels also pass the BS1203 tensile test on the glueline, in addition to the BS1455 knife test. Samples tested along the grain of the face veneer *with* the weathered face in tension, gave a bending strength of 15 per cent lower than similar material tested with the weathered face in compression. Samples tested *across* the face grain, with the weathered face in tension, showed a bending strength 5 per cent lower than with the weathered face in compression.

In addition to the phenol resins, the familiar urea formaldehyde types, fortified with other chemicals, are used to form powerful bonds. These combinations are known by their initials:

UF	Urea formaldehyde
UF/MF	Urea formaldehyde fortified with melamine
UF/PF	Urea formaldehyde reinforced with phenol
PF	Phenol-formaldehyde
PF/MF	Phenol formaldehyde reinforced with melamine
PF/RF	Phenol formaldehyde reinforced with resorcinol
R/F	Resorcinol formaldehyde (resorcinol is red in colour and could stain delicate veneers)
M/F	Melamine formaldehyde

Special pore fillers must be used in the finishing process or the resins may be incompatible with the finish.
UF/MF will produce a moisture resistant bond.
UF/PF will produce a boil resistant bond.
PF/RF will produce exterior bonds and marine application bonds.

Hot melt adhesives

These are mixtures of synthetic polymers with added resins and waxes to control their viscosity and adhesion. They are solid at normal workshop temperature and at high temperature they become liquid. The hot melt is applied to the groundwork and the veneer is applied and immediately put under pressure only until the joint cools.

Unlike other adhesives which rely on solvent evaporation or chemical reaction, hot melts rely on cooling only. They begin to soften at around 212 to 248 degrees Fahrenheit (100 to 120 degrees Centigrade), but because of the heat loss in assembly time it is more usual to apply the hot melts at 374 to 410 degrees Fahrenheit (190 to 210 degrees Centigrade)—but not above this temperature as they have limited thermal stability.

Hot melts will re-heat and should never be used where the bond will be exposed to re-heating above 140 degrees Fahrenheit (60 degrees Centigrade).

Hot melt film

This is specially formulated hot melt thermoplastic adhesive film, supplied with a siliconized paper backing for protection. The film is supplied in 100 yard rolls, 3 feet wide (83m²), and is simply cut to the required size with scissors. There is an indefinite shelf life; the film is five thousandths of an inch thick, water and heat resistant, transparent in the glueline, non staining, and gap filling.

The film melts at 86 degrees Fahrenheit (30 degrees Centigrade) but after curing will withstand temperatures up to 212 degrees Fahrenheit (100 degrees Centigrade). It has the advantage that it may be applied by hand veneering methods using an ordinary electric iron and it may also be used in a cold press, with heated metal cauls.

There is the further advantage that veneer matches may be laid directly to the groundwork, laying each part of the match separately. The film may be re-heated and re-laid in the event of blisters. It is clean and dry in use, there are no toxic vapours, and no cleaning solvents or special brush cleaners are necessary. In terms of edge veneering there is another advantage in that it enables the full range of natural veneers to be used as veneer edging instead of the few commercially available 'iron-on' edge veneers. Simply iron the film on to a leaf of veneer and lay aside until required. The coated veneer strip may be ironed to the panel's edge when required. If veneers are required for a porous edge, such as chipboard, first iron the film to the veneer, another film to the edge of the chipboard, then bring both surfaces together and re-iron.

Temperature and Curing

Most cold setting adhesives rely upon the diffusion of the water based solvent to effect the cure. A slight rise in temperature with a heated caul may assist in shortening the curing time but PVA softens when heated, and will have to remain under pressure until it cools, so there is really no advantage in heating PVA adhesives.

Those adhesives which cure by chemical reaction, can halve the curing time by every 50 degrees Fahrenheit (10 degrees Centigrade) increase in temperature. This is provided by heated metal platens, and one minute is added to the pressing time for every millimetre thickness between the heated platen and the glueline.

In many factories the platens (or metal strips used in edge veneer clamping) are heated by low voltage, high amperage current passed through a transformer. LV heating is widely used in the professional veneer shop.

Note: A very costly alternative is the use of radio-frequency electro-magnetic field (RF heating) supplied from an RF generator, which heats the glue precisely where required without losing heat through conduction in the wood.

In the case of hot melt adhesives, the coated surface must be kept hot and the adhesive fluid until the mating surface is brought under pressure and this is done by infra-red radiation or hot-air jets.

These high temperatures will seriously affect veneer matches, marquetry or parquetry assemblies causing open joints and most decorative veneering is therefore carried out in cold presses, with hot pressing chiefly used for laying veneers of one species, such as mahogany, teak, oak etc., or for plywood manufacture.

The pressure of the press must always be greater than that of the vapour pressure of the adhesive solvent at the operating temperature of the press. The temperature must never cause the adhesive to boil and create a foamed glueline as this is a certain cause of delamination.

In selecting the right adhesive for the project in hand, the veneer craftsman must consider these factors:

1.   Is the bond to be wood to wood, or wood to plastic or some other surface such as PVC foil?
2.   Will the surface be porous (wood) impervious (plastic) or one of each?
3.   Will the adhesive have to cope with oiliness, grease, gum, resin, or calcius surface; or one treated with carbon tetrachloride to remove natural greasiness?
4.   Will the required joint be a close contact or gap filling joint?
5.   Is the resulting bond to be flexible?
6.   Or subject to temporary or continuous loading, or stress or misuse?
7.   End-use? Will the panel be subject to high temperatures, drastic changes of humidity, dampness, strong direct sunlight, exposure, or marine use?
8.   What equipment have you available for glue mixing, and storage?
9.   Glue spreading, and pot life?
10.   Open assembly time and press loading time?
11.   What will the pressing or clamping time be? And how much time will be needed for the next sequence of operations?
12.   Can the glue line be heated to accelerate curing time?

12

Tapes & Taping

VENEER TAPES: There are a variety of extra thin, double gummed paper veneering tapes, which will not leave a staining residue after removal. Usual width about 1 inch (25mm).

In application, the tape is moistened for use and the paper will stretch and tack quickly. The tape is 'rubbed' on application and the heat generated by the friction of rubbing dries the tape, causing it to shrink and exert a pull on the joints.

Veneer tapes will be removed at a later stage after the veneers are laid, either by moistening and scraping, or papering, and it is also part of their manufature that after they have performed their intended main fuction, the tape will remove easily, without clogging sanding belts or pads.

Perforated veneer tape

This is used in corestock manufacture. The narrow tape is covered in perforations and is used for jointing corestock laminations. The tapes remain on the work and are bonded within the glueline. Perforated tape should never be used for decorative face veneering. Usual width ¾ inch to 1 inch (19-25mm).

Protective tapes

This is stronger paper tape, similar to parcel or packaging tapes. It is applied to the ends of veneer in storage to prevent splitting in handling. Once the veneer bundle has been trimmed ready for jointing, these tapes are discarded in favour of veneering tape. Usual width from 1 inch to 1½ inches (25-38mm).

Location tapes

These are also paper tapes, but applied for a different purpose. For example, if a large mahogany curl veneer is required for a door and also a drawer front from the same leaf, (or from any other matched jointed assembly) it is trade practice to affix a location tape across the assembly where the veneer will be cut across the grain, to ensure a clean cut without splintering. After the cutting operation, a half-width of tape remains on each part holding any tiny fragment or splintered part.

Edges, which may be subject to cutting operations after the veneer has been laid also have location tapes affixed.

Location tapes are usually wider than other forms of paper tape; usual width from 1½ inches to 2 inches (38-50mm).

Areas which will be bent over shaped cauls are also covered with a protective location tape to mark the spot and assist the bending operation.

Tapes are also applied to curl veneers on the weak side of the leaf where possible splits may occur in laying.

Straps

When two leaves of veneer are to be jointed together, veneer tapes are cut into about 4 inch (100mm) lengths and applied across the joint as 'straps'. One at each end of the leaf, and others at about 18 inch (457mm) intervals.

Large headed veneer pins are driven into the veneer leaf at each end and centre and tilted towards the joint. The veneer tape straps are applied and briskly rubbed until dry. The veneer pins are removed.

Hinge tapes

Having pulled the joint tightly together with straps, a long veneer tape is then applied along the complete length of the joint. When dry, the veneers may be folded back into 'pairs', using the tape as a hinge. This enables the pair of veneers to be cut at right angles across the grain.

Double taping

It is normal practice, when four piece matches or more complicated veneer matches are being taped together, for an already taped edge, to require taping with a second tape.

Obviously a build up of criss crossing tapes is to be avoided. When applying the long hinge tape along a length joint between two veneers, break off the tape at the intersection of the 4 inch (100mm) straps to avoid a double thickness.

When a veneer already has a protective tape on the edge, which now forms part of a joint to be taped, it can be ignored as a double thickness of veneering tape is permissible. Try to avoid a build up of more than two thicknesses. Where this is likely to occur, it is best to moisten and scrape off the existing tapes, and when the veneer edge is dry make the joint and apply a single new tape.

All taping must be on the face side and not the side to be glued, so that they can be removed after the veneer is laid.

Masking tape

This is available in various categories of adhesive strength and stretch. Only use the minimum stretch and strength types on veneers. It is chiefly used for temporarily anchoring joints before tape straps are applied. The masking tape is then peeled off and discarded. This is an alternative to using veneer pins to temporarily hold the joint.

Whenever masking tape is used it must be removed quickly. It cannot ever be sanded off as it tends to leave behind a residue, which will form into balls and tear into the grain if sanded.

Masking tape is also useful as a protective tape for applying across the ends of veneers to prevent splitting in handling, and it is best to cut off the veneer end complete with masking tape when trimming down to size. Usually applied in 1 inch to 2 inch (25-50mm) widths.

Pressure sensitive tape ('Sellotape' type)

This is available in the familiar transparent form in ½ inch (12mm) width up to ⅞ inch (22mm) wide, and also in various coloured forms. However, beware, as this tape adheres too well and should never be used on veneers. It has a variety of uses in the design stage, for fastening tracing paper or printed designs to leaves of waste veneer for example.

It is also used when cut into very small pieces about ½ inch (12mm) square to temporarily hold tiny inlay components in marquetry and parquetry work. But once the piece has been located into the main assembly, the adhesive tape is scraped off and replaced with veneer tape.

If allowed to remain on veneers, it tends to tear out the grain or to darken and discolour light toned species, or leave a staining residue on the veneer. When sanding off, any such residue forms into hard balls and tears into the grain. All traces of the tape must be removed, with a touch of lacquer solvent, before laying.

Double sided self-adhesive tape

This also has a limited use in veneering. When intricate jig cutting is taking place, such as parquetry diamonds, it is useful for temporarily anchoring already cut-out sections, which require further cutting.

The tape prevents fragments breaking off or splintering, and these pieces remain in situ, and can be rescued.

This tape must be scraped off and discarded before laying.

TAPING

Trimming

A trimming cut through veneers is usually made by a hand or power guillotine, or clipper, to reduce a bundle of veneer to an approximate length or width. But that type of dimensional cut is not good enough for veneer jointing suitable for matching. Regard trim cuts as being fractionally oversize to produce nominal widths and lengths.

Jointing

A jointing edge must be perfectly straight and true. In a factory, complete bundles are prepared with jointing edges in one of three ways: jointing guillotine; beam saw; or, beam spindle. In each case, the veneer is clamped under pressure. The guillotine operates in a downward and sideways shearing, scything action and cuts a complete bundle in one operation. A beam saw travels along a guideway beam the length of the bundle, and fine-saws the edge; the beam spindle planes the edge.

For the smaller craftsman without access to jointing equipment the bundle, cut to length, is compressed between battens, with a fraction of an inch protruding. The edge is then fine planed until the batten is 'kissed' by the plane for a perfect edge. While still under compression, the edges may be coated with a contact adhesive and allowed to dry. When brought together carefully, matching joints may be made without tapes.

More usually, leaves are matched in pairs. Two leaves of veneer are placed on the cutting board, and their pattern made to coincide exactly. Pin both leaves with veneer pins to ensure they do not move while a straightedge is positioned leaving about ⅛ inch (3mm) of the veneers protruding. Cramp the straightedge at each end and remove the veneer pins.

Use a veneer saw, or very sharp 'slashing' knife. With a bold stroke, cut through both veneers simultaneously. Keep one hand holding the straightedge in front of the knife to avoid any accidents should you slip.

If the veneers are brittle or the grain is very strong, there may be a tendency for the knife to wander in the grain despite the straightedge. In this case fasten a length of gummed veneering tape along the edge to be jointed and re-cramp. Cut through the veneer tape which will provide a clean cut and hold any tiny splinters which might otherwise be lost. Veneers which have been flatted, seldom give any trouble in jointing.

Examine the two jointing edges, by holding them against the light. If you are not satisfied with the joint because you can see points where daylight shows through, cramp the joint between battens, and shoot the edges with a plane with the iron set very finely.

Open the two leaves in book fashion and bring the edges together to form an exactly matched pattern. Fasten some 4 inch (100mm) lengths of gummed veneer tape straps across the joint at each end and at about 18 inch (457mm) intervals along the joint. Then fasten a length of veneer tape the length of the joint. Rub the veneer tape briskly with the rounded end of the knife handle. The friction evaporates the moisture from the tape, and as it contracts it will pull the joint tightly together.

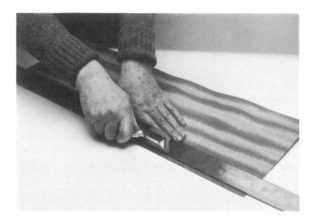

Fig. 124 Two leaves of sapele jointed with veneer saw and straightedge

Fig. 125 The leaves are taped together with short "straps" across the joint and long tapes down the joint

If you have used the contact adhesive method of gluing the edges while under compression, it will not be possible to fold the match, which will have to be stored in a flat condition until ready for laying.

The advantage of the taped joint, is that the tape is used as a hinge, and the pair of leaves may now be folded back, and cut across at right angles; or stored in less space. This is useful when you have to make several matches before commencing the laying sequence.

The small workshop should possess means of making joints other than in pairs, which is time consuming. A dimension saw with minimum set is effective, provided that the veneer bundle is clamped tightly between plywood. A straight line edger may also be used.

But an ideal set-up would be to construct a jointer which can be used with a high speed router, fitted with a straight faced tungsten carbide cutter—the type used for trimming plastic sheets is ideal.

Prepare two thick boards, slightly longer than your total press length. Make sure they are perfectly flat and with a very true edge run on one side, possibly prepared by a trade mill. Take extreme care with this, as all your future veneer joints and matches will only be as good as this sharp, true edge.

Obtain a length of non-ferrous metal such as brass or aluminium in right angle section about 3/32 inch or 1/8 inch (2mm or 3mm) thickness. Rabbet this into the top edge of the board. Countersink and screw the strip into the top edge of the board only—not the side edge.

A suitably prepared bundle of veneers—which have been previously flatted and taped, may now be compressed between the two boards, with the edge of the bundle protruding a fraction.

The top board is clamped in position with hold-fast clamps which are mounted on recessed holding bolts on the workbench, or with overhead struts. The struts or clamps must allow for a completely free passage of the router, which is held down hard against the board and inwards against the metal angle.

The veneers must be perfectly flat for this operation, or they may crack or split. As you apply pressure to the two boards before clamping, if you feel or hear any resistance, remove the veneers for flatting treatment.

13

Veneer Matching

THE two basic approaches to the conversion of veneers, depending upon their end-use in panel form, are utilitarian and decorative.

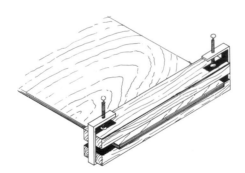

Fig. 126 A simple batten clamp for jointing

UTILITY MATCHING

Covers all interior work where the veneers to be joined together are required as compensating backing veneers, or to make up suitable widths for interior lamination, or where the result will not be seen; the veneer craftman's primary concern is the *elimination* of waste, and the final appearance is secondary.

Veneer wastage is an important factor and occurs in three ways: (a) cutting to length (b) trimming to width, and (c) odd leaves.

Length: Most veneers are available in lengths up to 8 feet 3 inches (2515mm). The temptation is to try to cut as many short lengths as possible from the bundle.

For example, if we required 32 lengths 24 inches (609mm) long by the bundle width, there are two options:

(i)   Cut up 8 leaves into 4 lengths of 24 inches (609mm) each, which would leave 24 whole leaves out of a 32 leaf bundle for another project.

(ii)   Cut off 24 inches (609mm) from the end of the bundle of 32 leaves reducing the entire bundle from 8 feet 3 inches (2515mm) down to 6 feet 3 inches (1905mm) and thereby reducing its future potential—for instance, it would no longer be usable for a flush door.

In the first example (i) you would have 8 sets of 4 leaves which would not match, but would have 24 whole 8 feet 3 inches (2515mm) leaves to use in future at their maximum potential. The ability to match veneers for interior work is unimportant.

The example given in (ii) would be the correct course only for decorative veneering.

Width: Practically every log has one good half and one not so good. The pith is rarely in the centre of the log and there is more wood to one side of the heart than the other. Therefore a log usually has narrow width bundles and wider width bundles on each side of the heart which may have been cut out at the mill.

For interior work selecting a bundle of the right width is all important and the craftsman has the options of either trimming waste or wasting odd leaves.

For example: we have a requirement to prepare 'lay-ons' (veneer assemblies jointed ready for laying) for six door interiors, 6 feet 6 inches × 22 inches (1981 × 558mm) which will require six assemblies 24 inches (609mm) wide, to allow for trimming after laying.

We examine our stock of suitable veneers and have a small bundle stock each of 32 matching leaves. Which would be the least wasteful to cut?

Veneer bundle width	Leaves to be jointed	Total width	Trimming waste	Total leaves	Odd leaves wasted
4½ inches (114mm)	6	27 inches (685mm)	3 inches (76mm)	36*	—
5 inches (127mm)	5	25 inches (635mm)	1 inch (25mm)	30	2
5½ inches (139mm)	5	27½ inches (698mm)	3½ inch (89mm)	30	2
6 inches (152mm)	4	24 inches (609mm)	—	24	8
6½ inches (165mm)	4	26 inches (660mm)	2 inches (50mm)	24	8
5 inches (177mm)	4	28 inches (711mm)	4 inches (101mm)	24	8
7½ inches (190mm)	4	30 inches (762mm)	6 inches (152mm)	24	8
8 inches (203mm)	3	24 inches (609mm)	—	18	14

*At a glance we can see that the 4½ inch (114mm) bundle width is insufficient for the job as we should have to break into the 5 inch (127mm) bundle and take four more leaves to make up the 36 required, and this would result in leaving only 28 leaves in that bundle.

The best width which gives the *least* trimming waste and the minimum number of odd leaves is the 5 inch (127mm) width, with only 1 inch (25mm) trim waste and two odd leaves.

However, if there was another use for eight matching leaves (in units of four) the 6 inch (152mm) wide bundle has two advantages. There is no trimming waste, and there are less joints to make.

The example above also shows that the 6½ inch, 7 inch and 7½ inch (165mm, 177mm and 190mm) wide bundles result in the same number of odd leaves, but an ever increasing trimming waste.

The 8 inch (203mm) width poses a special problem, with two advantages and a disadvantage: only two joints are necessary with three leaves and there is no trimming waste. If there was another use for the remaining fourteen leaves in units of four, the maximum savable would be twelve, leaving an odd leaf wastage of two leaves.

The example serves to illustrate the decisions facing the veneer craftsman when he calculates the maximum yield from his precious stocks.

To calculate the actual total veneer wastage, add the total number of wasted leaves, multiply by the length in feet and multiply this by the number of inches and divide by twelve. The answer is in square feet.

Assume the bundle length was 8 feet 3 inches (2515mm); taking the 5½ inch (139mm) width as an example, the trimming waste would be 30 leaves $\times$ 8.25 $\times$ 3½ divide by 12 = 72.1875 sq. ft. (6.70m²). Plus 2 odd leaves 8.25 $\times$ 5½ divide by 12 = 7.562 sq. ft. (0.7m²).

(Note: The wastage in the length is ignored for this exercise, since it would be common to all bundles.)

The total wastage on the 5½ inch (139mm) bundle would be 79.7495 sq. ft. (7.4m²).

This compares with the 5 inch (127mm) which would result in:

30 $\times$ 8.25 $\times$ 1 divided by 12 = 20.625 sq. ft. (1.91m²)

Plus 2 odd leaves = 7.562 sq. ft. (0.7m²) total 28.187 sq. ft. (2.61m²), which represents a total saving over the 5½ inch (139mm) bundle of 51.5625 sq. ft. (4.79m²).

Endless-leaf matching

We have seen how only ½ inch (12mm) in the width of a bundle of veneer can result in a large wastage factor. Therefore a more practical way has to be adopted for commercial production.

For all interior work where the final appearance is not important, the most economical method of veneer jointing is known as endless-leaf matching. Veneers are simply jointed together in full bundle width as rising from the stock, regardless of the actual width either of the veneers, or even of the panel to be covered. An endless width is jointed together and simply cropped off to suit the panel requirement, saving the offcut to be jointed again for the next panel without veneer waste.

Take a simple example. If the panel width requirement—allowing 2 inches (50mm) for trimming after laying, was 36 inches (914mm), and the veneer bundle was 8 inches (203mm), we would joint five leaves together to make a 40 inch (1015mm) width and trim off a 4 inch (101mm) offcut. The next panel would begin with the 4 inch (101mm) offcut and four more 8 inch (203mm) leaves. This will work with any multiple.

Bundle matching

For plywood laminations and corestock purposes, and even for compensating backing veneers for architectural panels which will not be seen, complete bundles of veneer of the same species, but not necessarily from the same flitch or log, are brought together in random widths, and the leaves endless-matched to make up panel widths without waste. To cover a panel of 36 inch (914mm) width, leaves of 4½ inch, 5 inch, 5½ inch, 6½ inch, 7 inch and 7½ inch (114mm, 127mm, 139mm, 165mm, 177mm and 190mm) could be used.

A small guillotine is ideal for jointing bundles. A hand operated type is sufficient in which the bundle of 32 leaves is clamped down beneath a pressure bar, and a long handled lever operates the knife, which shears off the veneers in bundle thickness ready for jointing.

The same machine is also used for the conversion of waney-edged bundles.

DECORATIVE MATCHING

Although wastage in any form is important, especially in the higher valued decorative veneers, it is true to say that the wastage factors which are considered of paramount importance for utility veneer matching, are of secondary importance when we consider decorative veneer matching.

The veneer craftsman's priority is now concerned with aesthetic considerations in achieving the best possible match to display his choice veneers.

Naturally, a thorough understanding of the various wastage options is still relevant, since the intrinsic value of rare and exotic burrs and curls, for example, makes their maximum utilisation extremely important and the desired effect must take priority every time, even at the expense of higher wastage.

It is the knowledge of veneer matching possibilities and technical skill in the application of matching methods, combined with the utilisation of available stock of veneers, that will minimise the wastage factor.

Figure jump

In the vast majority of decorative veneers, which are sold in bundles of 24, 28 or 32 leaves, the figure pattern seen on the surface of the top leaf in the bundle, is practically identical to the figure and markings on the bottom leaf of that bundle. Practically—but not in every case. In some cases, such as Japanese tamo, and cinnamon, I have seen the pattern on one side of a *single* leaf change from that on the reverse, making matches impossible.

Normally, the pattern 'drift' is infinitesimal, but even so, must be corrected, especially if eight, sixteen or thirty-two 'sunburst' pattern matching is desired.

Select a bundle which is oversize both in length and width and carefully examine the pattern visible at the edge of the bundle. Stagger the leaves sideways to align the pattern vertically from top to bottom; if the pattern is not very distinct and does not show on the side of the

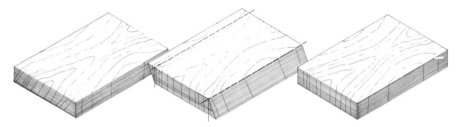

Fig. 127 Stagger and trim the veneers square

bundle, make a pencil or chalk mark in a few places on the edge of each leaf and line this up.

Trim the bundle from the top at its narrowest width, and check that the figure has now been perfectly squared up. Do the same at each side and also at the ends of the bundle. Also check to see that no leaves have been shuffled and replaced out of sequence, breaking the continuity. Number the leaves in chalk, with the letter F for 'face' when the bundle is received into stock.

When attempting to align bundles for multi-matches, like sixteen-piece sunbursts, or even thirty-two-piece, the problem becomes acute if the species to be worked has not got a distinctively marked edge pattern. Sunbursts are dealt with in depth later in this chapter.

Multiple leaf matching

Although the wastage options previously explained still apply it is of major importance that bundles for multiple matching are selected for their best matching effect and, therefore, the trimming and odd leaf wastage factors are of secondary importance.

It will not always be possible to select a bundle of rare or choice freak veneers in your desired width multiple, but the principle is there to follow whenever possible.

There are other considerations which have a bearing on the decision regarding the best bundle width when we turn to other aspects of veneer matching.

The most vital sequence in the whole process of decorative veneering is in the art of veneer matching; it is here that the veneer craftsman can express his virtuosity. He can make a diligent search through his available woods to find the best combination of figure, grain, texture, markings and colourtone to determine the best visual effects to artistically display his veneers.

The significance of grain is an important aspect of display because of its light refraction properties. Rather like the stripes of a newly mown lawn or of velvet and other fabrics, veneers will show a varying colour and appearance dependent upon the angle that the light source meets the wood.

Each leaf of veneer may be displayed in four ways, ie the smooth face side viewed from top to base and *vice versa*, and the reverse side, which has a loose or coarse face, viewed from the same two directions. When matching your veneers they could be marked as follows:

The face side, with the chalked mark at the top: F.T.
The face side, inverted with the chalked mark at the bottom: F.B.
The reverse side, with the chalked mark at the top: R.T.
The reverse side, with leaf inverted, marked at the bottom: R.B.

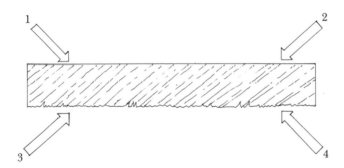

Fig. 128 The four viewing directions for every veneer:
arrows from top left indicate 1) Face side top (F.T.)
2) Face side bottom (F.B.) 3) Reverse top (R.T.)
4) Reverse bottom (R.B.)

In *single leaf matching* this is particularly important and therefore when arranging a single leaf of veneer in juxtaposition with another, always be aware of the *four* ways of making a match, and be sure to select the correct one to suit.

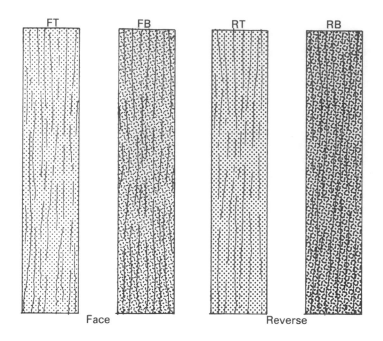

Fig. 129 Each leaf has four tones due to light refraction

The sliding match or slip match

This is where consecutive matching leaves of veneer are to be used to cover a panel to give the appearance of a piece of solid wood with all grain and figure and light refraction identical.

To achieve this, select only the very straightest grained or striped veneers, as the slightest deviation will cause the panel to have a leaning effect. Take sufficient leaves of veneer (all FT) and slide or slip them to the right without turning them over. (This is known in the trade as a 'dragged over' match). If carefully done, this match, when jointed will give the appearance of one very wide leaf of veneer.

However, if the grain or striped figure should not run truly perpendicular, but at a slight diagonal, the panel will have an unacceptable appearance and the cure is to take a wider bundle and trim it along the grain at each side to 'straighten' the grain. This provides trimming waste which is more acceptable than a poor match.

Another possible defect is when the bundle of veneer has a stronger figure at one side, and this cannot be trimmed off without undue wastage.

In a slip match, this would show a repeating pattern at every joint and emphasise the very fault that the slip match tries to conceal. One way to overcome this is with an *Inverted slip match.*

Fig. 130 The veneer hammer squeezes out trapped air bubbles and ensures a perfect bond

Fig. 131 Trim off surplus veneer overhang from corners towards centre

Inverted slip match

The veneer leaves are first 'dragged over' as in the slip match, all with face sides uppermost. Then alternate leaves are rotated through 180 degrees still keeping the face sides uppermost.

This has two results. Firstly, the alternate inversion of veneers brings the stronger pattern at the edges of the leaves together in pairs at meeting edges; and second, that the tonal difference will be evident. The overall effect will not be that of a single leaf of veneer, because the panel will have a definite pattern.

This type of match is acceptable only on condition that the attempt to match the figure at the edges in 'pairs' presents an aesthetic appearance and the light and dark leaf effect is also acceptable.

If the panel gives an unbalanced effect, the inverted slip-match should be abandoned in favour of the traditional book match.

Book match

The V match, or two piece match, refers to straight grained or figured book matches respectively. It is used where the veneers display a figure running at an angle to the edges, which would prove to be too wasteful to trim off; or where the figure is too pronounced. Two matching leaves are simply opened out like the pages of a book.

The left hand (reverse face veneer) 1RT, is jointed to the face side of the next consecutive leaf 2FT. The pattern must coincide exactly in the centre joint of the two leaves forming an identical mirror image.

The effect of light refraction will result in one veneer being lighter

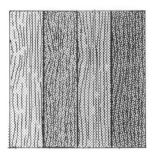

Fig. 132 Slip and turn book matches (straight grain)

Fig. 133 The slip match or sliding match "dragged over"

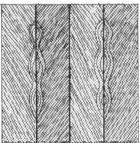

Fig. 134 The inverted slip-match

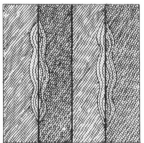

Fig. 135 Book matched fancy veneers

than the other; the appearance will reverse when either the source of light or the viewing position is changed. This does not detract from book matching, in fact this feature greatly enhances the overall tonal effect.

When preparing a two piece match, you must also consider the method of laying, and for all methods you will have to match, shoot and tape the joint to make a complete 'lay-on' assembly, except for the traditional 'hammer method' which uses hot scotch glue.

For hammer veneering, the two leaves are laid one at a time and the surplus veneer at the edges is trimmed off after the veneers have been laid.

To further illustrate this match, you will find a Butler's Tray two piece book match, simple veneering project explained in the projects chapter.

Fig. 136 Two piece book matched figured Brazilian rosewood

Fig. 137 Four piece book matched European walnut

Slip and turn match

This is simply a series of book matches on one panel. Consecutive leaves are slip-matched (dragged over) and then alternate veneers are turned over on their backs to form a series of perfectly matched pairs, (unlike pairs achieved by inversion), FT + RT + FT + RT etc.

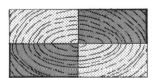

Fig. 138 Four piece match

The four piece match

Select four consecutive matching leaves of highly figured veneers. Arrange them so that the best figured portion of the leaves is at the bottom part of the leaf and either to one side or the other. Mark each leaf on both sides in chalk 1F, 2F, 3F and 4F on one side and 1R, 2R, 3R and 4R on the reverse.

Take leaves 1F and 2F and open them to form a two piece book match. Open them towards the direction of the main figure concentration. If the most attractive figure is at the bottom right hand corner of the top leaf, open the leaf 1F to the right, forming the match 2F + 1R. If the best corner was at the bottom left, open the match to the left to form

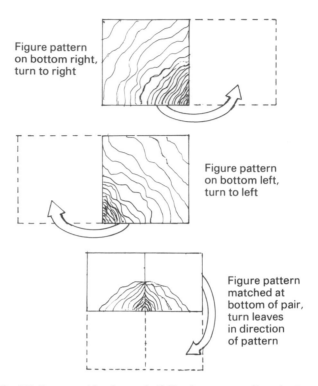

Figure pattern
on bottom right,
turn to right

Figure pattern
on bottom left,
turn to left

Figure pattern
matched at
bottom of pair,
turn leaves
in direction
of pattern

Fig. 139 Quartered book match (following pattern direction)

1R + 2F. Now take the next two leaves and open them in book fashion
either to right or left as decided above, to form either 4F + 3R or 3R +
4F. Now reverse the second match by turning it over in the direction of
the matched figure along the bottom edge. (not left or right but over its
horizontal axis).

This will form a book match either $\dfrac{2F + 1R}{4R + 3F}$ or $\dfrac{1R + 2F}{3F + 4R}$

In both cases the pattern jump is one in the horizontal direction and
two in the vertical direction, with opposite corners balanced with face
and reverse veneers, to provide the correct light refraction.

It is possible to make several transpositions of the four veneers to
achieve different visual effects depending on which of the four edges
offer the most attractive combinations. In every case, ensure that the
correct pattern jump is maintained and with balanced face and reverse
corners.

Angled mirrors

In order to test the best effect of a veneer bundle for a four piece match, without cutting into the veneer stock, a pair of mirrors are used. The top leaf of the bundle may be searched all over its surface at different angles to see at a glance the final effect of four piece matches. Hinge a pair of mirrors together—even a small pair of handbag mirrors will do—a more permanent practical aid would be two pieces of cheap mirror glass (not plate glass) about 9 inches × 4 inches (230mm × 100mm) and mount them on plywood, hinged at one end. Ideally, make a protractor strip, marked off at 30, 45, 60 and 90 degrees, and the mirrors can then be used for creating parquetry matches. Hold the mirrors vertically, opened at 90 degrees, and pass them slowly over the face of any veneer leaf, and you will see reflected in the angle formed by the mirrors, the effect of a four piece match.

Using only one mirror will show the effect of a two piece match; a 45 degree angle will show an eight piece, and a 22.5 degree will reveal a sixteen piece sunburst match.

Test the top leaf on a bundle of fancy figured butts, burrs, swirls and curls, or crown cut figured veneers such as walnut, rosewood, elm, ash, teak, myrtle, maple etc.

When you have obtained the desired effect in the mirrors, chalk along the baseline of the mirrors and cut the veneers to this line to produce the match you saw reflected in the mirrors.

Until experience is gained in matching veneers, it may be difficult to visualise which features will convert into excellent matches without using the mirrors.

Sometimes, a little quirk of figure at the edge of a leaf can result in an attractive match; an ugly knot in the centre of a leaf may have swirling figures around it, but the knot may blind you to the wonderful effect the swirl might provide if separated from the knot. Part of the fascination of veneering lies in the discovery of beautiful matches.

Making the match

Many amateurs find it difficult to cut through four veneers exactly at the same position to effect a match, and for this reason rely on the hammer veneering method in which the leaves are left oversize, and laid one at a time separately.

However, most forms of veneering—certainly all professional veneering—requires that the leaves are jointed together into a veneer 'lay-on' assembly, and laid as one piece.

As the four leaves must not move even a fraction during the cutting and jointing operation, they must be fastened tightly together along the edges *not* to be jointed.

Carefully examine the leaves, locate one special feature and insert a veneer pin through the identical spot on each leaf. Then use an office

Fig. 140 Align four matching leaves and cut the first joint

Fig. 141 Fasten straps of veneer tape across the joint to pull it tightly together, and one long tape down the joint

Fig. 142 The completed four piece book match reverse side (face side is taped)

Fig. 143 Inlay motif being fitted papered side uppermost

Fig. 144 Paper scraped off motif for clarity only

Fig. 145 Veneer match is trimmed square

Fig. 146 Chisel off border margin veneer before the adhesive cures

Fig. 147 Boxwood lines and crossbanded border surround are fitted and taped

stapler to staple the four leaves through the edges and ends which will not be jointed. Only staple them in two or three places, as the staples must be removed again.

Most craftsmen manage to achieve the same result by taping the leaves together at the surplus edges and ends, but either way, the leaves must be fastened tightly together.

They are then placed on the cutting board, with a straightedge along the long edge to be jointed. The straightedge may be clamped at each end on long matched leaves.

Use a veneer saw, which provides a square edge, to cut through the four leaves. Compress the four leaves between two battens and clamp them tightly together; shoot the four edges with a finely set plane.

Release the veneers from the jointing clamp, and also from the fastenings at the ends and edges (staples or tapes etc).

Open leaves 1RT and 2FT and pull them tightly together with short veneer tape 'straps' about 4 inches (100mm) long fastened *across* the joint with another tape right *along* the joint.

Repeat the above sequence with leaves 3 and 4, but remember to *invert* them to read 3FB + 4RB, *at the centre joint.*

Now fold both pairs of veneer back against their veneer tape 'hinges', to form a set of four leaves again for making the centre joint at right angles.

Temporarily pin, staple or tape the farthest edge to ensure no movement during the cutting operation. Place on the cutting board and using the straightedge and veneer saw, cut through the four veneers at right angles to the tape joints. Check the angle carefully with a square. Release the pins, staples or tapes etc.

Once more, affix short veneer tape straps *across* the joint and one long tape along the joint. Also affix protection tapes for handling purposes around the other edges, and ensure that all tapes are on one side of the assembly only — the side which will eventually be seen.

If you wish to include a marquetry motif, lines and a crossbanding border surround, there are two ways to proceed: firstly, the completed 'lay-on' assembly will be slightly undersize (smaller than the ground-work) to enable you to true up the veneers after laying, by using a cutting gauge parallel to the edge of the groundwork, and removing a tiny surplus before fitting the inlay lines and border crossbanding.

The second method, is one that most professionals use and requires more skill, and that is to make the four piece match the correct size, fit the bandings and border to the assembly, and accurately lay it in one operation without margin for error.

A marquetry motif may be included in the assembly whichever laying method is used, by aligning the motif against pencilled centre lines; release any backing 'waste' veneer from around the motif, usually left on for its protection.

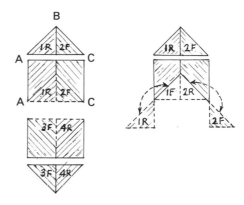

Fig. 148 Diamond matches. *Left:* Centre diamond with same face as adjoining quarter. *Right:* Top section separated into two triangles and reversed along hypotenuse to form centre diamond in contrast to the adjoining quarters

The diamond match

This popular match enables the craftsman to use very narrow bundles of striped veneers, such as sapele, oak, teak, elm or rosewood. These are slip-matched, all true faced, and made up into sets of four normal width veneers. Begin by 'dragging-over' the narrow leaves of selected veneer, after trimming a jointing edge along the striped figure. Number each narrow leaf with chalk and slip-match leaves 1, 2, 3 and 4 together. Chalk number 1F at the top of the face side. Repeat this with 5, 6, 7 and 8 to form leaf 2F; 9, 10, 11 and 12 form leaf 3F and 13, 14, 15 and 16 to form leaf 4F. The pattern jump will be four only between each newly formed leaf, so that any slight deviation of striped figure will be identical on each of the four new leaves.

Place the four leaves on the cutting board and trim off a triangular shape by cutting through the veneers at 45 degrees at each end, to form a rhomboidal shape as shown in the illustration.

Re-chalk the numbering on the face of each leaf, if the original numbering was trimmed off, and also number the reverse side 1R, 2R, 3R and 4R. Begin creating the match by jointing and taping leaves 1R to 2F along the mitred edges. Place a straightedge across the two leaves at A-C and carefully trim off the top triangle, which is then brought down and taped into the triangular shape along the line A-B-C to complete a rectangle. Next, take the pair 3R and 4F and joint them along the mitred edges; place a straightedge across the pair and cut off the top triangle and tape this into the bottom of the match to form a second rectangle, and turn this match over by pivoting the rectangle on its lower, horizontal axis (not to left or right) and tape the two rectangles together. The completed match reads $\dfrac{1R + 2F}{3F + 4R}$.

This provides a correctly balanced pattern jump, with light and dark corners of the diamond match formed by face and reverse veneers in opposite corners.

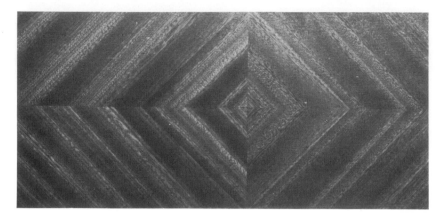

Fig. 149 Four piece diamond match in sapele

Alternative centre-diamond

The traditional diamond match described, arranges the striped figure in each quarter of the match to have a uniform visual appearance caused by light refraction.

The effect may be further enhanced by creating a contrasting centre diamond match.

After trimming off the top two triangles 1R and 2F, they are separated, brought down into their positions in the lower section, and then reversed. Hold each small triangle by its hypoteneuse and turn it over before taping it into position to form the complete rectangle. Do the same with the top section of the other half. See Figs. 148/150.

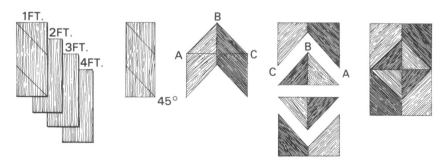

Fig. 150 The diamond match sequence of jointing

The overall diamond match will have the original appearance of $\dfrac{1R + 2F}{3F + 4R}$ but the inner diamond will be in contrast with the sequence $\dfrac{1F + 2R}{3R + 4F}$ and the pattern jump will have been maintained.

Fig. 151 Reverse diamond match

Reverse diamond match

This is a simple variation of the diamond match, which is taped together as previously described. Next, the assembly is cut through from top to bottom along the vertical centre line and the match re-jointed to form the pattern $\dfrac{2F + 1R}{4R + 3F}$. The resulting effect is an 'exploded' figure radiating from the centre of the panel outwards and can be very effective in some situations, especially when used in conjunction with normal diamond matches.

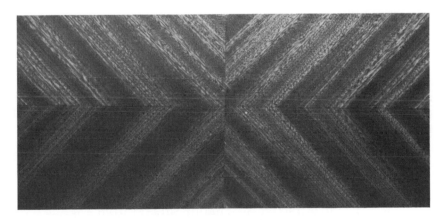

Fig. 152 Reverse diamond match in sapele

Reverse book match

Sometimes the figure of a four piece book match which is intended to form a diamond effect around a panel centre, would look much more effective with the 'exploded' treatment where the pattern radiates outwards from the centre towards the edges. If the mirror is placed vertically along one edge of a veneer, you will see the effect of a reverse book match. Test each edge in both horizontal and vertical directions for the best effect. If you prefer the result, simply cut through the match along either the vertical or horizontal joint and re-joint the match.

As an example, $\dfrac{1R + 2F}{3F + 4R}$ would become either $\dfrac{2F + 1R}{4R + 3F}$ or $\dfrac{3F + 4R}{1R + 2F}$

Fig. 153 The V match

Alternating squares match

This is an economical way to utilise very narrow widths of straight grained striped veneers. Chalk each leaf with the numerical sequence with F for face and R for reverse.

Narrow widths may be slip-matched together to make up the required width of each square. For example if the squares are to be 7

Fig. 154 Alternating square match

inches (178mm) then two leaves of 3½ inches (89mm) veneer could be jointed together, keeping all same faces together.

The veneers are then kept in correct sequence and cut into squares.

There are six ways to arrange each square on a panel, taking full advantage of the effects of light refraction.

Face, reverse, top, bottom, vertical and horizontal. It is therefore possible to make up attractive alternating squares from a single leaf of veneer arranged in the six ways.

The tonal effect of a multi-matched panel would be lost if an accurate sequence was not kept and the balance between face, reverse, top, bottom, vertical and horizontal was not adhered to.

In addition, if you used figured woods instead of straight grain, the pattern jump must also be considered.

The following suggestions are very effective:

Code: F = Face   R = Reverse
         T = Top   B = Bottom
         V = Vertical   H = Horizontal

$$\frac{1FTV + 2RH}{3RH + 4FBV} \qquad \frac{1RBV + 2FH}{3FH + 4RTV} \qquad \frac{3FTV + 4RH}{1RH + 2FVB} \qquad \frac{3RVT + 4FH}{1FH + 2RBV}$$

The alternating squares match looks best in squares of one species using such woods as oak, sapele, teak, wenge, rosewood or elm. It is also very effective when a blend of several closely toned woods, such as four or five mahoganies, are used. For example, choose veneers with interlocked striped figure such as sapele, utile, sipo, tiama, or African walnut, teak, afrormosia, and opepe.

Veneers with a strong ray figure add an extra dimension to the aesthetic appearance, such as 'raindrop' figured oak, lacewood, silky oak, etc.

Fig. 155 Alternating squares matched in figured oak

Harlequin squares

Multi-matching of a variety of different contrasting species can make up into very eye catching panels. Harlequin squares are ideal when creating a focal point of interest in a wall panelling scheme for a cocktail bar for example. The effect can easily be overdone and become tiring unless created with some restraint.

Herringbone matching

This is a very popular form of veneer matching frequently executed incorrectly. To illustrate the technique, select four matching consecutive leaves of pencil striped sapele. Place leaves 1 and 2 on the left and 3 and 4 on the right. Chalk them F1, F2, F3 and F4 and also mark the reverse sides of the leaves R1, R2, R3 and R4. Trim off the ends of leaves F1 and F2 at 135 degrees at each end. Cut off the leaves F3 and F4 at 45 degrees at each end. The cuts should be parallel, and in all cases the top edges of the leaves should be placed horizontally to the right.

Swivel leaves F1 and F2 so that the 135 degree bevelled edges are vertical. Slide leaf F2 to the right and turn it over to become R2, rotate it and joint the bevelled edges together to form F1 + R2.

Now take leaves F3 and F4. Pivot them so that the 45 degree bevelled edges are vertical. Slide leaf F3 to the left and reverse it to become R3. Rotate F4 and joint to R3 to become R3 + 4F. The next step is to joint together F1 + R2 and R3 + F4 to form a simple herringbone match. A straightedge is now placed across the top of the triangle, cutting across F1 + R2, and this piece is jointed at the bottom of the match; repeat with R3 + F4.

Fig. 156 Herringbone match (traditional)

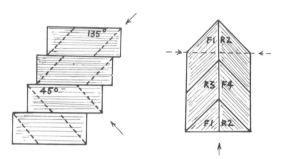

Fig. 157 Herringbone match (traditional)

Fig. 158 Herringbone match — alternative pattern (vertical & horizontal grain direction)

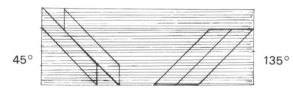

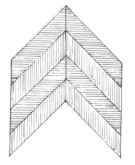

Fig. 159 Herringbone match — alternative pattern

The horizontal match

When you wish to create a herringbone match on two adjacent panels, it is necessary to achieve contrasts in both the vertical direction and also in the horizontal direction. For this we will need eight matching leaves to create a practice piece. This time, cut leaves 1, 2, 3 and 4 at 135 degrees at each end, and 5, 6, 7 and 8 at 45 degrees, with the tops of all leaves placed horizontally to the right. Reverse leaves F2 and F4, to become R2 and R4, invert them and joint to 1F and 3F. Slide leaves F5 and F7 to the left and reverse them; invert leaves F6 and F8. This creates the following herringbone match:

$$\frac{1F + 2R}{5R + 6F} \qquad\qquad \frac{3F + 4R}{7R + 8F}$$

There is a pattern jump of one horizontally across both panels, and a vertical jump of four, in addition to face and reverse matching, with top leaf matching due to the inversion of the leaves.

The triangular pattern jump

If a herringbone match was carried out with a 32 leaf bundle to the above sequence, it would result in the following:

1F + 2R	3F + 4R
5R + 6F	7R + 8F
9F + 10R	11F + 12R
13R + 14F	15R + 16F
17F + 18R	19F + 20R
21R + 22F	23R + 24F
25F + 26R	27F + 28R
29R + 30F	31R + 32F

When the top triangles are trimmed off and jointed at the bottom of the match it would mean that

$$\frac{29R + 30F}{1F + 2R} \qquad\qquad \frac{31R + 32F}{3F + 4R}$$

This provides an unacceptable pattern jump.

But if triangles 1F + 2R and 3F + 4R were to be cut off and jointed with 13R + 14F and 15R + 16F and the top triangles of 17F + 18R and 19F + 20R were trimmed off and jointed to 29R + 30F and 31R + 32F, this would provide four rectangles and form a break in the pattern of each door in the centre.

This is usually resolved by either the insertion of an inlay line or banding, or by creating a herringbone butt match.

Herringbone butt match

The problem of the centre joint is solved by taking the two rectangular sections for each door, and inverting them to create a butt match with an overall diamond appearance:

The doors would then have this appearance:

1F + 2R	3F + 4R
5R + 6F	7R + 8F
9F + 10R	11F + 12R
13R + 14F	15R + 16F
30F + 29R	32F + 31R
26R + 25F	28R + 27F
22F + 21R	24F + 23R
18R + 17F	20R + 19F

The centre diamond pattern would feature the top triangles.

1F + 2R	3F + 4R
18R + 17F	20R + 19F

This pattern jump is still rather large, but the diamond pattern renders this un-noticeable and avoids having to use a banding or inlay line.

The policy of simply inverting the two lower assemblies is therefore capable of improvement to make the pattern jump equalised throughout the match.

This is achieved by the herringbone reverse butt match.

The herringbone reverse butt match

In this perfect match, the lower halves of the match are not inverted, but *reversed* and the whole sequence is planned to produce an equalised pattern throughout the match as follows:

The lower doors are first assembled to read

5F + 6R	7F + 8R
13R + 14F	15R + 16F
21F + 22R	23F + 24R
29R + 30F	31R + 32F

The top triangles are jointed in to the bottom. The assemblies are then completely *reversed* and jointed to the top assemblies which now read:

1F + 2R	3F + 4R
9R + 10F	11R + 12F
17F + 18R	19F + 20R
25R + 26F	27R + 28F
29F + 30R	31F + 32R
21R + 22F	23R + 24F
13F + 14R	15F + 16R
5R + 6F	7R + 8F

The triangles meeting at the centre therefore are

$$\frac{1F + 2R}{5R + 6F} \text{ and } \frac{3F + 4R}{7R + 8F}$$

This provides an eight jump vertically throughout and only a four jump at the centre, with face and reverse matches throughout the pair of doors.

Irregular matching

When the veneers you have to work with do not permit such a careful study and arrangement, the irregular match provides an easy solution to the herringbone match. This is important when you have utilised very narrow bundles and slip matched them to make the match. The technique is to create the best herringbone butt match that you can contrive without concerning yourself too much about the eye catching central diamond feature of the panels, using the herringbone as a perfect background for an insert into the panel centre of a four piece match of burr or butt, or an inlay motif which will become the centrepiece and lead the eye away from the matching at the panel centre.

Sunburst matches

There are two basic types of sunburst matches, the slip-match and the book-match. The slip-match employs very straight grained striped material to produce a radial effect like the spokes of a wheel. Veneers which possess a figure which swirls off to one side of the leaf, produces a 'revolving' effect.

Fig. 160 Sunburst match

The book matched sunburst relies upon both light refraction and matched figure for its effect.

There are other types, such as 'slip and turn' in which all veneers are slip-matched, then alternate leaves are inverted; casual matching employs several different types of veneers, such as five mahoganies, for eye appeal.

The final effect for book matching is tested by the hinged mirrors closed down to 22½ degrees for a sixteen piece match or down to 11¼ degrees for a full thirty-two piece match.

Book-matched sunburst

There are three problems to solve. The first is the very accurate cutting required for a perfect fit as any small error in cutting suffers from a progressive accumulation and will multiply by 32. The second problem is the pattern jump, and the third is the centre point. Examine the veneer bundle carefully and compare the top and bottom leaves for an exact match by separating them and placing them together for comparison. Replace them in sequence and stagger the bundle sideways to ensure that the pattern at the edges can be trimmed vertically to form an exact match. Next, decide from the mirror-match where to draw the baseline for cutting.

Although narrow bundles may be used for economy's sake, it is sometimes best to cut diagonally across a wider bundle to obtain the desired effect. Any well marked lozenge shaped pattern with attractive concentrations of figure at the sides and at each end, will produce the desired effect.

If the pattern jump is marked but not too great, it would be pointless in fanning the leaves around in a circular match, because leaf number one would meet up with leaf number 32 and the pattern jump would spoil the sunburst match.

This is overcome with an eight leaf jump; reading in a clockwise direction with leaf number one at the top, 1-8; 17-24; 32-25; 16-9 and finally leaf 9 jointed to leaf 1 to complete the circle. If this pattern jump was still too large, opt for a small sequence reading from leaf one at the top in a clockwise direction, 1-4; 9-12; 17-20; 25-28; 32-29; 24-21; 16-13; 8-5 with 5 jointed back to 1.

Sixteen piece sunburst matches

It is best to use the pattern jump of four to create these matches, with the sequence starting at the top with no 1, and reading in a clockwise direction 1-4; 9-12; 16-13; 8 to 5 and complete the circle with 5 jointed back to 1.

In the case of book matches, alternate veneers would be reversed. For a slip-matched sunburst of narrow straight grained striped material, the pattern jump may still be an important factor. Keeping the veneers face side uppermost, fan them around to form a circle and judge the effect. If the pattern jump is marked, re-form the bundle, and slip-match to the right and left to keep to the above mentioned recommended sequences.

Fancy figured crown cut veneers, swirls, burry butts and curls make the best book-matched sunbursts; veneers with strong interlocked grain with a pronounced ray figure are also excellent for book matching or slip and turn inverted matching; plain straight grained oak, teak, elm, ash, rosewood and sapele are most effective when slip-matched.

Checkered matching
This is formed by assembling contrasting squares in traditional chessboard fashion. (See Figs. 161-166 overpage)

There are four types of checkered matches.

1. *True faced match*

Created from one species of veneer, kept same faced, where adjacent squares are in opposing directions at right angles to each other.

The two-toned result is due to light refraction effects. The best results are obtained by using very close striped, interlocked grain species such as sapele.

2. *Reverse match*

This also is matched from a single species, with adjacent squares at right angles to each other but *reversed*.

This greatly increases the effect of light refraction.

3. *Chessboard*

This classic, traditional match is achieved by the use of two different species, kept same faced. Try to avoid using black and white as this proves too tiring and effects the eyes of the players.

Brazilian rosewood and satinwood; laurel and avodire; harewood and rosa peroba; and walnut and sycamore, are examples.

4. *Harlequin checkers*

In this case a multi-selection of contrasting veneers is used, a different veneer for every strip. This type is only satisfactory for a small decoration and not for playing chess.

The technique of cutting and assembly of the checkered match is the same, except for the reverse match, where the jointing stage is different.

To make a checkered panel 12 inches (304mm) square for example, we will require nine strips 12 inches × 1½ inches (304 × 38mm) (five dark and four light).

For the True faced match, cut five strips 12 inches (304mm) long by 1½ inches (38mm) wide, and another four strips only 1½ inches (38mm) long by 12 inches (304mm) wide. Use either a 12 inch (304mm) wide bundle, or slip match narrower bundle veneers to make up 12 inches (304mm) wide. Keep the nine strips all true faces, and assemble them with veneer tape in alternate rows.

For the Reverse match, keep the five 12 inch (304mm) long veneers true faced, and turn over the 12 inch (304mm) wide veneers on to their loose reverse side in making the assembly.

Fig. 161 Two contrasting woods cut into strips

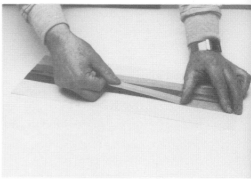

Fig. 162 Tape strips together

Fig. 163 Cut strips at right angles

Fig. 164 Arrange strips ready for staggering

Fig. 165 Taped assembly of strips

Fig. 166 Eight overhanging squares to be trimmed off

14

Inlay Bandings, Lines, Stringings & Motifs

MOST period furniture was enhanced by the application of inlays with the decorative veneers. There are several types commercially available today, all sold in 1 metre lengths; they are; Stringings; Flat lines; Square lines; Purfling and Bandings.

Stringings, flat lines and bandings are supplied in veneer thickness; square lines and purfling are usually sold in Imperial Wire Gauge (WG) measurement, in square section. The table below shows the measurements;

WG	Decimal of Inch	Millimetres
22	.028	.711
20	.036	.914
18	.048	1.219
16	.064	1.626
14	.080	2.032
12	.104	2.642
10	.128	3.251
8	.160	4.064
6	.192	4.877
4	.232	5.893
2	.276	7.010

Stringings

These are the finest inlay strips obtainable, and are simply veneers, cut into square section, 22 IWG (or 20 gauge in the USA.) They may be cut from any suitable veneer, but are usually available in boxwood, sycamore or dyed black.

Flat lines

Narrow strips of veneer, supplied in various widths either in imperial measure or metric, in ¹⁄₁₆ inch, ⅛ inch or ¼ inch (1.6mm; 3.2mm or 6.3mm). Available in boxwood or dyed black agba or peartree, etc.

Square lines

When in the finest gauges of 22WG or 20WG, these are known as stringings, but all other heavier gauges are square lines. The most commonly available are ¹⁄₁₆ inch, ⅛ inch and ¼ inch (1.6mm, 3.2mm and 6.3mm) similar to flat lines. Available in boxwood and dyed black agba or peartree etc.

Purfling

This is used chiefly for musical instrument inlaying, although not exclusively for that purpose. Purfling comprises a glued-up sandwich of three layers cut into a square section, and is usually ⅛ inch or 3.2mm square, in either black-white-black or reverse white-black-white combination. It is available in sycamore, holly with rosewood and ebony in addition to boxwood and dyed black.

Purfling is also supplied in mother of pearl, and imitation tortoise shell, plastics etc.

Fig. 167 Inlay bandings

Bandings

All bandings are of veneer thickness. Widths vary according to pattern, from ⅛ inch up to ¾ inch and wider. Imported metric bandings are offered in 4mm, 6mm and 10mm widths.

A very wide range of patterns is commercially available. One of the most popular types is the 'crossbanding', in which the grain direction runs across the width of the banding. These are usually offered in walnut, rosewood, tulipwood, satinwood, with a fine stringing of boxwood or dyed black (or both) at each side. Feather or herringbone patterns are favoured for bending around curves, as any pattern slip does not mar the work. Ladder or rope bandings, arrowhead, lozenge, diamond, elongated diamond, chess-checkers and Grecian key bandings are all popular. Three line bandings are also available, to match with purflings. The purflings are usually set in at the edges or corners of the work, and any additional bands used in the decorative face veneer wood match the purfling. These are in white-black-white or reverse combination.

APPLICATION

There are several rules governing the successful application of lines and bandings on a veneered panel.

1. A stringing or line is used to *divide* two surfaces, not necessarily to form a *contrast.* For example, if there was a walnut curl centre panel, with a striped walnut crossband surround, this might almost be sufficient in itself; the problem is that parts of the top of the curl leaf, might show fairly straight grain, and this could lose itself against the straight grain walnut of the surround. A fine line would neatly divide the surfaces.

2. It is possible to have a panel completely covered by a veneer match without a crossbanded border, but the *effect* of a border can be obtained by the use of a suitable banding.

3. On a very plain veneered panel, the banding itself could become the main decorative feature, by the intricate design used to incorporate it into the panel.

4. The outer edge of the banding, or in the case of stringings and lines, the veneer itself is either white or black. If the surround is light, the black line would be selected as the white would not show sufficient contrast as a dividing line. But on a dark rosewood background, the white line might show as too great a contrast. The black line, which is still in contrast to the lustrous dark brown of the rosewood, might still be preferred. Remember it is not a direct contrast that is required, but a line to mark the divide between two surfaces.

5. Restraint: The aesthetic sense of the craftsman comes into its own in the choice and application of lines. Great restraint is necessary to avoid the temptation to 'gild the lilly'. Much more so in the case of bandings which can dignify and grace the work if used with discretion or ruin and spoil or cheapen it, if overdone.

The banding should always be subordinate to the decorative veneers, and must serve to enhance them rather than compete with them. To compliment the panel by accentuating the overall design, but to remain part of an overall harmony.

6. True face: Examine the true face of lines used on one panel, as they may offer a different appearance when polished if they have been cut from the same leaf of veneer and accidentally turned over.

Craftsmen often prefer to cut their own lines. On a walnut panel, for example, a fine line of sap walnut would be preferable to a white line; an American walnut line would be better than dyed black.

CUTTING AND INLAYING

Double knife. The double knife comes into its own when cutting lines or the grooves to accomodate them. It is a home-made tool with two filed-up hacksaw blades in a wooden handle with a tightening screw. Insert a piece of line to be cut, and tighten. Use the double knife against a straightedge for straight lines, or freehand when the design permits.

Curves. To bend a line around a curve, steam it, or steep it in boiling water, and bend it across a heated pipe or dowel, working it back and forth gradually increasing the curvature.

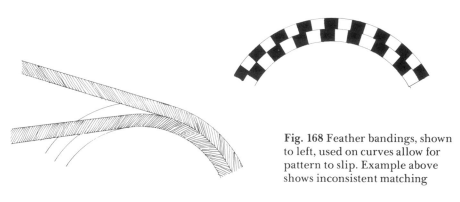

Fig. 168 Feather bandings, shown to left, used on curves allow for pattern to slip. Example above shows inconsistent matching

When cutting a curved line, use a pair of dividers of which one point has been flattened and sharpened to form a cutting edge. Put a scrap of veneer under the other point, and tape it to the surface to prevent any movement. When a banding is required for a curve, select a feather or herringbone type, and use a knife to separate the bandings down the middle. This allows the two 45 degree feathered angles to slip to the curvature without disturbing the pattern, which on any other patterned banding would look unsightly.

Criss-cross lines. When the pattern you wish to cut into the face veneer involves lines in the pattern which cross each other, always cut and fit one line at a time, before cutting the intersecting line. Never attempt to cut grooves into the face veneer which criss-cross, as tiny fragments will break off and become lost.

Double-line. One trick of the old masters, was to glue the veneer required for a line to a waste veneer and then cut the line from the two layer sandwich.The required line was glued into the groundwork with the waste line above it to provide pressure in laying. Afterwards, the top line was chiselled, or scraped and sanded off.

Pattern Balance

Care should be taken to match the pattern of the banding itself. It is not sufficient to start at one corner of the veneer assembly, and use part of the one metre length along one side, continuing along the next side with the offcut, and join the next banding to it, etc. The result would be unbalanced. The trick is to start at the corner. Select two bandings and study the ends. Adjust them together so that the patterns are identical and cut off the ends to coincide. Now mitre those bandings into the corner, allowing the rest of the banding to overlap the centre line of the panel.

Repeat the process with two more bandings in the diagonally opposite corner, again overlapping the bandings at the centre lines. The centre line cut is made to ensure that the pattern is equal and symmetrical on both sides of the cut. This is because the focal point of any banding layout is the mitred corners — if they are wrong the panel is ruined.

Inlaying bandings

If you wish to inlay a banding into a panel which has been veneered and trimmed square to the edge, select a cutter for the router or use a scratch stock that is the exact width of the banding, and set it to cut a groove slightly less in thickness than the banding. This enables pressure to be brought to bear on the banding, and for finishing flush.

If you have not got a cutter the correct width of the banding, use a smaller width cutter and use this to run the groove set to the inner edge of the groove (marked out with a cutting gauge) and then run a second groove with the cutter set to the outer edge.

Do not use the router into the corners. It is best to mark the corners with the chisel and remove them, rather than rely on the cutting gauge and router.

Main feature

When the intricate pattern of the lines or bandings themselves are to form the main decorative feature in an otherwise plain surface, for example, the traditional Grecian key pattern, (although there are plenty of more interesting ones), begin in one corner and make the first routed cut.

Repeat this sectional cut in each corner before making the next cut. Always work in a good light. An 'Anglepoise' spotlight or car trouble-light are good aids for spot illumination.

Edges

When fitting square lines or purfling right on the edge of the panel, to be seen from above and from the side, use a cutting gauge first from the top, and then at the side. Next use the chisel to start the rabett at the corners, and finish off with the small bullnose or rabett plane.

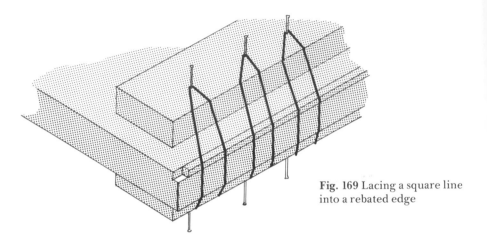

Fig. 169 Lacing a square line into a rebated edge

Laying with crossbanding surrounds

It is customary, when inlay bandings or lines are to be laid with crossbanding surrounds, for the face veneers to be laid undersize, and for the inlays and borders to be fitted later as a second operation.

This is because the slightest slip in the press, and the narrow crossbanding border surrounds will not be parallel to the edges of the panel. The surplus is removed with a cutting gauge and the bandings and borders fitted true to the edge and laid separately.

First mitre and fit the bandings in position, temporarily held with veneer pins. Next cut and fit the crossbanding veneers and tape in position. Incline the veneer pin heads towards the panel centre to ensure a tight fit. Veneer tapes are then run the length of the banding and crossbanding, so that they act as hinges, to allow both the banding and border surround to be lifted up to apply glue to the groundwork for laying. Press the surround into the glue, and fasten more short lengths of tape as straps taken around the thickness of the panel and fastened to the back of the panel, before pressing.

This ensures that nothing moves while the assembly is being brought under pressure. The crossbanded border surround will over-hang the panel for a subsequent trim off. The action of pulling anchoring tapes around the edge to fasten underneath the panel could result in breaking the crossgrained edge veneers. Avoid this by fixing small glueblocks, the width of the overhang, immediately below the tapes, to provide support. The blocks and tapes can be discarded later.

If the stringings, lines or bandings are to be laid together with the assembly, it is essential that a yielding wad of baize, felt, thick card or linoleum is used to take up differences in thickness to avoid blistering.

MAKING INLAY BANDINGS

Making banding is a challenging and fascinating craft but the principles are basic. The trick is to contrive the composition of the mosaic, so that *end grain* is never exposed. It is the *sidegrain* that is revealed in the banding.

To make a walnut crossbanding veneer for example, with a sycamore and black walnut stringing at each side you would need two leaves of black walnut 36 inches x 10 inches; (914mm x 254mm); two leaves of sycamore 36 inches x 10 inches (914mm x 254mm) and some solid walnut 6 inches (152mm) long plus sawcutting allowance (say 1½ inches) (38mm), as thick as you can find, by any width that you can rub-join together to make up to 10 inch (254mm) overall width.

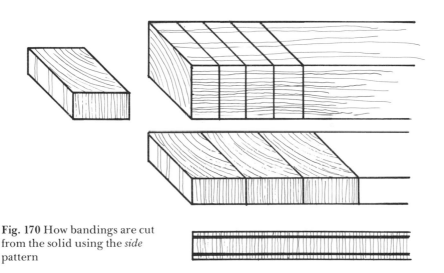

Fig. 170 How bandings are cut from the solid using the *side* pattern

Saw the walnut into ¼ inch (6mm) *long* strips, 10 inch (254mm) wide, by 1½ inch (38mm) thick. Now turn the strip on its side. Cut and assemble twenty-four such strips together, and you have a banding 36 inches (914mm) long, ¼ inch (6mm) thick and 10 inches (254mm) wide.

The assembly is covered with a polythene sheet and temporarily bound together with wide Sellotape. Then, end pieces are fitted to take the end clamps, followed by the three sash clamps. The surplus glue will not stick to the polythene.

When cured, clean-up both sides and lay the black walnut veneer, suitably coated with glue, and then the sycamore veneer into the press, followed by the coated mosaic core; followed by the second sycamore sheet, suitably coated and finally the second black walnut sheet.

The usual baize, and hot metal cauls, etc., are used to effect a good bond. After the panel has been allowed to cure, the block is taken to the sawtable and cut into 1mm bandings, with a fine teeth hollow ground saw.

When making bandings, it is the end grain which is glued to the outer veneers and the *sidegrain* displayed in the banding. It follows that providing you follow that simple rule, you can cut and assemble rhomboidal, rectangular or profiled shaped sticks to form any pattern that your ingenuity can conjure up.

INLAY MOTIFS

All traditional forms of marquetry decoration are now commercially available in the form of marquetry inlay motifs.

The motif is already assembled and is sold with a paper backing protecting the face side, and the reverse is toothed ready for laying.

Usually the motif is allowed to remain in a 'waste' veneer to protect it in handling and the waste is trimmed off before laying. In other cases, where the design lends itself, the motif is complete without a protective 'waster' around it.

The motifs are laid paper side uppermost, and this is scraped off and cleaned up later. They are applied in two different ways, either being 'let-into' the veneer assembly and laid as part of the whole face veneer, or inlaid into a routed ground, as a second operation, after the panel has been pressed. (In fact, many motifs are used in America as overlays on the surface, applied to the surface and allowed to stand proud rather than inlaid and levelled).

Some of the most popular patterns available today are round and oval patterae, sand shaded, shell, fans and corners, diamonds, bow-knots and ribbons or garlands, urns, vases and floral bouquets, musical instruments, military trophies, grotesques and chinoiserie, figure studies of classical Greek art, and mythology, and typically English sea-weed marquetry. Regency motifs are also extremely popular, incorporating brass inlays in mahogany or rosewood backgrounds.

Inlay motifs are extensively used on period furniture and reproduction furniture, and by tradition, incorporate dyed green and dyed black veneers in their manufacture, also the techniques of sand shading, which attempt to give the illusion of depth.

As marquetry decoration is intended as a form of level surface decoration and should always remain subordinate to the panel it is decorating, very great skill in application is required.

A typical example of the practical use of a small paterae circle with sand shaded sections, would be to avoid having to make extremely complicated joints at the centre of a panel.

If you have to create a sixteen piece sunburst match, with those sixteen veneers coming together at the centre to form hairline points, it is far more simple to cut off those points and slide the sixteen veneers to form a perfect match ignoring the centre, and then cut in a small circular inlay motif, thus eliminating the problem and much tedious and painstaking work.

In fact, it is the hallmark of a true craftsman, when he creates a perfect sunburst match *without* incorporating an inlay!

Motifs are usually cut from 0.8mm or 0.9mm thick veneers and are supplied already toothed on the back ready for laying. The problem arises when they are used as part of a veneer assembly which may have been made from thinner veneers. Unless the motif was reduced in thickness to that of the surrounding veneers, blisters could result in the final pressing.

For this reason, it is usual for motifs to be inlaid as a separate operation. Pencil guidelines are drawn on the papered side of the motif and on the face veneer. Work around the edge of the motif with a sharp knife. The trick is to cut a hairline whisker off the edge of the motif as you cut into the background veneer, and by cutting them simultaneously you obtain a perfect fit.

Remove the portion of groundwork around the cut line on the inside, using a gouge, and then use a router to remove the rest. The overall depth removed should be less than the thickness of the motif which must stand proud of the surface.

The motif can be laid with a protective paper cover and hot caul, with local pressure from clamps, or in the veneer press.

An alternative method is to cut out the outline of the motif from the face veneer, and use the 'waste' piece of face veneer to mask the groundwork when applying the adhesive by pinning it in position.

The face assembly is positioned over the waste piece and taped to it, while being pressed. Afterwards, the waste piece which has no adhesive beneath it, will lift out easily, and the motif can be laid without risk of blisters, or having to rout the groundwork.

15

Marquetry

The fascination of marquetry has always appealed to veneer craftsmen and readers wishing to pursue the subject in depth are recommended to read *The Art & Practice of Marquetry* W. A. Lincoln (Thames & Hudson).

Marquetry is the assembly of wood veneers to form a picture or decorative pattern.

The thickness of the veneer to be cut has governed the type of tool used for cutting the woods; in America where the standard thickness of veneers is 1/28 inch (0.9mm), marquetry has developed as a fretsaw operation, while in Europe where 1/40 inch (0.7mm) thickness veneers are used, the cutting has been done by knife.

Today, on both sides of the Atlantic, the knife and the saw are used, as techniques have been developed to exploit the advantages of both methods.

The Design

There is no recipe for producing an artistic marquetry design; the talent of the designer is the decisive factor. Most craftsmen rely on prints, photographs, paintings, etc., and adapt them for marquetry.

Every line drawn on the design will eventually have to be cut, therefore the aim is to use great economy in drawing the cutting line, avoiding jagged lines and acute angles.

Wood can best express itself as wood; therefore wooden objects, such as half timbered houses, oak panelled interiors, boats, trees, windmills etc, make the best subjects. Whilst others include landscapes, seascapes, costume and drapery, still life, portraiture, animals and birds and so on.

Designs that are copies of existing work, such as paintings, photo-

A selection of inlay motifs.

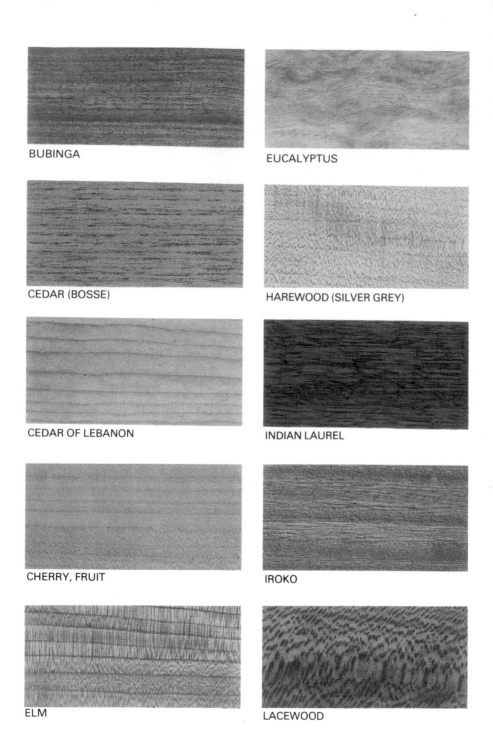

BUBINGA

EUCALYPTUS

CEDAR (BOSSE)

HAREWOOD (SILVER GREY)

CEDAR OF LEBANON

INDIAN LAUREL

CHERRY, FRUIT

IROKO

ELM

LACEWOOD

Wood Veneers.

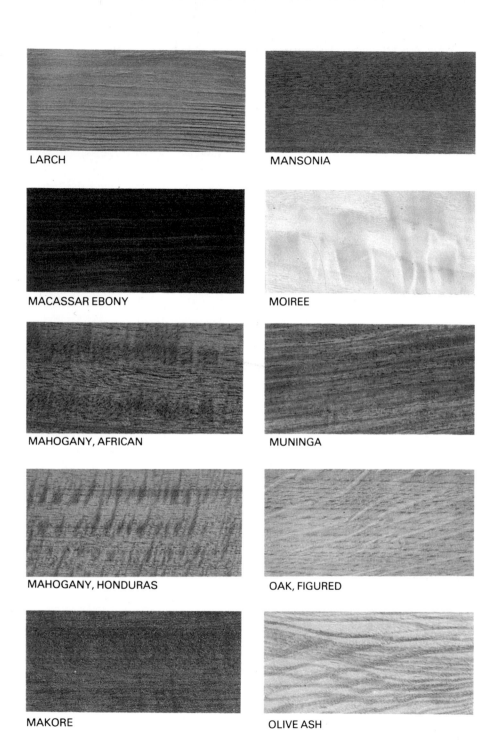

LARCH

MANSONIA

MACASSAR EBONY

MOIREE

MAHOGANY, AFRICAN

MUNINGA

MAHOGANY, HONDURAS

OAK, FIGURED

MAKORE

OLIVE ASH

Wood Veneers.

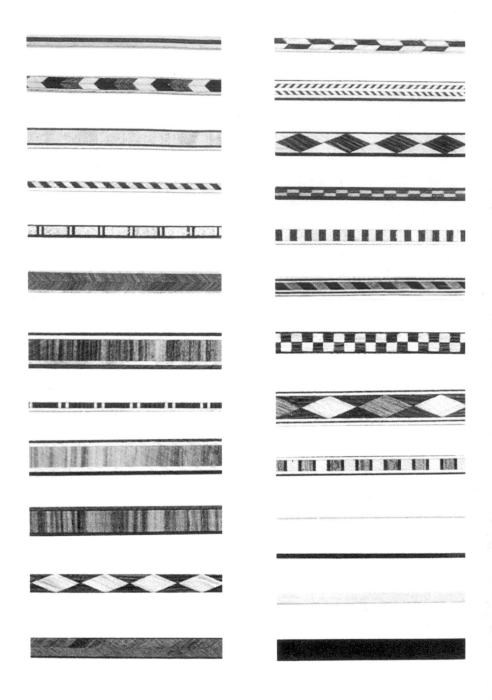

A selection of inlay bandings.

graphs, drawings etc., are produced in a number of different ways: direct tracing with tracing paper; carbon paper and stylus on to cartridge paper; frosted glass covered lightbox with holes ventilating the sides, the original is placed on top covered with tracing paper; projector: project a colour slide or black and white negative on to a screen and trace from the screen; photographic enlarger: put negative in holder and project the image on to a table and trace; pantograph: ideal for enlarging or reducing a print; squares grid: make a pencil grid of ¼ inch (6mm) squares over a protected original, and copy on to 1 inch (25mm) squares on cartridge paper; and photocopiers that have enlarging or reducing facilities.

Working in Reverse

The face side of the picture—the side visible when polished—is the underside when being cut and the side to be taped together, because the knife point ploughs a furrow in the veneer. It is necessary to reverse the design. There are three ways of doing this; firstly by making a tracing which can be seen from the back; secondly, by placing a plain sheet of paper beneath the design and a leaf of carbon paper beneath the lower sheet of plain paper, but with the carbon side *uppermost;* and thirdly, by making a pouncing (which is the traditional way) by inserting a needle in a cork and working over every inch of the design line pricking tiny holes as close together as you can. It is a tedious, time consuming job but well worth the effort. Roll up a felt pad and pounce black bitumen powder through the holes. Fix the powder by exposing the paper over a heat source. From the master pricking, you can make several original and reverse designs.

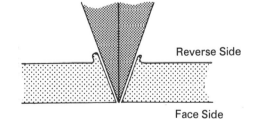

Fig. 171 The knife point causes "plough" on reverse side of veneer

Reverse Side

Face Side

FRETSAW CUTTING

The Double Cut

By this method, two contrasting veneers are cut simultaneously and the parts interchanged to provide two identical patterns; one with a light insert for the darker background, and a dark insert for the lighter background. Two contrasting veneers are selected with a third waste veneer placed underneath the two marquetry veneers, to take the swarf of the fretsaw. The grain direction of the waste veneer is opposite to that of the veneer above. The three veneers are slightly larger than needed for the required design, to provide a working margin. The design is glued to the top veneer and the complete 'sandwich' bound together with adhesive tape, or stapled through the working margin.

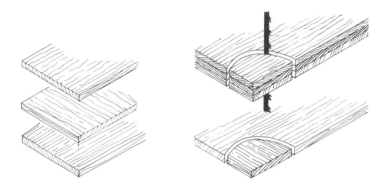

Fig. 172 The double cut on flat sawtable with robust saw. Sawcut visible

Large assemblies may be glued together with either scotch glue or PVA adhesive, and the sawn parts released later by the application of heat. Greaseproof paper or polythene may be included in the sandwich to make for easy separation later. A hole is pierced through the working margin and the fretsaw blade entered, with teeth pointing downwards from the top. The fretsaw is tightened using pliers if necessary.

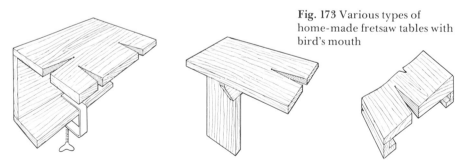

Fig. 173 Various types of home-made fretsaw tables with bird's mouth

Sawing is carried out on a bird's mouth V shaped fretsaw table, arranged horizontally, and the saw is held vertically. It is led up and down without pressure in smooth movements avoiding jerkiness. Wear a thimble to protect the forefinger of the other hand and use it to press the work downwards on to the sawtable at the point where the work is being fed to the teeth of the saw.

To turn the corners of the design, back out of the corner along the cut just made and approach the corner from the other direction. To prevent the design falling apart at an early stage of cutting, cut the small details or 'island' pieces first and work outwards towards the working margin. Hook up your apron under the sawtable to catch any tiny parts that may fall out during sawing. Lay the sawn parts out in trays until sawing is completed. When you are ready for the separation of the 3-ply sandwich parts, stand them on a hot plate for a few seconds and work between the layer with a flat kitchen knife. They will peel apart easily. Assemble them on to copies of the design and fasten them temporarily in position with balsa cement.

You now have two inlays, one light and one dark but identical in design. Cover the face sides with gummed veneering tape, or a sheet of kraft paper and when dry, turn both assemblies over with the open sawcut joins clearly visible, after discarding the design sheet.

These joins are now filled with either a matching wood stopping, or deliberately with a contrasting filler to the background colour when parts of the design need to be emphasised.

The back of the veneer assembly is cleaned of all glue and stopping traces, and smoothed perfectly flat ready for laying. The great advantage of this method for the beginner is the guarantee that all parts of the design will fit easily; the obvious disadvantage is that every part of the design has a sawcut space around it, either matched in or emphasised.

When these assemblies are to be laid on solid groundwork, both veneers in the design must be in the same grain direction as the groundwork, (but the waste veneer used to take the saw swarf would run in the opposite direction).

But when the assemblies are to be laid on veneer crossbandings the grain direction of the background must be opposite to the grain direction of the crossbanding. Note that fretsaw blades have rounded backs to enable you to rub the back of the saw against the cut just made when changing direction, prior to making a cut in the new direction.

The Bevel Cut

The next step is to create a marquetry assembly where the joins are as invisible as possible. The three layer sandwich is made as before, taking careful note of the grain direction required for the finished assembly.

The saw table is tilted, either to left or right by an amount which will compensate for the thickness of the fretsaw blade and also the thickness of the materials being cut.

The following range of fretsaw blades are the most popular for marquetry cutting and the 2/0 size is best for beginners to practise with. Use a simple protractor to get the angle of tilt approximately correct. Veneer saw blades have rounded backs and double teeth arranged in pairs with a tiny set.

Blade size	Thickness		Angle of tilt
2/0 coarse	.008 inch	(0.2mm)	14 degrees
4/0 medium	.0075 ,,	(0.19mm)	12 ,,
6/0 fine	.0066 ,,	(0.16mm)	10 ,,
8/0 very fine	.006 ,,	(0.15mm)	8 ,,

Only one inlay at a time can be produced by this method.

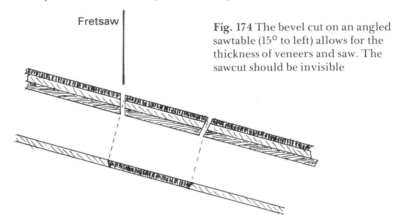

Fretsaw

Fig. 174 The bevel cut on an angled sawtable (15° to left) allows for the thickness of veneers and saw. The sawcut should be invisible

Feed direction and resulting shape

Table tilted to the left (left higher than right). If the work is fed in a clockwise direction towards the saw the shape will be smaller at the top than the bottom as in illustration Fig. 175 (a). If the work is fed anti-clockwise the shape will be wider at the top as in (b).

If the saw table is tilted upwards on the right hand side, and the work is fed towards the saw in a clockwise direction, the shape will be wider at the top (c) and an anti-clockwise feed direction results in a shape smaller at the top as in (d).

Therefore, this is put to advantage when using the bevel cut because sometimes you will require to let-in a piece from the botttom into an assembly, (for example when cutting a small piece into a picture) or you may wish to temporarily fasten an insert on top of an existing assembly and let it in from above.

As you see from the illustrations, you select the best angle of table tilt, and direction of feed, to suit your particular project.

In practice, a combination of the 'double-cut' and bevel-cut methods is used. A multi-layered sandwich of veneers is cut with a robust sawblade on the double-cut flat-bed saw table with the decorative motifs cut by this process fractionally oversize.

Fig. 175 The veneer is inserted into assembly according
to feed rotation and angle of saw table (N.B. *Scroll saw
bevel cutting* Dotted arrows show opposite rotation of
feed direction as the saw teeth point to the front, not the
back, as in fretsaw cutting)

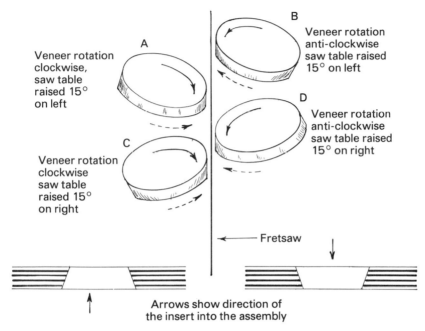

Arrows show direction of
the insert into the assembly

Then each motif, after separation, is laid and glued directly in
position on the base veneer with its underlying waste veneer, and
pressed until dry.

The work is then transferred to a bevel-cutting angled saw-table,
and using a fine sawblade, each motif is 'let-in' individually, into the
base veneer by sawing accurately to size on the required line.

This is exactly what led to the invention in France of the marquetry
'Donkey', which enabled the work to be gripped by foot pressure, and
the work held in a vertical position so that the sawdust did not obscure
the design line but fell away. It also left both hands free, one to turn the
work and change the feed direction, and by lateral side-play through a
toggle system on a rocker arm, bevel cutting was also possible.

The home-made swing-saw, or power fretsaw machine are both
excellent for bevel cutting. But there is one further complication for
craftsmen who possess a power scrollsaw, where the work has to be
pushed *away* from him and *into* the saw; the results show: a left hand
raised table and an anti-clockwise feed will produce (a); a clockwise
feed(b); with the right hand of the table raised an anti-clockwise feed
would produce (c) and a clockwise feed (d).

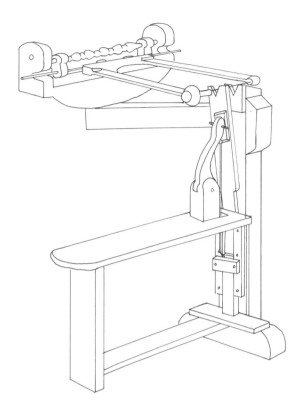

Fig. 176 The traditional marquetry cutter's "Donkey" or "French Horse"

Series cutting

This method calls for even more accuracy in cutting. Several copies of a line drawing are produced; some in reverse by the pouncing method, for the cut veneers to be assembled upon. Other copies of the design are cut up, one for every veneer and for every part of the design. These are gummed upon a pad of veneers up to a bundle in thickness. The pad of thirty-two veneers is compacted between thin plywood with the required design pasted on top, and the pad is nailed together through the oversized margin. The sawtable is kept flat and a robust blade may be used.

Sawing is carried out at 'half-mark', the sawyer aims to leave a hairline fraction of the needle sharp line barely visible on the insert veneer being cut. He cuts the inserts on the outside of the line and the background on the inside of the line.

In practice, many component parts of a design are cut by the series or double cut method to suit the design, and are let-in to the background by the bevel cut method. This permits the craftsman to deviate from accurate cutting without disastrous results.

The parts are kept in trays for final assembly on to a reverse design. When laid, the design will be uppermost and may be sanded off.

Marquetry pad method

The foregoing method requires very accurate cutting. This method enables the amateur craftsman to tackle making a marquetry picture or pattern, where the actual fretsaw cutting is relatively unimportant, and the saw could wander from the cutting line without serious consequences. By this method, in one single cutting operation, all parts will fit together perfectly.

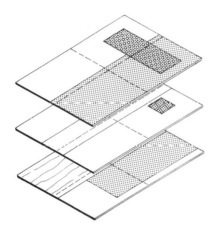

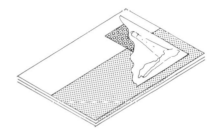

Fig. 177 The pad method. Veneers patched into alternate layers

Several leaves of waste veneer are prepared the full pattern size, with a generous margin around and with centre lines for accurate registration. The veneers are 'patched' into the waste veneers using a knife and straightedge in rectangular shapes ½ inch (12mm) larger in each direction than required for the picture part. These patches are made for every part of the picture in the correct grain direction, endeavouring to get as many as possible into each waster.

Because of the ½ inch (12mm) margin around each part, it is impossible to patch together two adjacent parts. Adjacent parts have to be positioned on other wasters to allow for the overlap.

The complete design is pasted on top of the sandwich, with a thin piece of plywood underneath to take the saw swarf. The pack is compacted, nailed through the margin and fretsawn. If the pack is too large for the fretsaw frame, it may be cut in half. The interchanged veneers will produce only one perfect picture.

A

B

C

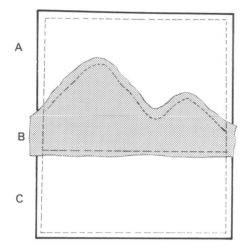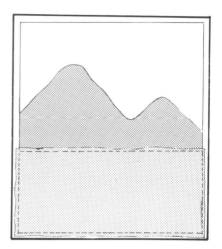

Fig. 178 The overlap method

KNIFE CUTTING
Overlap method
The design outline is traced on to the selected veneer and placed on the cutting board. Where veneer (a) will join veneer (b) a surplus of about ¼ inch (6mm) is left on veneer (a).

The next section of the design is traced to veneer (b) which is then cut exactly on the line where it will meet veneer (a) but with a surplus of ¼ inch (6mm) where it will meet veneer (c).

Veneer (b) is laid in its exact position overlapping veneer (a). Now following the contour of the edge of veneer (b) it is used as a templet to cut through the surplus of veneer (a) which is then discarded. Similarly, when veneer (c) is cut to size it is laid overlapping the surplus of veneer (b) and used as a templet to cut veneer (b) to fit. This is the basis of most marquetry kit sets. As each part of the picture is cut, it is then glued directly to the baseboard groundwork.

The window method
The name derives from the simple process of cutting a hole or 'window' in a soft waste veneer which then acts as a templet for cutting the veneer required to fill it. It is the method recommended and taught by the Marquetry Society.

The advantages of this method are:
(a) the effect of each piece of veneer on the picture can be seen before it is cut;
(b) several alternatives can be offered to the 'window' and tested for suitability;

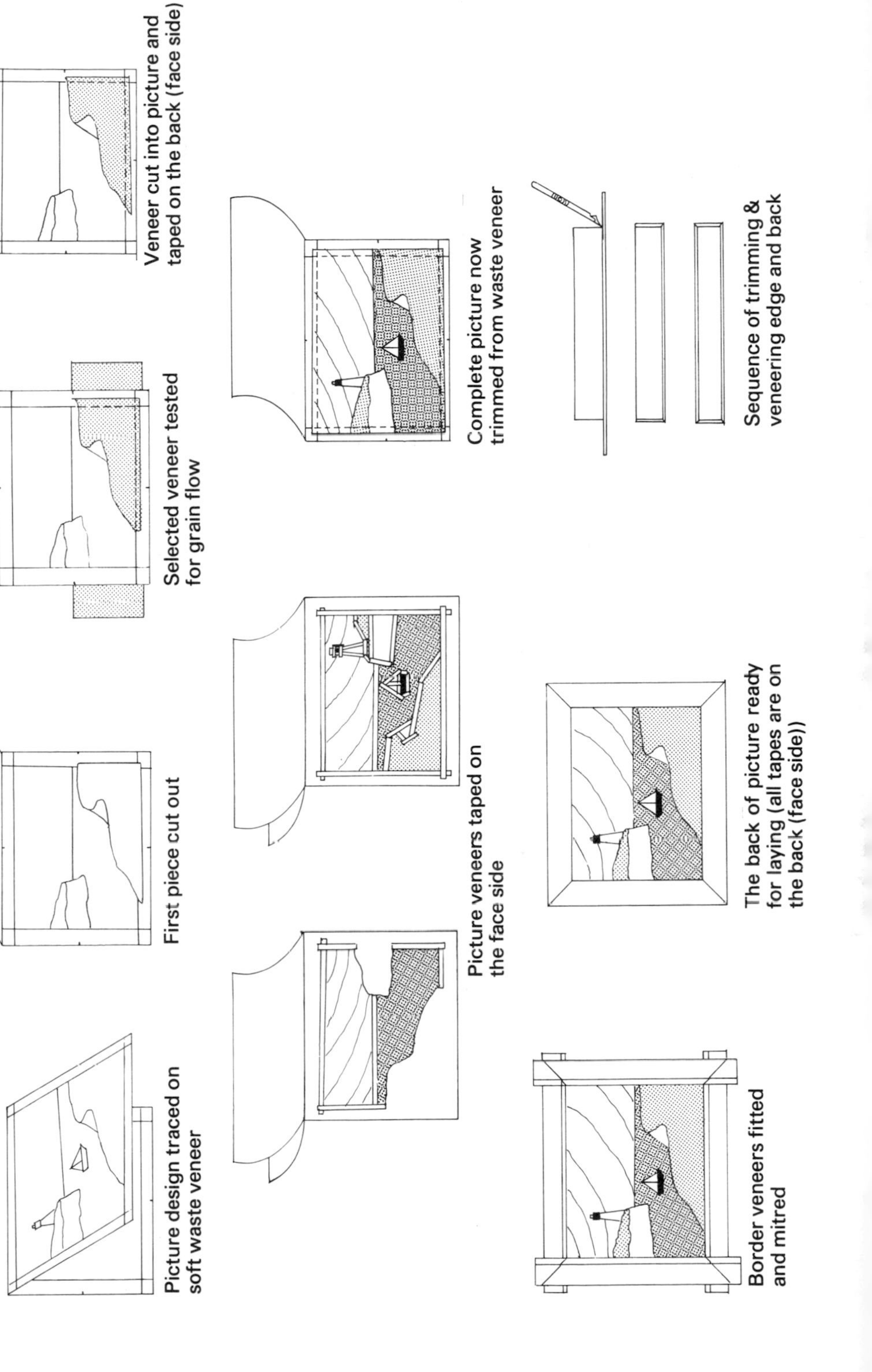

Fig. 179 Illustrating the window method

Picture design traced on soft waste veneer

First piece cut out

Selected veneer tested for grain flow

Veneer cut into picture and taped on the back (face side)

Picture veneers taped on the face side

Complete picture now trimmed from waste veneer

Sequence of trimming & veneering edge and back

Border veneers fitted and mitred

The back of picture ready for laying (all tapes are on the back (face side))

Fig. 180 Fasten the design on to the veneer

Fig. 181 Trace through the design, using carbon paper

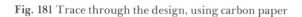

(c) each piece of veneer is cut from its mating veneer shapes and not from a design line;

(d) despite inaccuracies of cutting to the original design line the veneer parts will fit accurately;

(e) as the picture develops, modifications can be made to the design to suit the freak figure of the veneers as the overall effect of the composition emerges;

(f) for pictures with a predominating background comprising only one or two veneers, it is easier to use these actual veneers as the waster, and cut the picture directly into the background.

Procedure

The required design is taped to the top edge of a soft veneer waster and pencil centre lines are traced to ensure alignment. This waster will eventually be cut away and discarded and replaced by parts of the picture.

Next, trace the first part to be cut. Concentrate only on the largest pieces ignoring all medium and small details.

Remove to cutting board and cut out the first shape overlapping into the surrounding border margin. Place selected veneer beneath the 'window aperture' and manoeuvre to test for best grain flow direction. Fasten temporarily in position with Sellotape.

Mark the shape to be cut out on the required veneer by running the knifepoint around the edge of the window, using it as a templet.

Tilt the knife handle inwards so that the tip of the knife blade scores right into the corner and does not cut undersize due to the knife bevel. Remove the veneer to the cutting board and this time hold the knife so that the bevel of the blade is vertical. Rub white PVA adhesive around the edge of the veneer and insert into the window aperture. Leave under a weight, covered with a sheet of polythene, until the glue has set.

Repeat this process, and cut all the main background components of the subject into the frame of the waste veneer. Next, cut in the medium sized pieces, and finally the small details. Check if the picture is satisfactory and if not, modify it by rejecting offending pieces and cut in their replacements while the picture is in the 'veneer assembly' state.

The unwanted waste veneer is now trimmed off and discarded. Four narrow 'fillet border' inlay lines are fitted around the picture, overlapping at each corner, followed by four chosen border mount veneers.

Using a straightedge and craftknife, these borders and fillet veneers are mitred by cutting inwards towards the picture. If the direction of cut was outwards the border veneers might split.

The face side of the picture (the underneath—as all the work was

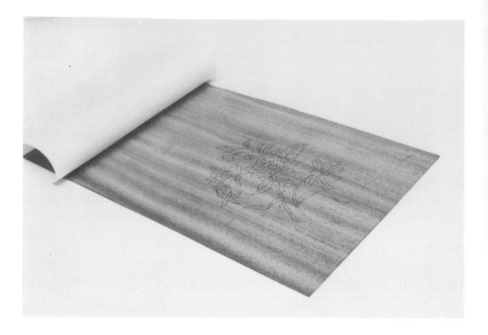

Fig. 182 The design outline ready for cutting

Fig. 183 Cutting the "window" in the largest sections first, tilting the knife handle inwards

done on the back of the picture in reverse) and the border joints are now protected with gummed veneer tape ready for laying.

Combination Methods

The window method also permits using combinations of all the other methods. For example, once the major parts have been cut into the waster, medium and small detail may be let-in by the bevel cut fretsaw method by placing the required piece on top of the waster and transferring the work to the fretsaw table. A jeweller's metal cutting piercing saw blade of about eight thousandth's of an inch wide is used for this work making almost invisible joints.

Progressive designs

For simplicity of working, it is possible to produce a series of progressive design overlays. The first overlay design would feature only the main parts of the picture. The second overlay would be placed in register, and used to cut in the medium and small parts. A third overlay in register, would contain minor tiny parts. A fourth might detail all parts to be sand shaded, and a fifth would contain those parts requiring fragmentation or mosaic techniques, where the small 'window' is simply filled with veneer fragments.

SHADING VENEERS

Sand shading

Most traditional veneer motifs are sand shaded to create three dimensional realism. The roundness of columns; folds in costume drapery, and in portraiture etc., and also in traditional motifs such as shells, oval patterae, urns, ribbons, figure studies, all benefit from sand shading treatment.

Its application is an aesthetic one, calling for personal judgment by the craftsman and successfully shaded work is one which does not appear to have been shaded at all.

Subtle tones which blend, merge and fade into natural wood tones are better than scorched, dark contrasting tones.

Clean, sharp-edged silver sand from the pet shop is ideal for the purpose. Pour about one inch depth (25mm) into a flat bottomed baking dish and heat over a gas ring or electric hotplate; regulate the heat down to a steady constant heat at a temperature which provides working comfort.

The veneer should not burst into flames even if left in the hot sand for a few minutes. In about ten seconds the surface above the sand on a scrap of veneer inserted on edge, should be unchanged, but with a gradual tonal change through the veneer in the sand without the bottom turning black by carbonization. That would be about right. The length of time the veneer must remain in the sand can be determined by constructing a tonal scale chart with the veneer you plan to use.

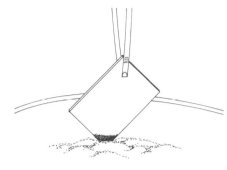

Fig. 184 Sand-shading veneers
in hot sand

Regulate the heat and using tweezers insert scraps of veneer on edge and count 5, 7, 10 and 12 seconds etc. As you remove each in turn from the sand, mark it and glue it to a tonal chart for easy reference. Don't leave veneers in the sand in the hope that a guess will result in the required shade. The golden rule is, it is better to increase the heat than the length of time. Also never leave the base of the veneer touching the base of the tray as it will almost certainly scorch.

The moisture content of the veneer is being lost while the scrap is in the sand; the quicker you can restore the moisture the better, so, immediately upon taking it out of the hot sand, damp with a sponge, wrap in clean paper and place under a weight to normalise.

The angle of entry governs the pattern of shading on the leaf. If a veneer was inserted vertically, there would be a marked tonal gradation; if the leaf was laid in horizontally the whole leaf would attain a uniform shade.

The height of sand is another variable. Half an inch of sand will darken the veneer much more quickly than a heaped up mound two inches (50mm) high where the top of the mould would not be so hot and would provide a tonal range.

A veneer may be masked, and sand poured over the veneer (and tossed back into the tray). This is repeated until the desired shape of shading around the mask is attained, then the mask is removed.

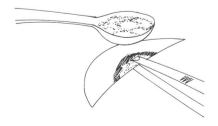

Fig. 185 Sand-shading veneer by
pouring on hot sand

Remember to mask *both* sides of the leaf, to allow for the assembly to be in reverse when assembled and turned over for laying on the face side.

Another method is to shade a leaf of veneer to different depths of shade around the edges, and to select the best for the job.

To decide if the tone is correct, you have to allow for surface charring. First lightly sandpaper the surface and then dampen it; this will remove any surface darkening and also restore the moisture and approximate to what the polished appearance would be.

The fact that the surface appears to be darker than the interior of the veneer is a good fault, as most people tend to over shade.

Dark woods always shade quicker and darker than light woods, which is why sycamore, holly, horse chestnut, birch and boxwood are the woods usually used for this purpose.

Pyrographic shading

Pyrographic pens are used to shade finished veneer panels. Using points which are interchangeable, a background 'flame wash' technique is sometimes used to darken a complete area, and this surface is either scraped away with fine pointed engraving tools or darker lines are etched in with heated pyrographic pens.

Although completely etched pictures can be made by this process, we are only concerned here with the pyrographic application on veneered panels.

Chemical Shading

Lapis infernalis—silver nitrate, is also used for shading. The silver nitrate is prepared in several dilutions with distilled water, and the required strength is brushed on the finished veneer part. It takes a little time for the water borne chemical to diffuse into the veneer; the effect is slow to appear, but when applied to marquetry floral subjects some exquisite results have been obtained.

OTHER MATERIALS

Many other materials are utilised by veneer craftsmen when creating traditional marquetry assemblies using fretsaw or power scrollsaw techniques. Tortoise-shell, mother of pearl, ivory, bone, celluloid, plastic, and a wide range of sheet metals such as pewter, copper, brass, silver, aluminium etc, are among the most popular.

Test the suitability of sheet metal by bending over a corner of the sheet: if it is soft it will stay bent; if it is very hard to bend up, the metal is 'half hard' and could be annealed; and if it refuses to bend at all, it is too hard.

Metal can be annealed by coating with soap on one side and heating over a flame; watch the soap turn brown and start to sizzle, then allow the metal to cool in the air; do not quench with water or oil. Use 20 swg

(0.914mm) with 1/40 inch (0.7mm) veneers or 18 swg (1.219mm) with 1/28 inch (0.9mm) veneers.

The Regency period used brass inlays into rosewood and mahogany furniture; and the famous Boulle work of Louis XIV period was cut from tortoise-shell and brass.

16

Parquetry

P ARQUETRY is the cutting and assembly of wood veneers to form a
geometric mosaic, and has a mathematical basis, being governed
by the laws of symmetry.

The veneers used are chosen for different reasons than those
selected for marquetry. For parquetry we need either plain veneers, or
narrow striped woods with parallel grain.

The tools required are a knife and straightedge, a drawing board,
tee-square and set squares, compass, a protractor, and a scale ruler.

Most parquetry craftsmen prepare a cutting board about 24 inches ×
18 inches (609 × 457mm) with a fence-stop about ⅛ inch (3mm) thick
screwed to the top edge, with spacers cut from hardboard. (See sketch)

Checkerboards

The very simplest form of checkerboard is the familiar chessboard
where two contrasting veneers such as walnut and sycamore are cut
into strips of each colour, and taped together in alternate rows. The
assembly is then turned through 90 degrees and cut across into eight
more strips of exactly the same width.

Alternate rows are advanced one square, and the assembly is again
taped together. The odd protruding squares are severed (as shown in
Figs. 161-166) and discarded to complete the chessboard pattern.

From this simple start a great many variations can be made. For
example, the veneers may be all of one kind but the pattern achieved
by alternating the grain direction which may run parallel to alternate
pairs of sides, or to alternate diagonals.

The strips may be formed from three or four colours; or a third
series of cuts can be made through the taped assembly to produce three
directional checkers comprising triangles.

Diamond cutting

There are basically two types of parquetry diamonds; the first in which the grain direction runs along the axis of the diamond in one piece and at right angles to it on the adjacent diamond; the second type contrives to bring the grain direction parallel with the left-upper and right-lower sides of a vertical diamond, and alternating in adjacent diamonds, to run in the opposite direction.

Quarter cut woods such as sapele, with an interlocked grain are best for this purpose, and also benefit from the effect of light refraction when the resulting parquetry is polished.

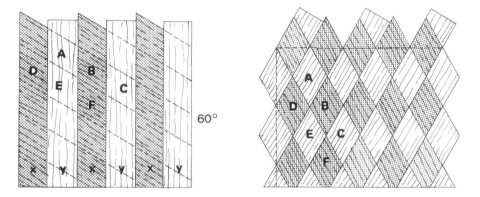

Fig. 186 How alternating grain diagonal diamond parquetry is cut

Diagonal diamonds

Cut a straight grained leaf of sapele veneer into 1½ inch (38mm) strips with the grain parallel to the edges of the strips. Cut another leaf into strips of exactly the same width (x) but this time cut diagonally across the grain at 60 degrees from the vertical (y).

Compress both sets of strips between battens and plane them accurately to a precise width. Assemble the strips alternately and tape them together.

Now cut across this taped assembly at 60 degrees from the vertical (y) into strips of the same width. Note the position of the rhomboidal shapes A, B and C in relation to D, E and F. The strip containing D, E and F is moved downwards one space to align with A, B and C.

Tape the assembly together again. Trim off square, by placing the straightedge along the tips of the first row of diamonds, and removing the surplus odd shapes, to reveal a completed parquetry pattern of alternating diamonds.

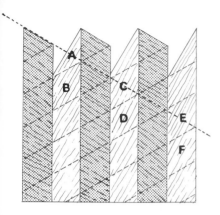

Fig. 187 How right angled diamond parquetry is cut

Right angled diamonds

The procedure is similar, except that the first set of strips are cut at 30 degrees to the vertical (instead of parallel to the grain), and the second set of strips at 60 degrees as before. The alternate strips are taped together. The assembly is cut at an angle of 60 degrees to the vertical, as before, into strips of the same width.

When these strips are moved forward by one space, the pattern will reveal diamonds with alternating grain direction in vertical and horizontal directions in adjacent diamonds.

Multiple cutting

By cutting through the assembly again, this time cutting the diamonds in half along one of the diagonals, and moving the strips forward one space, a multiplicity of geometric designs is possible.

Regular polygons

In any design where a regular polygon is required as the pattern, all the angles must be multiples of an angle which is itself a multiple of 180 degrees, which is referred to as the *modulus*.

The angles used are: for hexagons 60 degrees, octagons 45 degrees and 90 degrees; pentagons and decagons 36 degrees and 72 degrees; dodecagons 30 degrees, 60 degrees and 90 degrees; diamonds are always referred to by the smaller of the two supplementary angles they contain, ie, a 60 degree diamond is the same as a 120 degree. Any combination of angles can therefore be used, provided that they are compatible with each other, for example, 40 degree and 50 degree diamonds could be substituted for 45 degree diamonds, and would produce an eight sided symmetrical *irregular* polygon.

Hexagons cannot be mixed with octagons as they are incompatible, or pentagons with either. But squares can mix with both octagons and dodecagons because 90 degrees comprises both 30 degree and 45 degree multiples. Therefore any angle such as 27 degrees and 63 degrees will combine to make 90 degrees and will produce an irregular polygon.

Hexagons

This is the simplest pattern to produce with a modulus of 60 degrees. A 60 degree diamond may be cut in half, and remain both equilateral and also equiangular; three such diamonds combine to produce a hexagon.

Draw a horizontal line and divide it into any convenient number of parts to suit your project. Now draw two series of parallel lines at 60 degrees and at 120 degrees, and where these intersect, draw more horizontal lines until you have constructed a grid of equilateral triangles. Any two adjacent triangles make a diamond and any six meeting at a vertex make a hexagon.

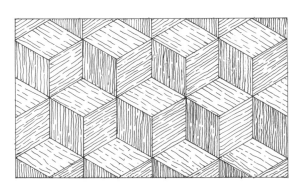

Fig. 188 Louis cube parquetry assembled from diamonds

Louis cube parquetry

Hexagons formed in this way form the famous optical illusion of 'reversing cubes' so popular in the Louis periods of French furniture, and utilises three different veneers to achieve its effect.

When any regular polygon has diamonds forming its side, it is described as a '2nd Order, or 3rd Order' polygon depending on the number of lengths of diamonds forming the side.

Interchanging Orders

A decagon, like the dodecagon (but unlike the octagon) can be expanded to the next higher order; five diamonds can be exchanged for two pentagons and one diamond without disturbing the pattern. Ten pentagons side by side will enclose a decagon. But pentagons cannot be built up by using diamonds alone, but may be built up by incorporating pentagons of a lower order.

A pentagon is constructed from one and a half 72 degree diamonds and half a 36 degree diamond! By substituting pentagons in pairs, for the equivalent number of diamonds the scope of design is greatly increased.

SYMMETRY

Parquetry is the science of transformation geometry and means that the pattern repeats itself in both directions at regular intervals.

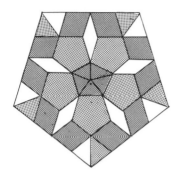

Fig. 189 Pentagon (4th order)

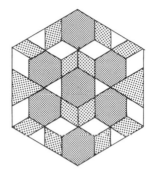

Fig. 190 Hexagon (4th order)

Symmetry can be described as rotational when the pattern matches in several places around a central pivot; radial symmetry is where the pattern matches like the spokes of a wheel.

A 'Catherine Wheel' pattern has rotational but not radial symmetry as the spiral curve meets at a vertex.

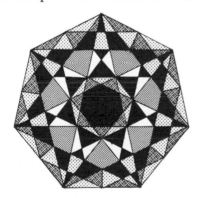

Fig. 191 Septagon (2nd order)

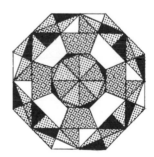

Fig. 192 Octagon (2nd order)

If the pattern can be moved in either vertical or horizontal directions and the pattern co-incides at regular intervals it has bi-directional symmetry; if in only one direction it is linear symmetry (as in the case of bandings).

In a two piece match the centre line is the axis of symmetry if both halves are mirror images. In the case of a four piece match (or an

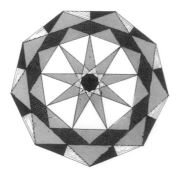

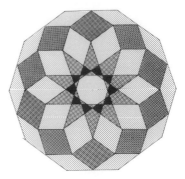

Fig. 193 Nonagon (2nd order)   **Fig. 194** Decagon (2nd order)

ellipse) it has two axes of symmetry. Shapes such as pentagons have five, hexagons have six and octagons eight etc. In parquetry therefore, any *pattern* without rotational symmetry must have at least *two* axes of symmetry and the veneers themselves must have rotational symmetry in colour selection.

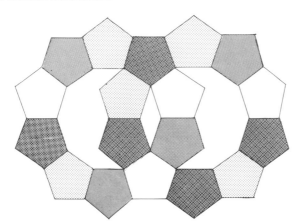

Fig. 195 Overlapped pentagons formed around centre diamond

SPECIAL CUTTING BOARDS

In the case of chessboards, and diamond parquetry cut from strips as previously described, the errors in cutting are self cancelling. An 89 degree cut would leave a 91 degree strip adjacent to it. But when parquetry cutting progresses beyond 'strip cutting', to individual shaped diamonds, a special cutting board is made by positioning hardboard stops in pairs, using contact adhesive. A steel straightedge can be lined up against the stops and this permits the accurate cutting of parquetry shapes.

A sheet of self adhesive plastic sheet is a useful aid, and the diamonds can be assembled directly to it.

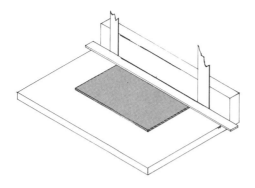

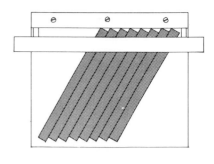

Fig. 196 Stripcutting board   **Fig. 197** Diamond cutting board

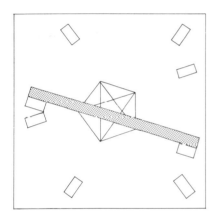

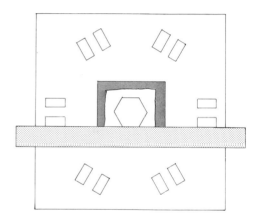

Fig. 198 Pentagon cutting board   **Fig. 199** Hexagon cutting board

VENEER MOSAIC DECORATION

As we have seen, parquetry decoration is a very accurate, precise, mathematical skill with its own laws. Far greater freedom of expression can be enjoyed with the much more ancient veneer mosaic art form.

The width of the visible glueline between the joints in parquetry or marquetry, is next to zero; the cutting of every joint critically accurate. But in veneer mosaic, each individual piece (known as tessera) is an irregular shape, conforming to no law of symmetry or mathematics, and the joints between the tesserae are wide and visible—in fact are emphasised to form an integral part of the overall design.

Veneers may be used for veneer mosaic in various ways. Firstly, by laminating into thin 3-ply, colourful veneer offcuts, and sawing them into irregular tesserae. Secondly, by cutting veneers into square, or triangular shapes on a cutting board into 18 inch (457mm) lengths, and then snipping them with scissors into triangular or irregular shapes to suit a design plan as work proceeds. Thirdly, produce a range of colourful 'spills' about 9 inches (228mm) long and of various widths.

Have a grid of squares superimposed over the required design, and brush with adhesive. Lay the end of the selected spill on the design square and snip off the end with a sharp knife.

It is important to turn the grain of the tesserae in all directions as they are laid.

There are two ways of creating veneer mosaic pictorial effects. The first is to lay the tesserae in straight rows in both vertical and horizontal directions to form the background; but to use much more colourful tesserae in swirling contours in the subject of the picture to make the central motif pronounced.

The other technique arranges for the background pattern to flow outwards in swirling lines from the central motif to the edges, with a darker or lighter central subject motif.

There is also an element of symbolism in the use of tesserae. Triangular shapes depict grass; rectangular shapes create the impression of placid water etc. The technique makes possible some very modern decorative motifs and murals.

OYSTER PARQUETRY
One of the most attractive and peculiarly English forms of traditional parquetry veneering is known as oyster parquetry.

It is created from sawcut veneers, cut from small limbs of trees of such small girth or irregular bole, that they are unsuitable for commercial conversion into decorative veneers.

Oyster veneers are cut from green timber, or timber that has been steamed or boiled in a vat. Avoid timbers which suffer from drying stress which could contribute to splitting or distortion.

Wet veneer oysters are more easily controlled during the drying process than partially dried timber. This is very important because oyster veneers have a differential growth both tangential and radial in each oyster.

The limb is sawn at about 65 degrees tangentially to the pith of the log producing an oval veneer with a sloping grain, (which is less likely to lift when laid, than had it been cut at 90 degrees to produce a circular shape) and the decorative pattern of heart and sapwood becomes a stronger feature.

The green oysters should be laid up in small piles with each oyster separated by strips of wood, to allow a free circulation of warm dry air around each piece, and the pile weighted down to prevent warping tendencies.

The sticks used as separators should be about ¼ inch (6mm) thick, and aligned carefully above each other. They will dry out reasonably quickly, but some species tend to split from the pith. Put a couple of thicker oysters as 'controls' on top of each free standing pile. If these start to split, use a fine gardening spray to damp down the pile and slow down the drying process.

When dry, the oysters are trimmed into elongated polygons, which are jointed together to form the very distinctive oyster parquetry, sized on the back and covered with paper on the face side.

This was used in the past either to form decorative border surrounds to a panel, or to form the centrepiece of a panel.

In some beautiful examples, oystering was used to completely cover matched doors in pairs.

They are always laid with caul pressure.

Woods for Oyster Parquetry

Local grown woods are ideal, providing you avoid woods with a large ray figure which split out during drying.

Oak, sweet chestnut, beech, plane, mulberry, elm, etc. should be avoided. Walnut, olivewood, lignum vitae, blackthorn and kingwood are excellent. The garden lilac tree can produce a veneer similar to tulipwood with yellow and salmon red bands. Laburnum's greenish brown colour background, with wavy concentric lines of light coloured parenchyma makes a very attractive oyster veneer.

Similar growth, although tougher in texture, is found in robinia or false acacia; privet, peartree, whitebeam and even the rowan tree has interesting growth patterns.

There is one very important consideration when using sawn oyster veneers. The saw teeth cause teeth marks to appear on the veneer surface and may obliterate the true grain and figure. It should be planed on one side with a finely set toothing plane. If laid in the glueline without this precaution, the sawmarks will telegraph through to the smooth polished surface as the action of the adhesive will pull the wood down and repeat the uneven sawmarks on the surface.

Sawcut oysters have their compensations, they are easier to finish off with a smoothing plane or power sander without the attendant risks of rubbing through, a risk ever present with knife cut veneers.

17

Edge Lippings and Facings

THE end grain of plywood, laminated boards and solid core stocks may be veneered with veneers to match the face veneer. However; experience has shown that these edges suffer damage from chipping or delamination, especially if they are working edges.

It is preferable to cover the edges of panels with a solid hardwood strip. Wherever possible the edge lipping should match the decorative face veneer, but this is seldom practicable on highly decorative panels or those using rare or exotic veneers.

It is accepted trade practice to substitute a moderately priced or more readily available hardwood lipping of similar colour tone and any slight colour variation adjusted during the polishing stage; e.g. mahogany is used on rosewood panels, ramin on satinwood, etc.

The edge lippings of working edges such as the front edge of lids, closing edges of drawers, meeting edges of doors, etc., should always be lipped. The hardwood strip used, should be wide enough to allow for shaping to suit the needs of the project, such as rounding, bevelling, chamfering, fluting or reeding.

Lippings can be applied before or after veneering and there are advantages in both methods. Modern adhesives combined with the use of radio frequency techniques are widely used in commercial veneering plants, but the home craftsman relies on either tonguing and grooving or more commonly, pinning and gluing.

The advantage of lipping before decorative veneers are laid, is that the face veneers will completely cover the lipping and enable the exact matching of one panel with the next—without the thickness of the two lippings spoiling the aesthetic effect—as for example in a herringbone

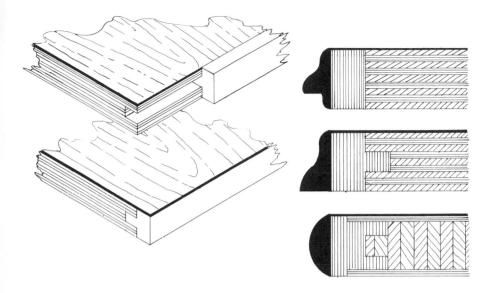

Fig. 200 Edge lipping applied before or after veneering (examples of moulded lipping shown in black profile)

matched pair of doors. It is also cheaper to apply lippings before veneering in that substitute timbers may be used. The finished effect is that of a solid panel.

The advantage of lipping *after* veneering, is that special effects are obtainable: for example, picture frame moulding formed by the lipping. Also, many lippings are utilised in furniture manufacture to form the handles for opening doors and drawers, while preserving a flush appearance. There is another definite advantage in that the possibility of the lipping telegraphing through to spoil the face veneer is eliminated.

This can result in two ways. If the lipping is not sanded perfectly flat with the panel before veneering, or if there is a differential in movement between the corestock and the lipping due to moisture content variance.

To prevent this, apply edge lippings with a radial face next to the core edge of the panel, to ensure that any minor shrinkage takes place in the thickness of the lipping and not in its width, which would affect both face and backing veneers.

The lippings or facings should be brought into the overall planned decorative scheme, either in contrast to, or in harmony with, the face veneers when the lippings are applied after veneering.

The Visible Edge

Which edge masters the other is important in edge veneering and even more so when lippings are applied.

When veneering a rectangular panel for example, you have to decide whether you want the end of the top veneer edging to be concealed by the side veneer edging—which will itself remain visible when viewed from *above*—or whether the top edge should overlap the side edge and remain visible when viewed from the *side*.

The sequence of applying the edgings is therefore important and is determined from the most usual viewing angle of the project. For example, a wall panel will be looked at from the front and therefore the face veneer or surround will conceal all edges, but the two side veneers would remain visible from the top or bottom.

When meeting a curved corner, always veneer the curve first before the flat surface, as it is easier to finish off the trimming on the flat surface after laying.

Lippings applied before veneering, may be butt jointed, pinned and glued, but lippings applied after veneering should be mitred at the corners. If the lipping is to be further worked after veneering, it should be sufficiently wide in section to permit shaping, rounding, bevelling, chamfering, fluting, reeding etc.

Circular Edges

These are often veneered with the grain of the face veneer in a vertical direction. The short length veneers are cut from the end of a bundle to produce consecutive matching leaves. Compress the bundle and shoot the edges between battens for jointing. Carefully butt them together on a sheet of paper brushed with glue, until sufficient pieces have been assembled to encircle the top.

Avoid finishing with half a width. It is better to reduce all the leaves a fraction, so that the final joint requires just a shave.

Remember to avoid the pattern jump on figured veneers, by temporarily pinning the veneers, paper side outwards, around one half of the circular top, and the other half of the veneers should be assembled in reverse order as in making sunburst assemblies. For example, if thirty-two pieces were to be used for the edge, you could make four strips of jointed veneers which would have this sequence: 1 to 8, 17 to 24, 32 to 25, 16 to 9 and No. 9 would be jointed to No. 1. This has equalised the pattern jump in units of eight.

The edging may be applied with contact adhesive or with cold resin glue, by wrapping around a webbing or leather belt or band caul, and tightening at the buckle. Webbing may be dampened and placed near to a source of heat which will speed the drying and cause the webbing to shrink.

If the edge is to be hammered, lay each piece individually and scrape off the glue squeeze-out from the mating edge as the next piece is laid.

Lacing

Another method of veneering the edge of a circular top is to cut two circles of plywood smaller in diameter than the tabletop. Fasten one to each side of the top with handscrews, taking care to protect the face of the top with felt or baize if the edging is applied afterwards — although it is usual to veneer the edge first.

Drive in a row of screws with their heads projecting, about 1 inch (25mm) apart all around the shaped plywood panels. If you use ¾ inch (19mm) ply, use 1 inch (25mm) screws and leave ½ inch (12mm) projecting to avoid the risk of penetrating through the plywood.

After applying the veneers to the edge, covered with a yielding wad of felt, lace the edge tightly using nylon cord, by wrapping it around a screwhead on the top, around the edge and around a screwhead below, alternately over and under the table top around the screwheads.

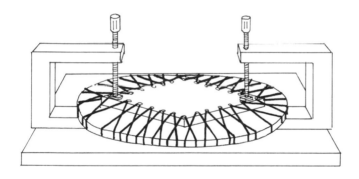

Fig. 201 How to lace the edge veneers on a circular panel

Bevelled Edges

Avoid cutting a bevelled edge to a point, as this will suffer wear and tear in usage. Veneer the four edges in the usual way as a first operation, and then cut the bevel to the four edges, leaving about ⅛ inch to 3⁄16 inch (3 to 4mm) of the original veneered edge showing, before commencing the bevel and this will take the rough handling.

Matching Sets

When making a cabinet or unit where the drawers, apron and edges are to have the appearance as though from one matched veneer leaf, it is important to make up the veneer match to the *overall dimensions*, and then carefully mark and cut every piece separately, and clearly number each piece in sequence to a master pattern.

THE SCRATCH STOCK

The lipping applied after veneering, which requires to be shaped, is usually moulded with a home made tool—the scratch stock. It comprises 2 pieces of hardwood about ¾ inch (19mm) thick, about 3 inches (76mm) wide and 6 inches (152mm) long. It is notched to form a handle and there are wing nuts or screws to tighten the two halves.

The tool holds cutters, filed up from old hacksaw blades, which are inserted and tightened. The notch runs along the side of the panel, and the cutter is worked backwards and forwards scraping away the wood, until the required depth of pattern is achieved.

Of course, this traditional home made tool has been replaced with the modern router plane, but the scratch stock is still found in the majority of veneer workshops.

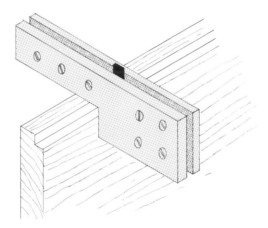

Fig. 202 A home made scratch stock rebating an edge for inlaying

When the cutter is set near the notch, it is used for shaping edge lippings. The cutter can be set further out for scratching grooves suitable for inlaying stringings, lines or bandings. It ceases to cut when the required depth is reached, and when used for inlays, the depth of groove has to be slightly less than the thickness of the inlay, so that it stands proud of the surface for finishing. Also, the inlay would not receive pressure when laying if the groove was too deep, and the glue would not hold.

A different type of scratch stock is required for cutting around curves or corners. The notch has to be rounded, so that only one point is in touch with the work, especially in hollow shapes.

When working with the grain, no problems are encountered, but when cutting across the grain in some woods, splintering could result. To avoid this, use the cutting gauge first to cut both sides of the groove, and the scratch stock to remove the wood across the grain.

Do not overrun the corners. Stop short of the corner and finish off with a chisel to cut the sides and finish off with the scratch. Always keep the scratch stock upright and do not tilt it when in use.

Tapered Legs

To inlay lines on tapering legs, a veneering box is made with a movable plate at one end. The leg surface to be inlaid is kept parallel to the sides of the box. The scratch stock is then guided by the edge of the box, to cut the grooves into the tapering legs.

Fig. 203 Box used for inlaying tapered legs, held parallel to sides

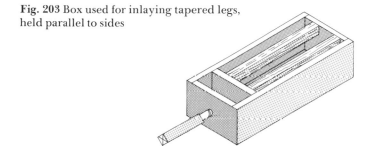

18

Laying Flat Panels

PREPARATION is perhaps the most crucial of all the sequences in the veneering process. If the preparation has been thorough, the laying techniques are straightforward and should be trouble free.

The veneers should be perfectly flat and if in the form of veneer matches, taped ready for laying. Most will have been given the flatting treatment previously described.

For the purposes of laying veneers, we regard the veneers as single 'lay-ons', even if jointed and taped into a veneer matched assembly.

The groundwork should be perfectly flat and true. It will have been carefully toothed with the toothing plane or scored with the teeth of a dovetail or tenon saw, worked diagonally across the panel from corner to corner. And any absence of teeth or saw marks on the surface would indicate a depression on the surface and the surrounding area will require levelling.

Different types of groundwork will naturally absorb adhesive in varying degrees and in general, wooden groundworks such as laminated boards with outer veneer casings, corestock with cross-bandings, plywood, etc., should be toothed and then sized with a coating of scotch glue diluted with water nine parts to one of glue. It is applied hot with a brush and allowed to dry out thoroughly during which time no dust or shavings are allowed to settle on the surface. When dry, rub the surface with coarse glasspaper to remove any tiny splinters or roughness of the keyed surface and brush with a soft brush or vacuum clean. The sizing will partially fill the pores of the woodwork and prevent undue suction from the bond.

Harder, impervious surfaces such as chipboard, tempered hardboard etc., do not require sizing. But the surface should be roughened with coarse sanding before applying the adhesive, except in the case of contact adhesion, in which the surface can remain as smooth as possible without keying to aid specific adhesion.

HAMMER VENEERING

This is the traditional method of laying veneers by hand, without presses or clamps. It is suitable for laying single leaves, veneer matches which have to be laid one leaf at a time, and for applying crossbanded border surrounds.

Elaborate veneer matches, marquetry, parquetry, etc., must be laid by caul with pressure. Curls and burrs should also be laid by the caul method as the action of the hammer may tear out the grain. The swelling of the veneers and subsequent shrinkage may cause joints to open if the shrinkage is unequal.

The workroom temperature should be around 70 degrees Fahrenheit (21 degrees Centigrade), with no cold draughts to chill the glue. Scotch glue is heated to about 120 degrees Fahrenheit (48 degrees Centigrade), in which you can just bear to insert your finger and it should run freely from the brush without forming into droplets. Set the iron at a steady heat, which will evaporate a droplet of water without spitting. An ordinary domestic electric iron is excellent for the purpose. Other tools required are a basin of hot water, a sponge, a veneer hammer, veneer pins and veneering tape; a sharp knife, straightedge, and G-clamps, if simple joints are to be made.

Brush a full-strength coat of glue, thinly and evenly to the prepared groundwork and the flattened veneer and allow both surfaces to tack. If the glueline is too thick it will be difficult to press out; too thin, and glue will soak into the wood pores. Wait until you can lay your hands on the groundwork without feeling the tack, and the glue has chilled — this will prevent the veneer from swelling. Remember that flake white powder added to the glue will prevent discolouration on light veneers such as sycamore if the glue penetrates porous veneers.

Lay the veneer on the groundwork and align with pencilled centre lines. Now work quickly over part of the veneer surface with a wrung-out damp sponge. Do not soak it. This prevents the iron from sticking and closes the veneer pores; it also increases the moisture content of the veneers to compensate for the loss of moisture when ironing. The dampening of the surface softens it and prevents possible blisters. Work the iron over the surface to melt the glue and draw it up into the pores of the veneer. If the iron is too hot it will cause glue penetration. Now use the veneer hammer—not like an ordinary hammer but in squeegee fashion—working along the grain in zig-zag movements, from the centre of the veneer leaf, out towards the edges and ends, to exclude all air bubbles from the bond and to force out the surplus glue.

Remember to work *along* the grain, as pressure exerted across the grain tends to stretch, and then to shrink the veneer. Take special care along the edges and ends, keeping two thirds of the working blade of the hammer on the flat surface and only allow a third to overlap the edge to protect the overhang from damage.

Use the hammer with light strokes at first, gradually increasing pressure. The glue will begin to chill and the technique is to keep repeating the sequence of dampening, ironing and hammering as often as necessary until the adhesion is complete.

When the veneer is laid, turn the panel over and lay it upon its face side on a clean cutting board, making sure that the board projects beyond the panel's edge and surplus overhang. Press down firmly, and trim off the veneer overhang with the knife. If the veneer has a strong grain, make a light tracing cut to establish the line, and a heavier severance cut. Wipe off the glue squeeze-out around the panel with a damp cloth and leave the panel to dry out in a warm, dry atmosphere.

Simple joints

One of the advantages of the hammer method, is the ability to make perfect joints. For example, to make a 2-piece match, select two matching leaves of veneer and pencil a line on each leaf, half an inch from the same edge.

Lay the first veneer as described above, lining up the pencil line on the centre line of the groundwork. The second leaf is then laid *overlapping* the first, with the pencil lines co-inciding. Clamp the straightedge along the top pencil line, and cut through both veneers with the knife, discarding the half inch veneer surplus from the top leaf, leaving the other half inch strip trapped below the joint on the bottom leaf. Make a quick pass along the joint with the sponge, then the iron to melt the glue, and the lower leaf will lift to enable you to peel off the unwanted surplus strip from the lower leaf.

If you cut the joint immediately after laying the second leaf of veneer, you will find that the veneer and the lower strip will lift together without difficulty and the strip will peel off easily. Re-lay both veneers for a perfect joint—if necessary repeating the dampen, iron and hammer sequence. Veneers which have been dampened, will want to shrink back to normality, so it is necessary to fix the joint by fastening a length of gummed veneering tape along the length of the joint and some four inch (100mm) straps of tape across the joint at about eight inch (200mm) intervals.

Also drive in a few veneer pins with large heads, and incline them towards the joint; this brings lateral pressure on the joint to keep it tightly closed. The taping and pinning operation would naturally

Fig. 204 Scotch glue being brushed on to groundwork

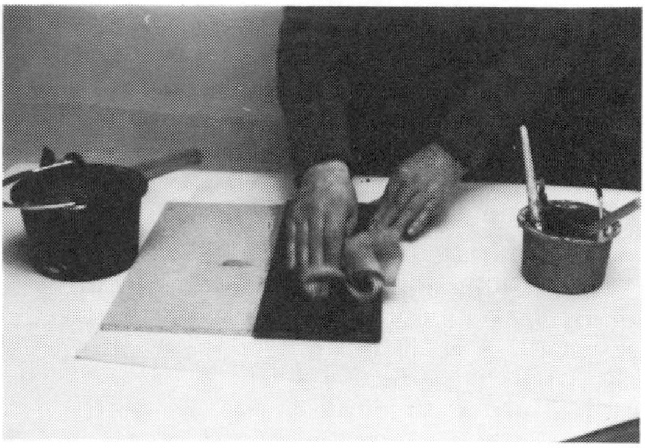

Fig. 205 Hot water being applied with damp cloth or sponge

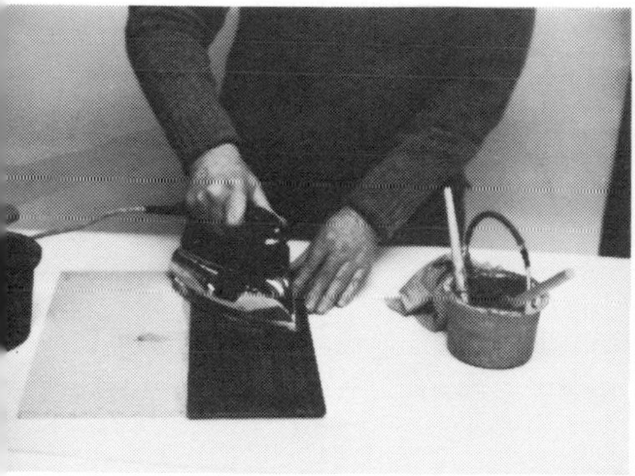

Fig. 206 Moderately hot iron applied to melt glue and immediately pressed flat with the veneer hammer

Fig. 207 Hot scotch glue being applied for the second half of the match

Fig. 208 After hammering, the centre joint is cut and the joint re-heated to release the lower trapped surplus strip

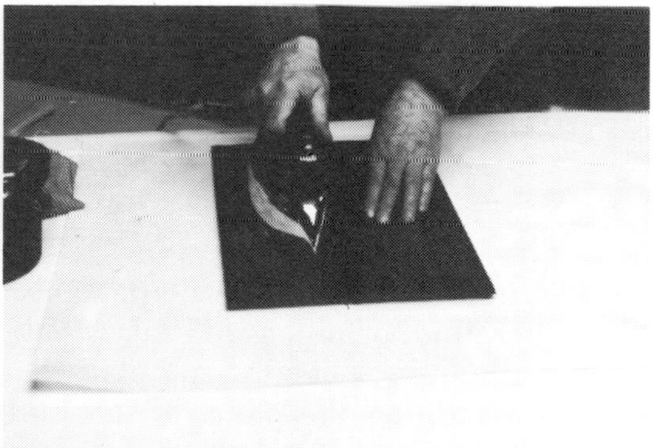

Fig. 209 The panel is laid with the iron and veneer hammer and allowed to cure

follow after trimming off the overhang and wiping off the glue squeeze-out.

When trimming off the surplus veneer overhang around the panel, remember that the veneer may shrink a fraction, and since the object at this stage is to wipe off the squeeze-out of surplus glue, trim off the veneer surplus a fraction oversize and leave the panel to dry out thoroughly.

The trimming cuts should always be made from the corner towards the centre of the panel to prevent the corners from breaking out. Trim the ends before trimming the sides.

Border surrounds

The word 'crossbanding' has been used to describe substrate veneers laid immediately beneath the face and backing veneers, upon corestock. When used in connection with decorative veneering the word crossbanding refers to the border surround, where the grain direction runs from the centre of the panel outwards towards the ends and edges.

Fig. 210 Crossbanded surrounds with centre or corner mitres

It depends upon whether the panel is to have a crossbanding surround, or not, as to exactly *how* the veneers are laid and trimmed. Without crossbandings, a plain panel would be laid with the veneers overlapping the panel all around the ends and edges to allow for trimming off after laying. But when a crossbanded border surround is to be fitted, the face veneer or veneer match, is prepared *undersize*, to fit into the border margin area, but not overlapping the edges of the panel. After the veneers have been laid, and the squeeze-out of glue wiped off, a cutting gauge is used to cut through the surplus veneer, parallel to the ends and edges, while the glue is still workable. When the crossbanding veneers are fitted and laid by the hammer method, they too, are allowed to overlap the panel for subsequent trimming off on the cutting board.

Cutting gauges, especially those with face strips, are not very useful for cutting around tight radii and are best for rectangular panels. For panels with curved corners, get as far as you can into the corner from each side with the cutting gauge, and finish off the curve with a knife, or purpose made dividers. Cutting dividers are made by flattening and then sharpening one leg to form a cutting edge. Put a scrap of veneer under the centre point; open the divider to the required radius, and use the sharpened cutting edge to cut around the radius.

The crossbandings laid around a radius are also hammer veneered. To avoid a pattern jump at the corners, and to have the veneer grain flowing uniformly around the curve, it is best to cut a number of small width veneers, and fan them around the curve, so that the grain direction turns through 90 degrees in small steps. Use a minimum of four veneers, each with a pattern jump of 22½ degrees, or better still, six veneers with a pattern change of only 15 degrees.

For a multi-corner assembly of crossbanding, it would be best to compress the small set of pieces between battens and shoot the edges; joint them on the shooting board, tape them together and lay them in a caul.

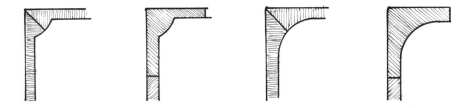

Fig. 211 Crossbanding borders

There are various types of crossbanding patterns. The Queen Anne style has simple butt jointed corners which line up with the butt joints of the framework. Most rectangular panels have mitred corners. In some, the grain direction of the veneer is vertical at the top and bottom and horizontal at both sides, with 45 degree mitres in the corners. But in other panels, the grain of the crossbanding is arranged at 45 degrees to run in the same direction as the mitred corner, and the crossbanding has a straight joint in the centre of each side.

When a moulding is to be fitted to the inner edge of a crossbanding, as in the case of a door frame, the veneers are not laid to overhang that inner edge, but are cut back slightly undersize, so that the moulding may be glued directly to the groundwork and not to the veneer.

After laying the crossbanding veneers, the panel is turned over face downwards on a perfectly clean and smooth cutting board, and the surplus veneer trimmed off before any attempt is made to cut the mitres at the corners. Leave the veneers overlapped and taped on the face side. Carefully cut the overhang from the corner towards the centre, making several light tracing cuts to sever the veneer rather than a single heavy cut. Then reverse the panel and cut the mitred corners from the corner inwards towards the panel centre to prevent breaking out the veneer at the corners. Protect the corners with veneer tape during the cutting procedure.

The drying out of a hammer veneered panel, especially when veneered one side only, will unbalance the panel and cause it to warp. To avoid this, it is best to veneer the back of the panel immediately with a balancing veneer before storing the panel to cure. Ensure free circulation of warm dry air during storage.

For repairing some traditional work, where the veneering was carried out on one side only, it is best to use a contact adhesive and avoid introducing moisture to the bond. After face veneering, tightly clamp the panel between battens until it is ready to be re-fixed into its framework.

Blisters

When the panel is dry, tap over the surface with your finger tips, or the end of a pencil, and you should hear a firm, hard, sharp sound to indicate a good bond.

If you should hear a soft, loose, pappy sound you have discovered a blister caused by trapped air or insufficient glue.

For the repair of blisters, see Chapter 23.

Rubber roller

Many craftsmen prefer to work with a 6 inch (152mm) roller instead of the traditional veneer hammer, or in addition to the veneer hammer. If used, the surface of the roller must have a yielding surface either of rubber, or similar material. It is much faster in use than the hammer and is to be preferred when laying multi-matches with contact adhesive.

IRON-ON VENEERING

'Glu-film' is a hot melt thermoplastic adhesive film which is available in 36 inch (914mm) widths in roll form, and has an indefinite shelf life. It is protected with a siliconised release paper backing and is cut with scissors to the required panel size.

The film is laid over the groundwork. An electric iron at a low heat is passed lightly over the surface of the release paper, which is then peeled off. Check that the film has no creases by smoothing it with the fingertips.

The pencilled centre lines on the groundwork can be seen through the transparent film.

Fig. 212 Four layer sandwich comprising (a) groundwork (b) glu-film (c) the veneer match (d) siliconised release paper backing

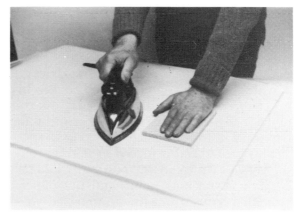

Fig. 213 Moderately hot iron melts glu-film below release paper and wooden block maintains contact as glue cools. Follow through with veneer hammer or rubberised roller

The veneers are laid in position and covered with the paper release sheet which will prevent the veneer from scorching. The electric iron is worked across the panel surface giving every part about a three second 'dwell' which is sufficient to melt the glu-film but not hot enough to scorch the veneer.

The correct glueline thickness of five thousandths of an inch is guaranteed, and the film is gap filling.

The procedure is similar to that of hot scotch glue hammer veneering, except that no dampness is introduced with no subsequent tendency to shrinkage.

Firm contact with the groundwork is maintained during the ironing phase, by following behind the iron with a smooth block of wood, until you can dispense with the iron and take up either the veneer hammer or veneering roller.

CONTACT VENEERING

Contact adhesive contains an inflammable volatile solvent therefore all work should take place in a well ventilated workroom away from any source of fire or sparks.

Spread the adhesive from the can with the comb provided in order to get a rapid distribution of adhesive over the panel. But this coating is far too thick for veneering, so follow up with the edge of a scrap of veneer, spreading the adhesive diagonally from corner to corner in both directions to ensure complete coverage. Check the surface against a good light to make sure it is shiny and no part has been missed.

Now coat the veneer in the same way. As no moisture is being introduced—the solvent evaporates into the atmosphere—it is perfectly safe to apply the adhesive to veneer matches.

Allow both surfaces to dry out thoroughly, and during this period keep both surfaces free from dust. After a few minutes it is possible to cover both surfaces with clean wrapping paper or a polythene sheet when 'touch-dry'. Leave for about an hour.

Drive a few veneer pins in the corner of the veneer leaves to hold them flat while the contact adhesive dries out.

After an hour, apply a second coat to both surfaces and repeat the procedure, allowing this also to dry out completely, for about half an hour. The surface has to be sufficiently dry not to adhere to a kraft paper separator 'slip-sheet'.

This 'slip-sheet' is placed over the groundwork to separate it from the veneers which are then carefully laid on top of the paper. By lifting both the veneer assembly and the paper separator, you can check pencilled centre guide lines unhurriedly.

Now ease the paper sheet out at the end nearest to you, about an inch, (25mm) and roller down the narrow strip of veneer now in contact with the adhesive.

Drive in a few veneer pins in that section to ensure that the veneers will not move out of alignment during the laying process.

Now withdraw the slip sheet in easy stages of about 8 inches (200mm) at a time, from the opposite end, and at the same time use the veneer hammer or rubber coated roller to press down on the veneer, working quickly from the centre of the veneers outwards towards the edges, forcing out all trapped air.

Remember to keep two thirds of the hammer blade or roller on the flat panel to avoid damaging the overhanging veneers.

It is useful to have a helpmate when carrying out this process, to hold the 'trailing edge' of the veneer up and allow the air to escape as you gradually work towards it. But this is not necessary for small panels up to about 36 inches (914mm) in length.

As you approach the end of the panel, and remove the paper slip-sheet completely, hold up the veneer and roller towards the edge. Do not let the roller go over the edge or you may splinter the overhang.

The operation of laying can be accomplished in a few minutes. The whole skill lies in keeping perfect alignment which is the reason for the few veneer pins at the beginning.

Thixotropic contact adhesives are of the 'gel' type and provide you with a second option. The first coat is allowed to dry thoroughly for an hour, but immediately the second coat is applied, the veneer assembly is placed directly on the groundwork *without* a slip sheet. The 'gel' allows time to slide the veneers quickly into perfect alignment.

The 'damp-iron-hammer' technique explained for hammer veneering is brought into use, and the heat rapidly evaporates the volatile solvent up through the pores of the veneer.

The technique is chiefly used with small panels upon which the alignment can be quickly checked at each corner before any possibility of the adhesive gripping. It is *not* a technique for veneer matches.

The 'slip-sheet' technique is universally used for laying plastic veneers and laminates to impervious surfaces because the 'gel' type cannot be evaporated by heat through the surface.

Contact adhesives are also widely used for applying edge veneers and decorative plastic trim to edges.

CAUL VENEERING
There are many types of decorative veneering where the hand laying techniques are not recommended.

The laying of curls, burrs, butts, sawcut veneers, oysters, elaborate marquetry assemblies and parquetry—are laid by cauls under pressure, especially veneers which by their nature are very porous, open grained, or have a tendency to tear out, such as curls.

Apart from the nature of the veneer, or its complicated assembly, you may wish to veneer both sides of a panel simultaneously to keep it in perfect balance.

Caul veneering is done in a simple press, the upper and lower parts of the press are known as 'cauls', usually panels of ¾ inch (19mm) blockboard slightly larger than the actual panel to be pressed. Then cross-bearers are required for top and bottom of the press, and these are either of wood or angle iron.

Wooden cross-bearers are cut from 2 inch × 1½ inch (50mm × 38mm) or heavier material depending on the size of the panel to be pressed. As the purpose of the bearers is to apply pressure across the *width* of the panel, but the actual pressure derives from clamps or bolts at the *ends* of the bearers, it could result in the bearers failing to apply pressure in the centre of the panel. To avoid this, the top bearers are usually slightly convex shaped tapering towards the ends, to ensure that pressure commences at the centre of the panel, and the air and surplus glue forced out towards the edges; otherwise, blisters caused by air pockets could result. The bottom bearers can be made either of the same material and shaped similar to the top bearers, or made from far stouter sectioned material to withstand the top pressure. The bearers must also be tightened in sequence for the same reasons. Tighten the centre bearers first, at each side, then the next set on each side, and those at the ends last, driving out both and glue from the bond at each end, as well as the sides. Ideally, press screws should be tightened simultaneously, and for large panels, it is best to have a helper to work at tightening the crossbearers on the opposite side of the press.

Fig. 214 Panel being pressed using clamps to ensure pressure equalised at ends and edges

There are four points to remember about caul veneering:

1. Keep the veneers dry. Apply the adhesive to the groundwork only.
2. Cover the taped side of the veneer assembly with a polythene sheet

to prevent the glue squeeze-out or glue penetration sticking to the blanket.

3.   The blanket or *wad*, must be a yielding material, such as thin felt, green baize, a wad of newspapers etc. Only use newspapers when the surface of the veneers is protected with polythene, otherwise the newsprint will offset on to the veneers. (The purpose of the wad is to take up any unevenness caused by criss-crossing veneer tapes used on the assembly, and to equalise the pressure).

4.   The introduction of heat.

Although caul veneering is usually carried out with cold setting glues such as PVA, cold synthetic resins, urea formaldehyde etc., where sustained pressure alone is sufficient to set and cure the bond, the introduction of heat to disperse the solvent, will rapidly reduce the press curing time.

In the past, the tradition was to stand the wooden cauls before a blazing fire; both sides of the caul had to be heated as wood is a poor conductor and is subject to rapid heat loss. This meant that the work had to be carried out in a sweltering heat at high speed. Today, there is no need for that! We do not heat the wooden cauls, but use sheets of aluminium or zinc for this purpose. The metal cauls are heated on a hotplate or over a gas ring, and will retain their heat much longer. Alternatively, some craftsmen use a combined heated caul and wad, by dispensing with metal plates and yielding blanket, and using instead a heated sheet of linoleum for both purposes.

Dry run

Before attempting to apply the adhesive and lay a panel in a press, it is good advice to carry out a dry run first. There are many small points to watch for, and it is best to have everything clear in your mind before applying the adhesive. For example, have you drawn pencil lines on the groundwork for perfect alignment? If using handscrews, have you opened them sufficiently for rapid application? Are you going to need a helper?

In nine cases out of ten, craftsmen who carry out a dry run are thankful afterwards that they did and the subsequent actual pressing was quick, effortless and the result perfect.

Sequence of assembly

As we have mentioned, most panels will require veneering both sides for balanced construction, however, in decorative veneering, it is not always good policy to perform simultaneous pressing.

There are several reasons why single face pressing may be advantageous.

1.   The pressure is designed to squeeze out surplus adhesive from the

glueline, which will exude out at the ends and edges and run down the thickness of the panel from the upper veneer, and form into a thick globule on the veneer overhang of the bottom veneer.

If you have edge lipped the panel with a solid facing before veneering the face and back, the squeeze-out will have to be removed quickly, otherwise, if allowed to cure and harden, will present a clean-up problem later.

2. The overhang surplus veneer will be difficult to trim off on the cutting board if hard glue squeeze-out is present in the corners formed by panel and veneers.

3. When a very special veneer match or assembly requires careful attention, it would be best to lay the backing veneer first as a single operation; remove the panel for squeeze-out clean-up and trimming off, and then to return the panel to the press for the important face veneering sequences. Thus giving your undivided attention to one part at a time.

4. When crossbanding borders are to be fitted, and the face veneers are to be laid undersize, the squeeze-out will occur on top of the panel, as well as the sides, and hence the need for a polythene sheet to prevent sticking.

5. There is always a risk of splintering a veneer overhang where a panel has these on two sides of the panel. It is best to focus attention on trimming one overhang at a time with its attendant problems.

6. When restoring antiques, the 'pull' of the face veneer may be countered by the framework of the cabinet, and the panel must be veneered one side only, and kept under pressure until ready for fixing to its framework.

Sequence A: Single Pressing (Oversize Veneers)

1. Lay the lower wooden caul on the bottom cross-bearers.
2. Lay the heated aluminium caul in the press.
3. Lay the wad in position.
4. Cover with polythene sheet to prevent sticking.
5. Lay the veneer assembly in the press, gummed paper taped side downwards against the polythene.
6. Lay in the groundwork, adhesive side down against the untaped side of the veneer. Check corners for perfect alignment.
7. The upper wooden caul.
8. The upper bearers, tightened in sequence from centre outwards.

Note (a) Have a soft brush handy to brush the surface of the aluminium heated caul before laying it in the press.

(b) The above sequence is only used where the veneers are oversize, with an overhang to be trimmed off later.

Sequence B: Single Pressing (Undersized Veneers)

When crossbandings are to be fitted to the face veneers and the assembly is kept undersize for trimming off with a cutting gauge later, the sequence of laying must be reversed, otherwise you will not be able to see the alignment of the corners of the veneer assembly in relation to the groundwork.

1. Lay the lower wooden caul on the bottom cross-bearers.
2. Lay in the groundwork pencilled lines uppermost and adhesive side up.
3. Lay in the veneer assembly, undersize, taped side uppermost, check the corner alignment with the groundwork.
4. Cover with polythene sheet.
5. Lay in the wad.
6. Lay in the heated metal caul.
7. Now the wooden caul.
8. Place the bearers in position and tighten them in sequence.

After the metal caul has cooled, and the panel has been under pressure for a couple of hours, the second operation is to remove from the press and clean off the glue squeeze-out. Return the panel to the press omitting the heated metal plate, and leave under pressure overnight for the glue to harden. This applies only to a panel which has been previously veneered with a backing veneer in one operation, and has now been face veneered in sequence B.

When both sides of the panel are to be veneered, the longer you leave the second operation, the greater the risk of the panel warping. The veneer assembly may have swelled when introduced to the moisture of the adhesive, (although the groundwork is never laid in the press until the adhesive has been allowed to tack) and sufficient time has not elapsed to allow for hardening and curing.

Therefore if you propose to veneer the other side of the panel as a second sequence when removing the panel which has been veneered one side for the squeeze-out clean-up and edge trim, the groundwork should be coated with adhesive immediately and the pressing sequence repeated according to requirements.

When double sided veneering is being undertaken in two separate pressing operations, it is best to lay the backing veneer first, as described in sequence A, followed by the face veneer in sequence A for oversized assemblies, or sequence B for undersize assemblies which will be subject to additional work later.

When both sides have been veneered, removed from the press for clean-up and overhang trim, the panel should be returned to the press and allowed to remain overnight to harden and cure.

Veneering two sides

When the simultaneous pressing of both sides of a panel is required, if the veneers for both faces are to be oversize, then the sequence of loading the press is optional. But when the backing veneers are oversize, and the decorative veneer face is undersize, the sequence is as follows:

1. Load wooden caul on bottom bearers.
2. Heated metal caul, brushed clean.
3. Wad.
4. Polythene sheet.
5. Oversized backing veneers, check alignment.
6. Groundwork coated with adhesive in 'tack' condition.
7. Fit glue blocks and straps. See notes (a) and (b) below.
8. Position face veneer assembly, check alignment.
9. Fasten veneer tapes, or drive in veneer pins and nip off heads.
10. Polythene sheet.
11. Wad.
12. Heated metal caul, brushed clean.
13. Top wooden caul.
14. Tighten top bearers in sequence.

Note (a)   It is useful to have a few glue blocks, the same width as the veneer overhang, and to position them at intervals around the assembly at half a dozen places.

(b)   Gummed veneer tapes, in short lengths of about 6 inches (152mm) are affixed to the backing veneer, in the same locations as the veneer blocks. After laying the groundwork in position with the face veneer assembly, the gummed paper tapes are brought up and over, and are fastened to the face veneers to anchor them and prevent any possibility of the veneers slipping out of alignment, as sequences 10-14 are carried out.

(c)   Glue blocks and tapes can be dispensed with if you drive in a few veneer pins and nip off the heads. These are located in the area which will be subsequently removed by cutting gauge for the fitting of crossbanded borders.

When the metal plates have cooled after a couple of hours, the assembly is removed from the press and the glue blocks removed, the backing veneer overhang trimmed off, and the squeeze-out glue surplus removed.

The panel can be tested for blisters on both sides; these can be corrected immediately and the panel can then be returned to the press to cure, without the heated plates.

When the simultaneous pressing of both sides is required for oversize veneer faces, the squeeze-out of surplus adhesive is the problem. This sequence is best employed when: (a) you intend to veneer the eges afterwards; (b) you want to fit an edge moulding or lipping, after veneering; or (c) where you have already fitted an edge lipping fractionally oversize, to allow for a clean-up trim after veneering.

The timescale will decide the best sequence. Since laying the veneers is the most vital part of the whole operation, the craftsman would lay the backing veneers in the morning, clean up and trim the edge overhang by lunchtime; lay the face veneers in the afternoon; clean up and trim by tea-time and return the complete panel to the press before close down and leave overnight.

Veneering two panels

When it is desired to veneer two panels in one operation, with one face each it is possible to use only one wooden caul and two metal cauls. The wooden caul must be larger than the two metal cauls and the veneers both oversize; both groundworks must be identical in size otherwise there will be unequal distribution of pressure, and blisters will result. Here is the sequence:

1. Bottom bearers, larger in section than top bearers.
2. Groundwork laid directly on bearers, glued side uppermost.
3. First veneer assembly, taped side uppermost, check alignment.
4. Polythene sheet.
5. Wad.
6. Heated metal caul.
7. Wooden caul.
8. Heated metal caul.
9. Wad.
10. Polythene sheet.
11. Second veneer assembly, taped side down.
12. Groundwork, glued side down, check alignment with veneers.
13. Position top bearers and apply clamps.
14. Tighten down in sequence from centre outwards.

This sequence is recommended only when the panels are of small size, up to about 30 inches × 15 inches (762mm × 381mm). Above that size it would be advisable to have a wooden caul on the bottom bearers and another beneath the top bearers so as to distribute and equalise the pressure.

Dimension losses

During the pressing cycle, the adhesive solvents disperse, and overall dimensional losses result and continue during the curing cycle. It is therefore important in all manually operated screw presses to re-tighten the press at regular intervals to take up this slackening of pressure.

Edge pressure

On single and multi-screw presses, small toggle clamps are fitted at the edges for use on large panels. The central screw type of press tends to lose pressure around the edges, and the toggle clamps restore it. Therefore on smaller workshop assemblies, it is useful to apply a few edge clamps after central screw pressure has been applied. This will apply to any press with a central screw ram.

Clean up

Apart from the mid-sequence removal of the panel for cleaning off the glue squeeze-out and trimming off the overhang, and checking for blisters, the panel is allowed to cure in the press for a few hours, and then to be stacked in a warm dry atmosphere for a few days, while the hardening process continues.

No attempt should be made to remove veneer tapes, or to do further work on the panel until it has been allowed to restore itself to the moisture content of its environment.

19

Shaped Veneering

P ERHAPS the most difficult part of shaped veneering is to strike a balance between stretching one's own talent, and recognising the limitations of one's present capabilities. Tricks of the trade, acquired by trial and error, reward the craftsman by enabling him to tackle projects of an ever increasing degree of difficulty. And those problems that are sometimes encountered which challenge the ingenuity and inventiveness of the craftsman, are mostly overcome by improvisation. In this respect, later in this chapter, we shall be discussing the use of home-made presses such as pneumatic, sandbags and boxes, plaster, etc.

There are several factors to be considered before tackling shaped veneering projects: the type of groundwork; the degree of curvature; the type of equipment available; and the type of veneer decoration.

Groundwork

In Chapter 10, the various types of groundwork were considered. Groundwork bandsawn from the solid, or from laminated boards, would have the offcut pieces retained for use as cauls in shaped veneering. Brick and coopered construction groundworks, on the other hand have no cauls readily available and it would depend whether the project was a 'one-off' and the expense justified of making special cauls. In such cases, a set of cradles and tambours would be the best method, or, alternatively, any of the hand veneering methods.

If the groundwork has been bent by the steaming process, it is best to rely on contact veneering. Alternatively wooden cauls or sandbag cauls and clamps would need to be employed.

Laminated corestock presents no difficulty, because this would have been laminated in a press with cauls, which are ideal for the final stage of face and back decorative veneering.

Hollow frame construction groundworks, usually have thin hardboard or plywood skins affixed, which may be veneered in crossbearer and clamp press, bench bent on to saddles, or hand veneered.

Degree of Curvature

There are basically three types of shape: flat single curves, which are the most common found in cabinet making and the easiest to veneer by any of the above methods.

Serpentine shapes, which may be laid in cauls, cradles and tambours; saddles and clamps; or screw or platen press; bag press, etc.

Compound shapes, which can only be veneered successfully in a hydraulic platen press, dome bag press, or vacuum press.

Type of Equipment

If you have access to a commercial type press of the screw type, hydraulic platen, dome bag press, or vacuum press, then any kind of shaped veneering on any groundwork need hold no fears for you.

But if you have no modern or sophisticated equipment and have a small workshop, with only the basic tools and equipment the following factors will have to be taken into account:

Size of panel

Panels up to about 36 inches × 18 inches (914 × 457mm) can be veneered in a home made press comprising pairs of crossbearers fitted with handscrews or press screws; or presses of the centre screw ram type.

Larger panels up to 6 feet × 18 inches (1828 × 457mm) are best veneered by any of the three hand veneering methods, if the type of shape permits (ie. flat gentle curve only). Panels of 6 feet (1828mm) and upwards, require most pressure, and preferably from a home-made press using angle iron or R.S.J's with long bolts or press screws.

In general, most shaped veneered panels should be cauled or pressed in a tambour press.

Panel thickness

Thin groundwork, such as hardboard or 3-ply plywood, may have been shaped by bending and clamping between bearers of a slightly greater curvature than the final shape required. The decorative veneering would therefore be carried out in the same rig-up.

Alternatively, the panel could be screwed to a former, and hand veneered, with temporary clamps affixed until the panel had cured.

Thicker panels, requiring only a gentle flat curve, are veneered either by returning them to the rig-up that was used to form the groundwork, or a slitting technique used, as follows: the panel would be made with a flat groundwork, and then face veneered only. Before the panel had cured completely, during the clean-up and trim stage, the panel is transferred to a sawtable, and slit with a number of sawcuts

Fig. 215 Saddle for
hammer veneering

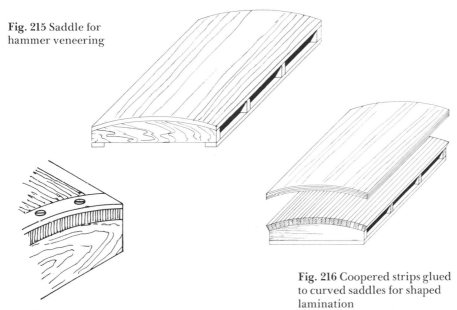

Fig. 216 Coopered strips glued
to curved saddles for shaped
lamination

Fig. 217 Hammer veneered thin
panel screwed to shaped saddle

made with a thick blade spaced about ½ inch (12mm) apart. Make the
sawcut through the thickness of the panel stopping short at the
crossbandings below the face veneer. Then test the curve by bending
after making a few sawcuts to see if the radius achieved is sufficient.
When you have cut the correct number of slits in the correct direction for
the bend, the panel slits will close and touch. If open gaps remain, you
have cut too many slits.

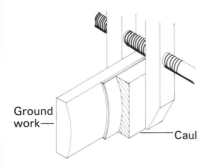

Ground
work—

Caul

Fig. 218 Caul for shaped frieze or
moulding

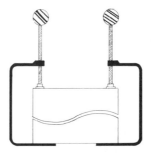

Fig. 219 Shaped wooden cauls
held with C clamps

Always protect the face veneer when bending the panel, by clamping a sheet of aluminium or zinc over the face to ease the tension of bending. Insert veneer strips on edge to fill any open sawcuts. Thoroughly coat the slitted surface with glue and allow to dry. Level off the protruding veneer in-fillings and veneer the back of the panel with crossbandings across the slits.

When dry, tooth the surface and coat with size; sandpaper the surface and veneer the back with the backing veneer, using one of the hand veneering methods, preferably contact adhesive.

Type of Pressure

For every 80 square inches (516cm²) of panel area, one press screw is required for a home made press. This would mean five sets of crossbearers, and ten press screws, for a panel about 4 feet × 16 inches (1219 × 406mm). Above that size, the rapid and simultaneous tightening of the press screws becomes a problem, even with a helper one would then require more powerful presses of the commercial type to cope with shaped panels of larger dimensions.

Temperature

The home craftsman works with cold setting glues such as PVA, aliphatic or adhesives of the urea formaldehyde type such as 'Cascomite One-Shot'.

The heat generated by heated metal cauls, about 120 degrees Fahrenheit (48 degrees Centigrade), is far below that used in hot presses, although sufficiently hot to accelerate the press time of cold setting adhesives.

Hot scotch glue and hot melt glue-film can also be used in home-made presses with heated cauls without scorching the veneers.

A workshop temperature of about 70 degrees Fahrenheit (21 degrees Centigrade) is essential.

Adhesive Time scale

The time scale problems of adhesives have a bearing on which you use for shaped veneering, taking into account the pot-life, assembly time, press time and curing time. This will decide the technique you use for shaped veneering; for all normal panel purposes you are quite safe in using any of the cold setting adhesives, and also with any of the hand veneering methods

Type of Decoration

The nature and type of veneer decoration may decide the method of laying. For example, when a panel is to be fitted with a crossbanding surround or inlay bandings, the slightest slip in the press would result in throwing the pattern out of true, parallel with the edges. It is very noticeable on narrow crossbanded borders.

Therefore, the first pressing or laying of the face veneer would be carried out with undersized face veneers, which would then be cut back with a cutting gauge for the border surround to be fitted as a second operation to ensure it will be parallel to the edges.

Very often this type of panel would be caul veneered first and the crossbanding applied by hand methods later.

IMPROVISED PRESSES
Pneumatic press

For small serpentine or even compound shapes an ordinary home made screw press can be converted into a pneumatic press for our purpose.

Obtain an inner tube of the type used on large tractors or aircraft tyres. These are made of thick rubber and can withstand very high pressures. Feed the inner tube through the press and connect to a foot pump or air bottle. Place a male former in the bottom of the press and arrange the corestock, suitably coated with adhesive, over the former. Inflate the tube, and ensure that it flows uniformly over the groundwork. This type of 'liquid' pressure can form the most complex shapes. When the glue has cured, deflate the tyre tube and repeat the operation with the decorative veneers.

Do not screw the press down tightly on the inner tube or you will cause a blowout. Only compress the tube slightly to spread the rubber sufficiently to cover the work.

The same technique can be used to re-veneer an existing piece when there is no male or female former, or caul.

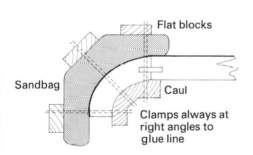

Fig. 220 Hot sandbag used as caul

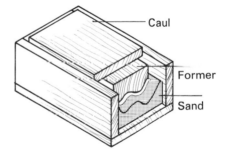

Fig. 221 The sandbox with male former

Sandbags

These are very useful for veneering awkward corners or sharp bends, and other difficult shapes. Fill a canvas bag with fine sand and heat it over a hotplate. The sand will retain the heat for a long time. The sandbag is thumped down with a mallet and fastened around the sharp bend or curve of the groundwork and fastened in position with clamps.

Sandbox

Construct a sturdy box to withstand considerable pressure. This is used for veneering existing corestock rather than for making shaped groundwork. About 5 inches to 6 inches (127-152mm) of fine sand is required.

Fill the canvas bag with fine sharp sand and heat on the hotplate. The sand acts as the female former. Make a hollow in the sand by thumping the groundwork into it to the required shape. Then cover the hollow with a sheet of polythene. Lay the face veneer down on the polythene sheet and apply gentle pressure to the glued groundwork, gradually increasing the pressure.

The veneering box can be placed into a screw press or press made with crossbearers and clamps.

Use a wirebrush to remove any particles of sand that might transfer to the face veneer should the bag split.

Rubber blocks

An alternative to the use of sand or plaster, is rubber. The prepared groundwork is glued, the face veneer pinned into position and the unit placed over a polythene-covered rubber block filled box. This is placed in the press and clamped until set.

Plaster

Formers can be made with plaster of Paris, reinforced with wire mesh or excelsior. Lightly grease the groundwork and embed into the plaster and remove before the plaster sets. Dry the groundwork and remove all traces of grease before applying the adhesive. After allowing an interval of several days for the plaster to dry thoroughly, it is then heated in an oven.

The veneers are pinned to the glued groundwork and gently inserted into the plaster mould. Pressure is then increased to form a clamp. Take care when exerting maximum pressure, too much will crack the plaster. At first it is a matter of trial and error.

Bran

A substitute for sand, plaster or rubber is bran, which is spread evenly in a box and heated. It is used in the same way and holds the heat effectively.

Cylindrical surfaces

The traditional way to veneer cylindrical surfaces was to soak the veneer to make it malleable; wrap it around the cylinder, to overlap, and bind it tightly with canvas webbing. This was also dampened and then exposed to a heat source which dried the wet webbing and melted the glueline. The webbing was left on until the veneer and webbing was dry, when it was removed and the joint cut with a straightedge and knife. The joint was re-heated, and the trapped lower strip removed, and re-laid with the hammer or hot cauled with webbing again.

The modern use of contact adhesives permits the veneer to be cut precisely to the correct length by revolving the cylinder on the back of the face veneer, to determine the required width.

By fastening a piece of masking tape to the cylinder, with a tack protruding, it will pierce a tiny hole in the veneer in two places as it makes one complete revolution. The veneer is cut to width on these marks and laid with contact adhesive.

Sash clamp press

Drawer rails or curved edges can be veneered with contact adhesive or cauled using an improvised sash clamp press.

Two sash clamps are cleated to a bench, with a saddle of the correct curvature at the other end; the veneer is protected with a heated metal strip caul, and the groundwork is protected by a batten against the clamp heads. A batten holds the whole rig-up down to the bench in case the work wants to ride up.

Moulded edges

The example of the sash-clamp device described above, could have a counterpart of the required moulding worked into the face and the metal heated caul omitted.

Strap cauls

Perforated steel flexiform bands, or nylon or webbing strap cauls, enable circular rims, oval and elliptical shapes to be veneered. The band encircles the work and is pulled tight through a screwhead, with self locking cams preventing the band from slipping.

COMPOUND TAILORING

The veneer craftsman determined to create a compound veneered shape, enters a world of stresses and strains not met with in other types of veneering. Try wrapping a piece of newspaper around a tennis ball! You will see that it creases, overlaps, and splits everywhere. A veneer, pressed over a compound shape will do the same.

The best way to proceed, is in easy stages. First, take a sheet of kraft paper, and lay this in the press over the male former, and close the press. Then open the press and examine the paper and you will find that it has creased in two different ways: on outside curves the paper has folded over upon itself as there was too much paper for the curve, and on inside curves, the paper will be torn, as it could not stretch itself to meet the demands of the curve.

Remove the paper from the press and lay it on top of the veneer to be pressed. Using scissors, cut small V shapes into the kraft paper where it has folded back on itself, so that the paper edges meet exactly. Save those V shaped pieces of paper to use as templets for cutting similarly shaped V's in the veneer. On the inside curves, where the paper is torn, you will have to eventually insert more veneer. But this is not possible when the veneer is flat.

Make knife cuts into the edges of the kraft paper in the exact locations of the splits and tears, and try to fit the paper over the contour of the former without further creasing. Try this once or twice until the paper will lie flat and can be smoothed neatly around, conforming to the shape.

Open out the paper on a flat surface, and use the paper as a templet to guide the knife as you cut through into the veneer making slits and V cuts as required. Protect the veneer with location paper gummed tapes, on each side of the splits and V cuts and across the ends.

Some craftsmen prefer to stick the paper to the veneer to prevent the veneer splitting when it comes under pressure. However, care must be taken that the paper does not stretch during adhesion, and for this reason it is to be avoided unless time is allowed for the swelling to be compensated for by eventual shrinkage.

Make a 'dry run' with the veneer before you actually lay it and you will find that the inner curves, where the slits were made will have opened up into V shapes which will require to be patched with inlaid pieces from matching leaves after pressing.

Clamping

Clamping pressure must always be at right angles to the glue line, no matter how irregular or shaped the work may be.

This is achieved by either cutting steps in the outer surface of the caul directly above the pressure point and parallel to the glueline; or by placing a wooden wedge, with paper below it, on the surface, to bring clamping pressure at right angles and parallel to the glueline. The wedge can easily be removed afterwards and the paper sanded off. Another way is to provide wedges in the jaws of the clamps.

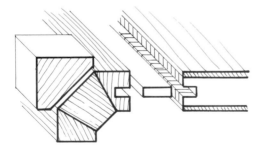

Fig. 222 Coopered ends should have temporary wood blocks fitted for clamping at right angles to glueline

Final check

Before commencing the pressing phase, always bring all pairs, sets, matches and other veneer assemblies together, and mark them in sets with chalk marks. It is so easy to take the wrong pair of doors out of sequence during the pressing operation and make a mistake which is irreversible.

20

Preparing and Repairing
of Veneers

A SMALL knot hole, patch of ingrowing bark or dead wormhole, in an otherwise beautiful leaf of veneer, is not sufficient reason to discard it. Small defects can be repaired.

A patch is used to repair a defect. It is usually an irregular shaped piece of veneer cut from a matching leaf (if that was free from a similar defect) or from a similar leaf from the same bundle, and kept for the purpose.

Cut the patch along the grain, keeping cross grain to a minimum. A jagged irregular shape is far better than an oval or rectangle, and will lose itself in the grain. Fasten the selected replacement patch veneer with tape to the underside of the face veneer and cut through both simultaneously with a sharp knife held at a slight angle to form a bevel cut. The patch being a fraction larger than the hole to take it. Or pierce the veneers with a needle, and enter a jeweller's piercing sawblade, with teeth pointing downwards, and fretsaw the required shape, holding both veneers down firmly on a cutting board, angled to take up the saw thickness.

Pay particular attention to strongly veined veneers or those with a pronounced marking and follow the contour of the natural line. If necessary cut a larger patch than strictly required to take advantage of any peculiar natural configuration.

Burr veneers especially, are often found with holes and defects.

Veneer punches are available in a range of sizes, and are used to cut an irregular shaped hole in both the leaf to be repaired and in the patch leaf. The punches should be sharpened by filing on the *outside* edge only, not the inside. The punch is placed over the defect making sure the shape is large enough to cover the defect, and the spring loaded ejector inside the punch is compressed so that the knife cutter touches the veneer. Strike a sharp blow with the mallet to the punch head, cutting the veneers through the first time; this will avoid the possibility of the punch moving if you have to have a second blow with the mallet.

Veneers requiring patching, must be previously flattened and dried. In the case of brittle burrs, place paper tape over the part to be cut out, and leave the paper on the patch until located in the repaired leaf.

Very often, highly figured veneers are received from the mill already patched by the manufacturer. Leave the tapes in position until after the veneers are laid.

Insertions

An insertion is a piece of veneer used to change the appearance of an otherwise sound veneer to correct a figure imbalance, or to achieve a figure match and its practice calls for a high degree of craftsmanship and knowledge of veneers.

For example, the leaf of veneer to be inserted must be held at the same viewing angle as the finished project will assume. A door will be viewed vertically, and a table horizontally. The effect of light refraction on the open and closed pore faces of the veneer are vital. An open pored insertion into a closed face veneer would stand out like a sore thumb.

Use the same general approach as for patching, by selecting a matching leaf, preferably from the same bundle, and following a predominating contour in the natural markings. A skilled 'inserter' can transform otherwise plain yew into very highly figured yew, using parts from other leaves. He can create highly decorative four-piece matches in veneers which may otherwise not really suit the purpose.

Precautions

Curls, are always difficult to handle as they possess in a leaf one smooth half and one rough. This is due to being back cut on a stay log.

Always 'prepare' the curls by placing protective paper tapes diagonally across the veneer from the centre along the curl figure on the rough side. This will prevent tearing out when laying and cleaning up.

Bird's eye maple and similar veneers should always be laid with the 'eye' down in the glueline. The 'eyes' actually taper with one face larger in diameter than the other due to being rotary cut. By laying the largest part of the cone shape in the glueline there is no possibility of the eyes chipping out in the cleaning up stage.

Sawcut veneers usually have the fine arc of sawmarks on the faces. These must be removed by planing, otherwise they will telegraph through to the surface months after the work has been laid due to the action of the glueline pulling the wood down by suction. Fasten the sawcut veneer to the working board and set a toothing plane very finely to remove the sawmarks.

Blisters

Blisters are a common fault in the veneering process. Their causes and repair are fully covered in chapter 23.

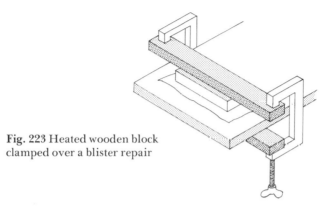

Fig. 223 Heated wooden block clamped over a blister repair

CLEANING UP

The panel should have been allowed to cure outside the press for a few days before any attempt is made to clean off the veneer tapes.

Upon inspection, the surface may reveal patches of glue penetration that occurred during the pressing and which might have been caused by end grain veneer, too thick a glueline, or too much heat. It will hamper the finishing process and must be wiped off. There may also be traces of the yielding wad used in the press, or fluff from the felt or baize, or paper.

Overhang

When trimming off overhang after pressing, always ensure that the cutting board is brushed free from dust, grit or chippings. Make a light tracing cut with a sharp knife before working over the cut again with a heavier severing cut, to prevent the knife wandering in pronounced grain.

As an aid to crossgrain trimming at the ends of the panel, fix a length of cellulose tape across the end of the panel beneath the cutting position, so that the knife point will cut through the tape. The tape will hold both the panel's veneered edge and the surplus trim-off and ensure a clean cut. Any fragment that does break out will be retained in location by the tape and can be glued back. The tape will peel off easily.

Sanding

Trimmed edges require sanding immediately. Wrap a sheet of garnet paper around a cork sanding block, and make a light pass across the trimmed edge, holding the block at an angle. This is a safety precaution to guard against the possibility of picking up a tiny sliver at an edge, and ripping it into a major tear out.

Always work away from the face veneer with the cork block; push the block from the face veneer down over the edge, and never work the rubber backwards and forwards.

The next step is to remove all surface problems. Use a cellulose sponge and a bowl of clean, hot water with no additives. The idea is to wet the paper tapes but not the veneer surface. Squeeze out the sponge and dampen a short length of the tape, allowing a minute or so for the water to penetrate through the tape. Lift the corner of the tape and try to peel it off. You will probably find it tears apart leaving a stubborn residue on the veneer which requires further dampening. Use less water this time.

To aid this tape removal, use a suitable sharp edged tool. All sorts of tools are suitable: kitchen knives, old razor blades, plane irons, a broken hacksaw blade, or a chisel held vertically.

The craftsman uses a flexible cabinet scraper—not the hook type of wallpaper scraper, unless you round off the corners to prevent digging in. The scraper is held with both hands, with thumb pressure in the centre to slightly flex the scraper. It is held at an angle and used with a scything action. Make sure there is a well-burred edge on the scraper.

Watch the veneer grain as you scrape; although you are concentrating on removing paper tapes, try to work along the grain and not across it. On multiple assemblies, work diagonally across the grain. On interlocked veneers, try working from each end towards the centre. Most single layers of tape will peel off easily. Assemblies with layers of criss crossing tapes will require coaxing, however, never attempt to use a power sander for this purpose. The paper tends to roll in balls and clog, resulting in veneer grain being torn out.

It is important not to soak the veneer, as the use of metal scraping tools might result in iron mould stain on veneers with a high tannin content, such as oak, obeche or afrormosia.

After removal of the tapes check the surface against a good light for any nicks, dents and depressions caused in handling. (A droplet of hot water from an eye dropper allowed to rest over a dent will cause the wood fibres to swell and restore the wood to its proper level).

Wipe off traces of chalk marks, grease spots, etc. with naptha. Work along joints with a scraper to remove any glue penetration. Check for veneer pins protruding; nip off the heads and bury remainder. Mix some of the scraped dust with PVA adhesive into a wood stopping to fill tiny holes. Finally, brush the surface with a stiff bronze wire brush while the surface is still slightly damp from the tape clean up and allow the panel to dry out and restore its moisture content to workshop conditions, and for grain shrinkage to be completed.

Quality control

Quality is something which has to be built into the panel and not inspected into it afterwards! It is necessary to carry out a quality control check at every stage in the production.

Right at the start at the planning stage you check to see that the materials, groundwork and veneers, conform to top grades for quality, figure, gauge, moisture content etc. At the veneer preparation stage you check to ensure that the pattern jump and matching is correct; the joints are sound, and that patching and insertions are practically invisible; that light refraction problems are overcome; all veneers true face etc; and that the corestock, crossbandings and other groundworks are checked for uniformity of thickness, true and clean surface and correctly toothed. When the pre-pressing stage is reached, you check on the preparation of the correct mix of adhesive in sufficient quantity and the right quality to guarantee the spread-thickness of glueline. The moisture content, workroom and press temperatures are correct and pressures and clamps to hand. Finally, at the post pressing stage, that the panel is trimmed and edge sanded correctly, checked for blisters, loose edges, open joints, faulty adhesion, dents, tears, and glue penetration.

Corrections and rejections should be made at every stage and repairs made immediately, rather than leaving it to a final inspection before the finishing process, hoping that a final inspection will reveal any defects.

A stitch in time saves nine. A minor defect, easily corrected at the time, can save what could develop into a major defect which may be irrecoverable.

Fig. 224 Typical use of veneered wall panelling
See page 270

21

Veneered Panelling

THE OPPORTUNITIES for expansion in business for the professional and the advancement in techniques for the craftsman are nowhere better exemplified than in the use of veneers to make wall panelling.

For the professional veneerer many companies whose offices are due for re-decoration are approachable, for although the initial costs may be higher than decorating, the long term savings are likely to even out any investment. For the craftsman too, there may well be the opportunity to change his own decor by panelling a room or even just one wall of a room. The effect can be exceptionally attractive provided that sufficient care is taken both in terms of choice of timbers and in the practical work.

VENEER MATCHING

The extent of the beauty of full 8 feet (2438mm) leaves of veneer can now be seen to advantage in the following matching sequences:

Book matching: Figured veneers are usually book matched to preserve a balanced running symmetrical pattern of grain and figure, but will appear as light and dark strips, due to light refraction.

Slip matching: This is sometimes known as 'slid' or 'dragged-over' matching, of plain, straight grained material. This match preserves a uniform appearance as the veneers are all kept 'true face'. They are slipped to right or left to suit the overall appearance and location of the panel in the room.

Random matching: Veneers of the same species but not of the same log are used, and are slip matched to right or left, using bundles of various widths adjacent to each other. This eliminates 'odd leaf' and bundle trimming wastage.

Sometimes the pattern is arranged to present an overall grain pattern by deliberately mis-matching adjacent veneers. These random matched panels may be used vertically, horizontally or even diagonally.

Casual matching: This permits both slip matching and book matching together with the use of *inverted* veneers to provide light refraction appeal. This is usually from one species, but employing various width bundles from different stocks, deliberately mis-matched.

Multi-species casual match: Monotone

There is a casual match of many different species, all closely allied and blending to provide a harmonising colour tone, for example, four different mahoganies, or gold-brown woods. The result will lack aesthetic appeal if not selected skillfully. It has the advantage that a great many wood grains, figures, textures and markings can be displayed, but requires great restraint in selection and matching to avoid over doing it.

Fig. 225 Harlequin casual matched wall panelling

Fig. 226 Finger-jointed panel

Harlequin matching: Anything goes! This sets out to achieve a stunning effect by deliberately effecting colour contrasts, with spectacular results. The more kaleidoscopic the result, the greater the risk that this cynosure will become an eye-sore and be difficult to live with once the novelty has gone. It is ideal for the run of an exhibition, to create a focal point.

Butt header-matched: Header joints are used to 'stretch' veneer lengths to make panels of exceptional length.
Finger jointed: A more careful length match is achieved by finger jointing.

This is done by cutting deep zig-zag lines into the end of one leaf and jointing it with similar lines cut into the leaf to be jointed; by choosing the grain and figure carefully to conceal the finger joints, an effect of one continuous leaf is achieved.

Parquetry matching

Another modern form of wall panelling is to take a few narrow bundles of veneer and guillotine them into small rectangular shapes and edge-joint them to create a parquetry pattern of multi-toned veneers for wall panelling.

Veneer Mosaic

A very effective addition to the wall panelling is to form a panel area which is deliberately very plain, and enliven it with a wall mosaic mural.

This is achieved by the mosaic processes described in the chapter on parquetry.

BATTENING

The usual method of applying wall panelling is to fix softwood battens to the walls. Use 2 inch × 1 inch (50mm × 25mm) battens, treated with wood preservative. Attach them securely to the walls at 16 inch to 18 inch (400-450mm) intervals at right angles to the direction of the panelling; vertical panels will require horizontal battening, etc.). Architrave mouldings around windows and doors should be prized off, and replaced with battens. However, leave the skirting boards in place to form a recessed plinth, with the bottom batten fixed directly on top of it.

If you want the panelling to go down to the floor, check that the skirting is 1 inch (25mm) thick to match the battens, or pack it out to suit.

Check the level of the battens with a straightedge, and pack out with offcuts of veneer or hardboard where the wall is hollow. Slacken off the screws, insert the packing and re-tighten. 2½ inch (63mm) screws with No 8 or 10 heads are the best size with countersunk heads. Countersink the battens first, and then mark the walls for drilling and plugging.

The battens allow a free circulation of warm dry air to flow behind the panelling to avoid condensation forming.

When fitting veneered panels into a corner, place a piece of hardboard against the adjacent wall, and hold a pencil flat upon it, with the pencil point on the wall panel. Slide your hand down the wall and mark the panel with a pencil line to follow when cutting the panel to fit. When necessary, protect the grooved edge of a panel with the use of wood blocks and using a mallet, not a hammer, to tap home.

SUBSTRATES

Panel thickness for wall panelling is not critical and here are the most popular types of board.

Type of Board	Application	Fire Rating	Thickness in mm.
Hardboard	Partitions Door facings	Class 1	3 and 6
Chipboard	Panelling Joinery	none	6, 9, 12, 15, 18, 22, 25
Plywood	Panelling Door facings Furniture	Class 1 and 0	1.5, 3, 4, 5, 6, 9, 12, 15, 18, 22, 25
Blockboard	Panelling Furniture	none	12, 15, 18, 22, 25, 32, 38
Laminboard	Panelling Furniture	none	12, 15, 18, 22, 25, 32, 38
Panoflam F.R M1 Chipboard	Panelling Joinery Furniture	Class 1 and 0	10, 12, 15, 19
Marinite Asbestos	Panelling Partitioning	Class 1 Class 0 non-combustible	9, 12, 15, 18, 22, 25
Delignit F.R.C.W. Plywood	Panelling Joinery	Class 0	6, 10, 14, 18
Monolux Non-asbestos	Panelling Partitioning	Class 0 Non-combustible	9, 12, 15, 18, 22, 25
Flaxcore Hardboard faced	Partitioning	None	46, 49, 54
Flaxcore Asbestos faced	Partitioning	Class 0	46, 49, 54
Blockboard Solid core	Door blanks		38, 45, 50, 54

Note: Doors of 45mm and thicker should conform to *BS459 Part 3* and *BS476 Part 8*.
54mm thick doors to one hour firecheck *BS459 Part 3*.

Substrates for use in internal wall panelling should have a 'spread of flame' classification; the following lists cover all boards with CLASS '0' and '1'.

PLYWOOD, CHIPBOARD AND HARDBOARD,
(either impregnated or surface coated) **CLASS 0**

Celgard	4.8mm	Impregnated. Standard hardboard
Karlit FR	9, 12mm	High Density medium board
Lurifuge CL		Chipboard, clear intumescent
Masonite Flame Test	5.4mm	Hardboard
Nullifire WD		Plywood, chipboad or hardboard
		Clear or pigmented intumescent
Oxylene O		Plywood and Chipboard
Retroflame	3.2mm, 4.8mm, and 6.4mm	Plywood, hardboard chipboard
		Blockboard
Swan	3.2mm	Standard hardboard
Vestos		Plywood
Vestoply	4, 6, 9, 12, 18, 25mm	Plywood
Delignit FR	10, 14, 18, 22, 26, 30mm	Compacted beech plywood
Gifu		Plywood
Panoflam	10, 12, 16, 19, 22mm	F R Particle board

HARDBOARD **CLASS 1**

Athyboard Flameshield	4.8mm 6.4mm	High density medium board
Cape FR Fibre board	12, 18, 24mm	One face flame retardant paint
Guardex	3.2mm	Standard hardboard
Sundeala FR	3.2mm, 4.8mm, 6.4mm	Standard hardboard
Vestopanel	9mm, 12mm	Impregnated medium board
Vestoseal	3.6mm	Impregnated standard hardboard

SOFTWOOD, HARDWOOD, CHIPBOARD, HARDBOARD & PLYWOOD **CLASS 1**

Ignicide	1.5mm to 24mm	Impregnated plywood
Vellowboard	4.5mm to 25mm	Impregnated plywood
Celcure F		Softwood, plywood and chipboard
Celguard		Plywood and chipboard
Flameproof		Plywood and chipboard
Fyreprufe		Plywood, chipboard and hardboard
Oxylene		Hardwoods, plywood, chipboard and hardboard
Pyrolith		Softwood plywood, chipboard and hardboard
Retroflame		Plywood, chipboard and hardboard
Vestos		Plywood, chipboard and hardboard

PARTICLE BOARDS **CLASS 1**

Celogil FR	11, 16, 19, 22mm
Broby Amber	12, 15mm
Vestos	12, 15, 18, 22mm

FIRE PREVENTION
When planning wood panelling schemes, the veneer craftsman must also consider fire prevention. There are two main stages of a fire (a) ignition and fire growth; and (b) the fully developed fire.

The behaviour of panelling in the first stage is termed its 'reaction to fire'. In the second it is the material's contribution to the 'fire resistance of an element of building structure'.

Reaction to Fire: The reaction of panelling in the early stages of a fire are:
(a)   non combustibility
(b)   Ignitability
(c)   Surface spread of flame
(d)   Rate of heat release.

Non combustibility does not apply to veneered panelling, as *BS476 Part 4 1970 'Non combustibility test for materials'* shows that even when treated with flame retardants, panelling is classified as combustible.

Ignitability
This classifies panelling on a basis of flame spread and sustained flaming. Timber will ignite at about 270 degrees Centigrade as long as a pilot flame is present, but spontaneous ignition will occur at about 500 degrees Centigrade according to *BS476 Part 5 1968 'Ignitability test for materials'.*

Surface spread of flame
Veneer panelling falls within Class 3 of surface spread of flame as long as the density is at least 400 kg/m³. (Species below this density and insulating board, etc., are classified as Class 4). But all veneered panelling may be up-graded to Class 1 by either impregnation (in the case of commercially produced groundwork and substrates), and surface coating of veneers. Inherent Class 3 ratings of most veneered panels enable them to be used internally without special impregnated substrates, but it is best to up-grade them with a surface coating to Class 1.

Rate of heat release
Wood-based sheet materials fall far below the requirements set for Class 0 as specified in *BS476 Part 6 1968 'Fire Propagation test for materials'* unless factory-produced by specialists.

Fire resistance
This is the ability of an element to carry on performing its function in spite of being exposed to a fully developed fire. The test for fire resistance is *BS476 Part 8 1972 'Test Methods and criteria for fire resistance of elements of building construction'.* As far as veneer panelling is concerned the keywords are its predictable charring rate, and this is covered by *BS5268 Part 4 Section 4;1, 1978.*

Surface coating flame retardants

There are clear, un-pigmented varnishes and lacquers available for surface coating. These are for all conventional methods of application including brushing, spraying, and roller coating.

It is not advisable to thin the coating because a minimum application is necessary to achieve the effect. The manufacturer's instructions should be closely adhered to.

The substrate groundwork classification is most important, and this can easily up-grade the veneer treatment to Class 0.

Many coatings are designed to intumesce upon heating, that is, to swell up, then foam and char; by so doing they entrap a thermally insulating layer of gas against the surface. The foam impedes the passage of heat and oxygen to the substrate and the products of combustion from it.

Another type of intumescent coating, upon being heated, evolves gases or vapours which interfere with the chemistry of the flames.

Unfortunately, the necessity for high loadings of the coating renders the decorative effects of flame retardants inferior to conventional surface lacquers unless you select a water-clear transparent type and these are usually much more expensive.

JOINTING AND WORKING SEQUENCE
Joints

There are various ways to join the wall panelling together.

(a) Butt joint. This is the most usual way, by grooving both edges of the panels, and supplying a loose tongue.
(b) Tongue, groove and secret nail through the tongues.
(c) Tongue, groove and V joint—and secret nail the tongues.
(d) Emphasise the joint by revealing a batten.
(e) Open up the panels to display a contrasting insert strip.
(f) Rebate the edges to insert a matching or contrasting strip.
(g) Solid lip the edges, but veneer over where exposed.
(h) Solid lip the edges after veneering to either match or form contrast, or make a decorative profile.

Edges

The edges require careful thought. For example: the panels fitted inside a door to form a door frame can be exposed so that the door fits inside them, or the door can be hung to cover them; linings fitted inside a window frame can be left to show, or to be covered by the wall panels and concealed; at corners by a chimney breast, you should decide if you want the panels which recede into the alcove to show their edges or be concealed, and so on.

The procedure is to draw a plan of the room and show which edge has to 'master' the other (cover or conceal it). This is most important, as it governs the *width* of the panels. Also indicate where you intend to fit solid edge lippings to one, or both edges and mark whether they are to be applied before veneering in which case the veneers must be wider, or after veneering, in which case the panel size is smaller.

It is usual to groove both edges in continuous panelling and to fit a solid edge where it will be seen.

Veneer continuity

With wall panelling, it is not simply a case of ensuring that veneers are kept in log sequence to avoid a pattern jump, but the continuity has to be planned. For example the area above and below a window aperture, will have to match the panels on each side at the top and bottom. Panels above doors have to match those on each side, even though they may be full sized panels. For this reason, decide upon the best multiple width for the panelling to provide the minimum wastage, taking into account the shape of the room. Panels 4 feet (1219mm) wide may result in narrower panels at room corners, beside doors or windows. Calculate the best multiple to avoid narrow widths which can spoil the effect.

This is the main reason why narrow V grooved panels, or even random width V grooved panels are so popular, as they reduce wastage to the minimum.

Pattern jump

If you started cladding the wall at one side of a door and continued around the room in matched sequence, the pattern jump when you completed the circuit would be far too great.

The trick is to start at one side of a focal point, which will take the eye, and to work equally around from each side of it which will halve the pattern jump.

By skilful planning, allow the main walls to run in matching sequence, but try to make four balanced 'starts' to reduce the pattern jump into four. This is usually done in corners and alcoves. For example, leaves 1 to 8 up to a corner, 17 to 24 from the corner around to a window 32 down to 25 around to the opposite corner and leaves 16 to 9 back to the start. This equalises the pattern jump.

22

Preparation for Finishing

THIS IS A highly specialised subject, worthy of further reading by all veneer craftsmen. A basic understanding of the various processes will guide your approach to decision making.

Since we are concerned with finishing veneered panels, and solid woods, we have to consider these facts:

1.   The natural beauty of veneers is 'only skin deep'. We are dealing, after sanding, with a layer of wood only about 0.5mm thick.
2.   This thin layer will only withstand the minimum of abrasion.
3.   The veneer is absorbent, easily stained, and requires protection from dirt, accidental damage through heat and spillage.
4.   Below the veneer, is a layer of adhesive which must not be affected by the finishing treatment. They must be compatible.
5.   In multi-matched assemblies of veneer, the surface will require a different treatment than that given to similar species in the solid.
6.   The surface treatment given to one species of veneer may be entirely unsuited to another if that species was resinous, oily or gummy etc.
7.   The treatment given to a plain panel may be different to that given to a similar panel containing an inlay motif.

An amateurish finish can mar the result of a really professional work of craftsmanship but it is equally true that a professional finish can enhance and increase the value of antique, scarred furniture.

Sadly, your work will chiefly be judged by the finish you give to it. Therefore one of the most rewarding aspects of veneering is the knowledge of how to provide your work with that professional finish.

Do not be deterred by the confusing and often conflicting advice of 'experts'. Certainly there is a place for technique and this can be mastered; but the 'know how' of choosing the right finish to suit your own capability is more important.

The effect of light

The finish applied to a veneered surface creates an optical effect resulting from substituting for the air above the wood, an optically more dense material. The dark parts of the grain are made to look darker, and the lighter parts only slightly darker, thereby increasing the contrasts and making the grain and figure more attractive.

When a ray of light passes through a prism, it produces the colours of the spectrum; blue, red and yellow, the primary colours. Combinations of the primaries produce the secondary colours, orange violet and green; for example blue and yellow make green; yellow and red make orange and red and blue make violet. When primary and secondary colours are mixed together we get tertiary colours.

Light may come from all manner of sources and we can even see the source, but what we actually see is *reflected* light from the surface the light shines upon. Dispersion of light occurs when light rays fall upon a veneered surface, causing white light to break into its constituent colour rays.

Reflection

A high gloss surface will give a more accurate reflection by maintaining a close relationship between each light ray; a matt finish breaks up this close relationship and the light rays are reflected in all directions.

Some light rays are not transmitted back to the eye, but are absorbed by the matt surface.

Refraction

Refraction is the bending of light rays by the nature of the surface from the angle of incidence of the light source.

If a pure red, blue, and green light were shone on to a surface it would appear as white light; the white being complete reflection of all three primaries, at one third density.

Therefore, surfaces *appear* to be coloured, only because they reflect light. A rich red mahogany surface appears so, only because it reflects red light rays.

In a white light, the surface absorbs the blue and green rays and reflects only the red. It will also appear red in a red light, but black in a blue or green light.

Intensity

The 'redness' of a mahogany surface, for example, will also depend on the type and intensity of light. If a dark colour is placed next to a light colour, the darker colour appears deeper in tone and the lighter colour even lighter by contrast. Therefore, it is the quality of light that modifies the colourtone and hue.

Patina

The patina of age, and the effects of infra red and ultra violet light rays, cause some woods to darken and others to fade. This is why great care should be taken not to position a cabinet or veneered surface where it is viewed in partial light or in light and shade.

The emotional effects of colour are subjective. Reds are warm and friendly, yellow and golds are stimulating and cheerful, and greens and blues are tranquillising. Fortunately, in the wood spectrum we are chiefly concerned with the yellow — brown — red categories.

The workroom

The first consideration then, is plenty of light in the workroom. It is best not to have a light hanging down over the workbench, but to flood the light upwards on to a white ceiling to dispense with shadows.

The polishing room should not be the same room as the clean-up room where you have sanding dust, etc. in the atmoshere, and the temperature should always be around 70 to 75 degrees Fahrenheit (21 to 23 degrees Centigrade) and evenly distributed. There should be a means of air extraction to take away odours, fumes and volatile solvents — and a good fire extinguisher standing by just in case. Have a metal tin with a tight lid available for the disposal of waste materials.

Sanding

It cannot be over-emphasised that if your veneered panels are perfectly flat and true you are more than half way to a perfect finish.

There are several points to watch when commencing the sanding operation.

Firstly, the open pores of the veneer will fill up with the sanding dust. In multi-matches, the dark dust from one veneer may be carried into the open pores of adjacent lighter toned veneers which could cause discolouration when the first coat of polish is applied. Secondly, many natural woods such as padauk, rosewood and rosa peroba, contain natural pigments, which will stain light veneers such as sycamore, horse chestnut and obeche.

These points are especially important when inlay motifs containing dyed veneers are used, dyed-black sanding dust will discolour any other veneer it comes into contact with unless properly sealed.

Thirdly, abrasion across the grain of veneer will cause a fuzziness due to minute scratches on the surface which will blurr the vividness and mar the result of the finish.

Use an old hairbrush or other soft brush, and get into the habit of regular brushing the surface between sanding each time. Make sure that every particle of sanding dust is removed, even if it means working over the surface with a small vacuum cleaner.

Try to work along the grain, although this is not always possible, as for example, with a crossbanded panel. Use a cork rubbing block in short flat strokes on the crossbanding, *with* the grain, before papering the main panel, using a finer paper to remove any overlap of fuzziness around the edges. Highly figured burr veneer panels can be sanded in a circular movement.

When using a cork rubbing block—or, for that matter, any power sander—it is important that you keep at least two thirds of the block or machine on the work at all times and overhang the panel by one third at the edges.

Power sanders require skilled handling. Powered belt sanders, reciprocal or straight line sanders can wreck a veneered panel in fractions of a second if handled incorrectly.

If the tool is tilted slightly, or there is a slight hesitation at the end of its run down a panel, this would double the sanding time at the ends and rub through to the crossbanding.

A rotary sander is not so powerful, but most craftsmen try to use too much pressure on it; the machine is heavy enough and only requires guiding.

A few loose grains of grit caught up on an orbital sander will scour deep ridges in the face veneer. Provided that you never lay the sander face down—always on its side, and always brush and vacuum the surface between sanding with different paper grades, the orbital sander is to be preferred.

The right paper to use for finishing is open-coat silicon carbide paper, eg. *Lubrisil* type. Alternatively, garnet paper with aluminium oxide as the abrasive. Begin with grade 150, and change to 220 and then to 320. The secret of successful finishing is to work through progressively finer abrasives.

Finally, when you have the surface as smooth as possible to the touch, and have brushed and vacuumed it clean, wipe the surface with a damp cloth or tack rag soaked in white spirit, which will remove all remaining traces of dust, and the solvent will evaporate quickly leaving the surface ready for the next finishing stage.

Stopping

This is sometimes known as filler. Examine the surface carefully in a good light for any signs of dents, nicks, open joints, splits, tiny holes etc. These are now filled with a wood stopping. There are various types available in a wide range of wood tones. They may be intermixed to obtain an exact match for any required shade. White or yellow may be added to lighten; brown or black to darken to the desired shade.

Stopping should always be applied one tone darker than required as it will dry lighter. It is packed into the defect and allowed to stand proud of the surface to dry to allow for shrinkage as it dries out. The surface may then be block-sanded smooth, brushed free of dust or vacuumed. For external veneering, always use special waterproof stopping. Polyurethane finishes require special PU stoppings.

Both interior, exterior and special stoppings are intended for use on veneer surfaces which are otherwise sound and supported. If you have a damaged edge which is unsupported, this will require a catalytic wood stopping.

Very small indentations or tiny holes may be filled without using wood stopping at all. Simply scrape the veneered surface to form dust, and mix with white PVA adhesive into a paste, which will form a self colour stopping.

Grain fillers

If the pores of the veneer are not filled, the surface will remain open grained and in some cases an open grained finish is desired. But for the majority of veneer work, whether you want the top coat finish to be high gloss, satin matt, or matt, you will almost certainly want the surface to be *smooth*. In other words, whatever the degree of *shine*, you want it smooth and the only way to achieve this is either by applying successive layers of polish or to fill the grain with a grain filler.

It is very important to use a grain filler recommended by the finish manufacturers, as the filler must be compatible with the finish. Heatproof finishes require heatproof fillers; waterproof finishes— waterproof fillers; catalytic finishes—catalytic fillers etc.

Fillers are usually available in two forms: either natural 'transparent', which are intended for you to colour to suit your project, or in a wide range of wood tones, ready-mixed, to match up with wood stopping. For most interior furniture purposes craftsmen use the ready-mixed toned oil-bound paste grain fillers, or oil-bound 'transparent or natural' paste grain-fillers which may be coloured with oil-soluble aniline colours.

Resin-bound fillers are used with all catalytic finishes, available in a range of wood tones.

The chief requirement of a grain filler is that it does not sink in the grain as its volatile solvent evaporates. It should not show in the grain nor impair the clarity of the grain.

As it is impossible to lighten a veneer to match another, the correct way to achieve a match is to select a veneer a tone lighter than the one to be matched, and to stain it down to match before using any grain filler.

Always test the stain or stain-filler on a scrap of veneer from the project. Apply each of the sequences to the scrap before commencing on the main project.

The filler is prepared according to makers' instructions and agitated well to ensure that the ingredients are thoroughly mixed. The filler is then applied to the veneer with a stiff bristle brush, packing the filler well into the grain in both directions and finishing off along the grain. It is allowed to dry out thoroughly and set, after which the surplus is removed with a coarse rag, sacking, canvas, or wood wool, vigorously rubbed in a circular movement and finished off along the grain. The surface is then block sanded, brushed clean of dust or vacuumed.

Readers requiring more information on the various types of stains and finishes and their preparation and application should refer to one of the appropriate books recommended in the Bibliography at the end of the book.

23

Repair and Restoration

VENEERED FURNITURE will eventually be in need of some form of repair or restoration. The first consideration is, how far is the repair justified?

Amateur restorers in their enthusiasm tend to over-restore to the point where restoration ends and renewal begins.

The evidence of age is something to be treasured in furniture and is easily eliminated. The natural patina achieved by many years of devoted wax polishing, intermixed with layers of atmospheric grime, become welded into a finish difficult to imitate, but once removed, will demote an antique into a lower valued restoration piece.

The amount of restoration required is no indication of the value of the item. The degree of repair is another consideration. A simple repair to a blistered veneered surface might suffice, where a more permanent repair might involve extensive work to the veneers or groundwork.

A problem that museum conservation departments are faced with is when a piece of furniture has been 'restored' by someone who has added ornamentation alien to the original piece. The Victorians excelled at this type of mischief by replacing handles or adding decoration that didn't belong.

The golden rule is to remain faithful to the original. Enthusiasm should be balanced with restraint and work should remain within the limitations of one's own capacity.

The first step is to determine the type, extent and cause of the damage; the nature of the finish, type of veneer and groundwork, and whether a partial repair or a complete repair is necessary or justified.

There are three basic types of repair needed: repair and restoration of the finish; repair or renewal of the veneers; repair or renovation of the groundwork or frame.

REPAIR AND RESTORATION OF THE FINISH
The first step is to determine the type of finish on the piece. There are six basic types: Wax polish; Oil polish; French polish; Varnish; Nitro-cellulose; and Resin lacquers.

Test an unimportant surface of the furniture to identify the finish by a process of elimination.

It is almost certain that the surface has been wax polished over the original finish, by a generation of housewives. De-wax the surface with turpentine. If the surface then reacts to methylated spirits, it has a shellac or french polished finish.

Lacquer thinners has no effect on a varnished surface. Acetone will soften shellac, varnish and cellulose but have no effect on resin catalytic finishes.

It is quite possible on an old piece of furniture that it may have originally received an oil varnish finish and then waxed for a long period. A previous restorer may have stripped off the wax finish, effected a repair and french polished the surface. This could have been followed by more waxing.

For our purpose, we have to strip the finish down to the oil varnish or beyond. Cellulose may have been applied over shellac – never the other way around or crazing would result. If the surface responds to cellulose thinners, do not apply rubbers of cellulose by hand or you will work up the old surface.

Oil varnish may be applied over a shellac surface but never the other way around.

Wax polish, on the other hand, may be applied over all other finishes and is the usual maintenance finish.

It is therefore worth repeating that the purpose of reviving the finish is to remove the film of grime without unduly affecting the rich patina of age; to reveal the original finish by restoring its lustre.

Another point worth stressing is that the scars of long service and duty which the surface reveals such as minor blemishes, digs, scratches, burns, scuffs, heat or alcohol rings, ink or perfume spots, are honourable scars won in giving a lifetime of service.

It is part of the art of the professional faker to attempt to imitate these defects to 'convert' a clever reproduction into an antique!
Reviving the surface
Begin by washing the surface with liquid soap and water and rinse with clean water applied sparingly with a wrung sponge and dried off immediately with a chamois leather and a clean dry cloth. Never saturate with water—and work with speed.

Next, wash the surface with three tablespoonfuls of turpentine and a similar quantity of boiled linseed oil if the surface looks murky after the wash treatment.

Rub this in briskly, working a small area at a time until the cloth drags. Now wash with liquid soap and water for the second time, rinse, sponge, chamois leather and dry off with a cloth.

This wash treatment can produce surprising results. Items which were black with age blossom into their original finish with the patina intact. But any artificially contrived patina by an early restorer can be easily washed away.

Alternatively, after the first soap and water wash, if the surface is lifeless and dull, make up a mixture of equal parts of boiled linseed oil, vinegar and white spirit and this will remove all traces of grease or oiliness.

Here are other useful revivers to try:

(a)   Equal parts of camphorated oil and spirits of camphor.
(b)   One part of terebene; four parts boiled linseed oil and twelve parts of vinegar.
(c)   Equal parts vinegar and methylated spirit to make one pint to which 1oz. camphor is dissolved in the spirit, and 1 fluid oz. boiled linseed oil and 1oz. butter of antimony.

There are also a wide range of commercially available revivers.

Identifying the defects

The first examination is to see whether the surface damage is *on* the film, *in* the film, or *through* the film, into the veneer.

Begin by examining the film to determine if the problem lies *on* the film.

Aeration: A thick film of finish with any rapid drying material can arise by trapping the solvent beneath a partially dry top skin of the coating. This gives the appearance of a milky film. Where a heavy coating has been applied to open grained veneer air pockets in the grain try to break through the drying top film which cannot then flow to bridge the cavities, and a rim forms around the cavities.

Bleeding: This is caused when a stain or stain filler bleeds up through the succeeding coats.

Blistering: When water, grease or other foreign matter has been allowed to interpose between coats, or after the film was dry, by exposure to excessive heat.

Blushing: If the solvents have evaporated too quickly they can cool the drying film causing water from the atmosphere to condense on the film causing the film to whiten. On a dry film this can be caused by spilled water especially if the liquid is hot, such as tea or coffee. Raise the workroom temperature and use a blush retarder. It is also caused by draughts, or high relative humidity in the workroom.

Bronzing: Caused by the stain or stain filler being applied too heavily and not cleaned off properly resulting in a murky appearance.

Blooming: This causes a blueish appearance on varnished or lacquered surfaces and is caused by excessive rubbing, inadequate ventilation, oil in the film, or chemical fumes.

Bubbling: This is similar to aeration, caused by air pockets or solvents being trapped by a top coating which dries too quickly.

Caking: May be caused by insufficient lubricant used with pumice or rottenstone; the harsh quality of the abrasives or excessive heat generated by the felt rubbing block.

Checking: Hair-line checks in the film result when a quick drying film is applied over a slower one; or a hard film is applied over a soft one due to differences in the rate of expansion and contraction with humidity changes.

Chipping: Caused in many layered finishes, when the top coatings were applied after the undercoats had dried hard and very smooth.

Crawling: Where the top coat creeps after being applied over a waxed or greasy surface, or a thick film was applied in a cold workroom.

Crazing: Caused by any of the following: tensions in the dried film; when colour matching is achieved by mixing colours from different sources and the resins being incompatible, or with different rates of drying; successive coatings are applied too quickly leading to solvent retention; extremes of temperature in the workroom; and, if inert fillers are used with excessively thinned undercoats.

Cissing: This is a formation of craters in the film caused by grease or silicone spots on the surface before the top coat was applied.

Flaking: Caused by varnish being applied over a heavy coating of shellac.

Lifting: When one coat has the effect of a remover on the preceeding coat, caused by using incompatible coatings.

Orange Peeling: This results in a pock-marked appearance and is a spraying defect. It may be caused by high airline pressure and too fast spraying technique; spraying too closely and too slowly; too low an airline pressure; too great a pressure on the material.

Overspray: Sometimes known as dry spray. Caused by cellulose being deposited on the surface in a dry condition due to the gun being held too far from the surface, or too high a pressure. The cellulose dries off at the edges of the spray cone before it reaches the surface and creates a sandy appearance.

Pinholing: Tiny holes or pits appear in the film caused by improper filling of the pores in the veneer, or of insufficiently dry undercoats.

Pitting: Similar to cissing.

Printing: Caused by an imprint on a varnished surface.

Runs: Sags caused by excessive material being applied to vertical surfaces or topcoating which has been thinned too much.

Sweating: Glossy spots or streaks in a varnished film caused by premature rubbing or abrasion.

White in the Grain: Caused by trapped grain filler solvent, sometimes aggravated by using inferior lacquers with weak solvent mixtures and consequent low tolerance for excess non-solvents in grain filler.

Wrinkling: Excessive air pressure on too heavy a coat of cellulose can cause the surface to wrinkle. Also in acid catalytic or combination lacquers, where the film has sufficiently cured for the subsequent coat not to coalesce, but not enough to prevent solvent penetration, which lifts the partially cured film.

Two other film defects which are attributable to the veneer are caused by silica deposits in certain veneers bleeding through the film; and, incompatibility of the solvents of the finish material with the catalyst in the adhesive, which may cause bleeding through the film.

Repairing the finish

Examine the freshly washed surface against a strong light and if the treatment was successful the surface needs only refinishing.

Fine scratches

Surface scratches which do not penetrate through the film may be rubbed out with the finest grade garnet finishing paper, lubricated with boiled linseed oil, applied with a felt block. This may affect the surrounding colour. If so, rectify this with a couple of rubbers of garnet polish to the repaired area, toned with aniline spirit dye to match the surrounding surface. If the scratches were evident before the wash treatment, de-wax the surface before the repair and re-surface the whole area with french polish and wax.

Deep scratches

Cat's claw marks will penetrate through the film to the veneer. They should be filled with plastic wood, wood stopping or stick shellac and when dry scraped level. Lightly paper with garnet finishing paper lubricated with boiled linseed oil. Finish off with rottenstone and oil. Repolish.

Accident scars

A sharp blow can cause a deep jagged scar through to the veneer. Remove all splinters and smooth out the cut with a knife, and repair as a deep scratch. After papering, the scratch should be painted over using a pencil brush dipped in thin white shellac. The repair is then coloured to match the surrounding surface with a rubber of garnet polish with aniline dye added to match. When dry, the finish is brought up with pumice and oil, and rottenstone and oil.

Cracked surfaces

Minor cracks may be filled with plastic wood or wood stopping, but more serious defects require stick shellac or catalytic stopping all of which are available in wood tones. Select a tone lighter than the surrounding surface.

When burning in the shellac stick, work quickly to avoid damage to the old surface, and avoid overfilling as this may prove difficult to scrape off without causing further damage to the surface.

Allow to dry and level with a chisel. Rub smooth with pumice and water followed by rottenstone and oil, using a felt pad.

Stick shellac is opaque and will show up in the grain and must therefore be coloured out using aniline dye applied with a pencil brush along the grain.

Plastic wood and wood fillers take stains a tone darker than shellac, and should therefore be given a coat of shellac before the repair is coloured in the dye then repolished.

Worn edges

Lightly paper the worn edge with garnet paper grade 9/0 to remove the film of polish. Give the edge a rubber of garnet polish with aniline dye to match the surface. When dry, french polish the surface.

Rub through

Sometimes the stain is accidentally rubbed through. Apply stain filler to the area, or a rubber of garnet polish toned with aniline dye.

Mouldings

When worn edges also include shaped contours or lippings, but the felt pad cannot conform to the edge contours, apply a slush of pumice powder to the shaped edge and rub with a stubbly bristled brush dipped in boiled linseed oil.

Wipe off the oil at intervals to see the degree of lustre obtained, and finish off with rottenstone applied direct to the edge with a clean brush.

Water stains

These leave a chalky white mineral stain on the film. Wipe the stain with white spirit or turps substitute and if the stain persists, rub with lint free cloth moistened with methylated spirits. Do not damp the surrounding surface.

If the water stain persists, rub down the patch with a slush of pumice powder and water if varnished, or pumice stone and oil if the surface is shellacked.

Next apply a rubber of half and half shellac and methylated spirits, and finish off with camphorated oil. Remove the oil by wiping with vinegar on a clean cloth. When dry, repolish.

Milk spots and stains

The lactic acid in milk forms a ring in lacquered and varnished surfaces. It is removed with pumice stone and water as above.

Ink stains

Cover the spot with household bleach, rinse off with clean water and dry with a chamois leather. If it persists brush over the stain with diluted nitric acid and wipe off with camphorated oil followed by the vinegar wash. Persistent stains may then be tackled with pumice and water.

Beer and spirit stains

These appear as white alcohol rings. Rub the spots with turpentine with a sprinkle of salt added. Persistent stains should be papered out with garnet paper taking care not to rub through the stain below. Try painting out the ring with a fine pencil brush with light brush strokes along the grain, using aniline dye in white shellac polish. When dry refinish the surface.

Heat damage

Damage from hot plates, hot water spillage, electric irons, or from the piece being exposed to intense heat from a fire, cause varying degrees of heat damage.

Rub the affected area with linseed oil and turps applied with a rag. Or try camphorated oil applied vigorously and then removed with vinegar.

Small blisters caused by local heat can be rubbed out with flour grade glasspaper lubricated with linseed oil. Wipe off with white spirit.

Where the surface is not blistered, but the heat has caused discolouration of the film, rub out with pumice and oil with a felt pad, and check progress occasionally with white spirit.

When the patch is rubbed out, restore the lustre with the addition of rottenstone and oil; wipe with vinegar and dry with a clean cloth. Repolish.

Cigarette burns

It depends upon the degree of burn. Light surface burns in the film may be sanded, stain filled, and given a rubber of shellac. Deeper burns may require a build up of several coats of shellac coloured with aniline dye. Bad cases, which have burned through the film and charred the veneer require scraping and cleaning with a knife. Shellac stick is then melted to fill the depression, and a simulated grain painted in with a fine pencil brush using aniline dye in garnet polish. When dry the surface should be repolished.

Complete Refinish

There will be some pieces where the effort to effect several patch repairs would cost more than to strip and completely repolish.

Take the piece outside and take every precaution against splashing other parts of the item—as well as surrounding walls or floor.

Use a strong paint or varnish remover—most of which are inflammable or with obnoxious odours.

Follow the manufacturer's instructions; allow plenty of time for the remover to do its work and then scrape off the finish.

Complete the task by scrubbing the surface with methylated spirit or white spirit, then wiping clean to remove all traces of the wax evaporation retardant left by the remover. Allow to dry out overnight and lightly paper the surface with 9/0 garnet paper.

If the stained surface has been affected, re-stain and completely refinish the surface.

Patched Veneer Surface

If the defect has penetrated to the veneer surface and this requires patching, the newly repaired veneer insertion should be stained if required, and given a protective coating of shellac *before* the surrounding surface is cleaned. New veneer will not lose itself on an old piece of furniture unless it is stained to resemble the patina of the remainder.

For mahogany, use bichromate of potash stain, made by dissolving crystals in water and test for effect on a veneer scrap. The full effect of its darkening is apparent only after it dries out.

Oak furniture may be stained with Vandyke crystals to which a little Bismark brown water soluble aniline dye can be added if the colour is too cold, or, black may be added to darken the tone.

These additional tones should be mixed separately into a solution before being added to the original solution.

REPAIR OR RENEWAL OF VENEERS

Splits and cracks

Veneers which were not correctly flattened prior to laying can result in splits or cracks and veneers laid in the wrong grain direction, or on groundwork with a high moisture content may split.

Cracks will often occur in burrs and curl veneers where their grain direction co-incides with that of the substrate crossbanding, and in most cases this cannot be avoided. This is also true with marquetry, parquetry and elaborate veneer matches such as eight and sixteen piece assemblies which risk cracking when the grain direction coincides with the crossbanding below.

Any repair will depend on how badly the surface is split: scrape the surface of the face veneer to create a self colour veneer dust which is mixed with white PVA adhesive to form an invisible filler. Alternatively, a wide range of wood toned wood stoppings or plastic wood tones are available which can be intermixed. Stick shellac can be melted into badly cracked surfaces, using a hot soldering iron or heated metal spatula. The shellac is packed well into the crack and built up slightly proud of the surface until dry to allow for shrinkage. Scrape level with a scraper and paper smooth the following day.

If you decide to re-veneer the surface, prevent the future recurrence of the problem by brushing adhesive on the groundwork and stretching fine Japanese silk or muslin over the surface. This will form a perfectly neutral underlay to receive the veneers.

More prominent cracks may need to have a veneer insert. The more wild or strongly marked the veneer figure, the easier it is to effect an invisible repair. Never cut a square, rectangular, oval or circular patch; always cut a jagged, irregular shape which will lose itself in the pattern. Take a craft knife and cut along one of the prominent markings freehand. Cut the repair piece oversize. Next, soften the veneer by using a damp sponge and local heat from an iron. Then prize off the damaged or split veneer piece.

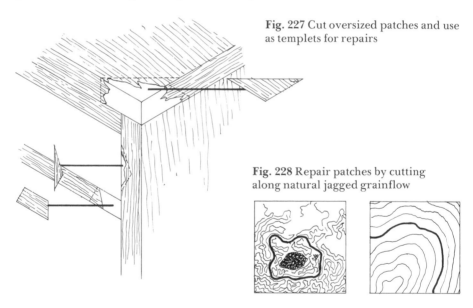

Fig. 227 Cut oversized patches and use as templets for repairs

Fig. 228 Repair patches by cutting along natural jagged grainflow

Use the oversized strip to act as a templet to guide the knife when cutting the replacement from similar veneer stock.

Alternatively, you can trace the outline of the required patch, on to the replacement veneer and cut it out first, and use this as the templet to cut around it into the damaged veneer for a tight fit before removing it.

Edge Veneers

The next most common defect in veneers is damage to working edges, such as the meeting edges of doors and the front edge of drawers.

This is particularly bad on edges which have been veneered direct to chipboard or other groundwork without first applying a solid edge lipping.

It is always best to re-veneer the edge rather than repair it. Try to cut a 45 degree bevel along the edge without touching the face veneer, and fit a triangular edge lipping to the working edge before applying the edge veneer, and the problem will not recur.

Holes

Sometimes a damaged spot or heavy indentation leaves a hole in the surface. Or perhaps a door lock or handle has been fitted incorrectly and the veneered surface has to be repaired over a hole. After the groundwork has been filled, the hole can be invisibly repaired using a veneer punch. (These and their use are described in the tools and equipment chapter).

The method is to search over a replacement veneer for a suitable matching figure and mark it clearly with centre lines or draw around the position of the punch.

Then tape the spot with gummed veneer tape before using the punch, which will aid the ejection and also keep any fragments held together.

Place the veneer on a cutting board, put the punch in position, and depress it against its spring pressure so that the cutter blade touches the veneer. Give the punch a heavy blow with a mallet and it will cut out the required shape. It is better to achieve this in a single blow rather than strike twice, as the cutter may move a fraction and spoil the patch.

Next, place gummed paper tape over the defect in the panel surface after carefully drawing alignment lines to guide the positioning of the veneer punch.

This time, do not expect the punch to eject the cut shape, which will be retained on the panel with glue. Dampen the patch and apply local heat to the spot then remove the unwanted piece using a skew chisel with a shallow spoon bend. It is important not to disturb the under-lying crossbanding veneer.

Multiple patching

If you do not want to attempt to cut a large patch freehand as previously described, another way is to use a series of punches of various shapes.

Cut and patch the first part and then overlap the second shaped punch and repeat the process. On some highly figured burr veneers, which often contain these bad patches, up to five or six overlapped patches can be cut in this way.

Yew is a veneer often full of small knot-holes which have fallen out and they make a very attractive feature. If they cannot be found and replaced from other leaves of similar material, use the veneer punch for repairs.

Trade houses often supply bundles of curls and burrs already containing veneer patches inserted by veneer punch. It is always advisable to buy more leaves than required for the project and use the surplus for patching requirements.

Always clean the groundwork of all traces of the old glue, when effecting repairs and avoid delaminating the surrounding sound veneer when applying heat. Skilful use of the chisel can avoid using heat at all.

Blisters

There are several causes of blisters in the veneered surface, which are pockets of air caused by delamination of the glueline.

This may be caused by bad jointing in the corestock or crossbanding; badly distributed adhesive; or inadequate pressure when cauling or clamping. Another cause could be that perhaps putty was used to patch a knot hole in the groundwork and this may have fallen out or delaminated.

If the blister only affects the face veneer, and it is sound or unbroken, slit the blister with the tip of a craftknife *with* the grain and insert fresh glue on the end of a sliver of veneer.

Place kitchen foil over the blister and use a domestic iron to heat the glue and re-lay. Remove the foil, cover the spot with polythene and clamp a heated wood block over the repair until it sets.

If the blister is fairly large, it may be necessary to cut an irregular V shape along the grain in order to peel back the veneer. To do this, cover the blistered area with a damp cloth or moistened pad of blotting paper, and heat with a domestic iron to soften the glue around the blister. This enables the dirt, grease or other matter which may have entered cracked or broken blisters, to be cleaned out and the old glue scraped away. (A useful scraper for cleaning out a broken blister is made by flattening the end of a nail.)

Fresh glue can be inserted, the veneer carefully relaid and ironed over foil as before and clamped over a wooden block (see Fig. 223).

Where the blister is caused by delamination of the groundwork, possibly by a putty patch in the corestock, drill a small hole right through the blister and through the groundwork. Use a glue injector or hypodermic syringe to force glue such as *Superglue* or instant contact adhesive below the defect. Do not use too much glue or this can increase the damage by loosening the surrounding veneer to make room for the excess glue. Put the blister under block pressure over-night to see if this has cured the deep seated groundwork problem before dealing with the face veneer repair.

If the blister occurs on an existing cabinet, clamping may be a problem unless you have the type of edging clamp that can be fixed to a sashclamp at right angles, and can bring pressure to bear in the middle of a flat surface.

If you make a temporary rig-up by using a car jack against a wall or ceiling, remember two vital precautions. Firstly, to spread the load by placing some 2ft. squares of plywood on the ceiling or wall to distribute the loading at that end and secondly, if the cabinet is hollow below the pressure point, or standing on feet, strut out the hollow or from the lower part of the cabinet to the floor, with bridge-struts to take the loading. In all such repairs it is largely a question of the craftsman's ingenuity.

True face patching

It is important when repairing matched veneers, to examine the veneer and establish whether the section being repaired is true face (tight closed pores) or reverse open pored. The examination is best done with a piece of the damaged veneer which you would have to clean up for the purpose.

Ensure that the repair is in the same face, otherwise it will stand out prominently when subsequently polished.

Also, when selecting a veneer for a repair, try to choose one with similar grain and figure characteristics, but a tone lighter in shade to allow for the darkening of the patch during the finishing process. The original cabinet cannot be lightened—it is far better to darken the patch.

Double repair

When it has proved impossible to locate a suitable veneer for a repair, the trade trick is to effect *two* repairs. Remove a portion of veneer from a relatively unimportant part of the cabinet to repair the prominent part, and use an approximate match to repair the unimportant part. It is a case of two good repairs being better than one bad one. Also the accurate identification of a veneer on a period piece may be very difficult with the face side ingrained with the patina of age and the other face disclosured with glue.

This is also true of modern furniture, as it is common practice for furniture manufacturers to colour-match such veneers as afrormosia, African walnut, agba, etc., to resemble teak, for example. Fortunately the restorer can use the same techniques to marry his repair to the original in the finishing processes.

Mitre repair

Where a surrounding veneer which is mitred at the corner of a panel is in need of repair, remove the complete strip and butt up the new veneer to the mitre joint and the repair will be invisible.

Another common fault is when solid framework has shrunk and split the veneers around a door frame. The repair is made by stripping all

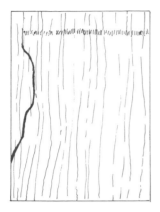

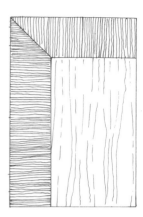

Fig. 229 Repair of veneer damage with new mitred crossbanding

the veneers from around the door frame, and replacing them with crossbanding veneers, possibly highlighted with an inlay line, with the object of making the veneer mitres of the crossbanding coincide with the solid wood mitres of the door frame.

Curved surfaces

These repairs are usually made with either the veneer hammer method, or heated sandbag acting as a caul. The usual rig-up employing a car jack from wall or ceiling is used, and struts are positioned slightly out of vertical and then tapped upright to increase pressure; or wedges are used at the ends of the struts for the same purpose, bringing sustained pressure on crossbearers.

Contact adhesives can be used without resorting to caul pressure if the curve allows. (See also *Cylindrical surfaces* in Chapter 19)

Mouldings

Damaged mouldings are usually repaired in a sandbox after embedding the moulding in the sand to make the impression. Lay a wad of paper in the impression, followed by the veneer and the glued moulding. Lay a heavy block of wood on top and apply clamp pressure.

If the moulding cannot be detached for insertion into a sandbox, a caul will have to be made. First cover the moulding with a piece of polythene sheet and make a plaster mould. Next, fold a few thicknesses of glasspaper to the same thickness of the veneer to be used, and pin this to the moulding.

Now rub the plaster mould several times up and down against the glasspaper and a perfect fit will result.

Tenting

Tenting is caused by water penetration. This often results from accidental damage caused by water spillage (from watering indoor plants etc) which seeps into the jointed veneer surface and delaminates the veneer. Joints and edges suffer most from this defect.

The first step is to dry out the panel. Do not use a very hot iron, but only a moderate heat as the moisture content of the veneer must not be affected as this would result in more damage.

Cover the affected area with blotting paper or clean paper and use the domestic iron to dry out the water damage.

This process may have to be repeated a few times until the veneer is dry and a normal repair made by inserting fresh glue after cleaning out the dried and contaminated old glueline. The joint is then relaid and clamped.

Bruises

Knocks, dents and bruises and other surface indentations can be raised by one of two methods: either fold pieces of damp rag over the bruise and heat the rag with a domestic iron and repeat this several times. Or, make many tiny needle prick marks through the bruised area, and place a water droplet over each tiny hole. Now touch each water droplet with a heated tool to vaporise them into steam. This will raise the depression without delaminating the bruised area.

Brass Inlays

When wood is heated it contracts; metal expands, forming into a loop or arched shape. If it is not possible to re-clamp the brass due to the recess being too small due to contraction, make a few fine sawcuts on the underside of the brass and file the ends to fit the veneer recess. Any modern 'superglue' will suffice provided that you work quickly and scrape off all traces from the veneers immediately.

Marquetry or Parquetry Repairs

Broken, damaged or missing parts of inlay motifs or parquetry assemblies can be repaired by using any of the marquetry techniques previously described.

The outline of the missing part is traced. To get an accurate fit it is best to lay a piece of tracing paper over the inlay and rub the surface with a soft pencil to obtain the outline. This can be emphasised by working around the outline with a thumbnail. Trace this outline to the selected replacement veneer, and place on the cutting board. Cut the shape fractionally oversize by angling the knife handle slightly towards the centre of the patch.

When the new part is placed in position use it as a templet to guide the knife and cut around it into the lower motif veneers. Carefully remove the fractional edge of the inlay veneer and insert the new piece.

If the motif is small enough or lends itself to being removed completely from the groundwork by heating and prizing off, it can be taped together and used as a window for repair by the window method and/or bevel cut fretsaw repair.

REPAIR AND RENOVATION OF THE GROUNDWORK

The most common problem with groundwork is shrinkage and distortion caused by central heating; swollen, twisted, cast, warped or split due to climatic conditions; or, neglect and accidental damage.

The shrinkage of solid timber takes place around the annual growth rings as the moisture dries out, therefore radially cut boards shrink in their *thickness,* and tangentially cut boards across their *width* and they will warp *away* from their heart side. Where this movement has been prevented by cross battens or screws, the board will twist, split or both.

Mitred wooden frames may have open joints. Often, timber of various species has been used for groundwork with varying rates of shrinkage. The most usual problem is the failure of the groundwork to have been constructed to allow for this movement.

Solid wood groundwork may be repaired in various ways. It may be flattened by mechanical pressure or by changing the humidity. But any attempt to dampen or steam the board and force it flat will be of no avail, as it will eventually return to its warped condition as it dries out.

Pull the board flat if it is not too thick or too hard, and secure with cross battens. Or veneer the back with the veneer in the *same* grain direction as the timber. Keep the panel under pressure until ready to fix immediately into its framework.

Bond another, thinner board to the groundwork with its heart side facing the original, and form a thicker panel after force flattening the original.

Table tops which are screwed diagonally through the rail should have the screws removed and replaced with buttons fitted in grooves or mortises to allow for future movement. If the top is screwed and plugged, enlarge the holes in the rail to allow the top to shrink.

If the panel is warped, but the veneer on the face is intact, the groundwork may be grooved. Make sawcuts along the underside up to two-thirds of the way through the thickness of the board, which is then clamped flat. Glue veneer strips into the sawcuts which should be about 1 inch (25mm) apart. Take care to avoid grooving along any joint in the original top.

Place small glueblocks between the grooves under crossbearers to enable long strips of veneer about 3mm thick to be glued in long lengths. When dry, the strips are planed level with the surface.

If the surface is to be re-veneered, saw the groundwork into strips, plane them true, and edge joint the strips with alternate heart side opposed, adding a further strip if necessary to make up the original width. By making the panel thinner than the original, it would then permit veneering both sides for a balanced construction.

Where groundwork has been affected by beetle infestation or fungal attack, cover the veneered face temporarily with hardboard for protec-

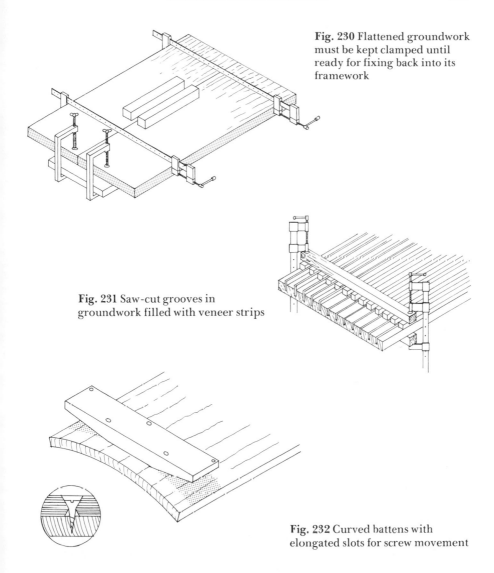

Fig. 230 Flattened groundwork must be kept clamped until ready for fixing back into its framework

Fig. 231 Saw-cut grooves in groundwork filled with veneer strips

Fig. 232 Curved battens with elongated slots for screw movement

tion and plane the back of the groundwork down to about ³/₁₆ inch (4mm) thickness, when it may be bonded to a new groundwork of laminated construction, veneered on the back.

When only one side may be veneered in keeping with the original piece, lay it on the heart side of the panel using a contact adhesive thereby avoiding moisture or heat.

A groundwork with severe curvature, will require battening on the back. Slightly curve the battens opposite to the curvature of the groundwork, and make elongated slots for the screws to pass through to permit future movement.

Broken joints

When a joint has come apart, shoot the joint afresh and reglue it. Rub both parts together placed on a flat surface over clean paper, with G clamps at the ends, and with sash clamps about one third from each end and one on the opposite side in the middle.

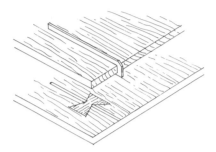

Fig. 233 Veneer strips or dovetail keys used to repair split groundwork

Splits

Splits along the grain may be opened up wider with a sawcut, and have inserted a tapered strip, with the grain, which should be glued, clamped and when dry, planed level.

Splits at an angle to the grain should have a dovetail key inserted, preferably on the underside. Take care that the two edges are kept in alignment, as clamping pressure could force one side higher than the other.

Knots and plugs

Knotholes can be patched with pellets in diamond or boat shapes with the grain in the same direction as the board. Never use dowels or insert plugs through the grain, as the long grain will not shrink with the groundwork and will remain proud of the surface.

Plywood and laminated board defects

The outer casings of plywood and laminated boards are usually of constructional veneers which are rotary cut. These often contain spindle or funnel shaped holes on the surface caused by hairchecks. When the constructional veneer was being cut from the log, tiny hairchecks run ahead of the knife towards the veneer surface on the underside and the thicker the veneer the more pronounced the hairchecks become. If the veneer shrinks in drying, they affect the surface, especially if this open pored torn side happens to be laid on the surface of the plywood or laminated board. A blunt rotary knife can tear (rather than cut) the veneer from the log. The pressure bar on the lathe can 'iron' the face of the veneer so tightly as to compress it, and case-hardening glueline problems result. A chipped veneer knife will cause raised scores across the face of veneers.

Badly jointed corestock will telegraph the defect through to the face veneer and overlapped or slipped joints in the core cause similar problems.

In these boards, the swelling and shrinkage caused by humidity changes is taken up by the gluelines. The thicker the glueline, the greater the pressure on the veneers; conversely, the thinner the glueline, the less stress on the outer casings.

Hard, brittle resin adhesives, such as urea formaldehyde, melamine, phenolic or resorcinol may shrink in hardening and produce checks or splits on the surface. The furniture would be modern if this was the problem and the easiest way to deal with this is to renew the groundwork if possible and re-veneer the piece.

There are six common defects to look for in man-made laminated boards and plywood.

1. Warping through unbalanced construction.
2. Hairchecks, tenting or open joints on outer casings.
3. Glueline delamination.
4. Scored veneer casings causing ribs and ridges.
5. Substrate veneers containing plaster plugs in defects.
6. Outer casing veneers laid wrong face outwards.

24

Veneering Projects for you to make

Project No. 1

LAMINATED VENEER BOXES. Although curved, shaped and compound veneering can involve complicated rig-ups, cauls and expensive machinery, it is also possible to enjoy making up shaped laminated projects with very little equipment and for the fun of working with veneers.

Here are instructions for making a range of laminated 'cubby boxes' from constructional and decorative veneers in 0.7mm birch or sapele.

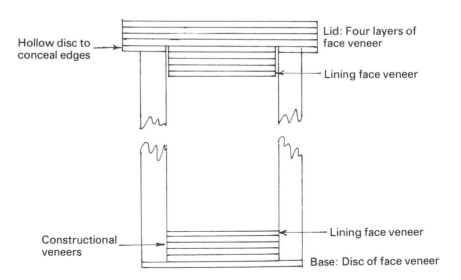

Fig. 234 Plan for cubby box

The first step is to select a suitable mould. Any container of the desired size with rigid smooth parallel surface such as a glass jar, bottle or tin. There should be no obstruction to prevent the laminated shape being drawn off after laminating.

If using a tin can with rolled ends, select one with no dents and fit the can with a veneer jacket around the middle to make it larger than the ends. To make a box 4 inches (102mm) in diameter and 2½ inches (64mm) high, a tin of fruit makes a good mould.

Fig. 235

1. Making the jacket

Begin with some short lengths of constructional veneer measuring 13½ inches (343mm) wide by 2¾ (70mm) long—if necessary joint and tape two or three small pieces together. Wrap this tightly around the tin, overlapping itself (Fig. 235). Bind it tightly with bands of Sellotape. Where the veneer overlaps, cut through the bottom veneer and discard the trapped piece and then Sellotape the joint securely.

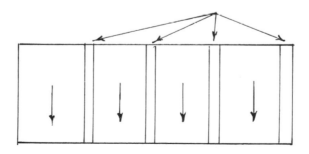

Fig. 236 Making the jacket. If necessary, tape, as shown at top arrows, to make up length. Ensure grain direction is constant (vertical arrows)

2. Laminating the cylinder

Next take a leaf of constructional veneer 65 inches (1650mm) long by 2¼ inches (57mm) wide sufficient to laminate the cylinder with 5 plies. Tape both ends of the strip with protective veneer tape.

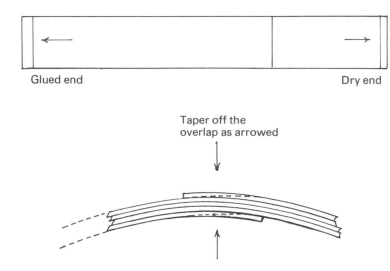

Glued end   Dry end

Taper off the
overlap as arrowed

Fig. 237 Laminating the cylinder

Apply glue only to the first 52 inches (1320mm) of the strip, leaving 13 inches (330mm) dry. When making other sized boxes always leave the circumference of the box dimension free of glue.

Wrap a sheet of polythene or kitchen foil around the jacket so that the cylinder does not adhere to it.

Next, wrap the veneer around the jacket, with the glue on the inside, starting with the dry end. Keep the starting edge well tucked in, and pull the layers tightly together as you roll the tin on a hard flat surface. Keep the sides parallel to produce flush square ends on the completed cylinder.

Place a scrap of veneer over the end of the veneer and bind the cylinder tightly with nylon cord or twine. The veneer scrap will prevent the end of the veneer from bulging. Check by turning, that the new cylinder has not adhered to the jacket.

Leave overnight. Next day, remove the binding. Sandpaper the ends square and flush by rubbing against a sheet of abrasive paper.

Taper off the ends of the constructional veneer both inside and outside the cylinder. Measure the internal diameter of the cylinder.

With a compass, mark off three discs of constructional veneer to form a base and one for the lining of the inside of the box.

Stick these four discs together with their grain at right angles to each other to form a plywood base, and clamp together.

Apply glue to the edges and push-fit the discs into the base of the box. Next, cut a disc of decorative veneer ¼ inch (6mm) larger in diameter than the cylinder, and veneer the bottom of the box, trimming off the overhang.

3. Fit inner liner

Make up a liner 13½ inches (343mm) wide by 2¼ inches (57mm) high from a decorative face veneer, cover with glue on one side, curl it around and fit it inside the box, face side inwards. It will overlap and this can be cut through and the joint perfected. Make sure the bottom edge fits snugly to the inner lining of the box by smearing glue on the bottom edge, Sellotape the butt joint.

When set, trim and sand the top edge of the box flush and smooth. and remove the Sellotape from the inside liner.

4. The outer shell

Measure the circumference of the cylinder with a tape measure. Make another veneer jacket, this time from decorative face veneers. This should be ½ inch (12mm) longer than the circumference and ¼ inch (6mm) higher.

This decorative shell can be a veneer assembly of parquetry, marquetry, or simply bands of different veneers; or simple counter-changed patterns; dots, diamonds, or any suitable motif.

It is glued, bound tightly around the cylinder as before, overlapped cut through and butt jointed for a perfect fit.

Fig. 238 Making the lid

5. Making the lid

The outer shell is then trimmed and sanded flush with the top of the cylinder. Measure the inside diameter of the top of the box in two directions at right angles and take the average. This is diameter 1. Now measure the outside diameter of the box and add on ⅛ inch (3mm), which is diameter 2. Now cut four discs of constructional veneer and one of lining veneer to diameter 1. Laminate these together at right angles to each other and clamp. When dry, sandpaper to form a perfect fit for the boxtop.

Next, cut four discs of decorative veneer to diameter 2, and laminate these together at right angles to each other, and clamp. When dry, glue both plywood discs together to form a complete lid.

Cut one more disc of decorative veneer to diameter 2, and cut a circle inside this disc to diameter 1. This ring is to decorate the top laminated edges of the box to conceal the thickness of the cylinder walls.

When this top ring has dried, it should be trimmed carefully to fit, and sanded smooth.

6. Decoration

Box lids can be decorated with an inlay motif, marquetry pattern of your own design, emblem, initials, or parquetry.

The motif should be made up to diameter 2, and when laid it should be laid at right angles to the top veneer of the lid.

Other shaped laminations

Once the technique of cubby box making is understood, it is possible to make up other curved convex shapes from suitable moulds, such as sweet jars, biscuit tins, canned foods etc.

Webbing clamps, straps, etc., can be employed to ensure tight clamping of odd shapes.

Hexagonal and other polygon shaped boxes are rather more difficult as the veneer requires to be 'creased' at the corners. This is achieved by covering the 'crease' location with veneer tape on both sides until ready for laminating. Perforated veneer tape may be left inside the laminations.

Project No. 2

Butler's Tray A two piece simple book-match

Dimensions: 18 inches × 12 inches (457mm × 305mm)

Cutting List   *Groundwork* 18 inches × 12 inches (457mm × 305mm) × 9mm plywood or chipboard

Crossbanding: 4 leaves 13 inches × 10 inches × $1/40$ inch (330mm × 254mm × 0.7mm) obeche

Backing veneer: 2 leaves 19 inches × 7 inches (483mm × 178mm) × 0.7mm veneer

Face Veneer: 2 leaves 19 inches × 7 inches (483mm × 178mm) × 0.7mm Brazilian rosewood

Tray moulding: 1 of 6 feet length (1829mm)
Handles: 1 pair 3½ inches – 4 inches (90mm – 100mm) to suit

Procedure   Read through these instructions carefully before commencing the project to form a clear idea of the overall procedure. This project will be laid by the hammer veneering method using hot scotch glue. It is not necessary to joint and shoot perfect matches, taped together. The matching and jointing is carried out on the actual groundwork as work proceeds one leaf at a time.

This project may also be produced by any other of the laying methods described in the book, and for our present purpose, the veneering will be undertaken in reverse order, commencing with the groundwork crossbanding, followed by the backing veneer and finally the face decorative veneers. This will provide plenty of practice in hammer veneering before tackling the face of the tray.

Draw pencilled centre line on the groundwork to form 18 inch × 9 inch (460mm × 230mm) rectangles. Take 2 leaves of crossbanding obeche each measuring 13 inches × 10 inches (330mm × 254mm) and you will see that they would cover an area 13 inches × 20 inches (330mm × 508mm). This is to allow for the wastage in jointing and the trim off at the edges.

Draw a pencil line ½ inch (12mm) from one 13 inch (330mm) edge and a similar pencil line ½ inch (12mm) from the opposite edge on the second leaf. Now make a dummy dry run. Lay the first veneer on

the groundwork, aligning the pencil line with the groundwork centre-
line; next, lay the second sheet, with its pencil line above the other two.
Check that you have ½ inch (12mm) of surplus material at each edge.

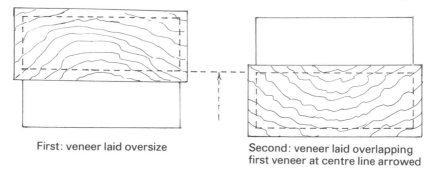

First: veneer laid oversize   Second: veneer laid overlapping
first veneer at centre line arrowed

Fig. 239 Overlapping matching veneers ready for cutting

Following the general hammer veneering instructions and coat the
groundwork with glue; lay the first leaf overlapping the centre line by
½ inch (12mm), and carry out the damp-iron-hammer procedure
forcing out all air and surplus glue at the ends and edges.

Then take the second leaf, coat the groundwork with glue, lay the
veneer in position *overlapping* the first veneer along the join, aligning
the pencil lines, and repeat the procedure damp-iron-hammer.

Next, take a straightedge and clamp it above the two overlapped
veneers exactly above the pencilled centre-line. Cut through both
veneers with a sharp knife discarding the ½ inch (12mm) surplus
from the top leaf and leaving the ½ inch (12mm) surplus of the
bottom leaf trapped below the joint on the bottom leaf.

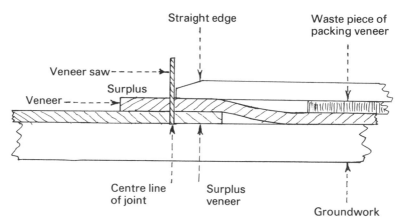

Fig. 240 Making the joint

Make a quick pass along the joint with a sponge; iron the joint to re-melt the glue, sufficiently to lift up the lower leaf and peel off the unwanted surplus strip from the lower leaf.

If the joint is cut immediately after the second veneer is laid, you will find that the veneer and lower strip will lift up together without difficulty and the strip will peel off easily.

Relay both veneers along the joint with the damp-iron-hammer procedure. Veneers which have been dampened and stretched in this way, will want to shrink back to normality so it is necessary to fix the joint by fastening a length of gummed veneer tape along the joint, and some 4 inch (100mm) straps of tape across the joint in three places.

Also, drive in a few veneer pins with large heads, and incline them slightly towards the joint which brings lateral pressure on the joint to keep it closed.

Trim off the surplus veneer overhang at the edges and wipe off the glue squeeze-out at the edges.

Turn the groundwork over and repeat the process on the other side. The panel may then be left to dry out before continuing with laying the backing veneer and face veneer.

The crossbanding veneers have been laid in the 13 inch (330mm) direction to maintain a balanced construction as the face and backing veneers will be laid in the 19 inch (483mm) direction.

When trimming off the overhang around the panel, remember that hammered veneers tend to shrink a fraction and at this stage the main purpose is to remove the glue squeeze-out.

Therefore trim off the overhang a fraction oversize to allow for minimal shrinkage as the panel dries out, no more than $\frac{1}{16}$ inch (1.5mm) all around. This will also prevent the panel being accidentally damaged and the edges torn or splintered.

These trimming cuts should always be made from the corner of the panel towards the centre to prevent the veneer breaking out. Always trim the ends of the veneer before trimming the sides.

When the panel is dry, the surface should be toothed to receive the decorative veneers and also trimmed down to size accurately.

The two backing veneers have pencilled lines drawn on them $\frac{1}{2}$ inch (12mm) from opposite edges as before; check the match with a dry run before actually laying them.

It is important now that the centre joint will display a precisely matched pair. For this reason, it is good practice to staple, pin or tape both leaves together, clamp between battens and shoot the joint, even though the pencil lines are to be drawn $\frac{1}{2}$ inch (12mm) from the newly shot joint; the resulting pattern should be an exact book match

The backing veneer is laid next by exactly the same procedure and finally the book matched face veneers. After trimming off the overhang and wiping off the squeeze-out, leave the panel for at least 24 hours to dry out before cleaning up, tape removal, and finishing.

Finally, cut and mitre the tray moulding to fit and affix the handles. If you prefer a modern tray, omit handles and employ a moulding suitably shaped with finger holds or recesses.

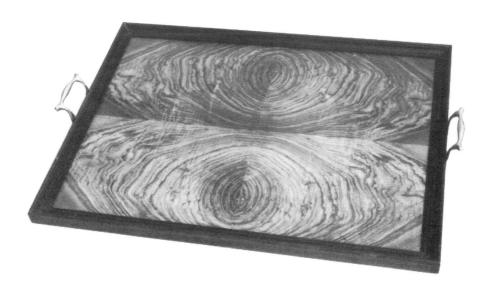

Fig. 241 Butler's Tray

Project No. 3

Four piece book matched table top

Dimensions: 36 inches × 18 inches × ¾ inch approx (915mm × 458mm × 19mm) (These dimensions are intended as a guide and may be varied to suit your own project)

Cutting List *Groundwork:* 35½ inches × 17½ inches × ⅝ inch (902mm × 445mm × 15mm) plywood or laminboard

Edge lipping: 3 lengths 39½ inches × ¼ inch × ⅝inch (1 metre × 6mm × 15mm) walnut*

Crossbanding: 6 leaves 19 inches × 12½ inches × ¹/₄₀ inch (482mm × 318mm × 0.7mm) obeche

Backing veneers: 4 leaves 19 inches × 10 inches (482mm × 254mm) × 0.7mm walnut veneer

Face veneers: 4 leaves 18 inches × 9 inches (457mm × 228mm) × 0.7mm selected highly figured walnut veneers

Crossbandings: 12 leaves 2½ inches × 9½ inches (63mm × 241mm) quartered striped walnut veneers

Inlay lines: 3 × 3 feet/1m lengths of ¹/₁₆ inches × ¹/₄₀ inches (1.5mm × 0.7mm) boxwood flat

Inlay motif: 1 oval motif of your own choice.

*N.B. walnut hardwood edging may be difficult to obtain. Normal trade practice is to substitute a cheaper hardwood stained to match.

Adhesive: Glu-film 48 inches × 36 inches (1220 × 915mm)

Preparation of groundwork: Plane, mitre and fit the edge lipping around the groundwork, by pinning and gluing or tonguing and grooving. Tooth the groundwork and edge lipping to ensure the surface is perfectly flat and ready for veneering. Joint and tape three leaves of obeche veneer together to form an oversized assembly for the groundwork, and another three leaves for the reverse side of the panel. Cut off sufficient Glu-film to cover one surface of the panel, place over the panel and peel off the protective backing sheet. Place the obeche veneers in position, replace the protective sheet and iron on the veneers.

Turn the panel over, on to the cutting board and trim off the overhang and clean off excess glue at the edges and ends. Repeat the process with the reverse side of the panel, and then allow the panel to dry out thoroughly before the next phase.

Prepare a four piece match for the reverse side of the panel.

Use the hinged mirrors to make the selection of the four figured walnut veneers for the back of the panel and chalk the position of the 19 inches × 10 inches (482mm × 254mm) leaves along the baseline of the mirrors and trim out four matching leaves. Chalk F1, F2, F3 and F4 on the bottom corner of each leaf, and also R1, R2, R3 and R4 on the reverse sides respectively. Check that the pattern exactly coincides on every leaf and tape them securely together along the edge which is not to be trimmed. It is essential that the leaves cannot move during the cutting operation. Some craftsmen prefer to use an office stapler to staple the four leaves together along the edge to be trimmed off later. Place the four leaves on the cutting board with a straightedge along the long edges to be jointed. On long matches the straightedge should be clamped at each end.

Use a veneer saw which gives a square edge for jointing, cut through the four leaves; then compress them between two battens and clamp them tightly together and shoot the four edges with a finely set plane.

When arranging the four leaves to form the match, try to arrange for the most attractive concentration of figure to appear at the bottom of the leaves. Take leaves 1 and 2 and open them like the pages of a book to form 1R + 2F. (If the figure was in the bottom left-hand corner). If the figure on your veneers formed in the bottom right hand corner, use the sequence described for the face veneers which would begin with opening the veneers to the right to form 2F + 1R.

Fasten veneer tape straps about 4 inches (100mm) long in three places across the joint, pulling the two leaves tightly together, with one long tape along the joint. Repeat the procedure by jointing together the two leaves 3R and 4F in the same way. Each pair will fold back on their tape hinges to form a set of four leaves for trimming square. Temporarily tape or staple them together to prevent movement on the cutting board, and make another sawcut through the four veneers at right angles to the taped joints. Clamp the newly cut joint between the battens and shoot the edges. Place the pair 1R + 2F on the workbench. Reverse the other pair by turning them over along their horizontal axis to convert 3R + 4F into 3F + 4R.

The four piece match now reads along the jointed centre line $\frac{1R + 2F}{3F + 4R}$ providing a one piece pattern jump in the horizontal direction and a two jump in the vertical direction, and a balance in opposite corners of face and reverse veneers.

Tape the new match together with long tapes across the centre joints and also tape around the edges to prevent splitting in handling. Make sure all tapes are kept to one side of the assembly for easy removal later. Now select the four highly figured leaves for the face of the tray. We will assume this time, that the best figure is concentrated on the bottom right hand corner of the leaves. Always follow the pattern direction and open the leaves to the right this time to form 2F + 1R. Joint and tape this pair, and then similarly open pair 4F + 3R to form the second pair. Return both sets of veneers to the cutting board for jointing, then clamp and shoot the four edges for the final match. Now reverse the second pair to convert 4F + 3R into 4R + 3F and joint this pair to 2F + 1R to form a completed match $\dfrac{2F + 1R}{4R + 3F}$ correctly maintaining the pattern jump and face and reverse opposing corners.

Lay the back of the panel first with the oversized match, using Glu-film. Touch the protective release paper lightly in each corner sufficiently to 'spot-weld' the match in position to prevent it from moving, before working over the surface from the centre out towards the ends and edges. After using the roller or veneer hammer, turn the panel over on the cutting board and trim off the overhang and wipe off excess glue around the panel.

The four piece match for the face of the assembly is made deliberately undersize and should measure only 35½ inches × 17½ inches (900mm × 445mm). Align the joints of the match with pencilled lines on the surface of the crossbandings, and iron on the four piece match with the taped side uppermost, working from the centre outwards as before. After laying, wipe off the excess glue from around the panel edges. Next, work around the panel with the cutting gauge, or straightedge and knife, parallel to the edges, and cut into the newly laid match, a strip 1¼ inch (32mm) all around the panel. This surplus strip of walnut veneer will peel off easily—if necessary aided by a quick pass with the hot iron to melt the glue—or strip it off with a chisel.

Now fit the boxwood lines around the veneer match, after checking to see that they are all true-faced by examining the ends of each line or feeling with the fingertips to determine the smooth side. Break one line in half and this will be sufficient for the two shorter ends.

The inlay lines are butted against the walnut veneers and fastened temporarily with a few small pieces of tape. The crossbanding veneers are kept same-faced and are slip-matched, butted against the boxwood lines and overlapped at each corner. Veneer tapes are fastened along the joints to cover both the lines and crossbandings so that they will hinge back against the tapes to allow fresh Glu-film to be inserted, after mitreing. A straightedge is placed at 45 degrees at the corners, and the mitres cut with a sharp knife. Cut through both thicknesses of walnut veneer and boxwood lines from the outer corner inwards towards the veneer match. Protect the veneer immediately beneath the mitre cut with a protection tape to prevent splitting out. Make a light tracing cut first, followed by a heavier cut to sever the veneers. Remove the unwanted trapped pieces and discard them. Fasten more tapes to secure the mitres, and lay the border surround.

Turn the assembly over on to the cutting board and trim off the surplus crossbandings. As these are all crossgrained the veneers should have a protection tape below the cut, and be cut carefully.

Next, align the inlay motif over the centre joints of the match and fasten with a couple of veneer pins. Cut around the outline of the motif with a sharp knife, using the motif as a templet. Melt the glue and strip out the unwanted walnut beneath the motif, and lay the inlay motif. Test the surfaces of the panel for blisters and repair any discovered by slitting, inserting fresh glue and re-laying. Allow the panel to dry out thoroughly before cleaning up.

When dry, dampen and remove the veneer tapes and allow to dry out again before finishing off the table top with polyurethane or french polish or any other desired finish.

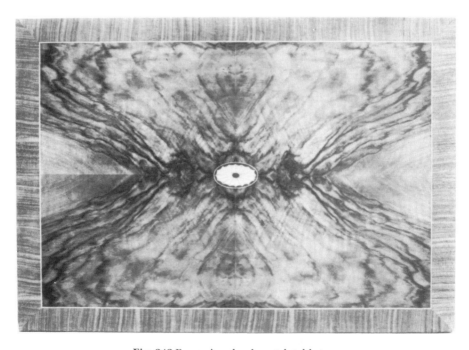

Fig. 242 Four piece book match table top

Alternative options

This project may be laid by the hammer veneer method, in which case each part of the match would be laid separately; by the contact veneering method with a slip sheet separator; by the caul method in a press.

If you wish to veneer the edge lipping, sufficient veneer has been allowed to cover this, and should be applied immediately before applying the crossbanded border so that the top edge of the lipping veneers are concealed. If you wish to substitute a ¼ inch (6mm) feathered walnut banding for the boxwood lines, increase the width of the setting to the cutting gauge to 1½ inch (38mm) when trimming off the surplus walnut around the edges.

Project No.4

A Chessboard

Dimensions   24 inches × 18½ inches (610mm × 470mm)

Groundwork: 23½ inches × 18 inches × ⅝ inch (597mm × 457mm × 15mm) Chipboard, laminated board or plywood.

Edge lipping: 1 × 5 feet (1525mm) and 1 × 4 feet (1220mm) of ¼ inch × ⅝ inch (6mm × 15mm) walnut hardwood or suitable substitute

Backing veneer:
(*Note:* Project No. 5 is a specially designed backgammon board to fit on the reverse side of this chessboard. If you wish to make a dual-purpose gaming board, omit the backing veneers and lay the backgammon board assembly on the reverse side)

2 matching leaves 25 inches × 10 inches (636mm × 254mm) or 4 matching leaves 12½ inches × 10 inches (318mm × 254mm) in figured walnut veneer.

Border surround: 8 leaves 4½ inches × 13 inches (114mm × 330mm) figured walnut veneer.

Chess-squares: 1 leaf figured sycamore 18 inches × 11 inches (457mm × 280mm) or two leaves 18 inches × 6 inches (457mm × 152mm) 1 leaf walnut burr veneer 18 inches × 9 inches (457mm × 228mm) or two leaves 9 inches × 9 inches (228mm × 228mm) 3 inlay bandings of walnut feather type ¼ inch (6mm)

Procedure   (An illustrated sequence can be seen in Chapter 13). Figured sycamore and walnut veneers have been selected for this chessboard, which provide a pleasant contrast without being too 'black and white' which would prove to be tiring for the eyes during play.

Other alternatives are pommelle mahogany and figured avodire; rosewood and satinwood; rosa peroba and harewood etc.

To begin, make a simple bench jig or use the straightedge and veneer saw on the cutting board to produce clean, square edges suitable for jointing. Cut *five* strips of figured sycamore veneer 16 inches × 2 inches (406mm × 50mm) and *four* strips of figured walnut burr veneer the same size. If you have a jointing batten clamp, cut the strips a fraction oversize and compress them between the battens, clamp tightly, and shoot the edges with a finely set plane, and check that the strips are precisely 2 inches (50mm) wide at both ends.

Take one sycamore strip and one walnut strip and tape them together alternately until you have assembled nine strips, five sycamore and four walnut. Make sure these veneers are all kept 'same-faced' and that none are accidentally turned over; also that all tapes are kept on the face side.

Turn the assembly at right angles in the jig, or on the cutting board, and saw through the strips to form eight 2 inch (50mm) strips each of nine squares. Now move strips 2, 4, 6 and 8 forward by one square to stagger the match and form the chessboard pattern.

Tape the assembly along every joint in both directions leaving the sycamore squares protruding at each end. Trim these off and discard them, leaving a 64 square playing area.

Now butt the inlay bandings around the assembly, taping them temporarily to the squares and overlapping the bandings at each corner. Place the straightedge over the double thickness of bandings at each corner in turn and cut through them at 45 degrees from the outer corner in towards the chess squares. Now tape the bandings firmly to the assembly.

Take the 8 leaves of 4½ inch long figured walnut border surround and joint them in matching pairs into 4 sets. These are fitted next, butting tightly up to the inlay bandings, with the centre of each pair aligned with the centre lines pencilled on the tapes. Protect the outer edges with tapes to prevent splitting in handling. Where these borders overlap at each corner, cut 45 degree mitres from the outer corners in towards the assembly and securely tape the mitred joints.

If you do not intend to veneer the back with the backgammon board, prepare a four piece book match for the back of the panel by cutting, clamping and shooting the joints, and then taping the match to measure 25 inches × 19½ inches (636mm × 496mm) approximately.

The edge lippings are now cut, mitred and fitted to the groundwork either by tonguing and grooving or pinning and gluing. The face and reverse sides of the groundwork must then be toothed perfectly level.

One of the main advantages of using contact adhesive for this project will now become apparent. No crossbanding veneers are specified for the groundwork when a backgammon board is to be laid on the reverse side, because the predominating grain direction of the chessboard assembly is in the 24 inches direction (610mm) and the main direction on the backgammon board face lies in the 18½ inches (470mm) direction.

For reasons of strength the groundwork was specified with its core and outer casings in the 24 inches (610mm) direction in the case of laminated board or plywood. For a balanced construction using normal adhesives crossbandings would be required under the chessboard to run in the 18½ inches (470mm) direction; but beneath the backgammon board in the 24 inches (610mm) direction. To overcome this dilemma (deliberately contrived as an example for this project series) there are two options.

The first is to change the grain direction of the border veneers of the chessboard so that they all run in the 18½ inches (470mm) direction, so that crossbandings could be applied to run in the 24 inches (610mm) direction. Secondly, to use a contact adhesive in which no moisture is introduced, on a board selected for strength in the 24 inches × 18½ inches (610mm × 470mm) dimension.

For this project we are able to dispense with crossbandings altogether and lay the project with contact adhesive, without unbalancing the panel, and to select the type of border surrounds that suits the project, and have the grain direction running in different main directions on each side of the panel.

Another reason why this project is to be laid with contact adhesive is that the playing area is a precise size, bordered by narrow 1 inch (25mm) surrounds at each side. It is therefore impossible to use a cutting gauge to trim the playing area parallel with the outer edges as this would mean trimming into the accurately cut squares.

The assembly has to be laid perfectly true, first time, with no margin for error. Apply the contact adhesive as previously described using a slip-sheet separator. Two coats are required with the correct drying out period between them. Then cover the groundwork with the slip-sheet and place the assembly in position, unhurriedly checking the correct alignment all around.

On the assumption that you are right handed (if not, reverse the next instruction), carefully fasten two veneer tapes from underneath the groundwork and bring them up and over and fasten them on to the right hand edge of the chessboard assembly.

Take the slip-sheet which protrudes at the left hand edge and ease it out until 1 inch (25mm), of the chessboard assembly at the right hand edge comes into contact with the adhesive. Drive two or three veneer pins along that right hand strip which is in contact, after passing the roller along the strip to ensure firm adhesion. Take care to keep ⅔rds of the roller on the panel and only ⅓rd off the panel, to protect the edge. The assembly cannot move out of alignment now. Slit the two temporary tapes and pull out the veneer pins. Now with the left hand, lift up the veneer assembly at the left hand edge, and withdraw the slip-sheet about 8 inches (200mm) and with your right hand holding the roller or veneer hammer, work from the centre of the panel out towards the edges, but do not go over the edge, which is oversize and overlaps the groundwork.

The slip-sheet can be withdrawn fairly quickly in three stages in a matter of minutes.

As an alternative to the above method, some craftsmen prefer to use two half slip-sheets, overlapping at the centre. The assembly is aligned and pinned securely on one half including the half slip-sheet, while the other half is withdrawn and rollered down. Then the other half has the pins removed and the slip-sheet withdrawn—the principle is the same. It is a good idea at this stage to work over the surface by replacing the slip-sheet on top of the finished panel, and use a moderately hot iron to make a few quick passes to complete the evaporation of the volatile solvent.

The project is now turned over on to a cutting board, brushed free of all dust etc., and the overhang is trimmed off, from the outer corners towards the panel centre, using light pressure first of all to establish a line and then heavier pressure to sever the veneers.

Fig. 243 Chessboard

Alternative options

A chessboard may also be laid using Glu-film or in a press. If Glu-film is to be used it is important to assemble the chess squares individually on to a sheet of paper with a pencilled grid of squares, using balsa cement (not PVA) to butt joint them together. Sufficient cement oozes beneath each square to keep it fastened to the paper, which will peel off easily when the assembly is laid. The Glu-film and the heat from the iron will not affect the balsa cement, but would delaminate PVA. However, professionals prefer the 'sliding-slip' technique described, which eliminates the progressive accumulation of cutting errors met with when cutting individual squares, as the strip method is self-compensating.

When laying the chessboard in a press, lay the backing veneer first and then the chessboard assembly as a second operation. Both should be laid oversize, and trimmed off later.

When laying both a chessboard and backgammon board, as both faces are of equal priority lay them in either order, but in each case, leave the assembly oversize and trim off the overhang before laying the second side. A simultaneous pressing of both sides—normal for professionals—requires skill and experience.

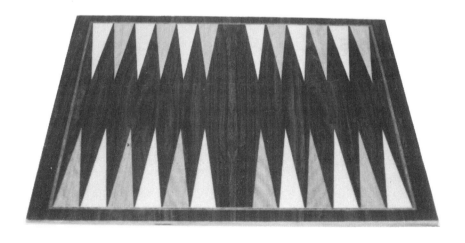

Fig. 244 Backgammon board

Project No. 5

Backgammon board

<u>Dimensions</u>   24 inches × 18½ inches (610mm × 470mm)

Groundwork: 23½ inches × 18 inches × ⅝ inch (597mm × 457mm × 15mm) chipboard, laminated board or plywood.

*Edge lipping:** 1 × 5 feet (1525mm) and 4 feet (1220mm) of ¼ inch × ⅝inch (6mm × 15mm) walnut hardwood.

*Backing veneer:** 2 piece match 25 inches × 10 inches (636mm × 254mm) or 4 piece book match 12½ inches × 10 inches (318mm × 254mm) in figured walnut veneer.

Face veneers: 4 leaves 19½ inches × 6½ inches (495mm × 165mm) 0.7mm figured walnut veneer.

Inlay triangles: 1 leaf satinwood 14 inches × 10 inches (355mm × 254mm) 1 leaf bird's eye maple 14 inches × 10 inches (355mm × 254mm)

Inlay bandings: 3 lengths ¼ inch (6mm) wide walnut feather; arrow; domino etc. at your option.

*Omit if the backgammon board is to be laid on the reverse side of the chessboard project.

<u>Procedure</u>   Take the four matching leaves of figured walnut and chalk mark them with face and reverse identification. Arrange them in the following sequence R1 + F2 + R3 + F4. which will equalise the pattern jump. Staple, pin or tape one edge together while the straight-edge and saw are used to effect a clean joint. Tape the four leaves together to make a match 19½ inches × 26 inches (495mm × 660mm). Pencil lines are going to be drawn on the walnut background veneer, and to ensure that they show up well, fasten a strip of paper veneer tape in the location and direction of the following pencil lines, which are drawn on the tapes.

First, draw a centre line across the assembly in the 26 inches (660mm) direction, with another line parallel to it 2 inches (50mm) above and another line 2 inches (50mm) below. This creates a central zone 4 inches (100mm) wide. On each side of the 4 inches (100mm) zone, draw two more lines at 6½ inches (165mm) about 1¼ inches (32mm) from the edge of the veneer at each side. Reading from top to bottom of the veneer match in the 19½ inches (495mm) direction you should now have a line drawn in the 24 inches (610mm) direction at 1¼ inches (32mm), 6½ inches (165mm), 4 inches (100mm), 6½ inches (165mm), and with a 1¼ inch margin (32mm) at the bottom. Next, tape and draw a vertical centre line in the 19½ inches (495mm) direction. On each side of this line draw more lines at 2¼ inches (57mm) and 9 inches (228mm) from it and this will leave a margin of 1¾ inches (45mm) to each edge. Reading from left to right, there is a line 1¾ inches (45mm) from the edge, another 9 inches (228mm) from the first, the centre line 2¼ inches (57mm) from that, then another 2¼ inches (57mm) on the other side of the centre line, another 9 inches (228mm) from that, with 1¾ inches (45mm) to the edge of the veneer.

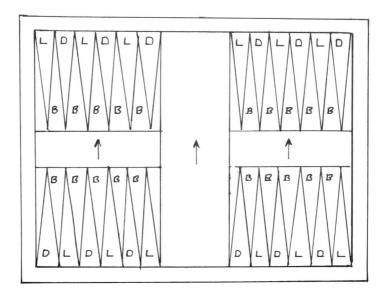

L=Light veneer   D=Dark veneer   B=Background veneer

Fig. 245 Layout for colour sequence

Looking at the assembly now, you should have four rectangles, one in each corner, measuring 9 inches × 6½ inches (228mm × 165mm). Carefully mark off 1½ inch (38mm) divisions along each 9 inch (228mm) baseline to form the base of 6 elongated triangles, the apex of each triangle touching the line 6½ inches (165mm) towards the centre of the panel, (see illustration). Keep all tapes on the face side of the

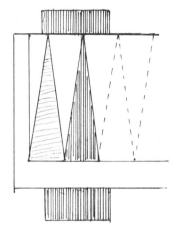

Fig. 246 Selected veneer seen through window

assembly. Using the 'window method' previously described, cut a hole in the walnut veneer around the outline of the first triangle. Place the satinwood veneer beneath the aperture, and adjust the flow of the grain into the apex of the triangle. Fasten the veneer temporarily with 1 inch (25mm) pieces of Sellotape on the underside, and transfer to the cutting board. Use the edges of the walnut veneer as a templet to guide the knife, tilting the knife handle inwards towards the centre of the triangle. Mark the satinwood with the point of the knife and release it. Cut out the triangle on the board, and then fit it back into the walnut assembly fastening into position with veneer tape on the face side. Fasten a protection tape across the assembly where the tips of the triangles occur. Use a straightedge to cut the sides of the triangles in the walnut, and the walnut aperture as a templet when cutting the satinwood or bird's eye maple. Repeat this procedure until all triangles are cut in and taped.

Now place the straightedge exactly along the line 1¾ inches (45mm) from each short edge (in the 19½ inches/495mm) direction, and trim off the walnut veneer. Save this offcut for re-use later. Do the same at the other edge, saving the offcut. Now place the straightedge along the baseline of the triangles and trim off the walnut veneer in the 26 inch direction (660mm), saving the 1¼ inches (32mm) offcut. Do this on both sides.

The inlay bandings are now fitted around the playing area, making sure that the corners match exactly where overlapped. Cut through both layers using the straightedge and knife at 45 degrees cutting from the outer corner inwards. Fasten the banding with veneer tapes. The walnut strips which were trimmed off and saved, are now refitted in their previous positions, but outside the bandings, keeping the correct face, grain direction and match with the remainder of the walnut.

Fasten both the bandings and the walnut surround with long veneer tapes.*

Laying   Adopt the same procedure as for the chessboard project. Coat the groundwork two coats and allow correct drying periods. Place a single slipsheet (or two overlapped half-slipsheets) over the touch dry contact adhesive. Carefully align the assembly and pin it to prevent movement. Remove the slipsheet in easy stages, rolling down the assembly from the centre outwards towards the ends and edges, using the left hand to withdraw the slipsheet and the right hand for holding the roller.

Place the removed slipsheet back on top of the assembly after removing the veneer pins, and make a few passes with the hot iron to evaporate any residual solvent from the bond.

If the backgammon board assembly has been laid on the reverse of the chessboard, this should be carefully protected with a piece of suitable material such as felt, hardboard, stiff cardboard etc.).

Finally, the panel is turned over on to the cutting board, after brushing free from grit, and the overhang is trimmed off.

*On the chessboard assembly, we used crossbanding border veneers. The backgammon board utilised the outer edges of the background veneers, as another option.

For the sake of overall unity, professional craftsmen would employ the same type of border surround on both sides of the panel, in this case the backgammon board would be fitted with crossbandings of the same type used on the chessboard.

Another option, would be to make the walnut background for the backgammon board from a four piece book matched walnut match and cut the playing area complete with bandings into the background, so that the book matched assembly also forms the border right to the edges. This would require four leaves 12½ inches × 10 inches (318mm × 254mm) instead of the four leaves 19½ inches × 6½ inches (495mm × 165mm) suggested.

Project No. 6

Modern parquetry wall clock

Dimensions: 22½ inches × 10½ inches × 2¼ inches overall (570mm × 266mm × 57mm)

Groundwork:9mm plywood hollow box, with centre division 11½ inches (292mm) from top and 10¾ inches (273mm) from bottom in 6mm ply.

> *Sapele Backing veneer:* 4 feet × 6 inches (1220mm × 152mm)

> *Face veneer:* Pencil striped sapele 3 square feet (0.27 square metres) (1 leaf 6 feet × 6 inches) (1828mm × 152mm) Black inlay lines 2 × 3 feet/1 metre × (3mm) flat

Extras: 1 silvered time ring (with self-adhesive backing) 1-Battery clock movement.

Preparation: Make up the hollow box, with central division and 9mm lid, 22½ inch × 10½ inch (570 × 266mm). Do not fix the lid to the framework as this will be the groundwork for the parquetry.
Follow the instructions for *Diagonal Diamonds* by cutting the leaf of pencil striped sapele into 2 feet (610mm) lengths—save one piece for the border surround.
Cut one 2 foot (610mm) leaf into strips 1½ inches (38mm) wide and parallel to the grain. Cut the second 2 foot × 6 inches (610mm × 152mm) leaf into 1½ inch (38mm) wide strips cut diagonally across the grain at 60 degrees from the vertical. Cut these strips with a straightedge and veneer saw very accurately. Assemble the strips and tape them securely together. Next, cut across this taped assembly at 60 degrees from the vertical into 1½ inch (38mm) strips again. Move alternate strips forward by one diamond. Tape the assembly together again. Place the straightedge exactly along the tips of the top row of diamonds and trim square, discarding odd shapes.
Trim the assembly exactly to 20 inches × 8 inches (508mm × 203mm) net size. Then cut it into two sections one 8 inches × 8 inches (203mm× 203mm) and the other 12 inches × 8 inches (304mm × 203mm).

Veneering the case: Use Glu-film and a warm electric iron. Begin by gluing the back edges of the box sides. Then the top and bottom sides.

Fig. 247 Box sides glued together, held with Sellotape at corner

Fig. 248 Top glued on and used to square up box

Draw pencil lines on the lid of the box 1⅛ inches (28.5mm) all around from the outside edges; and a ⅛ inch (3mm) line parallel to it inside to accommodate the inlay line.

Now iron on the first parquetry assembly 12 inches × 8 inches (304mm× 203mm) from the ⅛ inch (3mm) line at the bottom, 1¼ inch (31mm) from the bottom edge of the lid.

Next, take an 8¼ inch (209mm) strip of the ⅛ inch (3mm) black line and butt this snugly against the top of the parquetry, overlapping at each side into the ⅛ inch (3mm) lines.

Examine your battery clock movement and see the diameter of the hole required to accommodate the main shaft. Pencil a diagonal in the 8 inch (203mm) square to find the centre and drill the hole.

The 8 inch (203mm) square parquetry is now laid.

The next phase is to complete the fitting of the black inlay line, carefully snipping off the ends of the 8¼ inch (209mm) horizontal line already fitted. Leave them overlapped at the four corners.

Now cut the remaining leaf of pencil striped sapele into 1½ inch (38mm) strips across the grain 6 inches (152mm) wide. Glue and butt them tightly up against the ⅛ inch (3mm) black line, starting in the centre of the box sides. Lay each piece separately, and overlap the one laid before it by about ¼ inch (6mm). Use a sharp knife to cut through both layers of veneer in a straight line and discard the unwanted trapped lower piece.

Overlap the cross band border pieces at each corner. Place the straightedge at 45 degrees at the corner, and cut through the cross-banding layers and also the inlay lines from the corner towards the parquetry. Iron down the mitred corners.

It is possible to render any veneer self-adhesive and this is particularly valuable for edge veneering. Simply iron the Glu-film to a leaf of veneer by leaving the backing sheet on, and allow it to remain in place till the glue has set. The protective sheet is then easily peeled off, leaving the veneer already glued. The sheet is laid over the face of the veneer when ironing as usual, but this method has the advantage that the veneer, already glued, can be cut into strips and edges.

Trim off the overhang of the crossbandings; test for blisters and the case is ready for sanding and finishing.

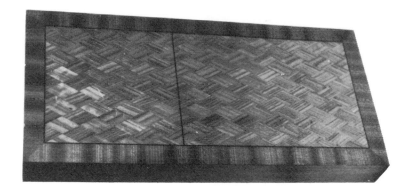

Fig. 249 Clockcase ready for finishing

To fit the time ring, centre it within the 8 inch (203mm) square section of parquetry at the top, and lightly mark its location on the veneer face with a soft pencil or chalk.

Slightly roughen the veneer within the two circles drawn on the parquetry to form a key for the time ring. Some time rings are not self-adhesive in which case apply PVA glue to the back of the ring and clamp to the face of the case inside the marked positions. Pierce and open the shaft hole with a knife.

The battery movement is fitted from the back of the case, by sandwiching the rubber ring between the movement and the back of the clockcase.

Gently screw the brass ferrule from the front of the clockcase slightly compressing the rubber ring. Fit the hands of the movement ensuring that the hour hand is pressed on to the spindle at 12 o'clock when the minute hand is also pointing at 12 o'clock.

Fit any suitable means of hanging: glass plate, chain, or hook — most battery movements have a plastic hook formed as part of the casing.

Fig. 250 Modern parquetry wall clock

Options:
(a)   Instead of diagonal diamond parquetry, you may prefer to use right angled diamonds.
(b)   Try making up other types of parquetry such as Louis cube, or regular polygons etc.
(c)   The clock face 12 inches × 8 inches (304mm × 203mm) is also ideal for veneer moasic, or oyster parquetry.
(d)   An inlay motif, or fraternal emblem could be inlaid.
(e)   A marquetry subject 12 inches × 8 inches (304mm × 203mm) could be used.
(f)   The veneering could be laid with Glu-film or pressure with clamps or in a press, with cauls.

Project No. 7

Sixteen piece Sunburst Occasional Table Top (Slip Matched)

Dimensions   24 inches (610mm) diameter by ⅝ inch (15mm) thick.

> *Groundwork:* 24 inches (610mm) chipboard or laminated board. Prepared from a 22 inch (558mm) octagonal shape, with tongued and grooved solid hardwood facings, bandsawn circular, to finish 24 inches (610mm) and suitable for moulding later if required.
>
> *Crossbandings:* As any veneer underlay will coincide with the face grain direction of a sunburst match in two places, it is best to cover the groundwork on both sides with fine muslin laid in glue.
>
> *Backing veneer.* 3 leaves 27 inches by 9 inches (685mm × 228mm) × 0.7mm mahogany veneer.
>
> *Face veneer.* 16 leaves 26 inches by 5½ inches (660mm × 140mm) of 0.7mm specially selected pencil striped sapele.

Procedure: Lip the octagonal shape, plane true and cover with muslin laid in glue; stretch in both directions and leave to dry. It is essential to tooth the groundwork to ensure that the hardwood edges and surface of the groundwork are perfectly level before applying the muslin. Cut, joint, tape and lay the backing veneers; wipe off excess glue, trim the overhang and clean off veneer tapes.

Chalk sequence numbers of every leaf of sapele on the face side only. Fan the sixteen leaves around like a pack of cards and check the pattern jump between leaf No 1 and No 16. If quite large, the pattern jump may be equalised by slip-matching to left and right. Working clockwise from the noon position, beginning with leaf No 1, the jointing sequence is 1-4, 9-12, 16-13, and 8-5, with leaf No 5 jointed to leaf No 1. The first step is to stagger the bundle and trim it to ensure the pattern shown on the edges is vertical. With pencil striped sapele it is not usually necessary to equalise the pattern jump but the technique is valid for a very large number of veneers.

Make a bench jig for cutting the sunburst segments, by gluing a couple of hardwood blocks on the cutting board for aligning the straightedge to produce a 22½ degree angle. Other methods of cutting

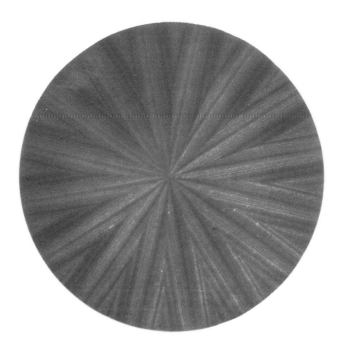

Fig. 251 Sixteen piece sunburst 'dragged over' slip match in sapele

the segments are to draw a paper templet on a sheet of stiff cardboard, (hardboard, metal or perspex would be equally suitable). If you have access to a guillotine, simply cut the bundle of veneers to the templet. If not, sandwich the bundle between two pieces of thin plywood nailed through the unwanted parts, and saw through. Before cutting the veneers, protect every leaf with a paper backing or veneer tapes, especially at the ends of the leaves where the fragile pointed tips will meet at the table centre. If the joints were cut on the guillotine or saw, no further work is necessary. If cut out by hand individually, each segment should be trimmed out a fraction oversize. The segments are then brushed with a coat of glue on one oversized edge; compressed between battens until dry. The 'wedge' shaped bundle is then turned around and compressed again and the edge shot with a finely set plane. The wedge of veneers is then turned back the original way, and the glue edges are planed off.

Another alternative is to stitch a nylon thread with a needle, right through the sixteen leaves and pull them tightly together before clamping and planing the edges. This is especially useful when using highly figured veneers as the needle point can be inserted in an identical feature on every leaf.

Assembly: The segments may be fitted temporarily to a paper pattern on which the design has been drawn, using balsa cement to butt joint the assembly. Sufficient cement will ooze out to fix the veneers to the paper sheet, but the paper will peel off easily, after the face side has been correctly taped. Otherwise the segments may be laid directly to the groundwork upon which a pencil outline of the pattern is drawn, using Glu-film and iron-on techniques. The veneers would require only one clean edge, and one oversize which is trimmed off with straightedge and knife one segment at a time.

Professionals and many amateur craftsmen use the 'window method' whereby the design is traced on to a waste veneer, which is cut out piece by piece, and replaced by the required veneer for the segment thereby guaranteeing a perfect match especially at the centre.

Laying: This sunburst top may be laid by any of the methods previously described in earlier chapters; hammer veneering; iron-on with Glu-film; contact adhesive with slip-sheet; or by pressure from cauls.

Project No. 8

Sixteen Piece Sunburst Dining Table Top (Book Matched)

<u>Dimensions</u> 48 inches diameter by ¾ inch thick (1220mm × 19mm)

Groundwork. Cut an octagonal shape 46 inches (1168mm) overall from a sheet of laminated board or chipboard. Tongue and groove hardwood facings to the edges and bandsaw to a circle to finish 48 inches (1220mm) diameter. The solid edges may be moulded later if required.

Underlay: If crossbandings were used, the grain would coincide with the sunburst match in two places. Therefore, after the surfaces have been toothed, both sides are covered with fine muslin laid in glue to form a key for the decorative veneering.

Backing veneer: 7 leaves 4 feet 2 inches × 7½ inches (1270mm × 190mm) × 0.7mm mahogany veneer.

Face veneer: 16 leaves 26 inches × 10 inches (660mm × 254mm) very highly figured burry-butt veneer 0.7mm thick. Look out for concentrations of figure at each end of the leaves and along the edges, also with some prominent feature in the leaf centre.

Procedure: We have to avoid a pattern jump of fifteen between leaf No 1 and 16. Examine the two leaves, after staggering the bundle and trimming out the required sizes.

If there is a marked pattern jump, use the following sequence: working clockwise around the circle from leaf No 1 in the noon position, use 1F, 2R, 3F, 4R−9F, 10R, 11F, 12R−16F, 15R, 14F, 13R−8F, 7R, 6F, 5R. Leaf 5R is jointed to 1F to complete the sunburst. Each pair of book matched veneers arranged with alternate face and reverse sides as shown. There are five methods of proceeding, each illustrating one of the aspects of sunburst matching.

1. Make a transparent plastic templet of one segment. This enables individual leaves to be studied and matching features aligned. This is one way to eliminate any pattern variation.

2. With a darning needle and nylon thread, pierce every leaf through a repeating regular feature such as a knot, and when the thread is

pulled tight, the bundle is properly aligned, the sixteen leaves may be trimmed, jointed and planed true, using a hardboard or metal templet.

3.   The bundle is threaded and aligned for pattern, then compressed between battens and the edges shot with a finely set plane. This only guarantees the mating edges of pairs. Therefore the groundwork is marked with the pencilled outline of the sunburst, and pairs are fitted to it and taped together, overlapping the adjacent pair. A straightedge is then laid across the groundwork lining up with the pencilled lines which are visible on the opposite side of the match, and an accurate joint is cut. The veneers would be laid by hammer or roller and Glu-film methods.

4.   Draw a full sized pattern on paper, and use a templet to cut each segment. The match is assembled temporarily direct to the pattern using balsa cement—only a few spots are used until veneer tapes are fastened along every joint on the face side, and the paper plan is peeled off and discarded.

5.   The 'window method' is used. The outline is drawn on to card or soft white sycamore veneer, casually jointed to the full width. The segment outline is cut out, and the required veneer for the match placed beneath the aperture and adjusted so that the figure matches precisely. The segment is then cut out on the cutting board and taped into the assembly. The next piece is cut from the waste veneer or card, and the edge of the actual segment is now used, together with the edge of the waste veneer, to cut the next segment, thereby assuring a perfect fit. The virtue of this method is two fold; firstly, the design is created piece by piece with great accuracy; secondly, each piece forms the templet for the next regardless of the original pencil line.

The actual design is made by simply drawing a circle, dividing it into four quarters; bisecting each quarter, and each of those units is bisected again.

The remaining problem in cutting lies in the centre of the sunburst where sixteen points come together to a fine point—a true revelation of your craftsmanship. To avoid problems before cutting commences, fasten protection tapes along the centre of every leaf of veneer, taking special care that the end to be cut into a point is well covered. Most professionals flatten their veneers and cover the whole leaf with paper on its face side. The hallmark of the veneer craftsman is to produce a sunburst match without a centre motif. But the way to solve the problem, if the points do break off, is to insert a circular inlay motif, or even a small centrepiece of burr veneer to create a focal point of interest, and convert a 'point' disaster into a strong feature.

Laying the sunburst assembly

The sixteen points at the centre of the sunburst match must be laid dead-centre of the table top. This was fairly easy to achieve using the hammer or iron-on methods, working directly on the groundwork.

When the table top is to be laid in a press, it is necessary to use a special technique to ensure very rapid alignment once the groundwork is covered with adhesive. Draw four pencil lines down the edge of the groundwork, to match corresponding lines on the laying-up bench.

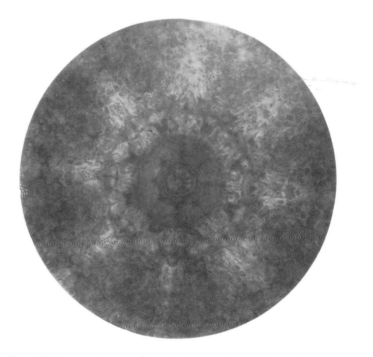

Fig. 252 Sixteen piece sunburst book matched table top in lacewood burr veneers

Also fix half a dozen wooden guide blocks so that the groundwork drops quickly into position and can be adjusted to the pencilled lines.

Also fix half a dozen taller glue-blocks, about ½ inch (12mm) larger than the diameter of the groundwork to allow for the overhang of the assembly.

Make two or three dry 'dummy' runs. Insert the groundwork and then drop the assembly into position. When you are satisfied that the alignment is perfect every time, make the final run.

Spread the adhesive, align the pencil marks and assemble the backing veneers first. When these are pressed, clean off the glue excess, trim off the overhang, and coat with adhesive on the face side, to receive the assembly. Drop the groundwork into its jig, align the pencil marks, lower the assembly into position as rehearsed, and drive in three veneer pins to ensure it cannot move before transferring the assembly to the press.

Many amateur craftsmen may not have access to a press which will accommodate a 48 inch (1220mm) diameter panel, and might like to use the contact adhesive method.

Coat the groundwork with two coats, allowing plenty of drying time between coats. Use *two* half slip-sheets allowing them to overlap in the centre, by about 6 inches (150mm).

Unhurriedly place the assembly in position over the slipsheets, using the laying up bench jig for location purposes. Drive in three or four veneer pins in one half of the table. Slowly withdraw one half of the slip-sheet and roller the veneer down. Withdraw the veneer pins and withdraw the other half of the slip-sheet, and complete the rollering without haste.

Always work from the centre of the panel towards the edges. After cleaning up and trimming the overhang, the outer edge of the table top may be bevelled, chamfered or moulded to suit.

Project No. 9

Traditional Curl Mahogany Door and Drawer Unit

Dimensions: Overall 27¾ inches × 18¼ inches (705mm × 463mm)
Door panel 18¼ inches × 18¼ inches (463mm × 463mm)
Drawer panel 8¾ inches × 18¼ inches (222mm × 463mm)
Unit frame ¾ inches (19mm)

Groundwork: Door panel 17¾ inches × 17¾ inches × ⅝ inches (450mm × 450mm × 15mm)
Flat or curved to suit unit, from laminated plywood.

Drawer panel: 8¼ inches × 17¾ × ⅝ inches (210mm × 450mm × 15mm)

Edge lipping: ¼ inch × ⅝ inch (6mm × 15mm) mahogany 7 lengths 24 inches (7 × 610mm)

Crossbandings: 6 leaves 19 inches × 10 inches (483mm × 254mm) 0.7mm mahogany.

Backing veneer: 2 leaves 30 inches × 10 inches sapele (762mm × 254mm) × 0.7mm

Face veneer: 30 inches × 18 inches (762mm × 457mm) 0.7mm to 0.9mm thick mahogany curl veneer. Select a curl veneer with a minimum 17½ inches (445mm) width at the narrow end.

Border crossbandings: 12 leaves 3 inches long × 10 inches wide (76mm × 254mm) × 0.7mm. Pencil striped sapele. Inlay lines: 4 lengths ¹⁄₁₆ inch flat boxwood (1.5mm) (or stringings if available).

Procedure: The door and drawer units both have working edges, and must be edge lipped all round. Tongue and groove or pin and glue; and mitre or butt joint the corners. This will bring the ground to the full size of 18¼ inches (463mm). The crossbandings are jointed and taped together for both sides of the panels, and pressed using the simultaneous method described in Chapter 18. The panels are laid oversize, cleaned, trimmed and allowed to cure before being further worked. When cured, the panels are cleaned of tapes, and both surfaces are toothed ready to receive the face veneers.

Next, the backing veneers are prepared as two separate oversized lay-on assemblies. Make a two piece book match 20 inches × 20 inches (508mm × 508mm) for the door, and one 10 inches × 20 inches (254mm × 508mm) for the drawer. These are pressed, cleaned off and trimmed and allowed to cure for a few hours before veneering the face sides with the curl mahogany.

There are three options open to the craftsman for dealing with the curl veneer door and drawer unit. One is to make up a lay-on for each component, including crossbanding and lines, into oversized assemblies to be laid in a single pressing. A second method is to caul both panels simultaneously laying one side only each with an over-sized lay-on, instead of individually laying them as in the first case.

The third option is when the face veneers are laid *undersize* in a single pressing, in order to use a cutting gauge around the panel, to trim the curl true and parallel to the edges before applying the boxwood lines and sapele crossbanded borders. The third method is the safest method and produces the best work.

The mahogany curl veneer should have been correctly flatted, and either fitted with protection tapes on its rough side, or preferably paper backed. The curl is cut into two pieces to ensure continuity of pattern across both the door panel and the drawer. One 16 inches × 16 inches (406mm × 406mm) and the other 6½ inches × 16 inches (165mm × 406mm). An advantage of this method is that you can use a smaller curl, 24 inches by 17½ inches (610mm × 445mm).

Oversized lay-ons

Butt the boxwood lines around the curl veneers of the drawer unit, overlapping at each corner, and fasten with temporary veneer tapes. Cut the sapele borders into 1⅝ inch (41mm) lengths and keep them all true faced, do not turn them over. Slip match them around the curl keeping each crossband the same way up—not inverted at the bottom of the panel. Cut and joint the crossbands together, and butt them to the boxwood lines overlapping at each corner.

Place the straightedge at 45 degrees, and mitre both the cross-bandings and the boxwood lines from the outer corners towards the curl veneers. Then securely tape the joints with veneer tape covering the curl, banding and crossbanding along the joints.

Now use a pair of dividers, one point flattened and sharpened. Place the other point over a scrap of veneer and mark the semi-circular shape at each corner of the curl veneer. Open the divider 1⅛ inches (28mm) and place the point in the centre of the mitre angle formed by the sapele.

Carefully cut out the four corner shapes and fit the boxwood lines around the large curl, overlapping at eight points. Fit the sapele crossbandings taking care to use the full 3 inch (76mm) length veneers at the corners. Keep all sapele crossbands same face and do not invert them either at the top or bottom of the panel.

Mitre the boxwood lines at each intersection, and secure them with tapes, before fitting the sapele borders. These are mitred at the corners, cutting towards the boxwood lines. Great care must be taken not to slip and cut through the boxwood lines.

The completed, oversized lay-ons must be pinned securely in the press to prevent the slightest movement as there is no margin for error. The task of fitting the veneer pins through the assembly into the groundwork has to be carried out accurately at high speed as the assembly is in contact with wet adhesive.

A laying-up bench jig is used, adjacent to the press, and rapid alignment comes with experience.

Fortunately, there is an easier way which most amateur craftsmen prefer as it removes the haste, anxiety and risk of error.

Undersized lay-ons

The curl mahogany is cut into two pieces, 17 inches × 17 inches (430mm × 430mm) and 7½ inches × 17 inches (190mm × 430mm). Draw centre lines on the groundwork and also a pencil line about ½ inch (12mm) from the edge all around the panels. Coat the groundwork with adhesive and place the curls in position paper side uppermost, align the pencilled guidelines, and drive a couple of pins into the curl to secure it.

Upon removal from the press, a cutting gauge is used to 'square-up' the curl, true and parallel to the edges, and this allows for any fractional movement in getting the panel into the press, loading the press with cauls, wad, etc.

Remove the panels from the press after a couple of hours, and the unwanted surplus shown by the cutting gauge can be trimmed off with a chisel long before it has cured.

The boxwood lines and crossbandings are now fitted. This provides three further options.

(a) The boxwood lines and bandings may be taped to the assembly and returned to the press after the application of fresh glue.

(b) The borders may be ironed on using Glu-film and roller or scotch glue and veneer hammer, or

(c) The borders could be applied using contact adhesive.

Continuity

The important point worthy of stressing with all wall units is that there must not be a pattern jump across units. The figure must flow across door and drawer units with an unbroken line.

When the wall unit has drawers or cupboards above or below, across a space (top door units and bottom drawer units with a shelf unit between), the figure must show continuity across the unit at the top, and at the bottom, and also vertically.

All doors and drawers and flaps must be prepared from matching consecutive leaves to an overall design which preserves continuity throughout the unit.

This traditional curl unit may be laid as a flat panel or for a shaped corner unit, laid in shaped cauls.

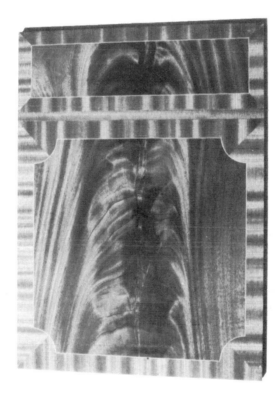

Fig. 253 Traditional curl mahogany door and drawer unit

Project No. 10

Pair of Wardrobe Doors with Herringbone Reverse Butt Match

Dimensions: 60 inches × 22 inches (1525mm × 558mm).

Groundwork: 2 pieces 59½ inches × 21½ inches × ⅝ inches (1510mm × 546mm × 15mm) chipboard or laminated board.

Edge lipping: 30 feet of ¼ inch × ⅝ inch (10 metres × 6mm × 15mm)

Crossbanding: 16 of 4 feet × 8 inches (1220mm × 203mm) × 0.6mm mahogany veneer.

Backing veneer: 16 leaves 62 inches × 6 inches (1575mm × 152mm) × 0.6mm sapele veneer.

Face veneer: 32 leaves 16 inches × 8 inches (406mm × 203mm) × 0.7mm pencil striped sapele.

Procedure: Cut and fit the edge lipping to both door panels. Tooth both panels flat and true and prepare mahogany crossbandings. Slip match, joint, tape and lay the crossbandings; clean up, trim off the overhang and allow to cure. Clean off tapes and tooth ready for face veneering. Chalk sequence numbering on every leaf on both sides 1F and 1R etc.

1.   Separate the 32 leaves into two piles, one for each door, which are designated door A and door B.

Leaves for Door A	*Leaves for Door B*
1, 2, 5, 6, 9, 10, 13, 14	3, 4, 7, 8, 11, 12, 15, 16
17, 18, 21, 22, 25, 26	19, 20, 23, 24, 27, 28
29 and 30	31 and 32.

2.   *Cut into 135 degree ends*   (Top of leaf to the right)
     1, 2, 5, 6, 17, 18, 21 and 22;   3, 4, 7, 8, 19, 20, 23 and 24.

3.   *Cut into 45 degree ends*   (Top of leaf to the right)
     9, 10, 13, 14, 25, 26, 29 and 30;   11, 12, 15, 16, 27, 28, 31 and 32.

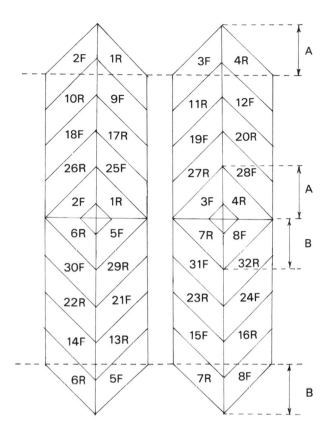

Fig. 254 Pair of herringbone reversed match doors

4. Begin with leaves cut to 135 degrees. Take leaves 1 and 2. Pivot them so that the bevelled edges are vertical. Slide leaf No 1 to the right and reverse it.Now invert it and tape leaves 2F to Leaf 1R, along their bevels. Repeat this with all the leaves shown in Step 2 above. Keep door A separate from door B.

5. Take the leaves with the 45 degree ends, beginning with leaves 9 and 10. Pivot them to arrange the bevelled edges in the vertical direction and slide leaf 9 to the right. Reverse leaf 10 and invert it. Then tape the joints to produce 10R + 9F. Repeat this procedure with all the leaves shown in step 3 above. Keep door A separate from door B.

6.   Joint and tape together the following herringbone matches.

Door A	Door B
2F + 1R	3F + 4R
10R + 9F	11R + 12F
18F + 17R	19F + 20R
26R + 25F	27R + 28F

7.   Place a straightedge across the top of the triangle formed by 2F + 1R and trim off. Re-joint this small triangle at the base of 26R + 25F.
Repeat this with 3F + 4R and tape this triangle into the base of 27R + 28F. This completes two rectangular assemblies for the top half of each door.

8.   Joint and tape together the following herringbone matches for the bottom halves of the two doors.

Door A	Door B
6F + 5R	7F + 8R
14R + 13F	15R + 16F
22F + 21R	23F + 24R
30R + 29F	31R + 32F

9.   Place a straightedge across the top of the triangle formed by 6F + 5R and trim off. Re-joint this small triangle at the base of 30R + 29F.
Repeat this with the top triangle of 7F + 8R and tape this into the bottom section of 31R + 32F.

10. Take the two matches made in Steps 8 and 9, and *reverse* them so that they read, when upside down:

30F + 29R	31F + 32R
22R + 21F	23R + 24F
14F + 13R	15F + 16R
6R + 5F	7R + 8F

Tape and joint them to the other two half doors to complete the herringbone reverse butt match.

The centre diamonds

Because of the re-matched centres, the butting triangles of each door form:

$$\frac{2F + 1R}{6R + 5F} \qquad\qquad \frac{3F + 4R}{7R + 8F}$$

In the centre of these triangles, a small diamond is formed comprising:

$$\frac{10R + 9F}{14F + 13R} \qquad\qquad \frac{11R + 12F}{15F + 16R}$$

The pattern jump horizontally across each door is only one; vertically the pattern jump is equalised throughout at eight on the main door panels, and four on the centre diamonds.

Also note that the maximum use of light refraction has been obtained by the alternation of face and reverse veneers.

Laying: The dimensions are deliberately a fraction oversize to enable the assemblies to be laid in a press with cauls, or by contact adhesive with a slip sheet.

25

Nomenclature

THERE are more than 70,000 different species of trees known to man. The largest wood collection in the world is housed in the Samuel James Record Memorial Collection at the School of Forestry, Yale University, Newhaven, Connecticut U.S.A., which comprises more than 50,000 species.

The International Code of Botanical Nomenclature sets down a standardised code of names in Latin, in order that scientists in every part of the world whatever their native tongue, can identify the species correctly.

The first name is assigned to a **genus**, and the second to a **specific epithet** to indicate the particular species of the genus.

The advantage of using the binomial latinised system is illustrated with the example of pinus woods. All pinus are true pines, (*Pinus sylvestris* is Scots pine). But Parana pine is not a pine at all, but *Araucaria angustifolia* belonging neither to the genus nor even to the family.

Botanically, every tree has a classification from which the generic and specific names are taken. The following example applies to English walnut.

Kingdom	Vegetable
Division	Angiospermae
Class	Dicotyledoneae
Order	Juglandales
Family	Juglandaceae
Genus	Juglans
Species	Regia

The botanical name for English walnut is therefore, (using the Latinised binomial system) *Juglans regia.*

In addition to the International Code of Botanical Nomenclature, the identification of timbers is complicated by the use of other names.

Pilot names:

These are listed in the *British Standard Nomenclature of Commercial Timbers (BS881 and BS589, 1974 etc).* Unfortunately these are only of value in Britain. Many other parts of the world have their own standard nomenclature, and some timbers are known by an entirely different name in Australia or America.

Wherever possible, in this book, the name used will be the Pilot name, with the addition of the Latin name for positive identification.

Trade Names

Very often these are names 'invented' by merchants and traders who wish to describe or even glamorise otherwise indifferent species, with a more romantic name.

For example ayan *(Distemonanthus benthamianus)* is often described in the trade as African satinwood, or Nigerian satinwood, in imitation of genuine satinwood from the West Indies *(Zanthoxylum flavum)* or East Indian satinwood *(Chloroxylon swietenia).*

Common Names

These are names in everyday common use and can also be misleading if they allude to a prominent characteristic. Any very heavy wood is called 'ironwood', and this name is given to more than 80 different species such as hornbeam.

Colour descriptions are very misleading. Black Italian poplar, is white in colour. Indian silver greywood *(Terminalia bialata)* Andaman Islands, is neither silver nor grey. Australian blackwood is not black but brown.

Vernacular Names

These are names by which the timber is known in its country of origin, usually in the native language.

This produces the reverse effect. Instead of 80 timbers having the same common name, we now have scores of different local dialect names for the same timber; these vary from region to region and are different at each port of shipment.

Obeche *(Triplochiton scleroxylon)* from West Africa, has vernacular names of African whitewood; arere; ayous; samba, okpo, wawa.

Afara *(Terminalia superba)* is known variously as limba, ka-ronko; frake; fram; djombe; eji; ofram. In America it is given the trade name of korina.

Throughout the English speaking world, there is a divergence in timber names. In Australia, oak, ash and elm are entirely different from those species recognised in Britain and America.

But on the other hand, Britain and Australia agree on timbers which are known by entirely different names in America. The following are examples:

Britain	USA
Silky Oak *(Australian)*	
(Cardwellia sublimis)	Lacewood
Lacewood *(Platinus acerifolia)*	Sycamore
Sycamore *(Acer pseudoplatanus)*	Maple
Maple *(Acer saccharum)*	Sugar Maple

It is therefore unsafe to rely on the trade or vernacular names. Every country agrees on the scientific name, therefore the veneer craftsman would be wise to make a study of these in order that he may be able to specify the precise timber he requires.

THE TECHNIQUE OF IDENTIFICATION

How is a piece of wood positively identified? The wood scientist cuts a sliver from three planes of the wood sample which need only be an inch (25mm) square (a) the transverse cross section (b) the tangential-longitudinal plane (c) the lateral radial face.

The specimens for examination are about twenty microns (0.020mm) thick, and are dyed or chemically treated to aid examination and a strong light is passed through them.

Using a compound microscope in a laboratory, he studies the size, distribution and groupings of the cells; the size and arrangement of the rays; the type of soft tissue present; the presence or absence of tyloses; modifications to the cell walls, and the appearance and proportions of earlywood to latewood.

Macroscopic identification is open to everyone by means of a hand magnifer, with a lens optically corrected to ten diameters (ten power). Other more powerful magnifiers are available with built-in illumination up to 20 power and are ideal for laymen's use.

Most scientific authorities use and issue dichotomous lens keys for the swift identification of timbers.

In his book "What Wood Is That?" Herbert L. Edlin describes 14 keys for easy identification:

1. General colour
2. Colour of heartwood
3. Growth rings
4. Pores
5. Grain (on longitudinal surfaces)
6. Rays
7. Hardness
8. Weight
9. Smell
10. Bark
11. Leaves
12. Country of Origin
13. Sapwood
14. Class of Use

The Forest Products Research Laboratory issues a lens key featuring 450 hardwoods, and also an Atlas of End-Grain Photomicrographs at X10 magnification of most hardwoods.

Colour

For our purpose, the colour description given in the following list is of the heartwood; the sapwood colour has been ignored.

This is important because in certain veneers the sapwood is equally important for decorative purposes as the heartwood. Indeed, some species contain a high proportion of sapwood with only a small heartwood section.

In other cases, logs of the same species and from the same source may vary in colour due to soil differences and other local conditions. Therefore, the colour description is intended only as an approximate general guide, based upon the normal appearance of regular stocks.

Usage

As a general rule, the veneer plant utilises its local resources, and if the plant is in Finland for example it will produce mainly for plywood and corestock.

However, the purpose of this section of the book is a guide to decorative veneers of the world, and the 250 species named may all be used for face veneering, even though degraded logs may be used for plywood or corestock purposes.

Timbers which are cut exclusively for corestock purposes have not been included.

Grain

When an asterisk has been placed against a species in more than one column, for example, 'straight grain' and 'interlocked grain', it usually means that the timber is chiefly straight grained, but sometimes interlocked grain may be found. When two or more types of grain are common, a description is used such as 'irregular' or 'crossgrained'.

Texture and hardness

Veneers do not fall neatly into broad classifications, either in relation to their hardness or texture; the coding is intended as a general guide.

Supply and price

This book was written and first published in the U.K. and therefore the availability and price guide columns will refer mainly to the U.K. Readers in all parts of the world, will find that veneers which are produced locally, will be more readily available and at a lower price.

Government embargoes on the export of logs, and seasonal shortages, changes in fashion etc., may also affect the demand and supply situation, so that veneers which are freely available and cheap today, may become scarce and expensive through market force conditions.

Therefore before planning a project and preparing your decorative veneer specification, check the availability of your selected veneer.

General Remarks

Many veneers are hard, brittle, fibrous, crumbly or otherwise difficult to handle and lay—but once laid, may take an excellent polish.

Others are easy to handle and yet provide a resinous, or open pored coarse surface which is difficult to work into an excellent finish.

These remarks are not intended to discourage you from using the species, but in the case of, say, an oily surface, you may decide to finish with oil and wax rather than attempt a high gloss finish.

Collector's Sets

Most veneer craftsmen prefer to build up their own permanent portfolio of rare and exotic wood veneers. A collector's set becomes an valuable aid when planning future projects and when seeking to match a veneer for a restoration repair. Architects and designers will find them a handy desk reference when considering specifications for panelling schemes. They also make excellent teaching aids for 'know your woods' recognition classes.

There are three ways to begin.

(a)   There is a set of 45 samples 3 inches × 1 inch (76mm × 25mm) which form a useful wall chart for quick reference.

(b)   The collector's set of 50 rare and exotic woods measure 4½ inches × 3 inches (114mm × 76mm), but complete with more than 60 labels with basic information including trade and botanical names, common names and country of origin etc. This enables the supplier to select 50 woods from those currently available. (See Fig. 255).

(c)   The set of 40 wood veneers 3 inches × ⅞ inches (76mm × 22mm) mounted and named in a concertina folder taken from H. L. Edlin's book *'What Wood is That?'* is available from Stobart & Son Ltd. (See Fig. 256).

(Larger sized veneers up to 12 inches × 4 inches (304mm × 101mm) or 36 inches × 8 inches (914mm × 203mm) are also available from specialist mail order stockists. See also *Timber Monographs* page 393).

It is an excellent idea to mount the veneers on a display panel; but only sand, seal and polish one half of each specimen. The veneer can then be compared in its natural and polished state and for this reason the labels are usually sent un-mounted so that the sets can be mounted in the appropriate manner, depending on their end-use, before labelling.

Fig. 255 Veneer collection by the Art Veneers Co. Ltd.

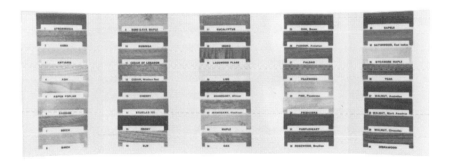

Fig. 256 Veneer collection from 'What Wood Is That?'

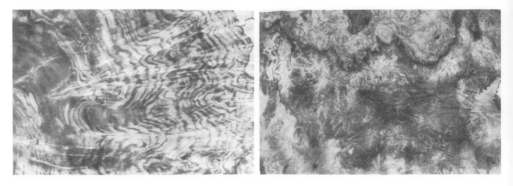

Fig. 257 American walnut burry butt

Fig. 258 Oak burr

BURRS

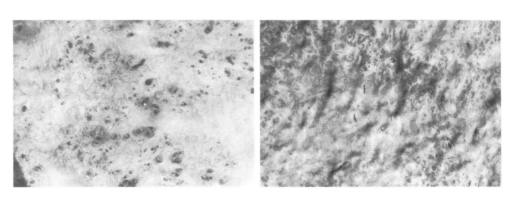

Fig. 259 Poplar burr

Fig. 260 Elm burr

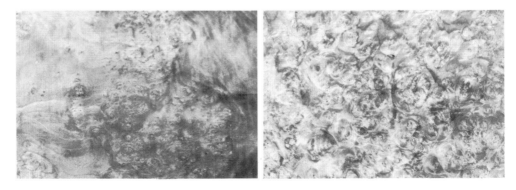

Fig. 261 Lacewood burr

Fig. 262 Walnut burr

Fig. 263 Castello   **Fig. 264** Half rounded Bolivian rosewood

CROWN AND STRIPED

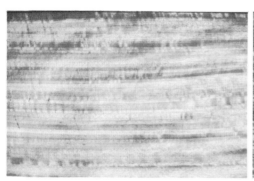

Fig. 265 Eucalyptus   **Fig. 266** Indian rosewood

Fig. 267 Avodire   **Fig. 268** Afrormosia

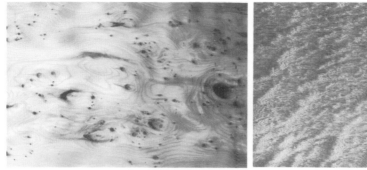

Fig. 269 Yew tree

Fig. 270 Pommelle

CURLS AND FREAK FIGURES

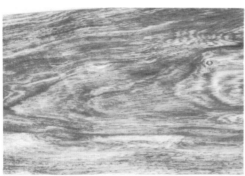

Fig. 271 Eccentrically cut
Brazilian rosewood

Fig. 272 Walnut curl

Fig. 273 Mahogany curl

Fig. 274 European walnut curl

APPENDIX A

TWO HUNDRED AND FIFTY wood veneers from all over the world including many rare and exotic types are listed in the following pages in alphabetical order of their pilot names.

Also provided, for easy identification, are their scientific names as listed in the International Code of Botanical Nomenclature, together with their family names.

To aid selection, in *Appendix B,* the list has been grouped into 24 different colour tones.

SPECIES	Family	Origin	Colour	Useage			Grain				Texture			Hardness			Supply				Price			Remarks	
				Decorative	Plywood	Corestock	Straight	Interlocked	Wavy/irregular	Spiral	Fine, even	Medium	Coarse	Soft	Medium	Hard	Rare	Spasmodic	Moderate	Plentiful	High prices	Average	Cheap	Works well	Takes finish
ABURA *Mitragyna ciliata* subaha; bahia, elilom, maza	Rubiaceae	Tropical W. Africa	Reddish brown to light brown	*	*	*	*	*				*		*					*				*	*	*
ADJOUABA *Dacryodes klaineana* ollem, igaganga mouvendo, ossabel safoukala	Burseraceae	W. Africa	Grey or pink		*	*	*				*					*			*			*		*	*
AFARA *Terminalia superba* White afara, limba, Ofram, korina, frake, limbo, akom, chene, eghoin	Combretaceae	W. Africa	Light yellowish brown. Irregular grey black markings	*	*	*	*	*	*			*			*					*		*		*	*
AFRORMOSIA *Afrormosia elata* kokrodua assamela	Leguminosae	W. Africa	Brown or yellow	*	*		*	*				*				*			*			*		*	*
AFZELIA *Afzelia spp:* doussie, apa, aligna, chamfuta mussacossa, mkora	Leguminosae	W. Africa	Light brown	*	*			*					*			*		*				*			*
AGARU *Dysoxylum decandrum* paluahan, bagulibas, buntugon	Meliaceae	Tropical Asia, Australia, and the Phillipines	Light yellowish brown	*	*				*		*					*		*				*		*	

Name	Family	Origin	Colour	Notes
AGBA *Gossweilerodendron balsamiferum* moboron, tola, tola branca, ntola, mutsekamambole	Leguminosae	W. Africa	Yellow pink to red	*gummy
AINI *Artocarpus hirsuta* anjili, ainee, pejata	Moraceae	India	Old gold with russet tinge with dark brown lines	lustrous
AKOSSIKA *Scottellia spp;*	Flacourtiaceae	W. Africa	Pale yellow with darker streaks	silver grain qt'd
ALDER *Alnus glutinosa* common alder, aune, black, alder, els, erle	Betulaceae	Europe Russia N. Africa W. Asia and Japan	Light reddish brown	
ALDER, RED *Alnus rubra* Western Alder	Betulaceae	Canada, Pacific coast to USA	Pale yellow reddish brown	*(knots, burls, used for wall panelling face veneers)*
ALMACIGA *Agathis philippensis*	Araucariaceae	Philippines	Pink-buff	
ALMACIGO *Bursera simaruba* red gombo, gumbo-limbo chaca. W. Indian Birch	Burseraceae	W. Indies, Mexico C. America N.S. Amer.	Whitish, Yellow to light brown	
ALMON *Shorea almon*	Diptero-carpaceae	Philippines	Reddish light brown	
AMARI *Amoore wallichii* lalchini, galing libor	Meliaceae	Andaman I. Burma Bangladesh N.E. India	Reddish brown	
AMBEROI *Pterocymbium beccarii* por-lekeng, kelumbuk	Sterculiaceae		White to cream	

SPECIES	Family	Origin	Colour	Useage: Decorative	Plywood	Corestock	Grain: Straight	Interlocked	Wavy/irregular	Spiral	Texture: Fine, even	Medium	Coarse	Hardness: Soft	Medium	Hard	Supply: Rare	Spasmodic	Moderate	Plentiful	Price: High prices	Average	Cheap	Remarks: Works well	Takes finish
AMBOYNA *Pterocarpus indicus* narra (Phillipies) padauk (Burma)	Leguminosae	South East Asia	Varies from brown with red markings to red with black markings	*				*		*	*(burr veneers especially attractive)*						*				*			*	*
AMOORA *Amoora rohituka* lota amara, galingasing thitni, chaya-kaya	Meliaceae	Southern Asia	Deep red		*		*	*					*		*					*			*	*	*
ANDIROBA *Carapa guianensis* crabwood, krappa tangare	Meliaceae	S. America W. Indies C. America	Reddish brown	*	*	*	*	*								*	*						*	*	*
ANGELIN *Andira inermis spp.* kuraru, koraro, yaba, rode kabbes, angelim partridge wood	Leguminosae	C. America W. Indies	Yellow-brown to reddish-brown	*			*				*(distinctive wavy bands make attractive face veneer)*		*		*		*				*			*	
ANINGERIA *Aningeria spp* agnegre. landosan mukali, kali, mukangu, muna, osan.	Sapotaceae	Tropical Africa	Beige with pink tint	*	*		*		*			*			*				*			*		Silica content	
ANTIARIS *Antiaris toxicaria* oro, ogiovu, ako. chen-chen, kyenkyen kirundu, diolosso	Moraceae	West, Central and East Africa	Yellow	*	*	*	*				*(quartered sliced face veneers, or corestock only)*	*	*						*			*		*

Name / Species	Family	Origin	Colour													
ARARIBA *Centrolobium spp.* araríba amarelo, aleo amarelo.	Leguminosae	South America	Orange to red with red to purple streaks	*				*	*				*		*	*
ASH, European *Fraxinus excelsior* English, French, according to origin. Olive Ash	Oleaceae	Europe N. Africa W. Asia	Cream to biscuit	*	*	*	*	*	*	*	*			*	**	**
ASH, Japanese *Fraxinus mandschurica* Tamo	Oleaceae	Manchuria Korea Japan	Light brown to biscuit	*	*			*	*	*	*(wild dark brown to black streaks known as Olive Ash)*		*	*	*	*
AVODIRÉ *Turraeanthus africanus* apeya, appayia, apaya, wansenwa, engan, esu, lusamba, songo.	Meliaceae	W. Africa	Golden Yellow	*	*	*		*	*	*	*(quarter cut face veneers have highly mottled figure)*		*	*	*	*
AYAN *Distemonanthus benthamianus* Movingui, ayanran, barré eyen, oguéminia	Leguminosae	W. Africa	Bright to golden brown	*	*			*	*				*		*	*
BAGTIKAN *Parashorea malaanonan*	Dipterocarpaceae Philippines		Grey to light brown	*				*	*				*		*	*
BAROMALLI *Catostemma spp.* baramanni;	Bombacaceae	South America	Beige to brown	*				*	*(distinctive ray figure on quartered wood)*		*		*		*	
BASSWOOD *Tilia americana* American lime	Tiliaceae	Canada Eastern USA	Cream to biscuit	*	*			*	*				*	*	*	*
BEECH, EUROPEAN *Fagus sylvatica*	Fagaceae	Europe	Biscuit to light tan reddish brown when steamed	*	*			*	*	*			*	*	*	*

SPECIES	Family	Origin	Colour	Useage — Decorative	Useage — Plywood	Useage — Corestock	Grain — Straight	Grain — Interlocked	Grain — Wavy/irregular	Grain — Spiral	Texture — Fine, even	Texture — Medium	Texture — Coarse	Hardness — Soft	Hardness — Medium	Hardness — Hard	Supply — Rare	Supply — Spasmodic	Supply — Moderate	Supply — Plentiful	Price — High prices	Price — Average	Price — Cheap	Remarks — Works well	Remarks — Takes finish
BEECH, JAPANESE *Fagus crenata* buna	Fagaceae	Japan	Light brown	*	*		*				*				*					*			*	*	*
WHITE BEECH *Gmelina spp.* koko, arakoko, buti,	Verbenaceae	Australasia	White with grey tinge	*	*		*				*				*				*				*	*	*
BIRCH EUROPEAN *Betula spp.* Silver birch, White birch, Finnish Birch Flame birch Masur birch	Betulaceae	Northern Europe	Cream to biscuit	*	*	*	*				*					*						*		*	*
BIRCH JAPANESE *Betula alba*	Betulaceae	Asia China and Japan	Yellow-red	*	*	*		*			*					*		*			*			*	*
PAPER BIRCH *Betula papyrifera* American birch, White birch	Betulaceae	USA	Cream, white	*	*	*	*				*					*		*			*			*	*
WHITE BIRCH *Schizomeria ovata* crabapple, humbug, squeaker, bea bea, malafelo, hambia	Cunoniaceae	Australasia	Pale brown	*	*	*		*			*					*			*			*		*	*
BIRCH YELLOW *Betula alleghaniensis* Quebec birch,	Betulaceae	Canada and USA	Reddish brown	*	*	*	*				*					*			*			*		*	*

(Flame Birch and Curly Birch caused by grain deviations Masur Birch caused by Agromyzia carbonaria beetle attack in the cambium. When rotary cut this appears as highly decorative black flecks and swirls)

American birch, etc, Hard birch

(BIRD'S EYE MAPLE – see MAPLE)

	Family	Source	Colour											
BLACKBEAN Castanospermum australe Beantree, Moreton Bay bean Moreton Bay chestnut	Leguminosae	New South Wales and Queensland Australia	Browny grey, brown streaks	*	*	*	*	*	*	*			
BLACKWOOD, AUSTRALIAN Acacia melanoxylon black wattle	Leguminosae	Australia	Golden-brown red to dark brown with brown markings	* * *		*	*	*	*	*		(highly decorative fiddleback figure)	
BOLONG-ETA Diospyros mindanaensis ata-ata, anang, tamil-lalaki	Ebenaceae	Philippines	Black with greyish streaks	*	*	*	*	*	*	*			
BOMBAX, INDIAN Bombax malabaricum semul, cottonwood, letpan, simbal	Malvaceae	India, Pakistan Bangladesh Burma	Pale yellow, brown	* *	*	*	*	*	*	*			
BUBINGA Guibourtia spp. Kevazingo, essingang	Leguminosae	Cameroons Gabon	Lt red-brown veined with pink or red stripes	*	*	*	*	*	*	*	*	*	(Rotary cut produces wild figure known as Kevazingo)
CALOPHYLLUM Guttiferae Collophyllum spp. satin touriga, blush touriga, satin mahogany, kokilo, buni, pagura bunu gwara gwaro		Australia Malaysia Solomon Islands	Reddish brown	*	*	*	*				*		

SPECIES	Family	Origin	Colour	Useage			Grain				Texture			Hardness			Supply				Price			Remarks		Remarks
				Decorative	Plywood	Corestock	Straight	Interlocked	Wavy/irregular	Spiral	Fine, even	Medium	Coarse	Soft	Medium	Hard	Rare	Spasmodic	Moderate	Plentiful	High prices	Average	Cheap	Works well	Takes finish	
CAMAGON *Diospyros discolour* talang-gubat palo-negro	Ebenaceae	E. Indies	Jet black with pink, yellow, brown or grey streaks	*			*				*					*	*				*			*	*	
CANARIUM, AFRICAN *Canarium schweinfurthii* papo, elemi, abeul, abel, mupafu, mwafu, mbidinkala	Burseraceae	Africa	Pinkish brown			*				*			*		*					*		*				silica present
CANARIUM, MALAYSIAN *Canarium spp.* Kedondong	Burseraceae	South East Asia	Pink to red brown with yellow tinge		*			*	*						*				*			*		*	*	
CATIVO *Prioria copaifera* cautivo	Leguminosae	W. Indies Central America	Light brown golden lustre	*			*				*				*				*				*		*	gum streaks
CEDAR *Cedrus spp.* Atlas cedar, deodar Atlantic cedar, Cedar of Lebanon	Pinaceae	Europe	Light brown	*	*		*		*			*		*					*			*		*	*	
CEDAR, BURMESE *Cedrela toona* toon, yomhom, Burma cedar	Meliaceae	South East Asia, India Pakistan Burma Thailand	Reddish brown with darker streaks		*	*	*									*						*			*	

Name	Family	Origin	Colour	Notes
CEDAR, CENTRAL AMERICAN *Cedrela odorata* acajou, Honduras cedar Cigar box cedar	Meliaceae	Central America and Caribbean	Dark reddish brown	exudes gum
CEDAR OF LEBANON *Cedrus libani*	Pinaceae	Lebanon	Cream to pink with Lt. brown heartwood	
PORT ORFORD CEDAR *Chamaecyparis lawsoniana* Lawson's cypress	Cupressaceae	USA	Pale pink to brown	
CEDAR, SOUTH AMERICAN *Cedrela fissilis* cedro, cedro batata, cedro rosa, cedro vermelho	Meliaceae	South America	Dark reddish brown with purplish tinge	exudes gum
CEDAR (VIRGINIAN PENCIL) *Juniperus virginiana* Eastern red cedar	Cupressaceae	N. America	Red-brown with darker latewood line	natural defects
WESTERN RED CEDAR *Thuja plicata* Red cedar	Pinaceae	North America	Red brown to dark brown	acidic stains
CEDAR YELLOW *Chamaecyparis nootkatensis* Yellow cypress	Cupressaceae	N. America Pacific Coast	Yellow	
CELTIS *Celtis philippinensis* hard celtis silky celtis	Ulmaceae	Australia New Guinea Solomon Islands	Yellowish brown	

SPECIES	Family	Origin	Colour	Useage: Decorative	Plywood	Corestock	Grain: Straight	Interlocked	Wavy/irregular	Spiral	Texture: Fine, even	Medium	Coarse	Hardness: Soft	Medium	Hard	Supply: Rare	Spasmodic	Moderate	Plentiful	Price: High prices	Average	Cheap	Remarks: Works well	Takes finish
CELTIS, AFRICAN *Celtis spp.* esa, ita, ohia, ba, shiunza, chia, mudengwa, kiambo kerrua, chepkelet	Ulmaceae	W. Africa Central Africa	Straw	*	*				*		*				*			*			*				*
CHAMPAK *Michelia champaca* saga, sangra, sagawa	Magnoliaceae	Burma India	Yellow brown to olive brown	*	*							*		*				*			*			*	*
CHAPLASH *Artocarpus chaplasha*	Moraceae	Southern Asia	Yellow to brown, darker streaks with white chalk lines	*	*		*	*	*				*	*				*			*			*	*
WHITE CHEESEWOOD *Alstonia spp.* dita, milky pine, pulai	Apocynaceae	Papua New Guinea	Cream to yellow brown	*	*	*	*	*				*		*						*			*	*	latex
CHERRY, AMERICAN *Prunus serotina* black cherry	Rosaceae	N. America	Red brown to deep red brown with flecks	*	*		*				*					*			*		*			*	*
CHERRY, EUROPEAN *Prunus avium* wild cherry, cerisier kirsche, kers, fruit	Rosaceae	Europe, Russia W. Asia N. Africa	Pale pink brown	*	*		*				*					*		*				*		*	*

Name	Family	Other names	Origin	Colour														
CHESTNUT, HORSE *Aesculus hippocastanum*	Hippo-castanaceae		Europe Iran, India	Creamy white	*	* *(Can be treated chemically as harewood)*						*	*	*	*		*	*
CHESTNUT SWEET *Castanea sativa* Spanish chestnut	Fagaceae		Europe N. Africa Asia Minor	Beige-tan or biscuit	*	*	*					*	*	*	*		* iron stains	*
CHICKRASSY *Chukrasia tabularis* Chittagong wood, yinma lal devdari, yinma Indian Almondwood	Meliaceae		India Bangladesh Burma Andaman Islands	Yellowish red, to reddish brown	*	*	*			*	*	*	*	*	*		*	*
CHUGLAM WHITE *Terminalia bialata* Indian silver greywood chuglam, lein	Combretaceae		Andaman Islands	Grey-yellow to olive brown banded with dark streaks	*	*	*	*	*		*		*	*	*	*		*
CINNAMON *Cinnamomum tavoyanum* hmantheinpo	Lauraceae		South Tenesserim (Asia)	Brown with pink streak	*	*	*			*			*	*	*			*
COACHWOOD *Ceratopetalum apetalum* scented satinwood	Cunonaceae		Australia	Brown to pink-brown	*	*	*	*	*				*	*	*		*	*
COCOBOLO *Dalbergia retusa* granadillo	Leguminosae		Central America	Brown to rich red with streaks	*	*	*			*			*	*	*		*	*
COURBARIL *Hymenaea courbaril* jatoba, jatai, W. Indian locust. jatai amarelo	Leguminosae		Central and South America	Pink to orange brown with darker streaks	*	*	*	*	*				*	*	*		*	*
DIFUO *Morus mesozygia*	Moraceae		Tropical Africa	Golden brown	* *(mottled)*								*	*	*			*

SPECIES	Family	Origin	Colour	Useage			Grain				Texture			Hardness			Supply				Price			Remarks	
				Decorative	Plywood	Corestock	Straight	Interlocked	Wavy/irregular	Spiral	Fine, even	Medium	Coarse	Soft	Medium	Hard	Rare	Spasmodic	Moderate	Plentiful	High prices	Average	Cheap	Works well	Takes finish
DOUGLAS FIR *Pseudotsuga menziesii* Oregon Pine Columbian pine	Pinaceae	N. America Europe	Orange brown with early and latewood zone colour differences	*	*		*		*		*	*			*				*				*		*	resinous
DUKALI *Parahancornia amapa* mampa, naranja podrida amapa	Apocynaceae	South America	White to cream	*	*		*				*					*		*					*		*	*
EBONY, AFRICAN *Diospyros spp.* (crassiflora and piscatoria) Gabon ebony, Nigerian ebony etc.	Ebenaceae	West Africa	Jet black brown stripes	*			*				*					*		*			*					*
EBONY, MACASSAR *Diospyros spp.* ebenum; melanoxylon, tomentosa, tendu, tuki, batulinau, bulatinau	Ebenaceae	Southern Asia Philippines	Black with beige or brown streaks or stripes	*					*		*					*		*			*					*
EKABA *Tetraberlinia bifoliolata* ekop ribi	Leguminosae	Cameroons Gabon W. Africa	Pink with darker streaks	*				*	*			*	*		*			*			*					*
EKOUNE *Coelocaryon Klainei*	Myrtaceae	Gabon Congo W. Africa	Orange brown with darker markings	*	*		*				*	*		*				*					*		*	*

Note (Douglas Fir): *(flat cut and rotary cut veneers attractive)*

Name	Family	Origin	Colour											
ELM *Ulmus spp.* (*procera* – UK) (*hollandica* – Dutch) Wych elm.	Ulmaceae	Europe	Lt brown	*		*		*		*		*	*	
ENDOSPERMUM *Endospermum myrmecophilum spp.* New Guinea basswood, toywood	Euphorbiaceae	Australasia	Straw	*	*		*	*	*	*	*		*	*
ERIMA *Octomeles sumatrana* ilimo; binuang	Datiscaceae	Australia	Pale brown with purple tinge	*	*	*	*	*	*	*		*	*	*
EUCALYPTUS – see OAK TASMANIAN														
SILVER FIR *Abies alba & spp.* whitewood	Pinaceae	Europe	Cream to white with yellow cast	*	*	*		*	*		*	*	*	*
GABOON *Aucoumea klaineana* Okoumé, Mofoumou, n'goumi	Burseraceae	Equatorial Guinea, Gabon and Congo	Light pink to brown	*	*	*	*	*		*(quartered wood has stripe and mottle)*	*	*	*	*
GEDU NOHOR *Entandrophragma angolense* edinam, tiama, kalungi timbi, abenbegna	Meliaceae	Africa	Pink to red brown	*	*	*	*	*	*	*	*	*	*	*
GHEOMBI *Sindoropsis le-testui*	Caesalpiniaceae	Gabon	Red brown	*	*	*	*	*	*	*	*	*	*	*
GMELINA *Gmelina arborea* yamane, gambari	Verbenaceae	India Burma Africa	Cream to straw with pinkish tinge	*	*	*	*	*	*	*	*	*	*	* resinous

SPECIES	Family	Origin	Colour	Useage			Grain				Texture			Hardness			Supply				Price			Remarks		
				Decorative	Plywood	Corestock	Straight	Interlocked	Wavy/irregular	Spiral	Fine, even	Medium	Coarse	Soft	Medium	Hard	Rare	Spasmodic	Moderate	Plentiful	High prices	Average	Cheap	Works well	Takes finish	
GOMMIER *Dacryodes excelsa* tabonuco	Burseraceae	Puerto Rico and the Caribbean	Pale brown to rich brown	*	*	*		*			*					*			*			*		*	*	silica
GONÇALO ALVES *Astronium fraxinifolium* Zebrawood, tigerwood	Anacardiaceae	S. America	Red brown with darker spots & streaks	*				*	*			*				*	*				*				*	
GREVILLEA *Grevillea robusta* African silky oak	Proteaceae	Tanzania and Kenya	Golden brown pink tinge	*			*						*		*				*				*			*	(silver grain on quartered wood)
GUAREA *Guarea thompsonii & cedrata* bossé; scented cedar diambi	Meliaceae	Africa	Pink-brown	*			*	*			*				*					*		*		*	*	resinous
GUM, RED (AMERICAN) *Liquidambar styraciflua* Sweet gum, satin walnut	Hamamelidaceae	USA Central America	Pink to reddish brown	*	*		*		*		*				*			*				*		*	*	(mottled figure)
WESTERN HEMLOCK *Tsuga heterophylla* Pacific hemlock B. Columbian hemlock	Pinaceae	Canada and USA	Pale brown with purple latewood lines	*	*		*					*			*					*		*		*	*	
HEVEA *Hevea braziliensis* Para rubber tree	Euphorbiaceae	South America	Pinkish brown		*	*	*					*			*			*				*		*	*	
HOLLOCK *Terminalia myriocarpa*	Combretaceae	Southern Asia	Medium brown darks streaks	*	*	*	*	*	*			*			*			*			*				*	lustrous

Name	Family	Origin	Colour	Properties	Notes
HOLLY, EUROPEAN *Ilex aquifolium*	Aquifoliaceae	Europe W. Asia	Whitish	* * * * * * * * *	
HURA *Hura crepitans* assacu, acacu, possentrie, sand box	Euphorbiaceae	Central America Caribbean and South America	Cream to buff and golden to deep brown with streaks	* * * * * * * * * * *	lustrous
IDIGBO *Terminalia ivorensis* emeri, framiré, Black afara	Combretaceae	Africa	Yellow to light brown	* * * * * * * * * *	avoid contact with iron
ILOMBA *Pycnanthus angolensis* akomu, otie, walélé eteng	Myristicaceae	W. Africa	Pink brown	* * * * * * * *	
IMBUIA *Phoebe porosa* canela, imbuya imbuia amarela	Lauraceae	South America	Olive to chocolate brown	* * * * * * * * * * *	
IPE *Tabebuia serratifolia* yellow poui, hakia, ironwood, wassiba	Bignoniaceae	S. America Caribbean	Olive brown with streaks & yellow lines	* * * * * * * * *	
IROKO *Chlorophora excelsa* odum, mvule, kambala bang, moreira, tule, intule	Moraceae	Tropical Africa	Yellow to golden brown	* * * * * * * * * * *	calcium carbonate
IZOMBE *Testulea gabonensis*	Ochnaceae	W. Africa	Yellow to grey	* * * * * * * * *	
JACARANDA PARDO *Machaerium villosum* Jacaranda amerello	Leguminosae	Brazil	Pink brown to violet brown	* * * * * * * * * *	

SPECIES	Family	Origin	Colour	Useage			Grain				Texture			Hardness			Supply				Price			Remarks	
				Decorative	Plywood	Corestock	Straight	Interlocked	Wavy/irregular	Spiral	Fine, even	Medium	Coarse	Soft	Medium	Hard	Rare	Spasmodic	Moderate	Plentiful	High prices	Average	Cheap	Works well	Takes finish
JARRAH *Eucalyptus marginata*	Myrtaceae	Western Australia	Dark red brown	*			*	*	*			*	*			*	*				*				*
JEQUITIBA *Cariniana spp.* abarco, bacu	Lecythidaceae	Brazil S. America	Yellow to pink brown with wild dark streaks	*			*				*				*			*			*			*	*
KAMARERE *Eucalyptus deglupta*	Myrtaceae	Australasia	Golden brown		*			*				*			*			*				*		*	*
KANDA *Beilschmiedia spp.* bitehi, nkonengu bonzale	Lauraceae	W. Africa	Medium to dark brown	*	*		*				*					*		*				*		*	*
KAURI *Agathis australis* Kauri pine	Araucariaceae	New Zealand	Orange to reddish brown	*	*		*				*				*					*			*	*	*
KEYAKI *Zelkova serrata*	Ulmaceae	China Japan	Golden brown	*			*					*					*							*	*
KINGWOOD *Dalbergia cearensis* Violetwood, violetta	Leguminosae	South America	Violet brown streaked with black or gold	*			*				*						*				*			*	
KIRI *Paulownia tomentosa* Foxglove tree	Scrophulariaceae	Japan	Silver grey to light brown	*			*				*			*						*			*	*	*
LARCH, EUROPEAN *Larix decidua*	Pinaceae	Europe	Pale red brown to brick red	*			*				*				*					*		*		resinous knotty	

KEYAKI — (fine burr veneers)

KINGWOOD — (only available in small-width 'billets')

KIRI — (peeled to produce scale veneers of micro-thinness)

Name	Family	Origin	Colour	Notes	...	resinous knotty
LARCH WESTERN *Larix occidentalis* Western tamarack	Pinaceae	N. America	Deep reddish brown with pronounced colour contrast		* * * * * * * *	resinous knotty
LAUAN RED *Shorea negrosensis* Philippine mahogany	Dipterocarpaceae	Philippines	Dark red		* * * * * * * *	*
LAUAN, WHITE *Pentacme contorta*	Dipterocarpaceae	Philippines	Grey-pink		* * * * * * *	* *
LAUREL, INDIAN *Terminalia alata* sain, amari, taukkyan	Combretaceae	India, W. Pakistan, Bangladesh, Burma	Dark brown to chocolate streaks black		* * * * * *	* *
LONGUI ROUGE *Gambeya africana*	Sapotaceae	Congo Africa	Brown-yellow, irregular dark stripes		* * * * * * *	*
LOURO RED *Ocotea rubra* determa, wane, teteroma, bewana, grignon rouge, louro vermelho	Lauraceae	South America	Red-brown with golden lustre and orange streaks	*(roe figured)*	* * * * *	*
LUNUMIDELLA *Melia azedarach* (Linn) Persian Lilac darachik, tamaga	Meliaceae	India	Reddish brown		* * * * * *	*
MADRONA (BURR) *Arbutus menziesii*	Arbutaceae	USA	Reddish brown	*(attractive burr veneer)*	* * * * *	*
MAFU *Fagaropsis angolensis* mfu, muremu, mukarakati	Rutaceae	Tanzania Kenya	Greenish grey with dark curls and streaks		* * * * * *	*

CMWV—M

SPECIES	Family	Origin	Colour	Useage			Grain				Texture			Hardness			Supply				Price			Remarks		
				Decorative	Plywood	Corestock	Straight	Interlocked	Wavy/irregular	Spiral	Fine, even	Medium	Coarse	Soft	Medium	Hard	Rare	Spasmodic	Moderate	Plentiful	High prices	Average	Cheap	Works well	Takes finish	
MAGNOLIA *Magnolia spp.*	Magnoliaceae	N. America	Straw with greenish tinge with purple streaks	*			*				*				*			*			*			*	*	lustrous
MAHOE *Hibiscus elatus* mountain mahoe, azul, majigua	Malvaceae	Central America Caribbean	Brown to olive with purple, blue or olive streaks	*	*		*				*					*	*				*			*	*	
MAHOGANY, AFRICAN *Khaya ivorensis* Benin, Lagos, ogwango ngollon etc.	Meliaceae	West Africa	Light red	*	*			*					*		*					*			*	*	*	thunder shakes
MAHOGANY BRAZILIAN *Swietenia macrophylla* araputange, acajou mogno, aguano	Meliaceae	South America	Reddish brown to deep red	*	*			*				*	*		*				*			*				*	
MAHOGANY, CENTRAL AMERICA *Swietenia macrophylla* Honduras, Mexican, Panama, caoba donureña	Meliaceae	Central America and Caribbean	Light orange brown with golden lustre	*	*		*	*			*				*				*			*		*	*	
MAKORÉ *Tieghemella heckelii* agamokwe, baku, abaku	Sapotaceae	Africa	Red brown to blood red	*			*		*		*					*				*			*	*	*	lustrous
MALAGAI *Pometia pinnata* malugay, agupanga, taun, kasai	Sapindaceae	Philippines and South Pacific	Pinkish Brown to red brown	*	*		*	*			*				*					*			*		*	

Name	Family	Origin	Colour	Notes
MANNIBALLI *Inga alba* prokonie, bois pagoda, bois sucre	Leguminosae	South America	Red brown with darker streaks	
MANSONIA DARK *Mansonia altissima* ofun, bété aprono	Triplochitonaceae	West Africa	Grey brown with deep purple heart	(selected logs have deep purple heartwood)
MAPLE *Acer saccharum* rock maple, hard maple sugar maple etc. (Bird's eye)	Aceraceae	Canada and USA	Creamy white sapwood; tan heartwood with fine latewood lines	(Produces Bird's Eye Maple (rotary cut) also fiddle-back, blister mottle, and curly butt maple)
MAPLE JAPANESE *Acer mono*	Aceraceae	Japan	Creamy white sapwood reddish tinge	
QUEENSLAND MAPLE *Flindersia brayleyana & spp.* maple silkwood	Rutaceae	Australia	Brown-pink	(lustrous striped figure in quartered veneers)
MARBLEWOOD, ANDAMAN *Diospyros marmorata*	Ebenaceae	Andaman Islands	Grey brown with black bands	
MAYAPIS *Shorea squamata*	Dipterocarpaceae	Philippines	Light red	
MEDANG *Dehaasia nigrescens*	Lauraceae	S.E. Asia	Red-brown with olive tinge	
MENGKULANG *Heritiera simplicifolia* chumprak, chumprag kembang	Sterculiaceae	Malaysia	Red to dark brown	(quartered surfaces large ray flecks)

SPECIES	Family	Origin	Colour	Useage			Grain				Texture			Hardness			Supply				Price			Remarks		
				Decorative	Plywood	Corestock	Straight	Interlocked	Wavy/irregular	Spiral	Fine, even	Medium	Coarse	Soft	Medium	Hard	Rare	Spasmodic	Moderate	Plentiful	High prices	Average	Cheap	Works well	Takes finish	
MERANTI (Dark Red) *Shorea pauciflora* seraya	Diptero-carpaceae	S.E. Asia	Dark red with streaks	*	*			*	*				*			*			*				*		*	resinous
MERANTI (Light Red) *Shorea acuminata* seraya, lauan	Diptero-carpaceae	S.E. Asia	Light red to pink	*	*				*				*			* *(ray flecks)*				*			*		*	
MOABI *Baillonella toxisperma* djave	Sapotaceae	Nigeria Gabon	Rich red to red brown	*	*		*		*		*					*				*			*	*	*	
MTAMBARA *Cephalosphaera usambarensis*	Myristicaceae	East Africa	Orange red to brown	*	*		*		*		*				*					*			*	*	*	
MUNINGA *Pterocarpus angolensis* ambila, mukwa, kiaat, kajat	Leguminosae	Africa	Chocolate brown with red streaks	*			*		*			*		*				*			*			*	*	
TASMANIAN MYRTLE *Nothofagus cunninghamii* Tasmanian beech, Myrtle	Fagaceae	Tasmania and Victoria	Pink to red brown	*	*		*		*		*					*			*			*		*	*	
NARGUSTA *Terminalia amazonia* fukadi, coffee mortar, almendro, cochun, white olivier, guayabo	Combretaceae	Central America and Caribbean	Yellow-brown with reddish streaks or striped	*			*		*		*					*				*			*			lustrous

Name	Family	Region	Colour	Notes
NARRA *Pterocarpus indicus* (Burrs known as Amboyna)	Leguminosae	S.E. Asia	Orange to deep red	
NIANGON *Tarrietia utilis* ogoué, wishmore, nyankom	Sterculiaceae	West Africa	Pink to red brown	resinous
NIOVÉ *Staudtia stipitata* m'bonda, m'boun, kamashi, nkafi	Myristicaceae	West Africa	Orange brown darker markings	
NYATOH *Palaquium maingayi* njatuh, padang	Sapotaceae	South East Asia	Red-brown	
OAK, BROWN	Fagaceae	Europe	Brown	*(Fungus Fistulina hepatica causes oak to turn brown)*
OAK, EUROPEAN *Quercus petraea* English, French etc.	Fagaceae	Europe Asia Minor N. Africa	Straw	*(rays produce silver grain)*
OAK, JAPANESE *Quercus mongolica*	Fagaceae	Japan	Yellow-brown	
OAK, PAPUA NEW GUINEA Indonesian chestnut gunung, berangan	Fagaceae		Pale brown	*(small fleck figure on quartered wood)*
OAK, RED *Quercus rubra*	Fagaceae	N. America and Canada	Pink to brown	
OAK, SHE *Casuarine torulosa spp.* forest oak	Casuarinaceae	New South Wales	Orange, brick red to dark red	*(broad flake ray figure)*
OAK, SILKY *Grevillea robusta* and *Cardwellia sublimis*	Proteaceae	E. Africa New South Wales	Red-brown	*(ray flake figure)*

(striped dark flecked rays)

SPECIES	Family	Origin	Colour	Decorative	Plywood	Corestock	Straight	Interlocked	Wavy/irregular	Spiral	Fine, even	Medium	Coarse	Soft	Medium	Hard	Rare	Spasmodic	Moderate	Plentiful	High prices	Average	Cheap	Works well	Takes finish
OAK, TASMANIAN *Eucalyptus spp.* Alpine ash, stringybark	Myrtaceae	Australia	Pale brown with pink tinge	*	*		*	*	*			*				*			*		*			*	*
OAK, WHITE *Quercus alba*	Fagaceae	Canada USA	Orange brown with pink tint	*	*		*						*							*			*	*	*
OBECHE *Triplochiton scleroxylon* arere, wawa, samba, ayous	Triplo-chitonaceae	West Africa	Pale yellow	*	*	*	*	*			*			*						*			*	*	*
OGEA *Daniellia ogea* oziya, faro, copal hyedua	Leguminosae	W. Africa	Golden brown reddish	*	*	*	*	*	*				*											*	*
OKWEN *Brachystegia eurycoma & leonensis* meblo, naga, brachystegia	Leguminosae	W. Africa	Golden brown to dark brown stripes	*	*		*	*				*				*				*			*	*	
OLIVEWOOD *Olea hochstetteri* musheragi	Oleaceae	Kenya Tanzania	Buff, with irregular brown and black streaks	*			*				*							*			*				*
OMU *Entandrophragma candollei* heavy sapele, kosipo, atom-assié	Meliaceae	Equatorial Africa	Reddish brown with purple tinge	*			*					*						*				*		*	*

OAK, TASMANIAN: (attractive block mottle or fiddle-back)
OAK, WHITE: (rays produce silver grain)
OGEA: lustrous
OLIVEWOOD: (marbled appearance and the burrs exceptionally attractive)
OMU: (ribbon striped figure, or moiré figure)

Name	Family	Region	Colour									
OPEPE *Nauclea diderrichii* husia, badi, bilinga	Rubiaceae	Equatorial Africa	Golden brown *(striped roll figure)*	*			*	*	*	*	*	*
OVANGKOL *Guibourtia ehie* amazakoué, anokye hyeduanini	Leguminosae	West Africa	Orange brown with grey to black stripes	*		*	*	*	*	*	*	*
OZIGO *Dacryodes buettneri and spp.* ollem, igaganga, adjouaba, mouvendo, ossabel, safoukala	Burseraceae	Africa	Grey-buff to pink	*	*	*	*	*	*	*	*	*
PADAUK ANDAMAN *Pterocarpus dalbergioides* Andaman redwood, vermilion wood (USA)	Leguminosae	Southern Asia	Varying from pink with red lines, through brick red, to deep purple *(roe figure or curly pattern on quartered veneers)*	*		*	*	*	*	*	*	*
PADAUK BURMA *Pterocarpus macrocarpus* pradoo, mai pradoo	Leguminosae	Burma Thailand	Dark red and brown	*		*	*	*	*		*	*
PADAUK, SOLOMONS *Pterocarpus indicus* warara, linggi, liki, rosewood (Papua New Guinea) Note: AMBOYNA is used to describe the burr veneers.	Leguminosae	South East Asia and Pacific islands	Golden brown to blood red *(fiddle-back, mottle, curls etc.)*	*	*	*	*	*	*	*	*	*
PALAQUIUM *Palaquium galactoxylum* Cairns pencil cedar moordooke	Sapotaceae	Australia	Pinkish-red brown with darker streaks	*		*	*	*	*		*	*
PALDAO *Dracontomelum dao* dao New Guinea walnut	Anacardiaceae	New Guinea Philippines	Brown-grey with greenish tinge and irregular brown to black streaks *(broken ribbon figure)*	*	*	*	*	*	*	*	*	*

SPECIES	Family	Origin	Colour	Useage			Grain				Texture			Hardness			Supply				Price			Remarks	
				Decorative	Plywood	Corestock	Straight	Interlocked	Wavy/irregular	Spiral	Fine, even	Medium	Coarse	Soft	Medium	Hard	Rare	Spasmodic	Moderate	Plentiful	High prices	Average	Cheap	Works well	Takes finish
PALOSAPIS *Anisoptera thurifera carpaceae* Bella rosa	Diptero- carpaceae	Philippines	Yellow-buff	*	*		*		*			*	*		*				*				*		*
PAU MARFIM *Balfourodendron riedelianum* moroti; quatamba	Rutaceae	South America	Cream to lemon yellow	*			*		*		*				*			*				*	*	*
PEAR *Pyrus communis*	Rosaceae	Europe W. Asia	Pink-brown	*			*				*			*					*			*		*	*
PEROBA ROSA *Aspidosperma peroba* red peroba	Apocynaceae	Brazil	Rose red with darker streaks	*			*		*		*					*			*		*				*
PEROBA WHITE *Paratecoma peroba* Golden peroba, peroba de campos	Bignoniaceae	Brazil	Golden brown	*				*				*				*	*							*	*
PARANA PINE *Araucaria angustifolia* Brazilian pine	Araucariaceae	South America	Brown with Darker brown figure	*	*		*				*					*				*				*	*
SCOTS PINE *Pinus sylvestris* European redwood redpine, yellow deal	Pinaceae	Europe N. Asia	Orange to red-brown two-tone	*	*		*				*				*					*			*	knotty	*
WESTERN WHITE PINE *Pinus monticola* Idaho white pine	Pinaceae	Canada & N. America	Straw with reddish brown lines	*	*		*				*				*								*	*	*

Name	Family	Species / other names	Origin	Colour	Notes
PLAN-CHONELLA	Sapotaceae	*Planchonella torricellensis* (red) and *P. thyrsoidea* (white)	Australia Pacific Islands	Straw to red	
PLANE, AMERICAN	Platanaceae	*Platanus occidentalis* Sycamore, buttonwood (USA)	Eastern USA	Light reddish brown	*(quartered figure known as lacewood)*
PLANE, EUROPEAN	Platanaceae	*Platanus acerifolia* London planetree Lacewood (quartered)	Europe	Light reddish brown	*(brown ray flecks on lighter background known as lacewood)*
PODO	Podocarpaceae	*Podocarpus gracilior & spp.* yellow wood	W. Africa	Light yellow brown	brittle
POPLAR	Salicaceae	*Populus tremuloides and spp.* Aspen, cottonwood	Canada & USA	Grey-white with light brown tinge	
POPLAR	Salicaceae	*Populus tremula & spp.* Aspen, black poplar	Europe	Cream pink streaks	
PRIMA VERA	Bignoniaceae	*Tabebuia donnell-smithii* durango, palo blanco, (Mexico) San Juan (Honduras)	Central America	Yellowish pink	*(often with mottled or roe figure)*
PTERYGOTA	Sterculiaceae	*Pterygota bequaertii* Koto, kefe, awari	Nigeria Cameroons	Cream yellow	*(ray fleck figure on quartered veneers)*
PULAI	Apocynaceae	*Alstonia spp.*	S.E. Asia	Cream white yellow brown with bands on surface	latex

SPECIES	Family	Origin	Colour	Decorative	Plywood	Corestock	Straight	Interlocked	Wavy/irregular	Spiral	Fine, even	Medium	Coarse	Soft	Medium	Hard	Rare	Spasmodic	Moderate	Plentiful	High prices	Average	Cheap	Works well	Takes finish
PURPLEHEART *Peltogyne spp.* Amaranth (USA) koroboreli	Leguminosae	Central and South America	Deep purple (oxidises to dark brown)	*			*	*	*		*					*	*				*			*	*
(striped on quartered surfaces)																									
QUARUBA *Vochysia hondurensis* San Juan, yemeri, emery palo de chancho	Vochysiaceae	Central America	Pink to brown	*	*		*	*					*		*					*				*		
RAMIN *Gonystylus macrophyllum* melawis, ramin telur	Gonystylaceae	Sarawak and Malaysia	Pale straw	*	*	*	*				*				*						*		*		*	*
RIMU *Dacrydium cupressinum* red pine	Podocarpaceae	Australasia	Light straw to grey brown	*	*		*					*			*						*		*		*	*
ROBLE *Tabebuia rosea & heterophylla*	Bignoniaceae	Central America and S. America Caribbean	Light golden brown	*			*					*			*				*		*				*	*
(fine brown lines with attractive mottle on quartered veneers)																									
ROSEWOOD, BRAZILIAN *Dalbergia nigra* Jacaranda, Bahia rosewood palissander	Leguminosae	Brazil	Chocolate to violet with dark wild markings and marbled figure	*			*	*				*			*		*			*						oily*
(exceptionally beautiful figure in both crown and flat cut, and close striped figure on quartered)																									
ROSEWOOD, HONDURAS *Dalbergia stevensonii* nogaed (USA)	Leguminosae	Belize	Pink brown to purple with irregular black markings	*			*	*				*			*	*						*				oily*

Name	Family	Species / other names	Origin	Colour	Notes
ROSEWOOD, INDIAN	Leguminosae	*Dalbergia latifolia* E. Indian rosewood Bombay blackwood	India	Rose purple to deep purple with blackish lines	
ROSEWOOD MADAGASCAR	Leguminosae	*Dalbergia greveana* Palisander. Faux rose	Madagascar	Rose pink with darker red streaks	
SABICU	Leguminosae	*Lysiloma latisilique* jigue	West Indies	Brown to copper	*(roe figure)*
SAFOUKALA	Burseraceae	*Dacryodes pubescens*	Congo	Pink	*(ribbon striped figure on quartered veneer)*
SAMAN	Leguminosae	*Pithecellobium saman* algarrobo, rain tree	Mexico, Central America Caribbean	Brown with darker wild streaks	lustrous
SANTA MARIA	Guttiferae	*Calophyllum brasiliense* krassa, guanandi, jacareuba, koerahara	Central, & South America Caribbean	Yellow-pink to red with red brown stripes	
SAPELE	Meliaceae	*Entandrophragma cylindricum* aboudikro	W. Africa	Red-brown	*(pencil and ribbon striped figure on quartered veneer)*
SATINÉ	Moraceae	*Brosimum parense* muirapiranga	Tropical America	Rich red with golden sheen	
SATINWOOD AFRICAN	Rutaceae	*Fagara macrophylla* Olon, olonvogo, olon dur.	W. Africa	Yellow veined	

SPECIES	Family	Origin	Colour	Useage			Grain				Texture			Hardness			Supply				Price			Remarks	
				Decorative	Plywood	Corestock	Straight	Interlocked	Wavy/irregular	Spiral	Fine, even	Medium	Coarse	Soft	Medium	Hard	Rare	Spasmodic	Moderate	Plentiful	High prices	Average	Cheap	Works well	Takes finish
SATINWOOD, CEYLON *Chloroxylon swietenia* E. Indian satinwood	Rutaceae	India Sri Lanka	Golden yellow	*				*			*								*	*	*			*	*
							(quartered wood has ribbon figure, mottled or beeswing)																		
SATINWOOD WEST INDIAN *Fagara flava & spp.* San Domingan satinwood Yellow sanders; aceitillo	Rutaceae	Central America Caribbean	Golden yellow	*	*			*			*					*	*							*	*
											(mottled figure)														
SEMPILOR *Dacrydium elatum* malor	Podocarpaceae	Sarawak & Sabah	Light brown to pinkish yellow	*	*		*				*				*					*			*	*	*
SEPETIR *Sindora coriacea & spp.* makata	Leguminosae	S.E. Asia	Orange to red brown with darker markings	*	*			*			*	*			*			*				*		* (resinous)	*
SEQUOIA *Sequoia gigantea* and *sempervirens* Vavona	Taxodiaceae	USA California & Oregon	Rich reddish brown	*	*		*					*	*	*				*						*	*
							(most highly prized for the burr veneers known as 'Vavona burr')																		
SERAYA WHITE *Parashorea malaanonan 7 spp.* bagitan	Diptero-carpaceae	Philippines S.E. Asia	Straw to pale brown with pink tinge	*	*		*	*				*	*		*				*		*			*	*
							(ribbon figure on radial cutting)																		
SIMPOH *Dillenia spp.*	Dilleniaceae	Malaysia	Dark red brown with purple tinge	*	*			*				*	*		*					*	*				*
							(silver grain rays on quarter veneers)																		

Name	Family	Origin	Colour	Notes
SISSOO *Dalbergia sissoo* shisham	Leguminosae	India Pakistan Bangladesh	Golden brown with dark brown streaks	
SNAKEWOOD *Piratinera guianensis* letterwood, amourette bourra courra	Moraceae	S. America	Dark red to red brown black speckles stripes	
SPRUCE NORWAY *Picea abies* European whitewood	Pinaceae	Europe	White to cream brown	
STERCULIA BROWN *Sterculia rhinopetala* wawabima, aye lotofa	Sterculiaceae	W. Africa	Orange to red brown	
SUCUPIRA *Bowdichia nitida* sapupira, black sucupira	Leguminosae	S. America	Red brown with yellow markings	
SYCAMORE *Acer pseudoplatanus* sycamore plane; great maple	Aceraceae	Europe W. Asia	White to cream	*('fiddle-back', curly, mottled, figures obtainable; chemically treated silver grey harewood; also tan coloured 'weathered sycamore')*
TABEBUIA, WHITE *Tabebuia stenocalyx*	Bignoniaceae	Central America Caribbean	Cream-yellow to brownish	
TANGILE *Shorea polysperma*	Dipterocarpaceae	Philippines	Brown red	*(ribbon striped quartered veneers)* lustrous
TAUN *Pometia pinnata* kasai, awa, ako, tava, ohabu, malugai	Sapindaceae	Australasia	Pink to red brown	
TAWA *Beilschmiedia tawa*	Lauraceae	New Zealand	Cream	*(fleck figure on radial cut)*

SPECIES	Family	Origin	Colour	Useage: Decorative	Plywood	Corestock	Grain: Straight	Interlocked	Wavy/irregular	Spiral	Texture: Fine, even	Medium	Coarse	Hardness: Soft	Medium	Hard	Supply: Rare	Spasmodic	Moderate	Plentiful	Price: High prices	Average	Cheap	Remarks: Works well	Takes finish	Notes
TCHITOLA Oxystigma oxyphyllum lolagbola, kitola, chanfuta	Leguminosae	Cameroons, W. Africa	Light brown with black and yellow mottled stripe	*			*	*				*		*			*						*		*	gummy
TEAK Tectona grandis	Verbenaceae	India, Burma Thailand and S. Asia	Golden brown with darker brown markings	*	*		*		*				*			*				*		*		*		oily
TERENTANG Campnosperma spp.	Anacardiaceae	Malaysia	Grey pink to mauve	*				*			*			*						*			*	*	*	(speckled rays)
TERMINALIA Terminalia spp.	Combretaceae	Australasia	Orange brown	*	*			*	*				*			*		*			*			*	*	
TETRA-BERLINIA Tetraberlinia tubmaniana ekop	Leguminosae	Liberia	Red-brown	*				*					*		*				*		*			*	*	lustrous
THUYA BURR Tetraclinis articulata	Cupressaceae	Morocco N. Africa Malta	Golden brown	*						*				*			*				*				*	(twisted curls and knots in burr figure)
TIAONG Shorea agsaboensis	Diptero-carpaceae	Philippines	Light brown to red	*	*			*			*				*						*			*	*	
TINDALO Pahudia rhomboidea	Philippines	Philippines	Orange red with black streaks	*	*		*	*			*				*				*				*	*	*	(often with bird's eye figure)
TOLA Pterygopodium oxyphyllum tola manfuta, chimfuta	Leguminosae	Nigeria Zaire W. Africa	Light to medium red	*			*	*				*							*			*			*	resinous

Name	Family	Origin	Colour	(properties/uses — asterisked columns)
TONKA *Dipteryx odorata* kumaru, koemaroe	Leguminosae	Central America Caribbean	Red to orange brown with purple streaks	* * * * * * * * * very hard
TOTARA *Podocarpus totara*	Podocarpaceae	Australia	Red brown	* * * * * * * * *
TULIPWOOD BRAZILIAN *Dalbergia frutescens* Pau rosa, jacaranda rosa	Leguminosae	Brazil	Salmon pink with deep red close stripes	* * * * (small billets) * * *
UTILE *Entandrophragma utile* sipo, assié	Meliaceae	Tropical Africa	Reddish brown	* * * * * * * *
VIROLA, LIGHT *Virola koschnyi & spp.* banak, sangre, bogabani	Myristicaceae	Central America S. America Caribbean	Golden to red brown	* * * * * * * *
WALNUT, AFRICAN *Lovoa trichilioides* dibétou, eyan, dilolo apopo, sida, lovoawood Congowood (USA) Tigerwood (USA)	Meliaceae	West Africa	Golden brown dark striped markings	* * (ribbon striped on quartered veneers) * *
WALNUT AMERICAN *Juglans nigra* black walnut	Juglandaceae	North America	Purple brown	* * * * * *
WALNUT EUROPEAN *Juglans regia* akrut, thicha, akhor, khor	Juglandaceae	Europe Southern Asia	Grey-brown with darker brown streaks	* * (excellent decorative veneers) * * *

SPECIES	Family	Origin	Colour	Useage: Decorative	Plywood	Corestock	Grain: Straight	Interlocked	Wavy/irregular	Spiral	Texture: Fine, even	Medium	Coarse	Hardness: Soft	Medium	Hard	Supply: Rare	Spasmodic	Moderate	Plentiful	Price: High prices	Average	Cheap	Remarks: Works well	Takes finish
WALNUT NEW GUINEA *Dracontomelum mangiferum* Pacific walnut loup, lup	Anacardiaceae	New Guinea	Orange-brown with pink tinge	*				*	*		*				*				*			*		*	*
WALNUT QUEENSLAND *Endiandra palmerstonii* Australian walnut, oriental wood	Lauraceae	Australia	Light to dark brown streaked with pink, and grey-green stripes to tan	*				*	*		* *(attractive when quartered)*				*					*	*				*
WENGE *Millettia laurentii* dikela palissandre du Congo	Leguminosae	Zaire	Dark brown with darker close veining	*			*						*			*			*			*		*	*
WHITEWOOD, AMERICAN *Liriodendron tulipifera* Yellow poplar, tuliptree canary whitewood, Green Cypress burr	Magnoliaceae	N. America & Canada	Olive green	*	*		*				* *(burrs are attractive with fine light green veining)*				*					*				*	*
WILLOW *Salix spp.*	Salicaceae	Europe W. Asia N. Africa	Cream to pink	*			*				* *(block mottled figure with lustrous moiré sheen)*			*			*							*	*
YELLOWWOOD *Podocarpus guatemalensis*	Podocarpaceae	Central America	Orange brown	*	*		*				*				*					*			*	*	*

Name	Family	Origin	Colour							
YEWTREE *Taxus baccata*	Taxaceae	Europe N. Africa Asia Burma	Orange brown sometimes with purple streaks	*	*(highly prized decorative veneer, with in-growing bark and knots, and clusters of burrs etc.)*	*	*	*	*	*
ZEBRANO *Brachystegia fleuryana* zingana, zebrawood	Leguminosae	Gabon Cameroons	Light gold yellow with black stripes	*	*	*	*	*	*	*

APPENDIX B

250 VENEERS GROUPED BY COLOUR TO AID SELECTION

White to Cream
Beech, white
Beech, European
Bird's eye maple
Dukali
Elm, white
Holly
Horse chestnut
Maple, American
Maple, Japanese
Paper Birch
Poplar
Pulai
Spruce, Norway
Silver Fir
Sycamore
Tawa
White poplar burr
Willow

Cream/Yellow
Antiaris
Cedar yellow
Obeche
Pau marfim
Pterygota
White cheesewood

Cream/Pink
Adjouaba
Almaciga
American whitewood
Cedar of Lebanon
Olive
Safakoula

Straw/Biscuit
Ash
Ash, Japanese
Basswood
Birch
Celtis, African
Chestnut, Sweet
Gmelina
Mafu
Oak, European
Rimu
White Oak

Straw/Yellow
Afara
Akossika
Almacigo
Birch, Japanese

Cedar yellow
Endospermum
Palosapis
Ramin
White seraya
White tabebuia

Straw/Pink
Planchonella
Western white pine
Parana Pine

Golden/Yellow
Avodire
Ayan
Chaplash
Iroko
Podo
Satinwood, African
Satinwood, W. I.

Yellow/Pink
Jequitiba
Prima vera
Santa maria

Pink/Light Brown
Aningeria
American red gum
Canarium
Cherry
Coachwood
Guarea
Hevea
Jacaranda Pardo
Malagai
Meranti, light
Myrtle, Tasmanian
Niangon
Oak red
Peartree
Quaruba
Queensland Maple
Rosewood, Honduras
Rosewood, Madagascar
Taun

Pink/Brown
Gedu nohor
Larch
Illomba
Palaquium
Port Orford Cedar
Queensland Walnut

Pink/Red
Canarium
Cherry
Ekaba
Gaboon
Tulipwood
Rosa peroba
Mayapis
Mahogany, African
Steam Beech
White Luaun
Terentang

Orange/Red
Arariba

Kauri
Louro, red
Scots pine
Mtambara
Narra
Satine
Sterculia brown
Sepetir
Tindalo

Tan/Light Brown
Afrormosia
Afzelia
Agba
Aguru
Baromalli
Beech, Japanese
Cedar
Celtis
Elm
Erima
Gommier
Hemlock, Western
Hollock
Kiri
Longui rouge
Oak, Tasmanian
Oak, New Guinea
Olivewood
Ozigo
Sempilor
Tchitola
Western Birch

Golden/Brown
Aini
Amboyna
Champak
Difou
Ekoune
Grevillea
Hura
Idigbo
Indian bombax

Kamaere
Keyaki
Nargusta
Ogea
Okwen
Opepe
Roble
Sissoo
Teak
Thuya burr
Walnut, African
White peroba
Virola, light
Zebrano

Green/Brown
Magnolia
Whitewood, American

Olive/Brown
Ipe
White Chuglam

Orange/Brown
Cativo
Douglas fir
Mahogany,
   Central American
Niove
Ovangkol
New Guinea Walnut
Paldao
Sabicu
Padauk Solomons
Tonka
Terminalia
Yellowwood
Yewtree

Grey/Brown
Walnut, European
Bagtikan

Red/Brown
Abura
Alder
Amari
Andiroba
Angelin
Almon
Bubinga
Calophyllum
Cedar, Burmese
Cedar, South
    American
Chickrassy
Courbaril
Cedar, pencil
Gheombi
Goncalo alves
Jarrah
Larch western
Lunumidella
Madrona burr
Mahoe
Plantetree
Planetree, USA
Red alder
Red gum
Red luaun
Sequoia
Silky oak
Tangile
Tiaong
Tola
Tetraberlinia
Utile

Dark Red/Brown
Amoora

Cherry, American
Cinnamon
Cedar, Western Red
Kanda
Mahogany, Brazil
Makore
Manniballi
Medang
Mangkulang
Meranti dark
Moabi
Nyatoh
Omu
Padauk Burma
Saman
Sapele
Simpoh
Snakewood
Sucupira
Totara

Dark Red
Padauk
She Oak
Cocobolo

Purple/Brown
Kingwood
Mansonia
Purpleheart
Walnut, American
Rosewood, Indian

Dark Brown/Black
Blackbean
Blackwood
Brown Oak

Bolongeta
Camagon
Cedar, American
Ebony, African
Ebony, Macassar
Imbuyia
Laurel
Marblewood
Muninga
Rosewood Rio
Wenge

Freak Wild Figure
Red alder
Amboyna burr
Thuya burr
Angelina
Arariba
Bird's Eye Maple
Olive Ash
Masur Birch
Kevazingo
Goncalo alves
Louro red
Nargusta
Oak, Tasmanian
Olivewood
Tonka
Rosewood
Yewtree
Burrs
Butts   } all
Curls

GLOSSARY OF TERMS

Banding. An assembly of solid woods and veneers cut into decorative veneer patterns for inlaying, in one metre lengths up to about 18mm wide.

Blank. Solid wood strip for steaming and bending.

Beeswing. Highly decorative cross-mottle figure on satinwood.

Bleeding. Stain penetrating through top layers of polish.

Bundle. Comprises consecutive matching leaves of decorative veneer, in multiples of 4 for matching purposes, usually sold in 32 leaf bundles; also available in 24's, 28's, 36's and 40's.

Burrs. Wart-like growth on tree with clusters of dormant buds and knots producing highly decorative veneer.

Catalyst. A weak acid which, when mixed with resin, initiates a chemical reaction to polymerise and cure. Used with adhesives and finishes.

Caul. Thin plywood or metal sheet used in a press to distribute pressure over the surface.

Corestock. The middle lamination in plywood or laminated ground-work; hardwood strips in laminated boards.

Crossbanding. 1. Veneers applied to the outer casings of plywood or laminated boards immediately below the decorative face and backing veneers. 2. Decorative border surrounds in face veneers, applied crossgrained.

Crotch. The pattern formed on veneer at the intersection of a limb or branch with the main trunk.

Curl. Same as crotch. (q.v.)

Daylight. The number of openings in a press to receive panels, e.g. a press with 3 sets of platens is known as a 3-daylight press.

Doat. A form of wet rot fungal attack.

Donkey. A wooden fretsaw machine on which the operator sits astride, and operates a toggle armed frame containing the saw; the jaws of the holding clamp is operated by foot.

Dross. A flossy covering of fungus which forms on the face of many veneers; it wipes off and is not considered to be a defect.

Dressed. When a bundle of veneer has had leaves taken out of sequence (to improve the superficial appearance of the stock) and placed on top.

Equilibrium M/C. When a veneered panel (or stocks of veneers) are allowed to remain in conditions of local humidity to acclimatise their moisture content.

Facing. A solid hardwood strip used to decorate a working edge, similar to an edge lipping.

Fiddleback. A strong cross mottle figure traditionally used to decorate the backs of violins etc.

Fineline. A man-made veneer formed by bonding laminations of decorative wood veneers and re-cutting them into striped veneers.

Flatted. Buckled or overdry veneers which have been coated and pressed flat ready for matching or laying.

Flitch. A section of a veneer log cut on the bandmill saw to extract the best figure and yield from a log. The resulting veneers, tied in 'bundles' are kept in flitch sequence.

Groundwork. The base material upon which the veneering process is to be carried out.

Hammer. A squeegee hand-tool used in zig-zag motions along the grain to lay veneers. It is not used like a conventional hammer.

Hairchecks. Minute cracks or splits torn from the underside of rotary cut veneers by the action of the knife, and sometimes found on the outer casing of plywood etc.

Harewood. Chemically treated sycamore, maple etc. to produce a silver-grey veneer with complete colour penetration.

Harlequin. Used to describe a veneer assembly using multi-matched contrasting colours in casual selection.

Ions. Positive and negative electric particles which form when an acid or alkali is dissolved in water.

Lace. Attractive ray figure seen on surface of quarter radially cut veneers such as sycamore.

Laced. A method of applying pressure at an edge, by entwining cord above and below the pressure-point.

Lipping. Solid hardwood strip applied to the edge of a veneer panel to protect the working edge from wear.

Loose face. 'Face' and 'Back' refer to each side of a veneer; they are often referred to as 'tight' and 'loose' faces, the loose face being the reverse or back side.

LV heating. Low voltage heating.

Moiré. Description of decorative veneer figure similar to a watermark, or patterns in silks.

Mordant. A chemical additive to a dyebath to make the colour fast.

Overhang. The unwanted surplus veneer at the ends and edges of a veneered panel to be trimmed off.

Oyster. A tangential cut through the limb of a tree to produce an oval shaped veneer, with an oystershell apperarance.

Parenchyma. Food storage cells in the form of soft tissues which radiate from tree centre and appear as rays on quarter-cut veneers.

Paterae. A small 'sunburst' patterned inlay motif usually sand shaded. Used extensively on Adam furniture.

Patina. The aged surface of polished furniture created by successive layers of atmospheric grime and polish, and the natural weathering of the finish.

Phloem. The inner bark of the growing tree.

Pith. The small hole formed in the centre of a tree in the years of its sappy early growth.

Platen. The plates or cauls of a press—usually metal.

Pommelle. An attractive figure comprising tiny speckled figure, most usually found in mahogany.

pH factor. The measure of the intensity of hydrogen ions present in a solution.

Purfling. Square inlay lines sometimes formed with three layers used to decorate musical instruments.

Reaction wood. 'Tension-wood' is caused when a tree is stretched and 'compression-wood' when the fibres are compressed. Both forms are known as reaction wood.

Refraction. Light rays are bent by the surface, from the angle of incidence of the light source.

RF heating. Radio frequency heating of veneer presses.

Shakes. Cracks in the veneer surface across the grain.

Shelf life. The period a material may be kept in stock before it deteriorates.

Shell. Ray figure torn out by the veneer knife leaving the veneer surface with a loose ray figure.

Scratchstock. A hand made cutting tool used to cut a groove in a wooden panel to receive an inlay.

Stringing. An inlay line of square section in veneer thickness.

Substrates. All layers of a veneered panel below the decorative veneers i.e., corestock, groundwork, crossbandings.

Sunburst. A multi-matched pattern radiating from panel centre.

Tailoring. Preparing a veneer 'lay-on' for a compound shape by inserting V patches and cutting V shapes to allow for tension and compression in laying.

Tambours. Square section sticks, glued to canvass or threaded together to form a shaped caul for laying veneers in a press; or for making a roll-top desk etc.

Thunder shakes. Trees shaken by tropical thunder storms appear, in veneer form, creased and cracked across the grain.

Tiestrap. Used in a wood bending jig to hold the two handles in final position until the wood dries out.

Tight face. The best side of a leaf of veneer.

Toggle clamp. Eccentric clamps used to tighten low voltage heating elements for edge veneering.

Tracheids. Wood cells in softwoods or water conduction and mechanical support.

Tyloses. A foam like substance which grows in the pores of many trees.

UV Ultra violet light. Used for drying tunnels in finishing plants, also found in finishes with ultra violet light ray absorbers to prevent light discolouration.

Vascular cambium. A sheath like layer which completely covers the tree under the bark.

Weathered. The natural (or artificial) ageing of veneer caused by effects of ultra violet light rays which cause some woods to fade and others to darken.

Waney-edged. Veneer bundles which have not been clipped to a uniform width and are left with irregular shaped leaves as cut from the log. Usually only expensive or rare woods are sold 'waney-edged'.

Wane. The bevel on the cutting edge of a knife.

Window. A hole cut in one veneer to act as a templet to guide the knife or saw when cutting the underlying veneer.

BIBLIOGRAPHY

Adhesive Bonding of Wood Dept of Agriculture TB 1512 1975.

Adhesion and Adhesives R. Henwick & G. Salomon 2 vols Elsevier (Amsterdam) 1965.

Art & Practice of Marquetry W. A. Lincoln Thames & Hudson 1971.

The Complete Manual of Wood Finishing Frederick Oughton Stobart & Son Ltd., 1982.

Furniture Finishing; Decoration & Patching, Pattou & Vaughan 1955 and later editions Sterling Pub. Corp. USA.

A Glossary of Wood T. Corkhill, Stobart & Son Ltd. 1979.

Glulam: The Manufacture of glued laminated structures W. A. Chugg, Benn Bros., 1964.

History of English Furniture. 1. Age of Oak; 2. Age of Walnut; 3. Age of Mahogany; 4. Age of Satinwood. Percy McQuoid, London, 1938., Reprint by Dover Pub. Co., USA, 1970.

The International Book of Wood (numerous contributors) Mitchell Beazley, 1976.

Machines for Better Woodwork. Gordon Stokes, Evans Bros. Ltd., 1980.

Timber Properties & Uses W. P. K. Findlay, Granada 1975.

Timber, Its Structure, Properties and Utilisation (6th Edition), H. E. Desch (Revised J. M. Dinwoodie) The McMillan Press, 1981.

Timber Monographs. (3 volumes with 40 actual wood samples in each) E. Palutan, Mitan Publishers, Milan 1981; (Stobart & Son Ltd., London)

Understanding Wood R. Bruce Hoadley, Taunton Press, 1980.

Wood Finishing and Refinishing S. W. Gibbia, Van Nostrand Reinhold, 3rd Edn. 1981.

What Wood is That? H. L. Edlin, Stobart & Son Ltd., Reprinted 1983.

Practical Veneering C. Hayward, Bell & Hyman Ltd., 1962 and later printings.

Recommended reading:

Adhesives H. R. Hindley, Furniture Industries Research Association.

Wood Finishing H. R. Hindley, Furniture Industries Research Association.

Edge Banding with Low Voltage Heating. J. Pound M.I.R.E.A.I.E.E. (Pye, Cambridge).

Present Day Low Voltage Heating. J. Pound M.I.R.E.A.I.E.E. (Pye, Cambridge).

TRADA *Wood Information Sheets,*

TRADA Training Aids

  Macroscopic Structure of Hardwoods G. Hart

  The Examination of Timbers

TRADA Red Booklet series of 9 booklets *Timbers of the World.* (Hardback versions in two volumes by Construction Press)

  TRADA (Timber Research and Development Assn., High Wycombe, Bucks).

Index